# The Service-Oriented Media Enterprise

# The Service-Oriented Media Enterprise: SOA, BPM, and Web Services in Professional Media Systems

John Footen
Joey Faust

Routledge
Taylor & Francis Group

LONDON AND NEW YORK

First published 2008 by Focal Press

Published 2018 by Routledge
2 Park Square, Milton Park, Abingdon, Oxon OX14 4RN
52 Vanderbilt Avenue, New York, NY 10017

*Routledge is an imprint of the Taylor & Francis Group, an informa business*

Notices
Practitioners and researchers must always rely on their own experience and knowledge in evaluating and using any information, methods, compounds, or experiments described herein. In using such information or methods they should be mindful of their own safety and the safety of others, including parties for whom they have a professional responsibility.

Product or corporate names may be trademarks or registered trademarks, and are used only for identification and explanation without intent to infringe.

**Library of Congress Cataloging-in-Publication Data**
Footen, John.
   The service-oriented media enterprise : SOA, BPM, and web services in professional media systems /John Footen, Joey Faust.
      p. cm.
   Includes bibliographical references and index.
   ISBN 978-0-240-80977-9 (pbk. : alk. paper)  1.  Mass media—Economic aspects. 2.  Mass media and technology.  I. Faust, Joey. II. Title.
   P96.E25F665 2008
   338.4′730223—dc22                                                      2008000457

**British Library Cataloguing-in-Publication Data**
A catalogue record for this book is available from the British Library.

ISBN:  978-0-240-80977-9  (pbk)

Cover Design: Maria Mann
Cover Images © iStockphoto
Illustrations: Joey Faust

# DEDICATIONS

This book is dedicated to my children — Alexander, Danial, and John. And, of course, to my always patient wife Sharin for her love and support.

*—John Footen*

This book is dedicated to my family and friends, whom I have neglected in order to ensure its completion.

*—Joey Faust*

# TABLE OF CONTENTS

# ACKNOWLEDGMENTS

Writing a book is often an underestimated task. What cannot be underestimated is the appreciation that we feel toward all of those who have helped and encouraged us through the process. A book of this nature is largely built upon discussions with dozens of colleagues as well as the practical experience that comes from working side by side with them on projects.

We are especially grateful to Ugo Corda, Al Kovalick, and David Potter, who were helpful over and over again as we went through the process of creating this book.

Peter Adamiak, Eliot Graham, Jim Leys, Chuck Phelan, Peter Thomas, S. Merrill Weiss, and our many talented colleagues at National TeleConsultants as well as the MSAG group of AMWA, we thank you for all of your support.

# INTRODUCTION

We live in a new world today in the Media & Entertainment (M&E) industry. Change is coming at us from all directions and we have to be prepared to adjust many aspects of our business and technology to adapt. Whether it is the growth of new distribution mechanisms and the resultant business model changes or the growth of file-based technologies that allow us to fundamentally reexamine how we build systems, there is more change in the business today that must be dealt with at a faster rate than ever before.

So what does this mean for the integrator building systems in this era? Given the rapid adoption of software- and IT-based technologies, are there other aspects of IT technologies or processes that we can leverage? How do we best position our enterprises to be in the strongest position to react with agility to the problems we face today and the unpredictable problems of the future?

The answers do lie in technology that has not yet been widely adopted by M&E, but they also lie in changing the very process by which change is dealt with itself. Change has always been a part of the media business and it will continue to be, so this is a fundamental change of perspective.

Companies that adopt new approaches to deal with change first are going to reap benefits from understanding what to change, when to change it, and how to affect that change earlier than their competitors. It is critical that media enterprises begin addressing this aspect of their business immediately.

The goal of this book is to take a look at the technologies and methodologies that help address this change. The primary subject is the application of Service-Oriented Architecture (SOA) to the media enterprise. SOA is an architectural style and approach in which functionalities of the business are viewed as services that are discrete and reusable throughout the enterprise. Business Process Management (BPM), is another major subject discussed. It is a collection of methodologies and technologies that allow enterprises to analyze, describe, and automate these services into flexible business processes.

We also take a detailed look at Web services. Web services is the most popular technology available for implementing SOA in enterprise systems. All of this leads to the overreaching goal of the book— enabling the reader to begin to think about how best to apply these technologies and methodologies in their business and to enable what is called a Service-Oriented Media Enterprise. A Service-Oriented Media Enterprise is an enterprise that has adopted the precepts discussed in this book that enable it to have enhanced agility and visibility in all aspects of its business.

This book will examine in some detail all of the key subjects associated with service orienting a media enterprise. The intended readers include management and engineering professionals from both the IT side of the house as well as the engineering or technology departments. To a reader with heavy experience in IT, many of the topics covered in this book may be familiar. For these readers, the book contains many media-specific examples and problems that must be faced and hopefully offers a fresh, media-centric look at these topics.

For the reader with a media technology background, many of the topics discussed may be new or of recent interest. This book will provide a foundation in terminology that is familiar, while pointing the way to more detailed examination of the topics.

Chapter 1 is a review of the technology and business changes that are prevalent in the industry and a discussion of why they are leading enterprises toward the adoption of SOA and BPM. Chapter 2 covers the software integration approaches and technologies that have been used in the past and the common ones in use today.

Chapter 3 is a detailed examination of SOA. It covers in some detail the history, benefits, terminology, and philosophy of service orientation. Chapter 4 then delves into a key enabling technology for SOA: middleware. A description of what middleware is in this context, along with descriptions of key capabilities and applications, are provided. Chapter 5 looks at the most popular technology for integrating services today: Web services. From history to an examination of key standards such as WSDL, this chapter covers the gamut of this complex subject. Chapter 6 takes on the subject of BPM, which gives SOA its attachment to the operations of an enterprise. With a foundation of the key enabling technologies, this chapter also covers critical applications of BPM in the media space.

Chapter 7 is where these IT architectures brought together into the media facility and the Service-Oriented Media Enterprise are introduced. This part of the book is where the differences between the media industry and the standard application of SOA and BPM is heavily examined. An approach to addressing the problems brought on by these differences is also detailed. Chapter 8 serves as a guidebook on how to bring about a Service-Oriented Media Enterprise in a media company. The first steps that an enterprise should take through ongoing governance are discussed.

This book also contains a number of appendices that cover a diverse range of related subjects, including media-specific service examples and lists of other books appropriate to both the IT-oriented reader and the media technology professional. Detailed security, reliability, and federation information is provided to assuage any concerns a reader may have in these areas as well as specific information for the vendors of media technology about how to orient their products for services. There is also a fun exploration of possible futures for SOA specifically and software-based media technology in general.

Change is inevitable; and as the Boy Scout motto says, "Be Prepared!" At this time in the history of media technology, this motto has never been more applicable. It is hard to predict what the future may hold, and the contents of this book try to give you the information that you need to begin your preparation. Each of the subjects covered is worthy of its own tome, so don't expect this book to be the end of your journey. Rather, it is the beginning for many as they embrace SOA and BPM and begin to move toward a Service-Oriented Media Enterprise.

# 1

# BUSINESS AND TECHNOLOGY CHANGES DRIVING THE SERVICE-ORIENTED MEDIA ENTERPRISE

It has been said that there is an ancient Chinese curse, "May you live in interesting times." Well, perhaps it is not so much a curse for those who love to embrace change. Anyone who falls into this category should certainly be relishing this period in the media and entertainment (M&E) industry.

It can be argued that, like so many aspects of modern life, media is undergoing rapid and disruptive change. Even if a media professional has been in this industry for a mere 5 years, he or she has seen some breathtaking changes; 20 years or more and it is almost unrecognizable!

So while this is exciting, it is still the job of the people responsible for the design and operation of the facilities that support media enterprises — the media engineers and integrators — to find the best ways to enable their technologies to adapt with agility to this rapid change. Their businesses demand it.

The good news is that there are approaches to making this easier. These have been widely adopted by other industries and now can be applied to M&E. This book will explore these approaches and the technologies that support them. Service-Oriented Architecture, Web services, and Business Process Management can all be applied to address these rapid changes and turn any media company into a Service-Oriented Media Enterprise.

## 1.1 THE UNPREDICTABILITY OF CHANGE

Sometimes it is hard to clearly recognize the degree to which change occurs over time. Many changes happen each year in media facilities and often the person responsible for those changes is heads down in solving the problems of the day. It is rare that there is time to look back at how far a facility has come and how much further it may go.

Fig. 1-1 shows a conceptual diagram of what a typical media system looked like in a facility just 10 years ago. What were some of the characteristics?

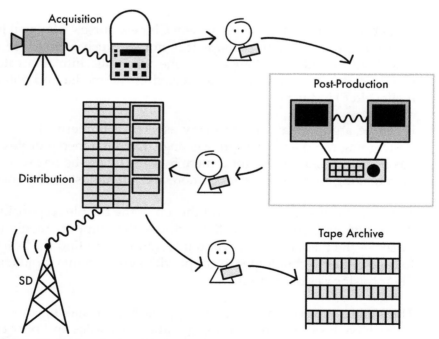

**FIGURE 1-1**  Typical media system, cir. 1998.

Facilities of that era were often primarily analog. Physical media abounded. Non-linear editing was available, but it was not pervasive. Some facilities used video servers but they were new and unreliable. Automation was mainly used to control tape machines. Interfaces between equipment were primarily proprietary and usually serial-based.

Of course, there was wide deviation in this description, but the point is that these systems included a lot of black box, proprietary technology and interfaces. On the one hand, this meant that individual boxes were purpose-built for their jobs and tightly interfaced, and on the other hand, change was difficult and slow.

Those systems met the needs of their day. Everyone then could point to a future where computers and digital would play a greater role. Filmmakers understood that a non-linear editing future was in store for them. Broadcasters could predict that video servers would have an impact. Change was coming, but it would come in a reasonable way. Or so they thought.

Fig. 1-2 shows how much things have changed in just 10 years. What people predicted would happen mainly did. Unfortunately many, many other things that were not on people's radar 10 years ago are now VERY important. Like what? How about the big elephant in the room — the Internet. The Internet has dramatically impacted almost every media company in our industry. In 1998 it would have been hard to see video on the Internet as too terribly critical. It's hard to see anyone saying that now.

How about mobile? In 1998, did many people have a mobile phone that even had a reasonable screen? What about the impact of commodity hardware and software technologies? The changing skill sets required to design and build media systems are undeniably moving toward information technology (IT). How about the pervasiveness of high definition (HD) in the United States? The coming of Internet Protocol Television (IPTV)?

Fig. 1-3 shows almost a single box. Is that where the industry will be in 2018? Will it all be software? Will holographic displays be a big thing? What about UHDTV, now undergoing SMPTE standardization? Will all the traditional media vendors be bought up by big IT companies?

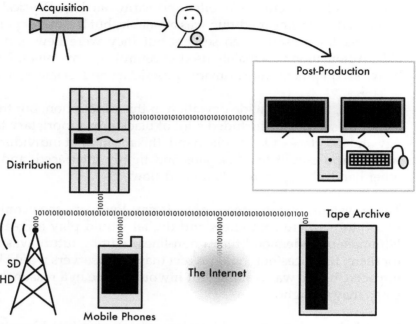

**FIGURE 1-2**   Typical media system, cir. 2008.

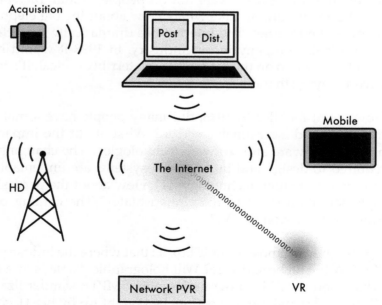

**FIGURE 1-3**   Typical media system, cir. 2018.

Will everything go wireless so that an equipment room doesn't have wires anymore? Will media in games be worth more than on linear TV? Who knows? How can anyone know exactly?

The point of all of this is that no one can know! Media enterprises are going to need to start thinking about how to build their facilities AND their business so that they can adapt to this kind of rapid change and be where they need to be when they need to be there. Media enterprises need to be able to count on their systems and their people to help keep them competitive as they face new threats and challenges.

## 1.2 NEW DISTRIBUTION PLATFORMS

Probably the biggest driver of change in the media industry today is the multi-faceted impact of new distribution platforms on traditional media companies. The power of these platforms on the media enterprise affects everything from the technology to the people to the nature of the business itself. It is easily argued that at no point in media history prior to this were there so many ways to consume the product that is produced.

Table 1-1 contains a list (not exhaustive) of common distribution forms in use today for motion media. This gives a sense of how many methods a media enterprise may have to consider.

The table does not list every consumer distribution form that has existed, let alone every professional system. It would be pages long if a comprehensive list were to be built. The history of each technology is long and complex and the dates selected are representative of key events in development. The important realization is that there are many formats coming more quickly and these must be addressed in some way. The table of distribution forms will likely look very different five years from now.

### 1.2.1 Television

The end of analog broadcasting and the beginning of all-digital broadcasting in the United States is one of the changes in distribution that is

**TABLE 1-1**

Common Media Distribution Forms Used Today

| Format | Year introduced | Format | Year introduced |
|---|---|---|---|
| 35 mm theater | 1892 | Windows media | 1999 |
| SD television | 1941 | PVR | 1999 |
| Imax theater | 1971 | IPTV | 1999 |
| VHS | 1976 | VOD | 2000 |
| Quicktime | 1991 | Flash Video | 2002 |
| DVD | 1995 | PSP | 2004 |
| HD television | 1996 | Digital cinema (DCI) | 2005 |
| Real Media | 1997 | HD-DVD | 2006 |
| 3 gp mobile | 1999 | Blu-Ray | 2006 |

certain to come. February 17, 2009 is a date that has been burned into the consciousness of every broadcaster. This date is when analog broadcasting ends, permanently. This is perhaps the main issue that the broadcasting industry has been dealing with in 2008 and will be into much of 2009.

As no transition of this magnitude is perfect, many broadcasters will have to deal with the aftermath. While there is much being done at the station in terms of equipment replacement, the digital transition is a great example of business issues being of even greater importance than technical ones. It has been far more worrisome and critical for broadcasters to educate the viewing public as to the change than it has been to replace equipment. It has been in the broadcaster's interests to educate the public . . . if the public is not educated, then there would be a greater chance of losing some viewers in the change-over period when their analog sets suddenly cease to work. No broadcaster could afford this. While the value of the spots, news stories, tickers, and other ways that broadcasters use to get the message out about the transition has not been insubstantial, it has been well worth the effort.

Although the transition to digital occurs on a fixed timeframe, HD is another matter. Perhaps one of the more persistent public myths about media change is that when the 2009 date was set, it was to mark the changeover to high definition television (HDTV), and not simply digital. In fact, the Federal Communications Commission (FCC) regulation does not specify the specific resolution of the video to be broadcast after the changeover, only that it be digital. Furthermore, it only applies to terrestrial transmission systems, not to satellite or cable.

HDTV has already had a major impact on facilities being built in the United States and Japan, and in an ever-greater degree in Europe and other parts of Asia. HDTV, also known simply as HD, is almost the flip side of the digital transition. Technical issues associated with producing and transmitting material in HD are significant, while there are not as dramatic business model differences in HD versus SD, or standard definition.

HD does, however, represent an interesting case for the integrator that would like to move toward a Service-Oriented Media Enterprise. Significant money is being spent in facilities worldwide to upgrade or change technology to support HD. This is a perfect opportunity to apply some of the precepts learned throughout this book and begin building service orientation at the same time.

HD certainly presents new creative challenges that must be faced with very high quality images, and these challenges will need to be helped along by technology and workflow changes. For example, it would not necessarily be appropriate to take a wide shot of a soccer match that was shot in HD and send it directly to a mobile phone. All of the action would not likely be visible. Instead, either a technological option (software that recognizes where important action is and crops automatically for mobile), or a workflow option (a separate edit session for the mobile version) will have to be brought to bear. Another problem to consider is that the same graphics that are perfectly appropriate in HD may not be appropriate in SD and may be completely unreadable on the mobile screen.

It is not only video that differs but audio as well. In addition to the obvious differences between 5.1-channel sound and 2-channel stereo, the content creator must consider the different environments in which the content will be heard (and seen!). There are big differences between a pair of headphones and a 300-watt home stereo system!

The media files themselves also represent a technical challenge for the facility aiming to move to HD. The uncompressed data stream of HD is about five times greater than that for SD. Compared to a mobile or

Internet stream, HD can be literally thousands of times more data per second. When converting to HD, facilities must consider the storage and networking requirements of such data as well as the appropriate compression schemes that make sense for their business.

All of this means that media professionals now have to really know more than just one medium to be in the media business today. Because content is going to end up on several platforms, engineers and enterprises alike need to develop a good understanding of each one on a technical as well as a business and creative level.

Perhaps the most dramatic impact on the business models of television has been the advent of the personal video recorder (PVR) or digital video recorder (DVR), the most popular example of which is TiVo. TiVo and other PVR's have introduced an extremely easy-to-use mechanism for recording content from broadcasts. Like Video Home System (VHS) tape before it, the PVR and DVR have allowed the consumer to choose to time shift when they see programs. PVRs have made that process extremely easy. If users can move around an Electronic Program Guide (EPG), they can operate a PVR.

In addition, these devices have integrated a wealth of other content into the TV. Home videos, pictures, music, games, podcasts, etc., are now all available in an integrated interface. Traditional "appointment television" is becoming less and less important.

Along with this has come one of the biggest challenges to broadcast television revenues. As content is prerecorded, it is easy for the viewer to skip commercials, and they do so with great frequency. The number of viewer eyeballs on ad content is the bread and butter of the broadcaster, and PVRs are reducing that number. Many experiments in advertising, some involving technological changes, are being tried to overcome this challenge.

IPTV is another distribution method, and a complicated subject that cannot be properly treated in the short space devoted to it in this book. It represents a new form of technical distribution, but it is unclear if there are any new business models or creative options that will come with it. It is a subject, however, that every broadcaster is watching closely for further developments.

Broadcasting or narrowcasting to mobile devices is also becoming a reality all over the world. A number of technologies that vary from country to country allow for this. Many aspects of mobile broadcasting are fairly similar to traditional broadcasting, but two major challenges arise for the mobile TV content provider. It is widely understood that audiences of mobile TV will not be willing to watch material as long as they would in other media leading to the development of a new, shorter content option called the "mobisode." Of course, regardless of the content, the small screen on mobile devices also presents challenges visually.

All of these problems must be addressed with both new technology and new business practices if the television industry hopes to succeed in this new era of broadcasting.

## 1.2.2 Motion Pictures

For the studios, one of the great new distribution changes is the rapid growth of Digital Cinema in the last few years. Before that, it seemed as though the digital distribution of content would never get off of the ground for the motion picture industry. And so, in 2002, the Digital Cinema Initiatives (DCI) was formed with the clear purpose of creating specifications that all corners of the industry could adhere to.

This created the need for new workflows throughout finishing and distribution chains. Many organizations have taken on these workflow challenges in unique ways, but there is no clear "right" way to handle digital cinema and thus many opportunities for media enterprises in this space.

The use of digital projectors in movie theaters has presented additional options that must be considered as well. For example, 3D cinema is growing in popularity again. Also, to what degree can revenues from live events such as concerts or sporting events be brought into the theater?

The home distribution market is also in flux. Today there are two new physical formats battling it out as replacements for DVD. Both HD-DVD and Blu-Ray deliver full HD video quality to the home in familiar pack-aging. Although each has its relative benefits and drawbacks, no clear winner has emerged for the consumer.

This is not the first time this has happened (see VHS vs. Betamax below), but it will likely be the last. Because Internet speeds have dra-matically increased in recent years, it has become clear to many that there may not be a need to physically distribute data any longer. As has been seen in the music industry, a greater number of videos are simply downloaded straight to people's computers. This trend is only likely to increase in years to come and the media industry can expect to see the importance of physical formats as a means of distribution decrease.

## FORMAT WARS: VHS VERSUS BETAMAX

It is said that HD-DVD versus Blu-Ray is to be the last format war. It is inter-esting to take a look back at the first. In 1975, Sony released the Betamax for-mat. In 1976, JVC introduced a competing format, VHS. While there were several other formats available to consumers during the period of this war — from Video Cassette Recording (VCR) to Super-Betamax to laser disks — these two carried the predominant market share and were the two formats most consumers felt they should choose between.

Betamax had several superior qualities. It was introduced by about a year before VHS. It had a higher resolution (250 lines vs. the 240 lines of VHS). It had lower signal noise and less chroma problems than VHS. And yet, it failed to win the war although every aspect of its picture was better.

It is often said that the availability of pornography was what allowed VHS to dominate. In fact, pornography content producers made content for both for-mats, and the pornography market has always been small compared to the larger media market. In reality the key factor that allowed VHS to prevail was its physical size! Not that it was better to simply have a larger cassette in VHS, but that the larger size allowed for more tape to be stored in a single cassette. This meant longer running times at all points in the history of the format. From the beginning size mattered. A movie could not be stored on a single Betamax tape (but could on a VHS) and when a VHS allowed a maximum recording time of 10.5 hours (NTSC), a Betamax could only achieve a maximum of 5 hours (NTSC).

As a footnote to that war, there was a similar war in the professional arena between Betacam, which had a Betamax-like cassette and MII, which used a VHS-like cassette. Betacam won that one!

### 1.2.3 The Internet

The Internet gets its own section here because it represents a major new distribution channel (and new challenges) for all media. Broadcasters need to address the Internet as a means of distributing content as well as a way to maintain a sense of community with their audiences. Studios also have begun to embrace the Internet as a distribution platform.

For much of its relatively short history it was considered a practical impossibility to distribute motion media content on the Internet. Low, dial-up data rates and inefficient video compression technology made a deadly combination for non-text content.

However, as broadband connections continued to proliferate, it became obvious that media could be distributed over higher-speed connections. The data rates available allowed decent picture quality — even streaming — over the first connections. Today, it is now accepted that content needs to be distributed over the Internet, because that is what consumers are demanding. Despite the fact that the Internet has been around for far less time than powdered wigs were popular, there is no doubt that it is not a fad!

This presents many challenges that need to be considered, the biggest of which is piracy. It has always represented a serious concern that grows by the day. There is great fear that the damage that was done to the music business through the use of peer-to-peer file sharing technologies such as Napster will also be done to the TV and Motion Picture businesses. This is not an unfounded fear — there have been several high-profile cases of movies distributed on the Internet, even before their release dates.

Many technological options have been created to try to address this problem. Watermarking, for example, places a marker (visible or invisible) directly into the content. This can contain forensic data that allows where the media was obtained to be traced. Fingerprinting media creates a "signature" of the content that can then be detected. This forensic technique can be used to help automatically detect copyrighted content. This has helped legitimate Internet content distributors to keep material they should not have off of their sites.

Another approach has been to consider changes to the business model for releasing material. Traditionally, media has been released in a series of "windows" to different distribution outlets. For example, a motion picture might be released first to theater, then Pay-Per-View, and eventually to DVD. Some content distributors have recently been experimenting with collapsing these windows to lessen the impact of some forms of piracy. Of course, pricing changes will also have to be considered, just as they were in music.

If content is to be distributed in digital forms (as is the trend), it will be important to examine the means by which it is protected. The general term for this is Digital Rights Management (DRM). Like many of the other subjects we are looking at, it is a complex topic in and of itself. There are some real challenges for the future in the creation and use of DRM technologies that are relatively transparent to users while being very secure regarding the content they carry. This is by no means a solved problem.

## CASE STUDY

### Working with New Media Distribution Companies

As the Internet becomes a larger part of the strategy for media enterprises, they will eventually come into contact with the many new media companies that are handling distribution in that arena.

One such company was very new to the professional media business. While its technological savvy regarding the Internet and IP distribution was clear, its ability to handle the high-quality distribution demands of the studios was in doubt. When preparing to launch its distribution site, this company initially decided that it would simply get tapes of the content and handle the encoding of these tapes to the Internet distribution format.

Wisely, the studios involved required that tests be done before the site was launched. They found, much to their chagrin, that the quality of the encoding, while technically correct, was not up to their standards. They knew, from recent experience, that a plethora of small changes to settings such as specific gamma correction was required to optimize picture quality.

So the distributor wanted to maintain control over the process to assure the technical quality of the material to be distributed on his platform. The content producers, however, wanted to be sure their product was of the highest quality possible. Eventually, the studios essentially trained the personnel from the distributor to better encode their material. As more expertise on these technical issues spreads, there is a growing trend for this encoding to be done back at the studio and the files to be sent to the distributor directly.

One Internet force that is taking the M&E industry by storm is the concept of Web 2.0. Web 2.0 can be defined as the catch-all term for the proliferation of user-generated content on the Internet. The IT pundits out there would defend it as a little bit more in-depth than simply a trend in content production (a concept which is explored in Appendix F), but that is its main touch-point with the media industry. Sites like YouTube have sparked a revolution in the eyes of many "wired" consumers that the era of big networks and studios creating big-budget movies and TV shows to entertain the masses is over, and the world has instead entered the era of peer-to-peer production. These consumers see the Internet as a massively parallel distribution mechanism that will solve all of the technical problems of getting content from point A to point B, and then all a 15-year-old video blogger needs to be the world's most popular producer/director is a $500 camera and a Digital Subscriber Line (DSL). While this is probably far from the truth, the media industry should still pay attention.

## WEB 2.0 WEB SITES

The Web 2.0 movement is an interesting one for media professionals to follow. Anyone interested in learning a little bit more about how it works should simply check out some of the flagship Web 2.0 Web sites out there:

- YouTube (http://www.youtube.com)
- Wikipedia (http://en.wikipedia.org)
- Digg (http://digg.com)
- Del.icio.us (http://del.icio.us)
- Flickr (http://www.flickr.com)
- Facebook (http://www.facebook.com)
- MySpace (http://www.myspace.com)
- Last.FM (http://www.last.fm)

User-generated content is becoming a much bigger part of every media outlet's programming. Not to mention the fact that services such as Joost (http://www.joost.com) that use user-generated (or at least tiny-studio-generated) media as their main source of content are becoming much more prevalent. Many news organizations, for example, are finding ways to leverage the cell phone videos from regular people on location of breaking news. Many networks are allowing users to practically dictate content. Even advertisers are running contests to have their customers create commercials for them! Web 2.0 is a big area that media enterprises are hoping to leverage to cut production costs. A huge investment in infrastructure is required for this to be successful, however.

## CASE STUDY

### Current TV

Web 2.0 can be leveraged within the media enterprise, as well. This is commonly done in IT by allowing employees to organize internal assets for the organization through rankings or semantics. Media has the opportunity to go much further with this by having consumers rank, organize, or even directly create content themselves.

One example of a media operation that has taken advantage of all three is Current TV, a cable and satellite network that has been on the air since 2005. Current TV gets most of its programming from its viewers. They allow viewers to submit content to be aired on the channel and then allow these viewers to vote on which content will be aired and when. This is classic Web 2.0, and it has been working very well for the network, which has been continuously expanding since its inception. Current TV's Web site is http://current.com.

## 1.2.4 Opportunities

Not everything is a business or technical challenge. Clearly, these new distribution platforms represent a significant new opportunity for additional revenue and this is truly exciting. Not only are there entirely new ways to reach an audience today, there are also new forms of content that can be produced that can generate completely new types of revenue.

Whether it is mobisodes for mobile or interactive content on the Internet, there are new realms to explore creatively and technically. The cost of content creation and distribution has been dropping dramatically. This can allow for more experimentation with an audience that is fracturing rapidly.

## THE LONG TAIL

Chris Anderson, of "Wired" fame, wrote an article about the long tail in 2004. He followed it up with a book, *The Long Tail — Why the Future of Business Is Selling Less of More*, published with Hyperion in 2006.

The basic premise is this: in a distribution system where the costs of locating and distributing content itself are low, more revenue can be generated from the many works for which the demand is low than from the few extremely popular works.

This theory seems to bear out in many places. From online booksellers such as Amazon to the growing popularity of niche content on video sharing sites such as YouTube, it seems that there are a number of opportunities for media enterprises to make significant money off of low-demand content.

This means potential changes for media companies in both business and technology. For example, many media enterprises have significant archives that can potentially be exploited even further for niche consumers. This targeted material—which would otherwise go to waste—can be leveraged to be profitable!

The new distribution platforms that are discussed in this chapter are allowing *The Long Tail* to become a reality for many media companies.

It must also be kept in mind that there are cross-platform opportunities as well. One platform can advertise for the other, while content can be optimized and sold across several platforms for the same material. Not only does this present a better experience for the consumer on each platform, but it allows for an integrated experience that can bring in more revenue from fans. For example, a TV show can talk to its audience about its corresponding Internet content, such as podcasts or Web videos while the Internet content can refer to upcoming mobisodes. The possibilities are truly endless!

Of course, as the many forms of content grow, so does something else: the importance of metadata! One of the key ways that audiences will connect with the content that they care about is through the metadata that is made available with that content. This is yet another challenge in our industry that needs to be faced and addressed in the years to come.

In the past, as new distribution platforms arise, organizations typically formed new departments or processes to address them so that initially rare skills can be concentrated and distractions minimized to the core business. Ultimately these separate silos become inefficiencies. As the new platform becomes an ingrained part of the business practice, it is important to examine whether enhanced organizational efficiencies can be found. An obvious potential place to look would be to examine how parallel production for multiple platforms can drive down costs and drive up quality.

One great example can be seen in how DVD content has evolved. Originally, the bonus content on DVDs was simply made up of excess material created during the production. Some original content, such as a director's track, might be created for the DVD, but nothing else. Now, it is not at all uncommon to see DVD content planned for and produced at the same time as the main content. Why the change? Well, initially, there was not much revenue from DVDs. As the revenue grew, so did the interest in creating the best content possible for the media.

## IMPORTANT NOTE

### The Value of Pre-Producing for Multiple Platforms

It cannot be stressed enough that multi-platform production should not be viewed as a burden. Although it is impossible to completely eliminate extra work when new content is produced for a different distribution form, it is possible to both reduce the labor and increase the quality to the consumer.

For example, if a producer were to shoot a documentary about tree frogs that would primarily be used for HDTV, shooting closer shots for SD and mobile might be taken into consideration. Some high-quality stills could be shot for the Internet, and clear sounds of the frog recorded for the radio program.

The best place to pull all of this together is in pre-production. When preparing for a shoot, understanding all of the distribution platforms intended for the material at the end of the day will help keep an enterprise from having to send someone out to capture content for a new platform that could have been done the first time around.

An extremely diverse set of topics are covered in this section very quickly. The point of all of this is to give a flavor of the many ways that new content distribution platforms are challenging the media industry. There are many other changes, besides new distribution, that have ratcheted up the need for agile media companies, however.

## 1.3  MEDIA CONSOLIDATION AND REGULATION

One of the other changes coming for the media industry is the rapid consolidation of traditional media companies. Note that this is specifically regarding the traditional media company. It is easily argued overall that media is fracturing as the costs of certain types of distribution go drastically down. Many "new media" companies are entering the marketplace, giving users the power to self-distribute in a way they never have before. These companies are (so far) unaffected by media consolidation, and probably have more to fear from a Google or Microsoft acquisition. However, within the largest media enterprises, there is clearly a need to address the impacts of consolidation.

As can be seen in Fig. 1-4, since the 1980s there has been a steady consolidation of media companies. An examination of the recent history of just one media conglomerate illustrates the trend.

In 1993, the Disney Corporation acquired Miramax. Their acquisition of ABC and ESPN followed in 1996, Fox Family Channel in 2001, and Pixar in 2006, not to mention their ownership of A&E, Lifetime, and other companies. All of this is added to Disney's existing organically grown holdings such as the Disney Channel. Similar stories of the growth of media conglomerates can be seen with GE/NBC/Universal, Viacom, News Corporation, and Time Warner in the United States.

So, on the one hand, the trend is toward consolidation of these kinds of media companies. This can be expected to continue for some time as new forms of media create the kind of competition that drives corporations to find efficiencies and eliminate rivals. On the other hand, there is a parallel growth of new players in media that is also expected create some fracturing. Google, Microsoft, and others are making moves in media. As the realms of IT and media slowly converge, more companies will no doubt follow suit.

While this presents some interesting questions from the perspective of social or political benefits resulting from such consolidation (and fracturing), it certainly raises issues as to how to best address the organizational and technical impacts and opportunities of these activities.

This problem is not unique to M&E. It is seen in a multitude of other industries. In every case, businesses must try to determine the best

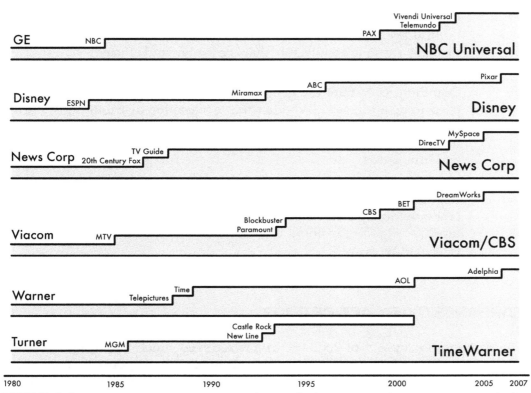

**FIGURE 1-4**  This timeline shows the consolidation of select major media enterprises over the last twenty-five years.

way to organize and gain the efficiencies promised by such business deals. This is a complex subject, but certainly there is room for systems architecture and technology to play a role as corporations suddenly find themselves with multiple enterprise systems to unify.

When two major media companies combine, there will certainly be duplications of functions in the combined organization. Some of these may be perfectly sensible. But, just like it is valid to look at how departments such as Human Resources and Accounting may be able to gain efficiencies from being combined, it is valid to look at how ingest, or editing, or transmission may be made more efficient. Some of this comes from how the people are organized; but also, efficiency comes from how systems may be integrated. It is not an easy task to figure out how to best architect the many systems in an enterprise. Certainly there will be dozens of legacy systems, entrenched work practices, and a multitude of new technology initiatives. It will take time to steer all of this into a system architecture that is coherent and efficient.

One thing is certain: the geographic distribution of the systems will need to be addressed. Whether that geographic distribution is a few city blocks away or on a different continent, special consideration will have to be observed with issues such as communications, bandwidth, and time zones.

Regulations are another area where the business of media is changing. Not only do regulations affect broadcasters in technical areas such as the 2009 digital transition, but they can also directly affect the business in other ways.

## SARBANES-OXLEY ACT OF 2002

The Sarbanes-Oxley Act of 2002 (SOX) has received much attention in the media space in recent years. This law was put in place in response to a number of large accounting scandals such those that plagued Enron. However, it affects all publicly traded companies, including many large and small media enterprises. While "SOX compliance" has been a big job in many corporations, it often does not directly alter the work of the media side of the house.

It is possible that this will change. Accounting rules change and evolve, and it is possible that the "value" locked up in media archives and other media assets may need to be more "auditable." If this happens, there could be a rather dramatic need for systems and process changes that will certainly affect media engineers and others throughout the enterprise.

Some forms of regulatory action may require system changes. At the Super Bowl XXXVIII halftime show, for example, there was a "wardrobe malfunction" during a performance with Janet Jackson and Justin Timberlake in which Janet Jackson's breast was exposed over live television. The incident received much publicity and resulted in the largest fine to that point for indecency from the FCC.

It also resulted in a number of broadcasters implementing technical changes such as video delay to help protect against similar incidents. When these kinds of things occur, the media engineer in a facility needs to react quickly. When regulations create a need for change — bringing new technology online or changes in workflow — it often comes more quickly than anyone expects.

Sometimes new regulations such as SOX create a need for greater visibility. Often, regulations will require some sort of reporting to internal entities or even to the government. In these cases, systems that allow for better automatic gathering of data in systems such as production systems can have value. Again, this is a technological change in response to a regulatory one.

The truth is, no entity in the media space is immune from the need to address changes brought on by the consolidation of media companies or changes in regulation.

## 1.4  NEW COMPETITION

Another major challenge that is driving changes is the advent of new competition for the traditional media companies. With so many new avenues of distribution, it was perhaps inevitable that major new companies would come along to play. Instead of simply ignoring these new threats or standing dumbfounded saying "Whoa! Where did that guy come from?!," media companies need to compete and partner on equal terms.

One of the first attempts at dealing with this competition was the merger between America Online (AOL) (an IT firm) and Time Warner (a media firm). While this was not a success, there are more recent examples that have been viewed favorably, such as the News Corporation acquisition of MySpace. In addition, several major companies have come to be perceived as powerful new players in media.

Google, with its powerful advertising platform for the Internet, is one such company. Its acquisition of YouTube was a major play into the media space. Additionally, Google has purchased the weblogging site Blogger and other companies which deal in content and content management. Google will be interesting to watch in the coming years for two reasons: first, it is a major force in the bread and butter of the broadcast space — advertising; and it is second only to General Electric (GE) in market value (among companies with major media holdings) at the time of this writing. That is a powerful place from which to compete.

There is another company new to media — with an even larger market value — that must also be reckoned with: Microsoft. With purchases of Lionhead Studios and Massive, among many others (not to mention homegrown Microsoft Network (MSN) and the partnership MSNBC), Microsoft is clearly a force in media. Additionally, Microsoft is interesting because it developed some key technologies of interest to the media space such as VC-1 (the Windows Media 9 format), now a Society of Motion Picture and Television Engineers (SMPTE) standard.

These kinds of companies enjoy distinct advantages over traditional media. They often do not have the kind of legacy technology base seen in most media companies. Also, union regulations that stifle agility are non-existent or lessened. There is also often a cultural difference that is well adapted to the new media space in which they are dominant.

They do face other challenges, however. Chief among these is that content remains king in media. New media enterprises are generally not as experienced with the production of professional media. They also simply do not reach the same kinds of audiences. The total viewership of the most popular clip on YouTube pales in comparison with the one-time viewership of even failing TV shows on major networks. These are factors that are likely to change over time, of course, but for now they serve as a barrier of entry for new media companies.

How to compete with these kinds of companies remains a real question. This problem is complicated by the new media distribution platform strategy that a traditional media company needs to develop. Regardless of what the answers will be (there is surely no one right answer, after all), one thing is clear: media enterprises will need to be agile and clear-headed to compete in the industry of the future.

## 1.5 CHANGING AUDIENCE

The ways in which the audience is consuming media is also changing with the availability of new media forms. The younger demographics are consistently turning to online forms of media and other new types of media over their older counterparts. For example, Fig. 1-5 shows the age ranges purchasing music online, which skews heavily to the lower end of the spectrum. In a few years, these people will be the majority of media consumers. This means new demographics need to be considered when selecting the platform for media.

As noted, the movement of audiences to new media is driving both new advertising models and the creation of media for a specific platform. In many cases this means more short-form material. After all, audiences seem to prefer short form when browsing on the Internet and on mobile devices.

Additionally, consistent with the growth of Web 2.0 (see Appendix F), there is an increasing desire for audiences to interact in some form with the media itself. One popular and simple example of this is the kind of interactive voting seen on shows like *American Idol*. This is a relatively simple interactivity to achieve, requiring only a phone bank and a tabulation system. More complex interaction has occurred in other media such as that on the Internet, where the full power of

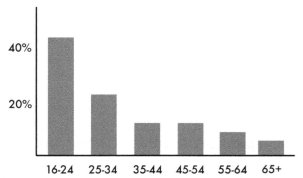

**FIGURE 1-5**   A comparison of music downloads by age in late 2005. The chart shows the percentage of total online consumers in a given demographic that regularly download music.
Source: Forrester Research, Inc.

Web 2.0 can be brought to bear. More and more, audiences are expecting to be a part of the experience.

Another area where the audience is changing expectations is the availability of content on the platform they want, when they want it. They are no longer happy with "appointment TV." The growing popularity of PVRs along with other forms of distribution means that each person will soon expect to be able to build their own "channel" of time-shifted, hand-picked shows. Of course, this does not apply to news and sports content, where a profundity of live content means the best experience is watching what's on right *now*.

Where will this lead in the future? Clearly there are trends toward greater interactivity and user participation. The "lean forward" experience of interactive media will clearly need to be accounted for in the content of the future and in the systems that support the production and distribution of that content. This does not mean that the "lean back" experience so familiar today will go away. Television, after all, did not kill off the movie theater! There is room for all sorts of distribution in the M&E industry of the future! It is also clear that anywhere, any platform consumption by consumers will only increase.

## 1.6  INCREASED ADOPTION OF INFORMATION TECHNOLOGIES

Not everything that causes change to be more rapid will be driven by the consumer arena. Some may be driven instead by professional technology. One change is the increasing adoption of IT technologies. Before, most of the technologies deployed in the media space were "black box" proprietary technologies that were purpose-built for the media space on specific hardware platforms.

In recent years, however, it became possible to perform many of the functions that had previously been performed by custom hardware in general-purpose computing platforms instead. Many of these applications today are pure software and can work on the desktop of readily available, standardized hardware. Thus, there is an increasing focus on software-based integration. Many of the support applications that these rely on (such as databases) are running on enterprise scale server technology. Media enterprises can expect even more functionality to move from the desktop to servers as media applications continue to follow the IT trend.

This means that now, more media than ever is moving on IP-based, standard IT networks. Quite a bit is still moved over physical media such as tapes, but clearly the trend is to push more and more media over the network within an enterprise. And this means disk-based media storage.

Even as recently as a few years ago, almost all disk-based storage that was used in media enterprise was proprietary in some form. At the minimum, little tweaks were required to firmware to achieve required performance from disk systems, thus requiring a proprietary platform. These days, however, the performance of disks is such that this is no longer necessary in many cases. Commoditized, standard IT storage is now a viable way to store much of the material in a facility.

These changes are making huge differences in the simplicity of hardware design and in the overall costs of building and maintaining such infrastructures. While it is hard to anticipate exactly when it will happen, one can expect to see little difference at some point between the IT data center and the media operations center. Much has merged already.

## IMPORTANT NOTE

### The Convergence of IT and Engineering Departments

If a media enterprise has not yet begun to look into combining these two departments, then it is important for them to start the process. The experience of organizations that have done this is a net positive. Certainly there are problems, but these are outweighed by the combined skill sets brought to bear on these problems.

In enterprises that have done this, chances are that the biggest complaint expressed by the employees is the desire to get more cross-training between the two, formerly separate departments. Managers should make this happen! While there is value in some degree of specialty, cross-training ensures that all of their eggs are not in the same basket while, at the same time, improving the morale of the team.

Merging is also occurring in the IT and engineering departments. In many enterprises, these two departments are merged into the same department. This is no surprise to anyone familiar with the growing influence of standard IT technology in the media space.

These two have traditionally been seen as separate departments. In many ways, this was how it always needed to be. The skills required to succeed in one department were very different from those required by the other, as are the cultural requirements for office support versus on-air support. Now that many media enterprises have combined the two, there has been no clear "winner" as to which management controls the combined department. In some cases it is IT management (or, at least, an IT manager) that has led the new department, and in others it is engineering. Either way, more IT skills are needed all around!

## 1.7  COLLABORATIVE, FILE-BASED PRODUCTION

Of course, what all of this adoption of IT technologies really means is the adoption of file-based forms of production. Assets are increasingly virtual now instead of physical, and this brings a whole set of new problems.

While the advancement of file-based production has mostly been done in a silo form, the industry is now seeing a greater adoption of end-to-end file-based workflows in media enterprises of all sorts. These workflows bring increased speed of production as well as increasing capability of collaboration, because multiple people can work on the same asset (sometimes at the same time).

As stated in the previous section, what is allowing this file-based revolution is the increased use of software-heavy technology running on commodity hardware. As software spreads to more parts of the enterprise, and as more vendors adopt compatible, standards-based file technologies, it becomes possible to bring together systems in a single workflow that may have been previously impossible.

## CASE STUDY

### The MXF Mastering Format

In 2005, Turner started off a project to create true interoperability among a large number of products with Media Exchange Format (MXF). Up to that point, specific implementations of the standard by different vendors were not completely compatible. It seemed that the huge standard had so many options that it was very difficult to get any two MXF implementations to deal with MXF files in the same way.

Turner gathered a large number of vendors of all types — from ingest to archive — and began a specification process. They followed this process up with a successful demonstration of a working system with files passing among many vendors at the National Association of Broadcasters (NAB) convention in 2007.

Turner moved forward with implementing this MXF Mastering Format at its London facility and, at the same time, the specification was turned over to the Advanced Media Workflow Association (AMWA) for finalization. The effort is still in progress, but it represents one of many necessary standardization and interoperability efforts that the M&E industry needs to undergo if it wants to garner more benefit from software-based technologies.

One reason that there is such increasing adoption is the sheer price advantages of leveraging IT hardware and networking technologies. As Fig. 1-6 shows, there has been a relentless trend of price decreases in IT technology. This is an advantage of commoditization, and enterprises can expect to see a similar trend in software technologies themselves as well.

One key aspect of this entire discussion is that the media business is highly collaborative. As such, media is often shared among many people and systems in a file-based workflow. This raises to the fore an obvious concern: security. Technologies such as watermarking and fingerprinting are very useful, but other technologies must be considered

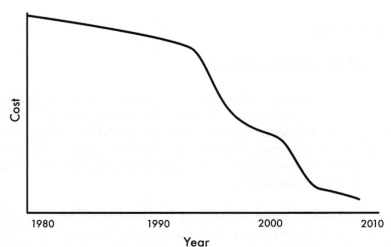

**FIGURE 1-6**   The pricing of enterprise IT has decreased continuously since it really came into its own in the 1980s.

as well to help ensure a secure environment when leveraging IT platforms. These include:

- Virus scanning
- Firewalls
- Identity management and password protection
- Encryption
- Physical security

## WATERMARKING

The term watermarking of course comes from the marks that have been made on paper for centuries to discourage counterfeiting. In the context of digital media, however, it refers to a mark (visible or invisible) that is made on the medium such that some identifying information can travel with it.

Watermarking really only has forensic value with respect to security. What is meant by forensic in this case is that the material has already escaped into "the wild" and a mark is needed to identify precisely from where it came. To make this possible in many media enterprises, the mark is changed at different points in the process to help identify exactly from where it had been copied.

For example, the mark might be changed between different points in the post-production process. In theater distribution, for example, a different mark could be used for each release print to identify the specific theater from which it was copied.

There are many techniques to make these marks. In the cases of invisible marks that are stored in the visible image, how much data stored is limited. Often times it takes some time to reconstitute the mark from the medium.

There are also several "attacks" that can be done against the medium to ruin the watermark which include distortions of the image, changing of color or luminance values, or degradation of the image. The most difficult type of attack to protect against and the most difficult to perpetrate is a collusion attack where the image is recorded multiple times from different sources to obtain many different watermarks. The frames are then "shuffled" into a new version. However, this type of infringement requires access to many different versions of the medium and therefore a significant breach of security.

A related technology to watermarking is fingerprinting. In fingerprinting, a mathematical value is determined that represents the media. This can be used to search for matches in places (such as illegal distribution sites on the Internet) to find where copyrighted material might be posted. This technology can also be proactively used by legitimate file-sharing Web sites to keep copyrighted material off automatically!

> Media enterprises should not forget to consider user management (a subset of identity management) as a serious consideration as they look at their architecture. How many systems in an enterprise still have valid logins for employees and contractors long gone? It is extremely common. So are those machines that have the default administrator password on them still! Don't forget the little stuff!

> There are many ways that collaboration is enabled in the enterprise. As the integrator looks at new technologies, enhanced collaboration should certainly be considered. Oftentimes, the value of performing technology integration in the first place is to enable greater collaboration among all of the participants in the full life-cycle of the media.

> Shared storage is certainly the most important technology to help enable collaboration. When media is stored securely in a shared location that

many users can access, it means that time is not wasted waiting for copies to be made at each individual location where the media is to be processed. This is getting to be a very common requirement in media systems. With the advent of Storage Area Network (SAN) technology in the media industry, there has been a growing demand for (sometimes quite massive) shared storage systems.

Communication technology in the form of emails, Instant Messenger (IM), Short Message Service (SMS), etc., also perform a well-established and useful function in collaboration. But media integrators should not think about only the human-to-human possibilities with these technologies. An integrator has an opportunity to enhance visibility throughout the enterprise by sending appropriate information automatically using these technologies. It is a common business requirement in software systems.

Portals and other Web-based technologies also are becoming a means to enhance collaboration with the workgroup. Portals allow for the integration of multiple screens of information, often from different applications, in the same interface. This allows quicker visibility to important information and faster, more accurate decision-making.

Collaboration in media has always been important. File-based technologies are making it easier, while at the same time enabling opportunities to apply some of the technologies and techniques common in the IT industry to the media space.

## 1.8 INCREASING AUTOMATION CAPABILITIES

While no one will ever eliminate the human from the workflow, there is certainly more and more of the workflow that is automated. This is mainly due to the increasing sophistication of automation systems. Early systems used a combination of proprietary hardware and standards-based machines to affect basic machine control. With the increasing power available to systems today, there is now the opportunity to do much more.

Automation has been able to spread into many areas . . . automation systems are involved in ingest, media management, playout, and archival of media assets. They control and interface with many kinds of devices from newsroom computer systems to graphics systems to video servers. These systems are now able to execute these functions in conjunction with complex business rules. Many even have workflow management features.

## CASE STUDY

### Enhanced Automation in the Newsroom

One candidate for increased automation that may be the least obvious is the newsroom. Newsrooms are sometimes viewed as the worst-case scenario for automation due to the chaotic nature of news production in general, especially in breaking news situations.

One major metropolitan broadcaster in the United States decided to take advantage of a rebuild at a green field location to explore how far they could take a number of technologies, including automation.

These days, there is a key standard for interfacing a number of technologies in the newsroom: Media Object Server (MOS). This is a well-supported means for allowing a newsroom computer system (NRCS) to communicate with many kinds of technology. This broadcaster wanted to leverage MOS to implement greater integration of the graphics technology to enable more seamless and automated playout during news broadcasts. One purpose for this was to decrease the staffing required for successful operation in the production control room.

This was achieved by using a desktop-based template graphics system that would allow the majority of producers and editors to be able to create their own graphics without the help of a graphic artist. This application was embedded in the newsroom computer system and tied via MOS to the script and eventually the rundowns. This reduced the need for a graphics operator to do most graphics and the complexity of graphics operation in the control room by stacking up the graphics in a simple way for the Technical Director.

The myriad factors that are driving the desire for increased cost reduction mean that anything that can be automated and remove the need for a human in the task is viewed very positively. As workflows have become more file-based and the sophistication of automation has increased, the opportunities for adding more automation to the process are numerous. Oftentimes these require new integration points.

Additionally, it is culturally possible to increase automation in the facility because people have begun to trust computers to do much more of their work. Computers are everywhere in daily life. This has led to increasing acceptance that computers will handle more things, even in media. Computers are perceived as more reliable than in the past. Whether or not this is true, this perception leads to a greater willingness to automate with computers.

This is something that should be taken advantage of. In many integration scenarios, the greatest problems are political or cultural. Perceptions matter. The modern integrator has to take all of this into account before making any architectural decisions.

Because of this, it is definitely worthwhile for them to check out the latest in automation technology. In conjunction with some of the technologies and techniques covered in later chapters, automation technology can be a very powerful tool.

## 1.9  CONCLUSION

Clearly change is in the air! The media industry has always faced change, but now it is more critical than ever that media professionals understand the nature of that change and be prepared.

This chapter covers the many reasons that now is the best time to architect systems and processes to react with agility. The key factors that make this need even greater than before include:

- Rapid growth of new distribution platforms
- Media consolidation
- Changing regulatory environment
- New competition
- Changing audience
- Increased adoption of IT
- Increased use of file-based, collaborative technologies
- Increased capabilities of automation

These factors mean that a new era of M&E is here. Certainly the media engineer working in this space knows that there are greater challenges and opportunities to be faced than ever before. It is critical that the industry finds a new way to address the problems it faces more quickly and more successfully move toward the creation of a service-oriented media enterprise.

## WHAT TO TELL YOUR BOSS

- There are many factors in the media industry, creating a demand for change at a faster rate than ever before. It is almost impossible to predict what will be the important technologies and business opportunities that the enterprise will be facing in 10 years' time.
- There are new technologies available today that present real opportunities for solving problems and creating new capabilities and efficiencies with a media organization.
- Information technologies are permeating the organization in every area. It is important to examine what new information technologies and techniques can help the media side of the organization further.
- Change is inevitable. It is important to ensure that the enterprise can adapt quickly.

# 2

# AN OVERVIEW OF INTEGRATION
# TECHNIQUES IN THE MEDIA INDUSTRY

It is often assumed that the media engineer's main job is the constant integration and maintenance of disparate media systems to keep a facility working. Sometimes it seems as if people see the media engineer as a crucial element of a working system, running around and patching holes all day long. The media engineer often sees himself or herself in this way as well. The truth is, by implementing good integration technology and process in a facility, media engineers can have very little to do, indeed. However, this requires a mastery of the art of integration (and it is an art) on the part of the engineer and support of good integration policies on the part of the media enterprise. As this is ultimately a book about new approaches to media integration, it is appropriate to ask the question: What's so great about integration in the first place?

## 2.1 THE BENEFITS OF GOOD INTEGRATION

The media enterprise that implements a solid integration policy and encourages appropriate hardware and software integration through capital projects and equipment purchases stands to gain a lot. Technology integration does not just solve technology problems; it also addresses many of the business problems that are often inadvertently caused by technology. If done properly, technology integration can help to increase collaboration, productivity, and visibility in an enterprise.

For example, many media enterprises (actually, in many enterprises of all industries) have developed organizational silos that separate business units from one another. Certainly it makes sense for different business units to be in separate domains of control, but many media companies have business units that do not effectively share information, have a hard time coordinating activity, or simply do not work together all that well. These isolated silos organically grow out of business culture or workflow, but may have technological causes as well.

Technology decisions, after all, often affect organizational planning. This is especially true if those decisions are made at an enterprise scale. The choice of an edit vendor may force how an editing department is organized. Or, more severely, the choice of a media system such as a newsroom computer system (NRCS) as the major communication medium among media professionals may shut out other departments that use a different technology such as enterprise instant messaging (IM) to communicate. Technology integration can alleviate these challenges. For example, integrating an NRCS with a corporate IM system would allow both media and IT departments to work the way they want and still communicate effectively.

Integration can also increase collaboration among these departmental silos. It does not take much to imagine the effect that shared storage between various creative groups in an enterprise can have on the quality of their output! That effect can be enhanced even more if the storage is able to integrate directly with the specific tools that each department uses.

In addition, because users of various systems (media or otherwise) often feel constrained by the boundaries that these systems impose through a lack of necessary functionality or a specific way of conceiving a business problem, technology integration can be used to increase the productivity of users and reduce the overhead of work created by unnecessary tasks and workarounds. Basically, manual labor that is caused by the limitations of technology can be minimized by maximizing the programmatic communication among that technology. This is one of the main reasons that enterprises integrate their technology, and it can take several forms.

In the media industry, the actual movement of media itself is a major source of workload inside a facility (even if that burden is carried mainly by production assistants and tape operators). A huge area of development in recent years has been in architectures that will reduce that need; in other words, create a tapeless workflow. This is entirely done through hardware or software integration, creating a huge logistical boon for a media facility. Any time a media system can get video into other media systems without the intervention of a human, an operator that would otherwise have to worry about that is free to do real work.

That benefit extends to data as well as media. Many business processes, especially those that cross organizational or departmental boundaries, will involve the duplicate entry of data. Everyone knows the story: one department prints a paper form from an antiquated scheduling system and hand-delivers it to another department, which types it into a completely different but equally antiquated billing system. Wouldn't it be nice if that data moved automatically from system to system because someone took the time to tie those two antiquated systems together? It is this promise of less duplicate data entry (which means less work for everyone) that drives much technology integration.

Another benefit of reducing human touch-points in an integrated system is the reduced possibility of introducing human error. That traffic operator that types scheduling data in a second time may make a typo on the twentieth or thirtieth form he or she has to do that day. This could charge the wrong advertiser and cause all sorts of trouble for the enterprise. However, if that double data entry is removed through integrating all scheduling systems, that danger goes away. This is just one way in which miscommunication can be avoided through the use of technology integration.

Another way is through the use of data validation. Instead of only moving data from system to system, the integrated environment can actually use system data to confirm data coming in. This can either happen by using aggregated data to restrict user input or by using semantics and data transformation on the back end to associate data fields with one another (an EDL entered into logging software actually becoming an editing timeline when opened in an edit suite, for example). This type of data management also reduces workload and eases business processes.

## CASE STUDY

### The Benefits of Integration

A major studio made the business decision to integrate many of their back-end systems with an existing, Web-based system that they implemented to manage ongoing projects. This Web-based system was the single largest source of data entry in the studio, because it was used at the outset of a major production project to get all aspects of production organized and continuously updated throughout production to inform all departments of changes and progress.

By integrating back-end systems such as editing, telecine, and scheduling into this Web-based project management system, the studio was able to use both client- and server-side data validation to reduce errors in data entry. Because the system knew which editing stations were available for a given project, it could provide the user with a drop-down menu of editing worksta-tions that was up-to-date and unique for every project. In addition, by inte-grating with the scheduling system, the project management system could present a list of people that producers could choose from to allocate responsi-bility. By implementing this system, the studio not only reduced the amount of up-front time required to organize production, but also increased the use of their project management system significantly.

Finally, software and hardware integration can actually help to make the lines of communication among system users clearer. Integrating two systems together means formalizing the ways in which those two systems can interact. If an automation system can only send a set number of commands to a video server, it is obvious what data is needed to make that connection work, and it is not expected that the automation system will have any additional responsibility over that server. This is different from human-driven processes, where nebu-lous boundaries and responsibilities may cause information-sharing problems among groups. Clear interfaces between systems and clear processes that dictate system use greatly increase productivity.

Using specific technologies that communicate with system users (such as e-mail servers, IM servers, or portals and task lists) can extend these clear interfaces into the human realm. Automatic notifications are a great way to leverage technology integration to improve human processes. For example, if a producer gets an e-mail when a particular media asset needs to be reviewed, it ensures that the producer gets to that task as soon as possible. Many software tools exist today that allow this sort of integration.

There are obviously many benefits to supporting hardware and software integration in the media enterprise. Unfortunately, too many facilities underfund integration projects or rely on vendors for this type of enterprise-wide integration. The benefits of good technology integration do not come to facilities that do not plan effectively for it.

## 2.2 WHAT IS INTEGRATION?

Okay, so, with all of the benefits of integration (benefits that are probably very obvious to those engineers who have been in this business and dealing with these issues for years), it is important to ask: What are the boundaries of this thing that is called "integration"? Are those that discuss its merits referring only to the modern concept of media software integration, or is this a science that has its roots in the earliest days of information theory? The short answer is the latter. Although, media professionals and IT professionals alike will find that the most benefit from an integrated system is felt when that system — and that integration — is done with cutting-edge technology.

As Fig. 2-1 illustrates, there are three "eras" of integration to be discussed. Obviously this book will focus on the latest phase: software-centric media system integration. However, it is important to cover all types

## The Evolution of Integration

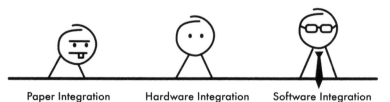

Paper Integration      Hardware Integration      Software Integration

**FIGURE 2-1**   The evolution of integration methodologies in the media industry starts with technology-independent integration that has existed for a very long time and progresses to the sleek integrated software systems of the present day.

of integration, because these exist today in the enterprise and, to a large extent, inform how future integration should be carried out.

The first "phase" of the integration evolution is what is referred to here as "paper integration." This basically means, at a high level, a technology-independent system that effectively passes the right information, at the right time, between various individuals and business units. Many media enterprises out there that have millions of dollars of fancy equipment on their premises have not yet mastered the art of paper integration and are suffering because of it. Good non-technical integration means that any-time there is more than one organizational unit in an enterprise (which encompasses almost every media organization), the touch-points among those organizational units are defined, formalized, and enforced. If an editorial group is giving a media asset a particular description as part of a logging process, and that description is not finding its way to the archive department even on a paper form, then that media facility is fail-ing at integration on a very basic level. This type of information manage-ment requires no technology . . . only people and good process.

And the truth of the matter is, in any media enterprise, paper integra-tion is all around! Anytime information needs to be exchanged and there is no technology solution for that exchange, the information will move through paper forms, phone calls, and e-mails. Paper integration is best done in a formalized way, however, so that the boundaries of what is and is not required of certain individuals is made clear to all parties. This avoids unnecessary pressure and overwork, and also helps the media enterprise to run smoother. Before starting on any extensive technology expansion, a media enterprise should ensure that all of its paper integration points are handled effectively. Chapter 6, Business Process Management: Definitions, Concepts, and Methodologies, dis-cusses some methodologies to do just that.

Once technology is brought into the mix, things begin to get interest-ing. For quite a while now, media enterprises have been integrating their systems using what is referred to in Fig. 2-1 as "hardware inte-gration." This evokes the hundreds upon hundreds of cables strung between routers and servers and whatever other video equipment is installed in a facility, carrying all manner of video, audio, and control data. Because much of what the media enterprise does every day was inappropriate for general-purpose computing platforms, it has only been recently that media facilities have been able to abandon dedicated hardware solutions for software ones, and so most existing system integrations use specific ports and protocols to accomplish their information sharing. This is effective when it is done in a specific way, but requires the support of equipment vendors to be successful. However, for many years this was all the industry had, and stringing coaxial and 422 cable became a major part of a media engineer's life.

Now, however, the industry has begun to move into the third phase of integration methodology: "software integration." The media systems of today are built on standardized computing platforms with standardized interfaces, and this means that the boundaries of what can and cannot be integrated into the larger system have blurred. Even media vendors that do not officially support a particular type of integration can be circumvented if they store their data in a database or use the TCP/IP stack to communicate. Many more types of integration are available in this phase, which opens the door to exploring new, combined functionalities in media systems. The potential exists for multiple asset management systems to pull from the same set of universally unique media identifiers, or for pricing data from a business system to mix with traffic and automation data to produce reports with dollar amounts for the finance group.

The boundaries of what can and cannot be shared with other systems become much more about what the purpose of a given system is, not just what interfaces it supports or what its physical limitations are. In a sense, software integration captures the best of both paper and hardware integration: it integrates pure business data, but in a way that is programmatic and automated. The new integration techniques discussed in this book are software-focused, and were in fact developed to deal with the wide array of integration options available to engineers managing modern, software-based facilities.

## 2.3 APPROACHES TO INTEGRATION

When considering an overall software integration game plan for a particular media enterprise, it is important to consider a number of factors (beyond simply budget). Some approaches to software integration provide greater functionality at the expense of implementation effort, while others will sacrifice cost and time to provide greater agility to make changes going forward. There are numerous tradeoffs and many options available to media engineers.

To simplify the discussion for the context of the book, this section considers three overall architectural patterns, so to speak, of software integration and discusses the merits of each. These three patterns are vendor vertical integration, best-of-breed integration, and custom or "house" solutions. They can be compared along several axes as seen in Fig. 2-2, including cost, ease of implementation, and agility. As usual with such things, the proper solution for a system in any given media enterprise is probably a combination of two or all of these patterns and is heavily dependent upon the business requirements to be

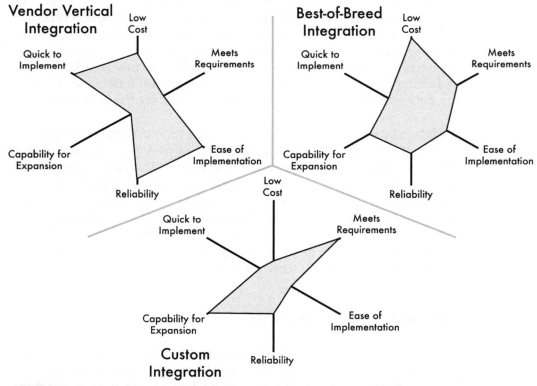

**FIGURE 2-2**  The three integration architectural patterns discussed in this section can be compared on a number of axes. The media enterprise will need to weigh the importance of each quality when considering system architecture.

fulfilled and the constraints of the integration project (although this book is biased toward agility-rich architectures such as SOA, because they are really a very good idea).

## 2.3.1  Vendor Verticals

Implementing a vertical solution to a problem, in this context, means finding a single system that addresses all or most business needs and adjusting the workflow and functionality to fit that available in the system. In other words, a vendor vertical architecture is one in which the system is supplied by a single media vendor (or, at least, a coalition of vendors in a supported configuration). It is the easiest architecture to implement (from a media enterprise's point of view, at least; it might be difficult for the vendor), but also provides, in most cases, the least appropriate functionality to address the business problem. An example of a vertical solution appears in Fig. 2-3.

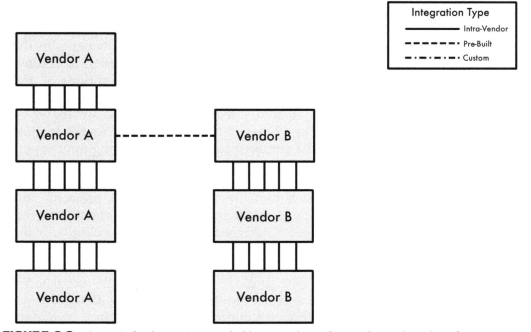

**FIGURE 2-3**   A vertical solution is provided by a single media vendor and tends to feature stronger integration between various system components than other architectures.

### 2.3.1.1 Advantages

Vendor vertical architectures have a number of advantages: they are simple to implement in a media enterprise, they are quick to deploy, and they offer a more consistent experience to the user than heterogeneous architectures.

Simplicity for a vendor-provided solution means that, in the media enterprise, a limited amount of enterprise integration is required to complete implementation of the system. Usually, no integration of any sort is required apart from initial configuration of the software/ hardware to correctly reflect the layout of the media infrastructure (component names and locations). The whole process can be very easy on the media engineer; this makes the pattern appropriate for situations where the enterprise is in a crunch, and cannot afford to spend cycles on component integration. Simplicity is also exactly what the doctor ordered for smaller media enterprises that do not need a sprawling solution to a straightforward problem — they would prefer to manage a few simple, vertical systems in their facility rather than one custom-integrated, complicated one.

In addition, buying a complete vendor solution has benefits in the speed with which a media enterprise can go from design to deployment. Often there are only a few supported configurations of any given media system, although sometimes very complex vendor tools are as complicated as custom integration but make up for it by directly addressing a wider range of possible business issues. In most systems, though, a media engineer can go from deciding upon a particular system to having it up and running. It is shopping, not development. This is very useful for greenfield projects that have a time crunch component (which sometimes feels like every project!). This architecture gets even speedier if there is an existing infrastructure in place that already supports the vendor chosen (for example, if the facility has systems by the same vendor).

Another major benefit of a single-vendor system is the consistency that users of the system experience when interacting with the various components. Vendors (hopefully) put a lot of effort into providing good user interfaces (UIs) for their customers that have a look, feel, and brand. More important, because the entire system is coming from the same place, there will be consistency over what things are named. Media assets will have the same identifier in all system components, terms for the same actions will be the same across all system components, and user preferences might even be shared across different views. This reduces the amount of training and support required for the system and therefore shortens the overall deployment effort.

### 2.3.1.2  Disadvantages

There are also a number of disadvantages to purchasing a complete system from a media vendor as opposed to introducing some customization or moderate integration effort. The main problems with such an approach are a possible increased cost, a functionality toss-up in terms of addressing real business need, and a reliance upon a single vendor.

Vendor reliance is arguably the largest disadvantage to a vertical solution and (in this era of high vendor and product turnover and effervescent support) can be a real headache for a media enterprise. Even in situations where the vendor chosen remains successful in the industry and in partnership with the customer, these architectures drastically increase the stake that a media enterprise has in the future direction of the vendor and its products. No one wants to be in a position where their central media systems are no longer manufactured and sparsely supported, or where the vendor does not support the product expansions or upgrades that the enterprise deems necessary. Vendor verticals are often difficult to integrate together, except in rare cases, and so choice of one vendor's system makes the enterprise wary to choose a different vendor for an adjacent system. Also, implementing a vendor vertical in an infrastructure with existing vertical solutions (from different vendors) in place may be a challenge. Getting the new vendor system to work with the existing vendor system makes the whole thing start to look a lot more like the best-of-breed pattern.

There may also be an increased total cost of ownership for the vendor system over a customized one. Because the media enterprise itself does not have ownership over the integration among system components, upgrades to single areas of the product have a tendency to ripple out, potentially to the entire system. Buying version 2.0 of a system component is not expensive in an architecture where that component is independent from other aspects of the system, but when all components are coupled together in a proprietary way, a little upgrade can turn into a big one! Vendor vertical solutions tend to trade off capital cost for implementation time and effort.

Finally, getting the necessary business functionality out of a particular vendor product is always a bit of a game of chance. Every media enterprise is different, and every media enterprise has a different way that it likes to work. Because media vendors need to focus on solving the most common case (or risk losing some of their potential customers), it is rare that a vendor system will be exactly the system that is needed to fill the hole in functionality in the enterprise. This means that the enterprise will need to make sacrifices in functionality just to find a product that works. Because of this, it is common in vendor-vertical-led infrastructures to have a series of undocumented workarounds and manual processes that fill the gap between what the enterprise needs and what the software or hardware solution provides.

A vendor vertical solution is appropriate for a media enterprise that needs a solution ASAP, and is willing to spend a little more up front to get that solution deployed. In addition, if the facility already features systems by that vendor or the enterprise stumbles upon a product that exactly meets their business needs, this is always a good idea to consider.

### 2.3.2  Best-of-Breed Solutions

Sometimes a single product does not even come close to addressing all the needs of a media enterprise. In this case, the enterprise may consider to pick and choose a series of products that cover the bases and use vendor-provided or in-house integration to link these products together into a working system like the one diagrammed in Fig. 2-4. This pattern of software architecture is called "best-of-breed." Best-of-breed solutions are often in the minds of media engineers, because they represent a good compromise between the expense and lock-in of vendor-provided solutions and the time and effort of custom development.

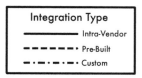

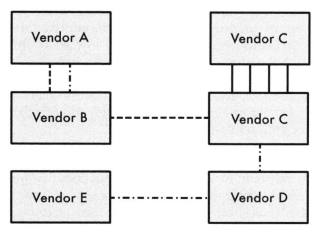

**FIGURE 2-4**   A best-of-breed solution uses components from many different vendors and integrates these components in the most effective way, whether that is standards-based, vendor proprietary, or custom-built.

### 2.3.2.1 Advantages

The three main advantages to a best-of-breed system in a media enterprise are the ability to achieve optimum functionality without development, the ability to achieve optimum cost, and the freedom of vendor neutrality.

There are minimal functionality gaps in a best-of-breed media system, because the media engineer designing the system is able to select products based on their ability to meet the needs of the business (although sometimes sacrifices must be made to ensure that the product will integrate with the rest of the system). For example, if a given vendor offers an asset management system with the right hierarchical storage management logic, but does not offer a good tape archive or an appropriate way to transfer digital assets into storage, a best-of-breed pattern would encourage the use of other products to address those needs.

The enterprise itself would be responsible for buying, finding, or building appropriate connections between these three components.

In addition to optimal functionality, there is also an optimal cost associated with these solutions. Because it is no longer restricting itself to a single vendor, the media enterprise has the opportunity to "shop around" for the right solution component at the right price. Unless an enterprise is already set up to pursue custom development (and therefore has a streamlined software department at a low cost), this pattern is the cheapest of the three. At the same time, however, a media engineer could spend much money and effort on integrating disparate system components together, so care should be taken to keep costs low throughout the integration phase (even though that has the potential to affect product selection).

Finally, a best-of-breed solution removes a facility's reliance on a single vendor, allowing them instead to select based on functionality and cost. This makes the entire system much more agile, because one component can be swapped out for another and not affect the versions or makeup of the rest of the system components. The integration connecting the system may be drastically affected by a single component change, but this infrastructure can then be changed to reflect the new orientation of the system.

### 2.3.2.2 Disadvantages

There are disadvantages to best-of-breed architecture as well. Because of the differing systems involved in constructing a true best-of-breed solution, enterprise integrators will need to deal with multiple vendor interfaces and interoperability, semantic differences among components, and potentially annoying support structures.

Buying lots of systems from different vendors and getting them to work together to solve particular business problems means implementing complex integration among these systems. Oftentimes there are established supported configurations, vetted by the vendors, in which two systems will interoperate. In other situations, there may be a standards-based method of communication (such as MOS; see Section 2.3.3 Custom Solutions for more possibilities) that can be leveraged due to its support by multiple vendors. There may also be areas where no integration solution exists yet, and the implementing media enterprise will need to develop (or outsource the development of) a communication link between systems. Regardless of the exact circumstances, best-of-breed infrastructures require the enterprise to design a solution that addresses all of the integration points in an architecture and buy or implement this solution. Compared to buying a single vendor vertical and deploying it immediately, this method takes a lot of work!

And it is not simply the technical communication that may cause problems in such a system. Because different software and hardware products have different ways of referring to the same data, there may be semantic or perspective issues to deal with. Two systems may have two different ways of considering the same information: they might both wish to give master IDs to the same assets or they might handle permissions and security differently. All of these eccentricities will need to be considered when implementing a best-of-breed solution.

Another difficulty that many an engineer has experienced when dealing with multi-vendor implementations is the blame game that arises out of the gray areas in various support contracts that come with the purchased systems. Especially in architectures that feature proprietary, vendor-supplied integration with various components, a problem with a connection between systems could spark a round of finger-pointing among the vendors involved. When this happens, more often than not, the media enterprise stuck in the middle loses. The media enterprise often cannot support these gray areas because it does not have the documentation, rights, or capability to open up the necessary proprietary components. This is a problem that is not shared by a vertical solution (where it is obvious which vendor must support the implementation) or by a custom solution (which can be completely supported in-house).

Even with these difficulties, a best-of-breed solution can represent the most effective way to get optimal functionality in an enterprise system. Because of this, most media enterprises today have a degree of heterogeneity in their infrastructures.

## 2.3.3 Custom Solutions

If all else fails, the media enterprise could decide to develop a software solution to a business problem itself. In fact, despite the connotation that custom software development has done so in many media enterprises, this might not even be a last-ditch effort in situations where business requirements are unique enough to make vendor-provided solutions prohibitive. Custom solutions, diagrammed in Fig. 2-5, may not include any purchased systems, although they could be the product of out-of-house development.

### 2.3.3.1 Advantages

Sometimes an in-house solution is the perfect fit in an enterprise that is already plagued with a number of incongruous vertical and best-of-breed systems. A custom system may even leverage functionality from some of these other systems in addition to the developed software. This allows for a number of ideal circumstances: exactly the business functionality needed to meet requirements and a user experience that can match the culture of the implementing enterprise.

Custom software provides ideal functionality for an enterprise because, well, why would it spend the time to build something that does not meet its needs? Unlike vendor verticals and even best-of-breed

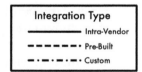

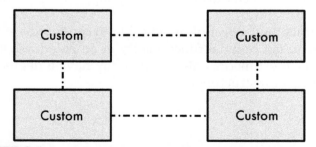

**FIGURE 2-5** A custom solution does not have any vendor dependencies. All system components are proprietary to the implementing enterprise, although interfaces can still be standards-based.

solutions, house software does not (or, at least, should not) feature functionality gaps that result in user workarounds and bad workflow. Any workarounds found necessary should be built into the custom system to make them "official" and keep system functionality ideal.

Custom software also provides an ideal user interface for the enterprise. A media organization may use some specific terms or concepts in its day-to-day business that are not shared by other enterprises, even competitors! Because these terms are probably also not shared by any media vendors, they would not work their way into any products purchased by the enterprise unless those products can be heavily configured to insert them. However, with custom software development, the way the enterprise likes to do business can be built right into the system. For example, if a post house develops internal "work orders" for itself and external "job orders" for its clients, a vendor-provided scheduling system would have to be customized to produce both of these programmatically. However, a custom solution could be built around these business objects, thinking of the data in the exact same way that the people in the organization do.

## CUSTOM SOLUTION CHECKLIST

The architectures discussed throughout the rest of this book can be considered a combination of the best-of-breed and custom patterns presented in this section. Therefore, techniques to elicit necessary business requirements for these systems are discussed throughout the book. However, when building a custom software solution for an enterprise need, there are a number of things that a media engineer should ensure:

- The enterprise software should meet the exact business need and not provide unnecessary functionality (to save effort and confusion).
- The enterprise software should not repeat any functionality that is already present in other systems, and instead leverage that functionality.
- The users of the system should have buy in on the functional requirements to make sure they will be happy with the end result.

- The user interface(s) should match the view most comfortable to the media enterprise.
- The enterprise must have a support structure in place for user problems and server-side difficulties or bugs.
- The developers should roll out the software slowly to make sure it works as intended and to provide time for training.
- The developers should elicit user feedback for later versions, since they have the benefit of being close to their users (in the same organization).

### 2.3.3.2  Disadvantages

Custom software development, especially at an enterprise scale, is unquestionably difficult and can be wrought with problems in an unprepared enterprise. Of the three patterns discussed, this one is hands down the most difficult to execute, and requires in-house (or contracted) development and support organizations. Because of this, many enterprises only resort to development in cases where no purchased solution will address business need.

A media enterprise hoping to develop a custom solution to a business problem will need to also develop the support capabilities required for the end product to work in the environment. There are no vendor support lines to call. Should users have problems with or feedback on functionality, they will need a place to go and a response that does not interfere drastically with their work schedule. In other words, in some media organizations (such as news), a 24-hour support hotline or some other such construct will need to be in place to have a workable system. This often requires too much effort for custom development to make sense in many organizations.

In addition to support staff, custom software also requires in-house development staff with enough experience to design and program a system that meets enterprise needs. Because most media organizations do not have such a staff on hand, contracting or outsourcing one may be required. However, even if the designers themselves are found, a media organization without any experience in product management or software development can still dig itself into a hole through poor planning.

Nominally because of these two concerns, custom development is the most expensive of the three patterns discussed. However, unlike with best-of-breed and vendor verticals, enterprises that start down the software development road will find it easier with each subsequent project. An enterprise support line can pretty much support two products as easily as one, and once the first system is under its belt, a software development department can begin to streamline its integration. So the potential also exists for custom development to be the cheapest of all three patterns. It all depends on the context and the experience of the enterprise.

To reiterate, the best solution for a given business problem may be a single vendor system, an integrated best-of-breed environment, a custom system, or some combination of these three. The specifics of the enterprise in question and its business needs will dictate the best course of action, and other factors, such as the details of specific technologies, will weigh in as well.

## 2.4 COMMONLY USED INTEGRATION TECHNOLOGIES

This is certainly not the first time in history this industry has needed to integrate. As seen in Table 2-1, there are a number of transport mechanisms and protocols in use today. While not comprehensive, it shows that the media industry already has a number of well-established mechanisms that need to be considered.

**TABLE 2-1**

A List of Some Common Transport Mechanisms and Protocols for Integration

| | | |
|---|---|---|
| RS-232 | Text files | MOS |
| RS-422 | Databases | NDCP |
| RS-485 | Ethernet | BXF |
| GPI | VDCP | Sony Control |

## 2.4.1  Transport Mechanisms

Transport mechanisms carry control information and data from one system or device to another. The media industry has primarily relied on mechanisms that were low latency and reliable due to the real-time nature of many applications.

One of the most pervasive of these transport mechanisms in recent history is the serial control transport that was actually adopted from the IT space. An RS-232 port is well known to anyone who can remember the old days before USB in PCs, when many devices would connect through the RS-232 serial port. RS-422 is a cousin of RS-232 that was based on balanced signals and thus could be run a much longer distance than unbalanced 232. RS-422 was and still is widely used in professional media products.

General Purpose Interface (GPI) is perhaps the most simplistic of all information exchanges. It only has the capability to act as a contact closure or other simple on/off mechanism commonly used to trigger events between two devices. For example, the pressing of a button on a production control switcher would send a GPI instantaneously to another device such as a tally light or a graphics device.

Another mechanism that was (and still is) used to carry information between media systems was the good old-fashioned text file. This mechanism was used in a custom way between different applications that had no other way to talk besides communal access to a file system. The files could be in some sort of standard form such as comma-delimited or fixed field length. Text files are used to transmit edit information/EDLs or any other document-style data like as-run logs.

## THE EDL

The edit decision list (EDL) is perhaps the most famous form of text file in media. In linear editing systems, it was the mechanism for moving the most basic edit information (reel and timecode primarily) from off-line to on-line edit systems. It was as simple in many ways as its cousin in film, the negative cut list. Today, the EDL as a document is still used in non-linear editing systems, although it may take advantage of a more complex medium (such as XML) and contain more information about transitions or clips used. Modern EDLs are used to transfer editing information from system to system, just as old EDLs were (although today these editing systems may be laptops running Final Cut Pro instead of their bulkier ancestors).

When EDLs were crucial to edit system usage, there were a number of popular formats (based on edit vendor) that were unfortunately incompatible and required translation to interoperate: CMX, Sony, and GVG are all examples. These file formats lost much of their importance in later years due to the rising popularity of non-linear editing systems and the growing sophistication of the image manipulation expected in edits. The ultimate successor to these formats in the modern era is the Advanced Authoring Format (AAF), a structured data format that represents both edit information and other metadata about media assets.

Another rather common mechanism for passing information between systems in the media space is through databases. This has been done increasingly by applications as the popularity of a common database interface like Structured Query Language (SQL) has grown. Like text file passing, database integration requires agreement among the participants as to where the data is stored. Sometimes stored procedures are placed directly on databases to affect manipulation of the common data by different applications.

One of the complexities associated with the use of databases as a means of exchanging data is the performance issues that arise when a large number of clients wish to access that same data. When faced with a multi-vendor environment where the vendors share a common database, it can be wise to consider whether the cost savings associated with using a single instance of a database are outweighed by the potential interference of multiple vendors on that common platform and the inevitable finger-pointing that follows. Instead, an integrator could choose to mirror the database across several instances, but then there are synchronization and data replication issues to worry about.

Despite all of these mechanisms, the most common way that applications interchange information today is via custom Application Programming Interfaces (APIs). The media industry, much like many other industries, currently has a dearth of standardized APIs available to it. Furthermore, some vendors consider their API to be highly confidential information and may be unwilling to share it readily with customers or third parties looking to integrate. These APIs are almost always accessed over TCP/IP on Ethernet.

## 2.4.2 Protocols

There are a number of protocols that have been very popular in media over the years. Perhaps one of the widest spread in recent times is the Video Disk Control Protocol (VDCP). This protocol was designed for use with the first generation of video servers, but even it was based on a highly popular protocol that came before it: the Sony VTR Control Protocol. VDCP was typically run over RS-422. The Network Disk Control Protocol (NDCP) was later developed with similar goals, but to run over TCP/IP networks instead.

Media Object Server (MOS) is a very popular protocol used in news systems. It is not considered to be a real-time control protocol like VDCP, and so is not expected to run on-air systems that require real-time response. It is XML-based, as it was developed relatively recently. Its main purpose is to pass around key information between a newsroom computer system (NRCS) and the many devices that must be orchestrated for the complicated dance that is a newscast.

When faced with getting information from one transport or protocol into another so that it can be understood by a different system, an integrator would commonly develop some form of gateway. A gateway uses physical interfaces to handle the differences in transport between two systems and would usually use some form of custom software to translate the data between two protocols. Gateways are still a common architectural concept in media integration and, as can be seen through the discussion of service gateways in Section 5.4.1: WSDL, one that will exist the future of media integration as well!

These are other forms of transport and other protocols used to integrate systems in media. The point of this section is not to give the reader a comprehensive reference, but rather a flavor of the kinds of integration methodologies that a modern integrator might encounter in "the wild." Knowledge of current and past media integration techniques is especially important for an integrator examining how to interface with legacy systems in a Service-Oriented Media Enterprise.

## 2.5  ACCIDENTAL ARCHITECTURE

"Accidental architecture" is a very descriptive phrase to describe the nature of almost any system that is out there in the real world today. An accidental architecture is one in which the overall plan for a facility's architecture does not exist (often despite best intentions!), and where the ways in which systems are interconnected grows organically instead of systematically over time.

Nobody sets out to build a tightly coupled brittle architecture. Usually a facility starts off life as a happy, greenfield site. In these cases, the architecture is probably not accidental at all at first, although it may be tightly coupled and brittle. As time passes, however, a number of projects will ensue, either because of changing business needs or because, over time, equipment simply needs to be replaced. As each project is done, it is usually done in isolation. Often there is no consideration to the overall facility architecture, either because there is no time or because the project does not have budget to address such larger concerns.

As each project is approached individually, the people involved are usually rewarded for doing the project with the least amount of money in the shortest amount of time. The end result is that this series of projects slowly mangles the look of the system architecture and dramatically increases the brittle, tightly coupled nature. See Fig. 2-6 for an illustration.

It's not that the system doesn't work. In each individual case, the project team has certainly accomplished the goals that it set out to accomplish. The system does work and it will connect to other systems as designed. It is just that expanding or otherwise changing now becomes a greater and greater challenge.

Perhaps the main offender in creating this kind of architecture in a facility is the vertically integrated system from a vendor. These tend

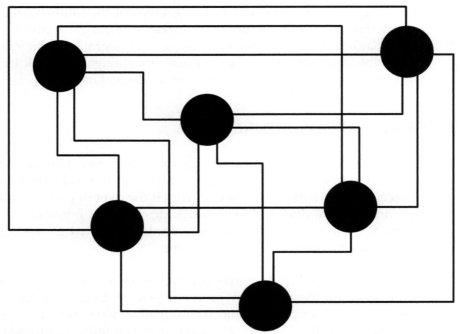

**FIGURE 2-6** Though an integrated architecture may be small and growing (shown here with only six systems), quick, thoughtless integration vastly increases the number of connection points. This is called tight coupling.

to be set up as islands or silos by the vendor because this is easier from the vendor's point of view. Many media facilities may have even dozens of these silos spread throughout the facility, each one working well for what it does, but probably not playing well with others.

Architecturally, these problems are made worse by the point-to-point style of integration that is used. In point-to-point integration, information is passed over a single connection directly from one device to another. Oftentimes, there may even be multiple point-to-point connections that are made between two systems to carry different kinds of data. The problem with this, of course, is that complexity grows as the number of connections grows.

This creates interdependence among systems. The good behavior of one system is usually required for other systems to properly operate. If one system has a problem, that problem can ripple through many systems.

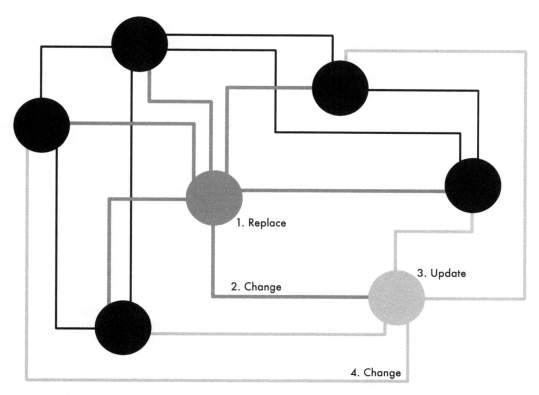

1. Replace

3. Update

2. Change

4. Change

**FIGURE 2-7**  A tightly coupled, accidental architecture can cause simple changes to have huge downstream consequences as one change ripples through the infrastructure, forcing other changes to keep a working system.

This "ripple effect" can lead to unexpected downstream consequences, as Fig. 2-7 shows. Sometimes a minor change in one system that nobody expected to have any effect on another system will have an effect. This is because, in many facilities, with so many connections between systems, it would require a superhero to keep track of them all! With such a risk, it is no wonder that many chief engineers are reluctant to make changes to systems unless absolutely necessary.

Furthermore, the presence of so many silos in a facility will mean that each individual silo requires its own administration. This is likely familiar to anyone responsible for these facilities who has had to deal with such a setup. Everything from users to the status of equipment is difficult to centrally manage. Instead, it must be managed in many separate places, none integrated with any other. Not only does this increase the amount of labor required, but it certainly exposes the facility to more administrative errors, such as expired users still on the system.

Because system architectures grow this way over time, it is unlikely that everything will remain properly documented. Nobody has the time to keep a single silo properly documented, let alone the interconnections. Any complex system that is attempting to respond to the business requirements laid out for it will inevitably develop a large amount of workarounds to get the job done. These are also likely to be largely undocumented.

So are what are the most important qualities of a system that has an accidental architecture?

One of the most obvious is that it is very difficult to change a system when it reaches end of life. Usually there are many individual interfaces that need to be considered to succeed at such a change. Because nobody wants to replace all of those other systems that it talks to, every individual connection needs to be rebuilt. And do not even consider putting in a second system from a different vendor to live side by side!

This problem is even seen when upgrades need to be done. Because of the tightly coupled nature of the architecture, a simple upgrade to one system can have impacts on several others, which can create further downstream consequences. This means that everybody feels the need to have a special lab with the particular systems and software in it that are in the production system, just to test that the upgrade will not create chaos for the rest of the staff. The presence of so many separate environments makes it even more difficult for an engineer to administer all of the systems in a facility.

Because of all of this, a facility ends up with the exact opposite of an agile system. The systems are not agile, they are fragile. This fragility is why the implementation of new functionality is ultimately discouraged in such enterprises. The pain that it can bring is often viewed as not worth it. Many an opportunity has been lost for positive change because of these problems. Because complexity increases as the square of the number of systems (see Fig. 2-8), everyone becomes happy just to tread water. In fact, it gets MORE difficult to make changes as new systems are added. So, at any point in time, the current state of the architecture is more organized than it will ever be again!

This is not what anybody sets out to do, but it happens all the time. There are a number of reasons for this, both business and technical.

Chief among the business reasons is the lack of appropriate budget to keep overall system architecture a priority. The budgeting process in

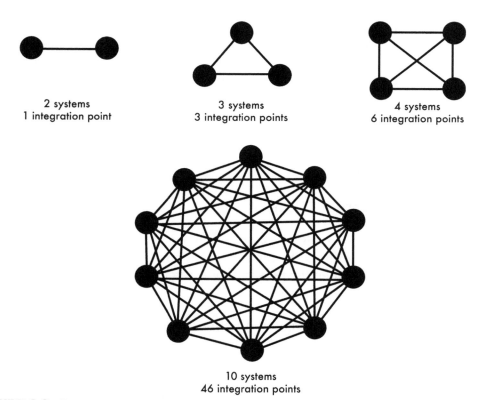

**FIGURE 2-8** Because every new system has potential connection points to every other existing system, a single addition may mean the addition of several new integrated connections. This is known as the n-squared problem.

many organizations is rather short-sighted and it is rare that attention is paid to the longer-term issues of system agility.

The way that enterprises are organized often will contribute to the problem as well. Different business units will each work to resolve their issues in a vacuum. Very few media enterprises have an overall technical governance organization that will take on the enterprise-wide view necessary to avoid silos.

Technically speaking, there is an obvious cause for accidental architecture: there is no single vendor out there that will do all things for an organization (despite their marketing claims). The need for multiple vendors, which has its own positive characteristics, also means that they will need to be interfaced.

What is also obvious is that there is a lack of fully successful standards and specifications to help with the interconnection and interchange between systems. This has been a concern for years, and organizations like SMPTE and AMWA are making moves to address this, but the past has certainly been filled with a large number of proprietary schemes.

## IMPORTANT NOTE

### Accidental Architecture Checklist

How would a facility know if it has an accidental architecture? All of them likely do! Engineers can check the following list. If more than just a couple of these apply to a facility then the prescriptions described in this book are just what is needed!

- Is the overall architecture ignored with each project that is done in the facility? Is no one responsible for governance?
- Does the facility have a multitude of silos integrated by sneaker-net or tapes?
- Are integrators afraid when small changes are made to one system about the effects it will have on other systems?
- When one system goes down, does it stop others from working?

- When someone leaves the company do administrators have to go to several systems individually to remove the user?
- If an analyst interviewed the staff about their work practices, would he or she find many undocumented workarounds?
- When a new system is added, do integrators have to consider the interfaces and impact on many other systems?
- Do upgrades fill the whole enterprise with dread because of the impact on the overall facility?
- When a system goes end of life do engineers want to squeeze every last drop out of it, not because of money, but to maintain their sanity?
- Does the facility lack a plan for the future of its systems overall? Is the future instead filled with many all-nighters, getting two systems to work together?

## 2.6 CONCLUSION

Media industry engineers are clearly not neophytes when it comes to integrating systems. This has been done in many different ways over the years. In this chapter, some of the history and the technologies were reviewed along with an assessment of where we are today.

And it isn't pretty, as anyone responsible for media facilities well knows. The following chapters will examine the prescription to these problems and explore ways in which they might be addressed. Things are unfortunately not going to get any easier. The future holds more than its share of new business challenges and opportunities that will need to be tackled. A reexamination of the very process by which facilities build and change their systems must now be done.

## WHAT TO TELL YOUR BOSS

- The importance of good integration is not going to go away in the future.
- Developing a new culture around the design, execution, and maintenance of systems is going to be necessary for the business to succeed.

- The accidental architecture in the facility took time to build and it is not going to go away overnight.
- Doing it right is actually going to produce immediate returns in reduced errors and improved productivity. It will also allow changes in response to new needs in the business to occur more quickly and easily in the future.

# 3

## SERVICE-ORIENTED ARCHITECTURE: DEFINITION, CONCEPTS, AND METHODOLOGIES

To effectively understand how Service-Oriented Architecture (SOA) fits into the media industry, a good media integrator has to know exactly what it is. SOA, for some, is not an easy concept to understand. It is hard to find two authors who agree on what SOA is. Many media professionals have probably heard the term bandied around in meeting rooms or trade show floors, and maybe even have a definition of their own that was cobbled together from various marketing snippets overheard at NAB or read in e-mail newsletters. Or maybe they understand SOA backward and forward and are just oh-so-anxious to hear yet another SOA evangelist try to describe it. The awful truth is that there is a lot of hype built up around the concept of SOA. It is the buzzword du jour, and because of that, it is a concept that garners a whole lot of skepticism in circles that have seen the rise and fall of many buzzwords.

SOA is more than just a buzzword, though. Hopefully this book can convince readers over the next few pages that in addition to being the latest enterprise technology craze, SOA is simply a good idea. It will be around in 10, 15, and 20 years. Maybe it won't be called SOA then and everyone will take it for granted, but it will be a key part of the way that large systems are designed, including media systems. So looking into SOA now is a great way to get a jump on what will ultimately be part of media's day-to-day reality.

## 3.1  INTRODUCTION

Service-Oriented Architecture is the result of an evolution in thinking regarding computer architectures. Maybe previous architectures did not impact the media world quite as much as this one because SOA's rise coincides nicely with the rise of computers inside the media facility and does tasks originally relegated to purpose-designed hardware. The best way to navigate this merger of two worlds is to know a little bit about the history of both. Appendix B covers a short, but relevant history of technology in media in a grand, sweeping way (for all of the IT folks out there), so this introduction will briefly discuss some of the technologies and architectural concepts that led to SOA.

SOA, remember, is not a specific technology. The main technology that supports SOA, Web services, is discussed in Chapter 5. SOA is a software architecture, and as such, its precursors are not specific technologies like Java, XML, or application servers, but instead are architectural concepts like object-oriented programming (OOP).

### 3.1.1  History of SOA

OOP is actually a great place to start a discussion on the history of SOA. It started a long time ago (back in the 1960s when dinosaurs roamed the Earth and TV stations were pulling video off of *tapes!*), but only about twenty years ago did it really begin to take off and revolutionize the world of mainstream software programming. Media integrators have to realize that SOA ultimately comes from the world of software. It may be widely applicable as a way to organize many different types of work in an enterprise, but it was all about software first. This is one reason why so many people get SOA confused with Web services, which is a software technology. OOP was the first time that computer users really started to deal with discrete and independent objects. A programmer could create a library that contained object definitions and the operations that those objects could do, and that library could be copied around and used in any number of different applications. In OOP objects are contained and reusable. These are key qualities in SOA as well.

OOP, due to its use of independent entities in programming, introduced a number of terms into the integrator's lexicon that became much more important and fully realized in later architectures. For example, software objects are "encapsulated." This means that to use a given object, integrators do not need to know intimate details about how it works, they just need to know the functions that it offers and their purpose. This is also a very important concept for SOA. Part of the definition of services is separating interface from implementation, which has its roots in the object-oriented era of software development. In addition, software objects introduce what is known as a "layer of abstraction" into the world of programming. Software programmers could think in terms of functions and procedures when writing objects, and then think in terms of objects when writing entire programs. This makes it much easier for them to write long and complicated programs that contain thousands and thousands of lines of code, because they are able to stash the code away behind these software objects. Readers will see the same thing in Chapter 5, but on a much grander scale. The SOA middleware layer introduces a whopper of a layer of abstraction into the mix.

The problem with OOP languages, and the reason that the IT industry is moving on to newer and greater architectures, is that they require a specific platform to work. A program that is written in C++ or Java, no matter how well it is designed and how efficiently it can fulfill its purpose, is only useful on C++ or Java platforms, respectively, and cannot cross over into the multi-platform space quite so easily. What was needed was essentially OOP at the application level. The next evolution in software architecture took the best practices of OOP such as encapsulation and abstraction, and let them work on an enterprise scale across many systems and platforms.

The first group to really take a crack at solving the enterprise application integration problem was Microsoft. Their approach, the Component Object Model (COM), allowed different software applications running on different platforms to exchange objects with one another. Essentially, it allowed otherwise incompatible systems to have a conversation.

There are many details to COM and its more fully realized successor, the Distributed Component Object Model (DCOM), but one of the more interesting and relevant topics to SOA is the idea that COM introduced an Interface Definition Language (IDL).

COM's architecture included an IDL as a way for COM components to specify to other COM components what sort of objects and operations they offer. Microsoft realized that the first thing to be done when integrating two very different systems is to give them a common language to speak. IDL was a way to do that, because it allowed a system to say, "This is what I can do." Then, other systems could see that interface and know how to use it. This idea is crucial to a working enterprise architecture.

There are two ways to accomplish this joint understanding among systems. One is to ensure that both systems adhere to the same functionality standard. This is the common practice in the media and entertainment (M&E) industry today, and can be seen in standards like MOS or the SMPTE S22-10 BXF. It works because both systems know every operation they need to specify and every data type they need to understand. The other way to accomplish intersystem communication is to establish an open language (like IDL) that allows each system to advertise its own unique functionality to every other system in the enterprise. Instead of forcing a system to adopt all of a particular communication standard, having a standard interface language allows systems to adapt to each other's interfaces. Standardized and published interfaces originated with COM, but with SOA and its common implementation technology Web services, they have really hit their stride.

The last architecture in this little history lesson is the common object request broker architecture (CORBA). It is very similar to COM and DCOM, but was established as an "open" alternative (don't want to let Microsoft hog the spotlight for too long!). CORBA took off in popularity beyond DCOM, and did have a few advantages over the Microsoft model. One of the main ideas that CORBA introduced to the integration world is the idea of "wrapping" a software component to give it a published interface. Wrapping has its place in SOA too, and it will be discussed in detail elsewhere in this chapter.

## CORBA

CORBA was developed as a standard in 1991 by the Object Management Group (OMG), a consortium made up of a number of technology companies and dedicated to the development of object-oriented concepts in the enterprise. It allows a programmer to write enterprise applications using any methodology desired, and then "wrap" that application to a standard interface using an IDL. These ideas are very similar to the ones advocated by SOA.

SOA started appearing as a term to refer to an architecture of business services right around the time CORBA was a major force in the enterprise integration world. Because of this, many people that were around and aware then intimately associate CORBA with SOA. Many people consider CORBA to be the first implementation of enterprise SOA, which is an accurate assessment. CORBA has been replaced by other technologies such as Web services as the preferred SOA implementation standard. While CORBA was standard and open, these new technologies leveraged widely adopted existing technologies such as XML and HTTP to do many of the same things CORBA invented new standards for.

Integrators will, however, still find CORBA implemented in many IT enterprises. It is also important to note that these CORBA networks do not go to waste, even if a more modern technology is used to build the SOA! CORBA is a well-conceived technology and offers all the functionality an enterprise could need, just in the wrong format. A service gateway could certainly be dropped into an existing CORBA network to allow it to plug in to a modern enterprise SOA.

So CORBA and SOA actually are fairly intimately related. New development does continue on the CORBA front, as well — the newest revision to the CORBA standard came out in 2003. Interestingly, the OMG is now focusing on industry-specific business models and processes. Their Web site is http://www.omg.org.

One final note: COM, DCOM, and CORBA are all technologies as well as architectural concepts. Their developers not only outlined suggested ways that software components should be used, but also the standards that would allow those components to be used in that way. It would be accurate to think of the COM or CORBA architecture as a subset of what is known today as SOA. This means that an enterprise could actually implement an SOA using DCOM or CORBA technologies!

## 3.1.2  Adoption in Other Industries

The term Service-Oriented Architecture has been on the scene since the days of CORBA (really, only a little over a decade ago). Because it is an architecture, and not a technology, a viable SOA could be created out of many computer technologies. And indeed SOAs have been in place for quite some time in many large enterprises. The point here is that SOA is not a *new* idea (at least in non-M&E industries), but at this point the IT industry has gotten really good at it so everyone is starting to take notice. It is useful to look at some other industries and how they have made use of the SOA paradigm.

SOA first started getting bandied around as an architectural concept in 1996 with the publishing of a Gartner report titled " 'Service Oriented' Architectures." However, the first major SOA installations are probably more closely aligned with the advent of the technology known as Web services (discussed in Chapter 5). SOA went hand-in-hand with CORBA technologies at the beginning of its life, but around 2003, the major IT vendors began packaging SOA products separately from CORBA. SOA began to stake out a claim of its own in the enterprise software world. It has followed a fairly steep rate of adoption ever since — good ideas in computing seem to catch on quickly. Today SOA is pervasive throughout the IT industry. The Evans Data Corp. even predicts that SOA adoption will double between 2007 and 2009.

In industries other than M&E (such as banking, insurance, healthcare, or finance), SOA has taken off as a way to architect enterprise systems. One interesting thing that is happening in other industries as SOA architectures become more popular is the development of industry-specific SOA standards. As industry-specific enterprises roll out service-oriented infrastructures, they are finding the need to define specific industry-wide objects and services to increase interoperability with other facilities. The prediction is that integrators will see much the same trend in M&E in the coming years. Indeed, organizations like the Advanced Media Workflow Association (AMWA) have already begun this work.

## SOA CASE STUDIES

SOA has been around for more than a decade now, according to most accounts. However, major enterprise adoption of SOA has only really started occurring in the last five or so years. Because any significant, enterprise-wide architectural change takes a couple of years to execute, the first case studies of SOA success are only starting to roll in from various industries that were among the first to adopt SOA principles.

For example, a major financial services firm recently used SOA to change their workflow and introduce more automatic processing of accounts, thus reducing the load on their staff and the mistakes of manual entry. The project took just under two years in total, and allowed the company to reduce staff and save millions annually. ROI for the solution was 18 months.

ROI for these solutions is living up to expectations, although the time frame may be a few years. SOA is a major commitment, which is why an entire chapter of this book (Chapter 8) is dedicated to the topic of moving toward an SOA in a media environment.

### 3.1.3 SOA in a Nutshell

Hopefully the point has been made that SOA is a force to be reckoned with. It is the rightful heir to the enterprise software integration throne. This is not just because SOA took the best practices from the architectures before it, but also because SOA is different and better than those architectures. It is rare to find a concise definition of Service-Oriented Architecture. That is because no such definition really exists. There are some very good definitions out there, but nothing that is widely recognized as *the* definition of SOA. This book will certainly contain a concise definition, but the definition comes with a disclaimer: the line between SOA and not-SOA is a bit blurred, and the best thing that anyone can say about it is that when someone understands SOA, that person will be able to look at a system architecture and tell whether or not it is service-oriented.

## THE OPEN GROUP'S DEFINITION OF SOA

One of the better SOA definitions out there is published by the Open Group (http://opengroup.org), and reads as follows:

> Service-Oriented Architecture (SOA) is an architectural style that supports service orientation.
> Service orientation is a way of thinking in terms of services and service-based development and the outcomes of services.
> A service:
> Is a logical representation of a repeatable business activity that has a specified outcome (e.g., check customer credit, provide weather data, consolidate drilling reports).
> * Is self-contained
> * May be composed of other services
> * Is a "black box" to consumers of the service
> An architectural style is the combination of distinctive features in which architecture is performed or expressed.

The SOA architectural style has the following distinctive features:

* It is based on the design of the services, which mirror real-world business activities, comprising the enterprise (or inter-enterprise) business processes.
* Service representation utilizes business descriptions to provide context (i.e., business process, goal, rule, policy, service interface, and service component) and implements services using service orchestration.
* It places unique requirements on the infrastructure — it is recommended that implementations use open standards to realize interoperability and location transparency.
* Implementations are environment-specific — they are constrained or enabled by context and must be described within that context.
* It requires strong governance of service representation and implementation.
* It requires a "Litmus Test," which determines a "good service."

This and other established definitions each paint a part of the SOA picture. Another part is painted in this chapter. To truly and completely understand the concepts and principles of SOA, integrators should seek out as many views of the architecture as they can. This book endeavors to present SOA in the most digestible way for the media professional, but certainly there are insights to be gleaned from other perspectives.

So now, without further ado, here is the definition of SOA, in a nut-shell, that will be referred to in this book:

> SOA is an architecture of independent, wrapped services communicating via published interfaces over a common middleware layer.

Short and sweet. Perhaps not entirely satisfying, because it weasels out of a nice, normal definition by using words like "wrapped," "services," and "middleware" that have SOA-specific connotations and to which Chapters 4 and 5 are dedicated. To get a definition without all that baggage, readers should check out the Open Group's not-so-concise version. Also, notice that nowhere in the definition does the word "software" appear. The term "SOA" may have come out of the software world, but it describes an architecture that can be implemented using hardware or even people and paper forms. No computers required! Of course, SOA still has its greatest usefulness in the world of software, because software technologies are really able to leverage the benefits of business agility and visibility that SOA brings.

SOA can be recognized when it is seen. Fig. 3-1, for example, is *not* an SOA. This sort of accidental architecture arises over time when there is no centralized planning to an infrastructure or specific project requirements and constraints create less than optimal integration plans. The systems in this diagram may very well be business services like the ones that appear in an SOA, but there is no common middleware layer over which they all communicate. Messaging is tightly coupled and distributed.

Fig. 3-2 also does not represent an SOA. These software systems are communicating over a common infrastructure, but they are not doing so in an independent, loosely coupled way. And because the implementation details of each system are crucial to the interoperability of the entire network, there is no "service layer" in this architecture. The software systems are not exposed as services.

Fig. 3-3 represents what an SOA really looks like. The middleware layer, the independent services, and the wrappers that the services use to present a common interface to the rest of the infrastructure are all crucial SOA components. Each of these SOA components will be discussed in detail in this chapter and in Chapters 4 and 5, but, in preparation for that, a brief definition of each follows.

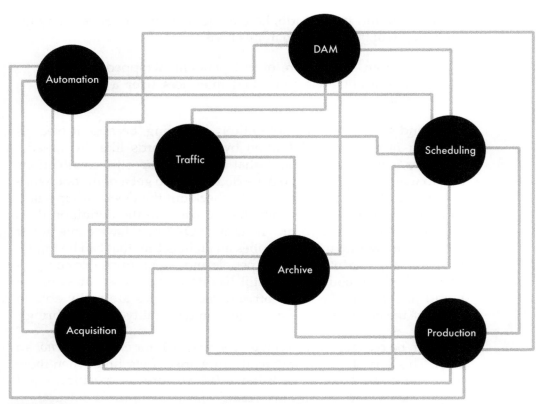

**FIGURE 3-1**  This figure represents an organically grown, tightly coupled architecture. None of the SOA benefits are felt in such an infrastructure.

Services are the bread and butter of a Service-Oriented Architecture (after all, it is right there in the name!). A service is any participant in an SOA that provides business value. Recall that services do not have to be software applications, but in an architecture where the middleware layer is implemented using software systems, each service is going to have a little software in it (even if it is, for example, the Producer Approval service) if only to present the service interface to the middleware layer. The important thing about services is that they are *loosely coupled*, or independent and self-contained. No service implementation can depend on any other service's implementation to provide its business value. Services do call other services — different classes of services are discussed later — but always through the service interface and never through hard-coded back channels. The interface a

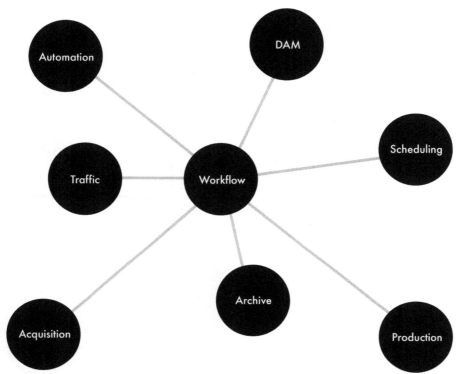

**FIGURE 3-2** This sort of hub-and-spoke architecture is closer than the tightly coupled architecture to the ultimate goal of SOA, but still lacks many of the central benefits. For example, there is no service layer of abstraction between the central entity and any of the outlying components.

service presents is the other important aspect of what defines a service. Just like its predecessors, SOA separates interface from implementation. The rest of the SOA does not care about how a service is implemented, just the business value it provides to the rest of the enterprise.

Wrappers are the components that sit between a service and the middleware layer and transform messages that pass through them. Wrappers provide a layer of abstraction between the service and the middleware layer, allowing an integrator to change either one without drastically affecting the other. This is crucial to the business agility message of SOA, which will be discussed later on. Wrappers, more often than not, are also the components that give services an implementation-independent interface. Who knows what sort of services will have to be implemented in an enterprise? Because most software

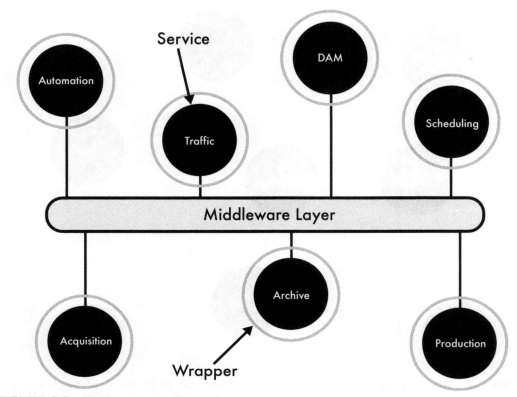

**FIGURE 3-3**    Finally, a depiction of SOA.

systems do not automatically come with a published interface that can communicate with the middleware layer, integrators are able to write wrappers to make these disparate systems into services.

Finally, the middleware layer is the catch-all term used to describe the communications infrastructure around a network of services. The middleware layer can provide a number of benefits to service communication such as business process automation, service directories, security and reliability, and data transformation. More often than not, a middleware layer is composed of multiple servers providing each of these different functions (although, in a hypothetical computer-free SOA, the middleware layer could also be the guy that routes, sorts, and stores messages sent between services). Middleware provides a lot of the visibility and governance benefits touted with SOA.

## 3.2 THE BENEFITS OF SOA

Service-Oriented Architecture provides solid business benefits to organizations that take the time and effort to implement it correctly. In fact, one of the main attractions of SOA (and the reason that all the IT pundits like it so much) is just how many different value propositions it has. This does not mean subtle, technical value, instead it means large, sweeping business value that makes marketing people do double takes. And, for the most part, SOA delivers on that value promise (although this book covers all the little quirks and imperfections as well). So, to get an appreciation for what SOA provides to the enterprise, and what has made this such a hot topic in the IT industry, it is important to walk through some of the benefits of SOA.

There are three main types of benefits that SOA provides to the enterprise:

1. Business agility benefits
2. Business visibility benefits
3. Organizational benefits

Media professionals may hear different IT pundits touting different SOA values than the ones discussed in this book. They may focus on reusability or componentization or something else when they speak about SOA. However, this particular way to examine SOA highlights the key benefits that SOA can provide to the M&E industry specifically. SOA brings along with it all of these benefits when implemented, but some may be more important than others. Everyone realizes that M&E could benefit from more reusability or more interoperability, but when an integrator is making the big SOA sell to the CTO or VP of Engineering, he or she will want to focus on benefits that have the most positive effects on the M&E pain points. And this section does just that.

## 3.2.1 Business Agility

The central benefit of an SOA is that of agility. SOA adds what software designers refer to as a "layer of abstraction" into an enterprise architecture through the use of wrappers and standardized interfaces. This abstraction boundary creates independence among components on either side, meaning that their implementations do not affect one

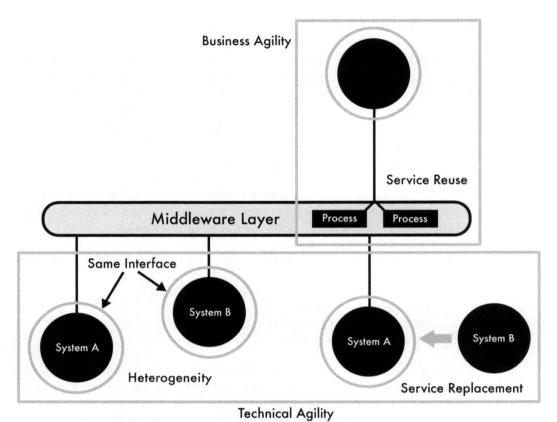

**FIGURE 3-4**    A representation of how SOA brings business and technical agility.

another. This is the enabling factor for business agility. This chapter even goes into detail about how SOA services create this layer of abstraction (and specifically how abstraction provides agility). Fig. 3-4 provides a depiction of the business and technical agility benefits of SOA.

Agility means that it is easier to change components of the SOA architecture than it is in tightly coupled architectures. Considering the sheer amount of business changes the M&E industry is currently undergoing, this would be an invaluable quality for an infrastructure to have. Integrators are able to change the implementation of a service without affecting other components in the SOA. Should they decide to add additional services to the infrastructure, these simply are added to the middleware layer without affecting existing services.

The service is an independent entity, and this is valuable when making changes to an enterprise architecture.

If, for example, an integrator decides to implement a new-fangled, software-based automation system to handle playout in a media enterprise, in a tightly coupled architecture, that automation system would need to get hooked up to the traffic system, the asset management system(s), the scheduling system, and also whatever sort of system monitoring network exists in the enterprise (Simple Network Management Protocol, or SNMP, for example). Rarely do two boxes work as soon as they are plugged together, so this represents significant effort on the part of the integrator to get each of these links up and running. In an SOA, however, the only link that needs to be created is the connection between the automation system and the middleware layer, because all of the other systems are connected to each other via the middleware layer. This reduces the overall amount of work that needs to be done, and therefore enables faster change. This is business agility.

In a tightly coupled architecture, each integrated connection is independent from every other connection in the system. However, the services/systems are dependent on one another to function in the overall workflow. Getting that automation system hooked up to the traffic system does not improve the amount of work it will take to get the automation system hooked up to asset management. Also, it does not matter what else the traffic system is connected to; these connections do not generally benefit the new connection created between traffic and automation. And yet, if an integrator had to switch out the traffic system with a different or upgraded system, there would suddenly be multiple connections to manage.

In SOA, integrated connections are dependent on middleware while services are now independent. Integrators only need to set up the link to the middleware layer once, but they have the opportunity to reuse that link for other integration projects. This makes each additional integration project easier than the last. In other words, if for the first SOA project an enterprise service enables and integrates its traffic and automation systems, it has three distinct tasks: connecting the automation system to the middleware layer, connecting the traffic system to the middleware layer, and writing the logic or processes into the middleware layer that dictate how these two services interact. Now, if the media enterprise decides to add a scheduling system to the SOA to integrate with automation, it only has two tasks: connecting the scheduling system to the middleware layer, and writing the integration logic that connects the scheduling system's interface to the existing automation service interface. If it were to then decide to integrate scheduling and traffic, it would only have one task: writing the integration logic. The wrappers and interfaces are already written. This is the flip side of business agility — a kind of technical agility.

The greatest benefit of agility in SOA is that SOA can help a media enterprise to implement heterogeneous vendor environments. The services in an SOA are not low-level, implementation-oriented entities, they are at a business level. This means that the interfaces presented by these services are not driven by the details of how the service is built, but instead by the business functions that the service provides. An editing system, for example, should provide the same business-level functionality to the enterprise, regardless of who makes it. Whether an enterprise is using a top-of-the-line editing suite running on dedicated, custom hardware or a consumer product running on a laptop, it is providing the same business service. True, the quality of the output will probably differ drastically between these two editing service implementations, but the functional requirements are the same: edit the piece, consume an EDL, produce a 10-second tease, etc. If these two editing systems performed the same business functions, they could be wrapped to expose the exact same interface.

In reality, a dedicated editing suite will probably be able to expose more business functionality than a producer's laptop, but assuming that one service's functionality is a subset of the other's functionality, then it does not matter to the rest of the SOA what system is implementing the core service functions. It only matters what interface the service wrapper exposes. A business process could call "edit the piece" on either service, using the exact same language, and it would get done. Now, in this case, the service client might care which of these two systems edits the piece, so there are business rules and other middleware components that will allow the user, and not the systems or the IT guys, to make that decision in an integrated enterprise. But, should the enterprise lose an editing suite, the user will probably be thankful that the integrated enterprise can just as easily pass off work to the editor's laptop during crunch time. And should the enterprise decide to replace all of the custom suites with commodity editing solutions (for whatever reason), that decision will not affect the other services in the enterprise. In this way, SOA helps enable agile, heterogeneous environments.

## CASE STUDY

### Using SOA to Reduce Vendor Dependence

One of the most often heard complaints in media enterprises are those associated with the reliance on a single vendor for key technology. Whether it is the sheer cost of equipment when one vendor "owns" the market, the inability to get certain features for a part of the facility, or the difficulty often seen with integrating the occasional piece of "third-party" technology — nobody likes to be dependent on a single vendor.

A post-production department at a major studio decided to do something about this situation in their facility. They noted that they had been completely dependent on a single large vendor for editing technology. When the time came for an expansion of the facility, they felt that the response they were getting from this vendor from the request for proposal (RFP) was not really competitive, and they felt the incumbent vendor was taking advantage of the situation.

They spent some time reevaluating the nature of the project and the best way to structure it to achieve their business goals. By including generic service definitions of what they wanted to achieve with their editing systems, along with accounting for integration efforts in the project itself, they were able to make substantive moves toward SOA in the facility.

This also allowed them to look more carefully at their growth needs. They were able to eventually expand their existing system from the incumbent vendor, while at the same time add new editing technology from a second vendor in an appropriate area. Because they ultimately integrated their growth needs with a common interface to their other systems, they were able to treat them as similar services at their business workflow level.

They have not, as yet, solved the problem of how to exchange media between the two systems as this was not an immediate issue. They are currently looking at how best to add a "media layer" to their existing SOA. No longer does one vendor have an absolute hold on them, and they are looking forward to bringing in more technologies that meet their needs using a service-oriented approach.

In addition to replacing services without affecting other services, SOA enables the flip side of agility: service reuse. Media enterprises often have tremendous repeat functionality: every department has an asset management system, every producer uses slightly different methods to track production expenses. A facility could probably save a good deal of time and money if it could leverage existing systems to provide new functionality. This is one of the promises of SOA. Instead of buying a new archive or asset management system for a department because infrastructure or political red tape prevents that department from making use of existing systems, a media enterprise can expose that system as a service, and then any group in the enterprise is able to write services and processes with that shared archive/asset management service in the back end. The human work to access and manage that system is still departmentalized, so political issues become more of a matter of working out the shared load on the system. SOA is an architecture that has the capacity for equal access across the entire facility; the reuse of services is one major benefit of that access.

SOA evangelists often talk about broad reuse in SOA as the ultimate goal of service reuse. Unanticipated reuse also occurs when one department in a service-oriented enterprise discovers a service offered by another department that they did not know existed but were able to use. Because SOA makes it just as easy to use a service in a different facility or area of the business as it is to use a service sitting right there, having individual project teams share resources not because they are told to, but because they can, is a real possibility. This sort of reuse will probably be rare in M&E except in a few of the largest enterprises. For example, in facilities that have lots of production teams working independently that are in charge of their own facilities, this kind of broad reuse could help out quite a bit. However, in most media enterprises, where a single operations group provides systems for any and all production teams, this kind of reuse naturally arises more than it will in an SOA.

As soon as the concept of SOA is extended outside the enterprise to the entire industry, reuse becomes a much bigger deal. Imagine discovering a post facility because they have advertised their service interface in a service registry (oh yes, whole businesses can be services, too) and taking advantage of their services. At the inter-enterprise level, the M&E industry is heavily federated. Federation is discussed further in Appendix E, but suffice it to say that when multiple facilities start exposing services, reuse of federated services will be a huge benefit.

This brings up an important point about service reusability and increasing reuse: this benefit of SOA is felt more strongly as more services get added to the architecture. Eventually, a facility can reach a "critical mass" of services that will make service reuse an easier option. After all, how can project teams make extensive use of services when only a handful of services exist at all? Initially, every SOA project will likely mean all new services, but as more services get added to the network, project teams will be able to take greater and greater advantage of existing service assets. When an enterprise hits SOA critical mass, no one will even have to tell or suggest to project teams that they connect to the SOA to achieve their functionality — it will be the most convenient way for them to complete their work. This is a big part of the ultimate promise of business agility.

## ACTION ITEM: FIND OUT HOW THE INFRASTRUCTURE AFFECTS AGILITY

Having an agile enterprise means the integrator is able to make changes more quickly as the architecture develops. So, over the course of the next few projects, a media enterprise should measure the amount of time a project takes to complete relative to its cost and scope. If it is building within the context of an agile SOA, the duration should decrease as the projects move forward. In a tightly coupled, point-to-point architecture, it will probably take more time to complete each subsequent project.

### 3.2.2  Visibility

Another major benefit of Service-Oriented Architecture is visibility, both into data and into the business. SOA allows a media enterprise to aggregate data from across the enterprise for analysis or monitoring, and also gives it a good idea of the real-time capacity and load of systems. SOA can help an enterprise to do all of that, as shown in Fig. 3-5.

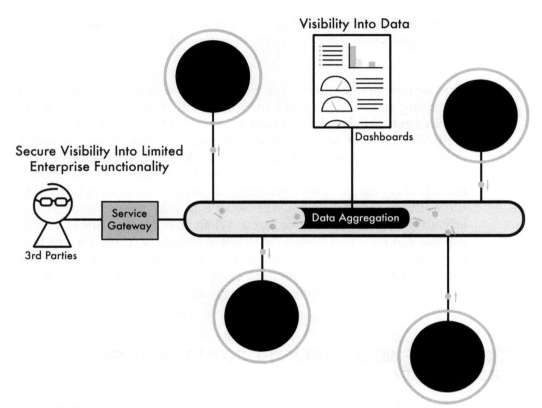

**FIGURE 3-5**   A representation of visibility within an SOA environment. Dashboards, gateways, and data aggregation all provide views into previously obfuscated data.

Who hasn't wanted a better idea of what was going on in their facility at any given moment in time? Better business decisions can be made with knowledge of what systems are currently doing and how well infrastructure has performed in various situations in the past. This is the promise of business visibility, and the primary enabling factor is data aggregation. To produce the sorts of business metrics that managers and system administrators want, they need to be able to look at data from multiple systems. For example, to determine what news stories are the most popular in a news organization, a producer may want to look at a combination of which graphics and clips are getting used more often and what stories the other producers are currently working on. This represents data from multiple systems that need to get aggregated into a single place where these metrics can be determined.

In a Service-Oriented Architecture, services measure and provide these data. The graphics, asset management, and newsroom computer services may be able to provide data about story popularity from their systems. The key is to be able to identify these data and get it out of the service and into the middle layer, the one place in an SOA that has visibility into all services and that can collect and analyze their data. The way to accomplish this is through intelligent wrapper design.

To externalize their data into the middleware layer, services need to be able to provide those data on either a real-time or as-needed basis. The details of what data that may be and how those data are formatted and exposed are business-function specific and will differ depending on whether it is a transcoding service, editing service, accounting service, etc. Again, wrappers provide the key to making these data visible. Sometimes getting the information needed out of an end system is a difficult issue that involves polling the system for data or performing a series of sequential calls like logging in, querying for an asset ID, using the asset ID to get specific asset metadata, and logging out. In an SOA, the wrapper is the place for these details, providing the middleware layer with a pure business level call to make getting the data independent of how the application providing the service is implemented. Because all service communication flows through the middleware layer, integrators are also able to get data out of messages moving from service to service.

What could such data be used for? Well, system administrators would certainly be interested in data about the health and current state of the services in an enterprise, and so data aggregated from services could be used to create enterprise dashboards to monitor the status of a facility's infrastructure. Here SOA is providing functionality similar to that of SNMP or other monitoring protocols, but on the business level similar to that of a "super SNMP." An administrator can notice that more work is coming from a particular department or production team (based on business data moving through the middleware) and react accordingly, even if all teams are using the same systems. Because SOA deals in business data, this sort of activity monitoring can be used to determine both technical (e.g., a system down) and business (e.g., resources not allocated efficiently) problems.

Management would also be interested in this sort of a dashboard. Imagine having a single portal screen with information about what projects are currently using equipment, all productions that are behind schedule and by how much, and averages of system usage (by production) over the last month. Because SOA is aggregating business data, and not simply technical data, such metrics are possible. End systems, like a scheduling system, may be able to determine a handful of metrics themselves because they have all the information anyway, but they are not extensible and systemic like an entire SOA, so their usefulness is ultimately constrained by the scope of that vendor or what data the system decides to display. SOA constraints are in service functionality not user interface. The management dashboard, incidentally, is a big sell for SOA in the IT industry; the idea resonates favorably with M&E management, too.

Using the business intelligence of SOA is a way to know the capacity and capability of a facility. Having aggregated statistics of system load allows for more accurate capacity planning. In addition, analysts are able to quickly determine areas of the business where there are functional gaps and bottlenecks. Instead of simply guessing about the aspects of the system infrastructure, SOA provides defined and accurate answers.

Another potential benefit of data aggregation in SOA is the ability to share business data with third parties. Media engineers may not agree, but it is not an entirely bad idea. Service gateways can be constructed as part of an enterprise's SOA that expose specific functions to authorized third-party users. This means that, in the right circumstances, a content provider could call a service to get a universally unique ID (UUID) for their content or a post house could call a service to get filtered asset metadata based on that UUID. The enterprise could even offer clips for download, at a price, to other media enterprises using SOA. SOA is a wonderful architecture for doing this because the aggregated middleware layer means that integrators only need to expose a single service gateway instead of exposing lots of individual systems for each externally facing function (or, even worse, constructing a tightly coupled, externally facing system that is difficult to change if it is decided that the public should not have access to certain data). With the increase in the use of new media, having visibility in the enterprise can help to correctly expose those portions of the enterprise that should be shared.

## IMPORTANT NOTE

### Service Gateways

Implementing service gateways in an enterprise is another great way to increase productivity, because having an outside-facing interface allows users to more easily outsource work to third parties. SOA can help take away the headache of figuring out how to securely and efficiently delegate work to outside facilities by providing those facilities with a standard way to connect and programmatically interface with an enterprise.

## ACTION ITEM: FIND OUT HOW MUCH VISIBILITY AN ENTERPRISE ARCHITECTURE PROVIDES

An architecture has visibility if its users are able to view and analyze running processes and business data that are meaningful to them. Visibility can be objectively measured by looking at what percentage of data is moving from system to system in an enterprise. If there are twenty systems in the facility passing control signals and asset information in forty different ways but only having a dashboard to view the status of the SNMP infrastructure, then that facility only has visibility into perhaps 3% of the work done there. If, however, the facility is orchestrating half of the system communication using business processes in a middleware layer (which gives the real-time status of any one of those processes), it has increased visibility to 50%. As it implements the next few projects, the facility should keep track of how visible the enterprise is. If it is implementing new systems into a unified SOA, users will no doubt see that visibility increase. However, in a tightly coupled, point-to-point architecture, each new system probably introduces more integration points than it allows to be viewed thereby decreasing overall visibility.

### 3.2.3 Organizational Benefits

In addition to the major benefits of business agility and visibility, SOA provides a number of corollary benefits to the savvy implementer. Services, with their defined and published interfaces, present a layer of

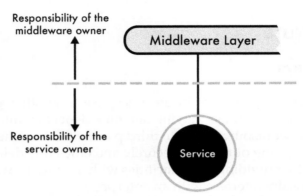

**FIGURE 3-6**    One of the benefits of SOA is the clear boundary lines between services and middleware that can assist media enterprises with scoping development and support.

abstraction beyond which implementation is independent from functionality. That layer of abstraction, along with the unified middleware layer, gives some clear organizational benefits when an enterprise has to manage multiple departments, all wanting interoperability.

Ownership is an area that is made clearer in a loosely coupled, service-based architecture. There is a clear service boundary in SOA — the service interface. Anything underneath the service interface is part of the service and anything beyond that interface is part of the middleware layer. This makes questions of ownership much more straightforward than with tightly coupled integration techniques. As shown in Fig. 3-6, the owner of the service has responsibility over writing the service to that interface, and the SOA team or whoever has ownership over the middleware in the enterprise is responsible for writing processes and integration to that interface. There remains some middle ground in the initial design and any periodic revisions of the interface itself, but this situation is much improved over the "who's job is it" world of non-SOA integration techniques.

One area in particular where clear-cut SOA services come in handy is when dealing with vendors. One of the largest barriers to best-of-breed integration and vendor heterogeneity is the issue of who is responsible for supporting any integration that occurs within the enterprise. Many vendors will support a laundry list of standards that their product already exposes, but when vendors are involved in the integration of several larger software systems, the lines get a little blurry. For example, some vendors will offer to do custom integration of their products, but ongoing support for these solutions ultimately lands in the customer's hands or is uncertain. SOA provides a clear precedent in allowing vendor-led integration: write to and support to the service interface.

When vendors do not and will not expose an SOA-compliant interface for their products, then the integrator will have to write a custom wrapper to get to that interface. With custom wrappers, a media enterprise is in the same boat as with vendor-provided integration when it comes to vendor support — the enterprise gets only what the vendor offers — but thankfully SOA's business agility means that integrators only have to rewrite the wrapper, and not any of the integration logic, if and when the vendor changes interfaces or upgrades their product. If the vendor is the one wrapping his or her own product, then the media enterprise will have an SOA interface document that the vendor will need to support. Either way, the job is easier than having to support the entire integration infrastructure.

If a media vendor is looking for ways to meet the needs of the service-oriented enterprise, then Appendix D, which was written especially for vendors, is a must-read.

These sorts of organizational concerns also come into play when integrating different departments in the same enterprise. The question of whose budget an integration project falls under is certainly not a new issue to any M&E professional, but SOA can help make solving that problem a little bit easier. Writing independent services and integrating them over a middleware layer means that each department providing a service has responsibility over writing, exposing, and supporting that service (again, up to the service interface). The logic behind how the interface functions can also be dictated by the department. Because SOA interfaces are written at a business level, requests for additional functionality are confined to business topics (e.g., "I need to be able to send assets to you for cataloging and this is the information that's important to me," and not "I need you to support a specific cataloging standard in your system"). In addition, as is covered in the Chapter 6 Business Process Management: Definitions, Concepts, and Methodologies, it is very possible to set equivalent divisions around integrated processes living in the middleware layer.

SOA provides an integrator with many benefits in the areas of organizational governance and control over services. But what about the middleware layer itself? Due to its position at the heart of an SOA, one would think that some sort of centralized administration would be necessary to support the middleware layer. To a large extent, that is right. The responsibility of keeping the middleware up-to-date and running in large organizations should fall to a dedicated SOA team or integration department. However, if desired, many aspects of process management that live in the middleware can be distributed to various departments thanks to standardization of middleware technologies.

Most SOA advocates revel in middleware's potential for centralized administration. Having a dedicated team (as discussed further in Chapter 8, Moving toward a Service-Oriented Media Enterprise) means having a single place to go for integration questions and issues. Middleware technology is much easier to support than a confusing web of tightly coupled system connections, and much of the logic over how individual services should be used is encapsulated beyond the service boundary. So SOA, in a sense, attempts to promote the positive benefits of centralized administration while reducing the negative aspects of it.

With a centrally administered middleware layer, integrators are able to aggregate data from across the enterprise, and have a place to produce dashboards and business metrics for managers. They would also be able to ensure that the correct responsibility is given to service providers to define and support their own interfaces while at the same time looking for opportunities to expose services from different departments and technologies using the same interfaces. A middleware layer gives all of the benefits of looking down on an entire infrastructure and ensuring that it is designed in an efficient way. There is no danger of accidental architecture creeping into an SOA when a dedicated SOA team is used to manage the middleware layer and provide a safe environment for different departments to integrate with one another.

There is one final benefit worth mentioning from implementing an SOA in your enterprise: an SOA makes project specification and design an easier process.

When planning for a new implementation project in a facility, the engineer determines the business requirements for any new systems, writes them up, and either provides them to an internal team to design and construct, or maybe hires a systems integrator or vendor to do the design and installation for them. Essentially, they figure out what business service they need in the enterprise, and they get someone to build it. Maybe the engineer has a good idea of what technology or specific product will fit the bill, maybe not. SOA (which expresses individual components of an architecture in terms of business service) can make this whole process easier.

Look at the RFP. In an SOA, users think about the functions of their systems in terms of services. Thus an RFP, in SOA terms, is an expression of what services are needed to achieve desired business functionality. Perhaps the enterprise wants to provide a new distribution channel that will host content on a Web site. In an RFP, an enterprise would specify that you need a service to edit existing content for the Web and a service to push edited content to the Web. The RFP would express how it wants to use these services, and what other services it has that can be leveraged to help with this work. In essence, the RFP is specifying an enterprise's needs by specifying a service interface.

## CASE STUDY

### New Kinds of RFPs

Adopting a service-oriented approach to a facility can pay real dividends in many aspects of running a media enterprise. One broadcaster found that the time spent detailing business processes and service definitions really paid off in their next project.

This broadcaster was looking to overhaul the way that media was managed throughout the sports broadcasting areas of their enterprise with a view toward later expansion into other areas such as news. Media was handled in several different, incompatible systems that had organically grown as they had increased their sports coverage over the years. These systems were frustrating to operate and difficult to maintain.

When considering how to approach an update to this technology, it was decided to do a full analysis of the current workflow and then to develop a view of an ideal workflow with a view toward service orientation. The analysis took a little less than 6 weeks, nearly 50% longer than in similar projects.

This information was combined with non-functional requirements of the organization (such as video format, etc.) into a new kind of RFP. This RFP actually focused on the workflow as a series of use cases for the system. Each use case was documented fully in a standard way and the service definitions were described for the services that would be expected to implement this workflow.

As it turned out, this kind of RFP, while taking a little longer to write up front, actually shortened the whole project, because this was the clearest that requirements had been defined in advance. This made it much easier for the vendors to clearly understand how they could fit into the picture and propose the best possible solutions to the broadcaster without feeling like they needed to present every solution. The broadcaster could more quickly develop an appropriate gap analysis of desired features with proposed technology to understand where things fell short. This meant that selection of vendors and development of contracts occurred more quickly.

It also meant that integration points were better understood up front. This avoided the post-award negotiations so often seen between vendors. In the end, not only did the project get executed more quickly, but the project was considered a success due to the ability of multiple, well-integrated vendors to provide a more complete solution.

That is right: the Service-Oriented RFP is simply a list of service interfaces that need implementation. SOA separates the implementation from the interface, so it does not matter to the rest of the enterprise how these services are implemented. It only matters that they meet the specification of the interface that the rest of the enterprise uses. No more needing to run on specific platforms, no more needing to integrate with these specific vendor's products already in place, just "these are the business services that I need you to expose." This makes it easier on the integrator because he or she can use whatever platform or technology is most convenient, and it makes it easier on the facility because there is less worry about using a specific technology just to make everything work. SOA enables true best-of-breed solutions.

## 3.3  SERVICES

Now down to the nitty-gritty of Service-Oriented Architecture. There is the concise definition from earlier — SOA is an architecture of independent, wrapped business services communicating via published interfaces over a common middleware layer — but now it is time to take a detailed look at what is meant by the various SOA buzzwords within the definition (business services, wrappers, and middleware layer). The next section will be devoted to the exploration of wrappers and service exposure, and middleware gets its own chapter (Chapter 4). This next section will take a look at the concept of business services.

### 3.3.1  Definition

So what is a service? Because it is in the name of Service-Oriented Architecture it is obviously a crucial aspect of the whole concept. But when someone says "business service," what exactly are they talking about?

This turns out to be a trickier question to answer than one would think because of the vaguely defined boundaries between what is and what is not a service. To understand the key point of the definition, readers must think of the common usage of the word "service": a person hires someone to perform a service for them, a waiter or waitress will serve a customer at a restaurant, one gets service done on their car. A service is a transactional arrangement that brings value to the customer. It has inputs and outputs. For example, a restaurant patron gives his or her waiter the name of an item on the menu and a tip, and the waiter gives that person a plate of food and probably refills the coffee once or twice. Homeowners give their satellite TV provider $70 a month, and the provider gives them 500 channels of content. A producer gives a freelance cameraperson a day's wage, the cameraperson gives the producer a few hours of raw footage.

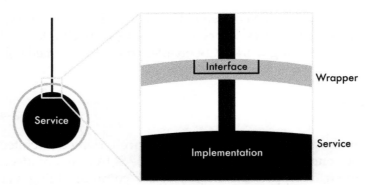

**FIGURE 3-7**   The main characteristic of a business service is that it has an implementation that is separate and independent from its interface.

A service in an SOA is looked at in much the same way. It is a black box entity that has inputs and outputs and provides some business value. It also has a service description or interface associated with it so that the user knows what inputs to give the service and what outputs can be expected. This is known as "calling" the service. It does not matter what application, system, or person is inside that black box doing the work to produce the service's business value. Just like CORBA before it, SOA offers service interfaces that are independent from their implementations (shown in Fig. 3-7). That interface is known as the "wrapper," and this is why independent, wrapped services are discussed in an SOA.

A service must provide business value. Not everything that has a transactional interface with inputs and outputs that is separated from its implementation is necessarily a business service. For example, a Java object that offers the ability to change an integer into a string is probably not a service. It may be part of a larger service that takes many prices in and produces an invoice, but it is rare to find a situation where an integrator would want to expose this function as its own service. Also, a service that takes in a budget amount and outputs a major motion picture in 10 to 12 months is a poorly conceived service. This is mostly because movie producers do not think transactionally like this (at least, most of them do not). They want more interaction with the movie as it is produced, which makes "produce movie" a poor choice for a business service. Services should not be conversational.

The question is, when is a service really just a piece of a larger service, and when is a service really more than one service? When should an application expose a single service, when should it expose multiple services, and when should it work with other applications in a tightly coupled way to expose a single, loosely coupled service? The answers to all of these questions are honestly up to the individual media enterprise, but there are some best practices that will help to ground generic exploration of business services. For example, it helps to think of the business function that is closest to the ideal service in M&E: transcoding.

## MEDIA'S MOST NATURAL SERVICE: TRANSCODING

When the IT think tanks of the late 1990s were envisioning SOA, they had in mind a particular application — the integration of the type of business system that is crucial to the business, easily explainable, and captured inside a single application. The people management functions of SAP and PeopleSoft are perfect examples of this "killer app" of SOA. Unfortunately, in M&E, many business functions do not have the same one-to-one relationship to applications as IT does. Oftentimes, media professionals use many software components to accomplish their work, and much of what is done is outside of the context of software at all! This puts M&E on the outskirts of this SOA killer app, which may have contributed to SOA's slow adoption in the industry.

Transcoding is, however, one business function in M&E that is perfectly aligned with the most accessible aspects of SOA. It is a business-level service, because it is something understood even by the managers who direct business goals in a facility. It is also often carried out by a single software system called a transcoding engine. In addition, transcoders are already heavily integrated components in most media architectures, so vendors in this space have provided a number of interfaces that can be wrapped to expose services. Transcoding captures a sweet spot for SOA in M&E.

Another way to help understand the concept of a business service is to consider the various qualities that a business service has: encapsulation, abstraction, and business value.

Business services are encapsulated. This essentially means that they are black-boxed and independent from one another. From the "outside" of the service, one cannot determine any details about how the service is implemented and exactly what happens when that service is called. When an integrator is implementing an SOA in a facility, this service encapsulation could be an aspect of the system that is installed (if it were service-oriented or presented an interface that exposed business functionality), or the integrator could encapsulate the service manually by writing a wrapper that shields the service's implementation from the rest of the enterprise. The act of wrapping is what turns any generic application or system into a business service, because it provides that encapsulation.

An SOA is composed of services and middleware, and the only connection that a service has to the rest of the facility is through the middleware layer. The service presents a published interface to the middleware layer. The middleware layer (and, through it, other services) refers only to that interface, and not to any implementation-specific details of the service. This means that if a service changes — assuming the change does not alter the business functionality that the service provides — integrators only have to worry about adjusting that single connection (the wrapper) so that the new implementation exposes the existing interface. This is how encapsulation leads to business agility, one of the main benefits of SOA.

Services — and therefore service interfaces — are defined at the business level, so the only changes that affect the interface in a well-designed service are business-level changes. This is called abstraction. As Fig. 3-8 shows, abstraction and encapsulation are two independent

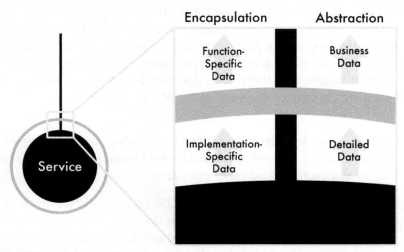

**FIGURE 3-8**   The difference between encapsulation and abstraction is subtle, but crucial to a thorough understanding of SOA theory.

benefits of SOA. When services are abstracted they are defined at a "higher level" than many interfaces that applications expose. Abstracted services offer business-level operations such as fulfilling work orders, processing assets, or archiving material instead of lower level operations such as setting fields, opening a file for processing, or deleting a record. Here again is a gray area around the definition of a service: How abstract is abstract enough to meet the criteria of having a "business-level" interface? The short answer here is that it is best to have services at varying levels of abstraction in an enterprise. This chapter looks into a few best practices surrounding service decomposition, or the breaking down of systems into the services that they expose.

Abstraction also provides the benefits of business agility associated with SOA. An abstract service has an interface that is defined at a different level than the actions that enable it (not necessarily a more generic level from the integrator's perspective, just different; there may be no functional difference between deleting an asset and removing a database record, or there may be many more steps associated with deleting an asset). It is easier to change the implementation of an abstracted service than one that exposes an interface written at the same level as its implementation. If a second asset management system is added to the enterprise, integrators would have to add another "remove database record" service, but this second system could be folded into the "delete asset" service. Assuming the interface remains the same (i.e., no additional business-level data is required to be input to the service to remove the asset from the second system), no other components of the architecture need to change. Compare this to the tightly coupled architectures discussed in Chapter 2 that have interfaces that depend upon specific implementations — SOA makes change easier. Creating an abstract service call also tends to bring attention to the business value associated with a service operation, and so abstraction of business services flows naturally into building services that offer defined business value.

Including business value as part of the definition of business services is a tall order. To a systems integrator in a major enterprise, it is often hard enough to prove that you offer business value to the company, much less the services that you will be exposing! At the very least, it certainly ups the ante for service definition, because integrators can no longer remain safe in the easy world of "blaming the vendor." If a system has a given purpose in a facility but does not have a good interface to programmatically expose that purpose to the rest of the facility, it is the media enterprise's responsibility in an SOA to find a way to wrap it (even if that wrapping is to e-mail a user to access the system manually). This forces integrators to think about what purpose a system has in their facilities, and how they would want that system to ideally look to the rest of the enterprise. The reason that business value is a part of the definition of SOA is because it forces participants to ask the big questions about how business works instead of treading water with tightly coupled integration. It may mean more work up front (it almost certainly does), but facilities will feel the benefits of that work sooner than in other architectures, because they will have a good grasp on the business functions and the way that they like to operate; not the way the vendors they have chosen like to operate.

So what does it mean to offer business value? One way to think about it is to take a functionality centric view of service operations. For example, many applications that expose programmatic interfaces will include operations that may be necessary but are not functional. Operations like "login," "logout," or "get user info" are great examples of these. The Application Programming Interface (API) documentation that goes along with that application may dictate that users should log in before making any API calls and log out when they are done. This may make sense from a programming point of view (the concept of session security is certainly not bad), but it does not make much sense from a business point of view. These operations do not offer business value because they are not functional. The purpose they serve is logistical — users have to log in before they can make a functional call. This forced causality is another red flag for business value; any time an integrator says that one operation must come before or after another operation, services are not created that offer independent business value; therefore the enterprise falls short of providing true "loose coupling."

The SOA solution to these logistical operations (or APIs with forced causality) is to fold them into the wrapper. When making a single call to the service, the wrapper that is mediating between the SOA and the underlying implementation should translate that into several calls to the application: one to log in, one to call the functional operation, and one to log out. This focuses on the functions, and therefore the business value that the underlying system or systems provide instead of focusing on the logistics of calling that system. There may be a good deal of gray area in what constitutes business value, but a media enterprise should never see a "log in" service. There is just no business value there.

This discussion of business value provides a good excuse to begin to sort the universe of services into different types. There are many ways to type or class business services, but looking at the business value question provides some insight into functionally different ways that services might be implemented. Think again about the idea of SOA services that are equivalent to the common usage of the word "services." When a service is "invoked" in the real world by ordering a coffee or getting a pool cleaned, there are two different ways this might happen. One is transactional. The customer gives the order and money to a barista and, in return, gets coffee. The customer is either not doing anything else in between ordering and receiving the coffee (the transaction is *synchronous*) or the customer places the order, then makes a few phone calls over in the corner of the café, and then receives the coffee when his or her name is called (the transaction is *asynchronous*). Either way, a user gives something and gets something back in return. The other type of service is one-directional. A customer calls the pool service and gives them an address, and does not receive anything back (well, maybe a confirmation — a common architecture for SOA services as well), and then, eventually, that customer's pool gets cleaned. Someone essentially calls the service and then continues with a daily routine — fire and forget. These concepts are illustrated in Fig. 3-9. Synchronous, asynchronous, and one-directional messaging translate directly to methods of service exposure, and when discussing decomposition of services, integrators will want to know how, functionally, the service will be used. This is not a logistical or operational question, but a business one.

Good engineers (like all of the readers surely are) are asking themselves at this point: "Are there any exceptions to these rules of encapsulation, abstraction, and business value in services?" Of course there are. Having services at different levels of abstraction and providing different levels of business value (including services that are not very abstract or do not provide a lot of business value) are all part of building a realistic SOA. Ultimately, the best services to put in an enterprise are the ones that describe the way that enterprise really does business. The best way to get the benefits of business agility and useful visibility is to expose services that match the way the enterprise thinks. That

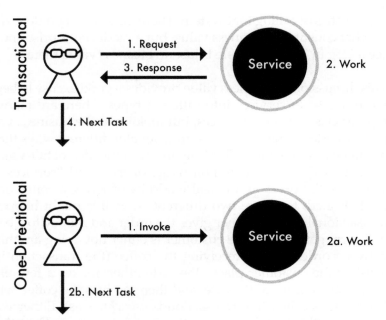

**FIGURE 3-9** Service calls can either be transactional, which means that the requester of the service expects a response, or they can be more one-directional, where the work of the service does not affect the next steps of the requester.

way, when it is necessary to replace a system or add a new system, it will be easy to translate that system into a business service that thinks the way the rest of the enterprise thinks instead of trying to translate it into a business service that thinks the way existing random services think. To that end, no one should accept a service interface as is in the enterprise just because it will save the time or money it takes to wrap it so it presents an appropriate interface. Sure, there are budgetary considerations here. Maybe there is no time or money to do that for all new systems and the integrator feels lucky enough to get one that is generally service-oriented, but that integrator should keep wrapping that service on his or her to-do list for when it is affordable. The bottom line is SOA is not about integration options and choices led by the vendors and systems chosen, instead it is about the architecture leading the choice of vendors and systems. Do not take the easy way out and expose inappropriate services. It will only mean more money and more work down the line to undo the tightly coupled accidental architecture that such choices tend to lead to.

## 3.3.2 Service Implementation Choices

The M&E industry has only recently started to use computer technology in areas where other industries have been using it for a long time (for example, SANs). There are many reasons why the M&E industry is more conservative than most, but the main reason that media is so "old fashioned" is because it is such a craft-based industry. Computers cannot be relied upon to color correct or edit in the same way that banks can rely on them to balance accounts. Many media engineers probably are not sure of SOA's applicability in M&E because there are so many people directly involved in media business processes and not enough automated computer systems. Well, just because the language and best practices of SOA come out of the enterprise computing world does not mean that only enterprise applications can present themselves as services. Service-Oriented Architecture advances methodologies that are widely applicable.

This section will look at different common service implementations — highlighted in Fig. 3-10 — whether those are enterprise applications, people, or whole facilities. The only prerequisite needed to be a service in an SOA is the ability to be wrapped to present an interface that conforms to the selected standard of the middleware layer. In the common case (and indeed, in every case considered in this book), that middleware layer will be implemented using enterprise software tools such as application servers and Enterprise Service Buses (ESBs). Services in such an SOA must use wrappers that present a software interface compliant with these tools. This means that, even though all kinds of things can be services in an enterprise, ultimately the goal is to get that information into a software format.

The most obvious type of service implementation is a software application. A software application might be wrapped to present a service interface if it provides some discrete business value. Considering that most applications are created to do just that — provide specific business value to the user — it is common to see enterprise applications wrapped as services in an SOA. For example, transcoding servers, media management applications, or automation systems could all be wrapped to expose one or more services to an enterprise. Remember though, that a service needs to be encapsulated, abstracted, and it must provide business value. So, applications that do not meet these requirements (such as

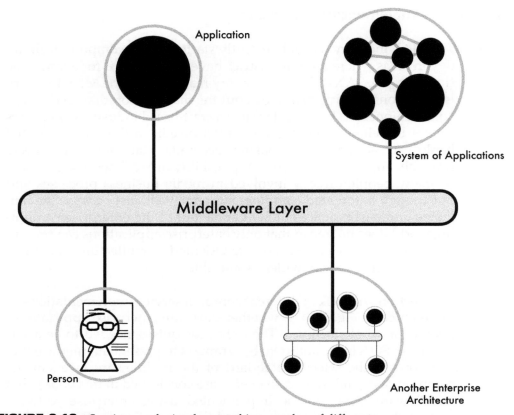

**FIGURE 3-10**   Services can be implemented in a number of different ways.

a component of a larger suite of applications that is tightly coupled to other components in that suite or an application that does some incredibly low-level task such as formatting scheduling data into iCal) are probably not good choices for directly exposing services.

When attempting to expose an enterprise application, it is best to try and leverage existing interfaces in the application by writing a wrapper that calls one or more of these interfaces. If this does not meet all needs (if the application provides some business value that is only accessible through an application-provided UI and the vendor of the application is not willing to work on the service enablement effort), integrators could then try to access the data that application writes to disk or to a database directly. Or the enterprise could allow the end user to continue to use the application directly and wrap that user as a service. Media enterprises will find the latter method to be the most useful, especially in M&E, which has so many custom applications that do not offer robust programmatic interfaces as well as many processes that do not lend themselves easily to automation.

When faced with an application that seems to be naturally paired with other applications (such as vendor-provided suites of systems), integrators should consider that perhaps it makes more sense to expose the entire system of applications as a service. This is another possible implementation of a service. Recall that in SOA, a service's interface is independent from its implementation. From the point of view of the rest of the enterprise, it does not matter what is beyond that interface. Integrators will probably have more options when they design a wrapper that wraps an entire system of applications instead of just a single application. The wrapper could call various programmatic interfaces on each component of the system to achieve the desired service functionality (just as with a single application), but this means that the wrapper architecture is very tightly coupled with that specific system configuration. If the location of one of the servers is changed, for example, the system will not only have to get reconfigured, but the wrapper will also have to be rewritten. A better architecture (if it is possible with the system wrapped) is to configure a single system component to serve as the "gateway" to the rest of the system and only have the wrapper communicate with that single component. This way, any system configuration changes can be done within the bounds of the system and will not ripple out to the service itself. Because this is not always possible, integrators may have to settle for a more tightly coupled design. Or, as in single applications, they may have to screen-scrape or poll databases to get the information needed. Either way, an enterprise is still better off than having that entire silo of applications tightly coupled to the rest of the infrastructure. An enterprise has to do what it takes to expose the right business interface.

When thinking about the resources that provide the most business value in your enterprise, the media engineer's mind no doubt immediately goes to the people that work in the enterprise. No one yet lives in a world where large chunks of the daily workload can be automated and given to computers to complete. People, especially in M&E, tend to directly handle the vast majority of the business processes in a facility. That means, in the context of an SOA, that they are services. And, just like other services, they must be wrapped to present a published interface to the rest of the enterprise. Wrapping people, however, is a unique challenge.

Ultimately, any interaction between people in an SOA taking part in the data aggregation, security, and automation capabilities of the software-based middleware layer must get back into the digital domain. The main way to do this is to formalize communications that would otherwise be informal. To inform people of their tasks, instead of sending out e-mails or leaving phone messages, implementing a to-do list in a Web-based portal will ensure that when an individual finishes a task and clicks the "complete" button, that status is known by the business processes running in the middleware layer. Employees will no doubt like the visibility into their tasks that such a portal would give them, and this will make adjustment to that system easier. The key when implementing UIs to an SOA like this is to provide the users with concrete business value, otherwise they will continue to use informal, tightly coupled methods of communication that do not bring the rest of the enterprise SOA benefits. And why should they use an SOA portal if they get nothing out of it? Just as every service must provide business value in an SOA, so too must every individual feel business value. The way to do this is to leverage SOA benefits inside people-based services. For example, if a media enterprise wants to create an editing service that will effectively wrap its editors, it should not give them mindless extra tasks such as entering data about their editing session into a form so that data can be formalized into service messages. It should instead get whatever data it can automatically (such as how long the editor was editing, what video assets were used in the edit, or the editing station where he or she sat) and return valuable, interesting data (such as a task list, producer instructions, and newly available assets) back to the editor. More often than not, a Web page or portal is the desired way to interact with human resources in an SOA and have that server handle messaging tasks to and from the wrapper/middleware. Other options include wrapping specific end systems that people use and designing small-footprint applications that will sit on users' end systems to receive and respond to data. Because many people in a facility do work outside of the context of a network-attached computer system, it is often difficult to avoid inserting unnecessary tasks to get data into an SOA. Only do this when necessary, and make a point to provide business value back to users so that they will appreciate and use the SOA infrastructure.

The final type of service implementation is when a media enterprise decides to expose whole service-oriented departments, facilities, or enterprises as services. Essentially, this means exposing an SOA as a service! This can happen at a micro level when a production team or a purchasing department is wrapped to present services to the rest of the facility, or it can happen at a macro level if the enterprise decides to link into another company's externally facing services as part of its SOA. This type of service exposure is one of the most discussed in the IT world, because it is the one with the most challenges. When interacting with business services exposed by other business entities on the Internet, security becomes a very big deal. In addition, it is harder to guarantee that these services will be exposed to be directly useful to an enterprise. Integrators may have to wrap them a second time to use them inside the network! Though there are more things to think about when consuming or producing business services across organizational boundaries, there are plenty of examples out there of enterprises that do it right.

## GLOBAL SERVICES AT GOOGLE

Getting one's head around the concept of a business service, especially one that provides you with the functionality of an entire enterprise somewhere out there in the world, is not an easy task. The best way to describe something like this is through examples. Thankfully, there are many companies offering such services today! One great example is the search giant Google, who offers the public many ways to programmatically interface with the services they offer. These offerings are found at http://code.google.com/apis.

Because they are a search company, these services center around searching the Internet and returning data to the user. The important thing to note when looking at Google's offered interfaces is how they are aligned by the business services they offer. There is one interface for each type of offering they have, whether it is to use their maps or news or even YouTube. These interfaces, where applicable, are implementation independent as well, using technologies such as WSDL, SOAP, and REST to achieve this.

Because of the simplicity of their offerings, Google is a good example of the ways in which one might service-orient an entire enterprise to allow other companies or individuals to more easily take advantage of what can be done.

There are plenty of reasons someone might want to consume services from other enterprises, especially in M&E, where freelancing and the outsourcing of work are a way of life. There are plenty of reasons to expose services to others as well — a network making functionality available to its affiliates, a post house offering a contract submission and negotiation service, or a sales department allowing electronic submission of advertisements are all good examples. The best way to expose such services to the outside world is through the use of a service gateway that will filter and secure inter-enterprise service communication. This ensures that only the chosen functionality is made available to others, and that this functionality is made digestible to other enterprises. Appendix E has more information about this and other architectures.

### 3.3.3  Classes of Services

What are some best practices surrounding the definition and design of business services in an SOA? To answer this question, a layered model of service structure is outlined in Fig. 3-11, which serves as a framework for any SOA facility. There are many such layered models that have been published. Using a reference model like this one to frame a discussion of Service-Oriented Architecture is a good idea for three reasons: first, it provides a common terminology with which to discuss service classes; second, it provides a visual representation of the various layers of abstraction that are present in an SOA, which helps integrators to understand where these layers fall; and third, it focuses the efforts of service component development because it offers distinct "levels" for components to be written to. Many vendors will present their version of a layered SOA model for these very reasons, so it is appropriate to use a layered model for the discussion here.

The best solution to offering reusable business value in services is to have business services at many different "levels" within your enterprise: some encapsulating lower level tasks like moving files from server to server, and some encapsulating higher level tasks like ingesting assets. A representation like that seen in Fig. 3-11 partitions the possible world of services into distinct classes to help an integrator figure out where in the SOA universe various business operations fall. This layered model of service classes is not a part of any official SOA specification; it is simply this book's version of a diagram that represents the layers of abstraction in a services environment.

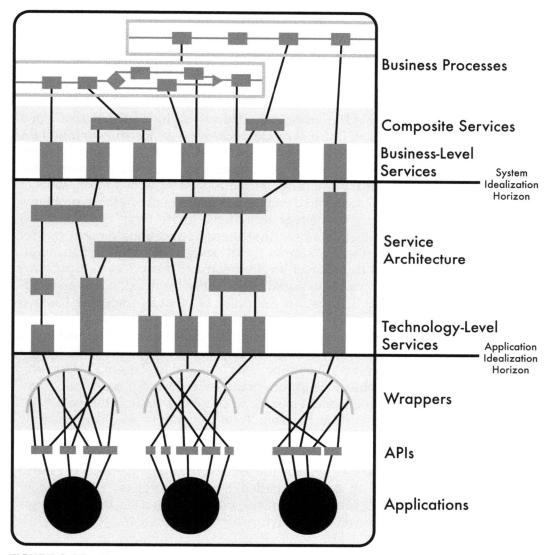

**FIGURE 3-11** The service model used for this exploration of SOA features multiple levels and two abstraction horizons. This model may not exactly match other models used to describe SOA, but assuming that the best practices and architectural concepts are the same, all models are equally valid.

This section examines this layered structure and discusses the various SOA classes and what services, processes, or architectural components might fall into them. Each of the features of the above service model is considered.

The first aspect of the service model to note is the appearance of two "horizons" — the application idealization horizon and the system idealization horizon. These horizons bound the three primary layers of abstraction in the service levels model: the application domain, the service domain, and the business domain. These domains are effectively three large "bins" into which every component in an SOA can be sorted. Many SOA models choose to only include one horizon — or a "service" horizon. But this model includes two horizons to highlight an important aspect of Service-Oriented Architecture: that SOA integrators must worry about both wrapping individual systems and applications and presenting reusable, system-wide, business-level functionality to the facility. Instead of tackling both of these problems at one time, many SOA integrators choose to first wrap applications to expose the business services that those applications present (represented here by the application idealization horizon), and then wrap whole suites of these lower level infrastructure services to expose the business functionality required of the entire facility (the system idealization horizon). To illustrate this point, say that an enterprise has two media asset management systems for online storage, and it wants to present the business service "search for online asset." Because it is a business-level service, this enterprise does not care about which asset management system the online asset is stored in. This is a classic unified search problem. First, integrators would wrap each individual media asset management system to present a "search for asset" service at the application horizon. Then integrators would orchestrate these two services together using business rules to present a unified search service at the system horizon. One horizon abstracts an individual application or system as a service, the other abstracts the infrastructure itself to present unified business services. Each type of service will be examined in detail, but first, what do these horizons mean for the overall infrastructure?

### 3.3.3.1 The System and Application Idealization Horizons

The job of an integrator is to make multiple distinct applications work with one another. In any integrated architecture, therefore, there are components that are considered applications, and other components that are considered "infrastructure." Service-Oriented Architecture is no different, thus the service model includes an application idealization horizon. Any component that is part of the application falls below this horizon, and any component that is part of the infrastructure falls above this horizon. Therefore "technology-level services" — the highest-level interfaces provided by any one vendor's system in an SOA — exist at the horizon.

This chapter has discussed what types of service implementations might exist in an SOA. Vendor systems, suites of systems, portals for human interaction, and entire SOA architectures could all be the underlying implementation behind a service interface. Each of these implementations might expose interfaces at varying levels of abstraction. Applications especially tend to expose technology-level services at the application idealization horizon. For example, a transcoding application might expose a "transcode asset" service while a wrapped post-production department might expose a "prepare package for playout" service (which will no doubt include some form of "transcode asset" within its implementation). One good way to envision the application idealization horizon is to see that it distinguishes between individual contributors and workers in an architecture and the infrastructure components that unite and connect these individuals.

The purpose of the application idealization horizon is to provide technical agility to an infrastructure. Technical agility is the ability to change out individual applications and systems without affecting any other systems, connections, or business processes. By having a layer that abstracts application functionality, an enterprise is able to upgrade or replace the application below that layer and write the new wrapper to that existing interface, thus ensuring that no other component needs to change. Technical agility is an important benefit of SOA, as has been discussed, and having an idealization horizon at the application level is a valuable part of any Service-Oriented Architecture.

Other types of service implementations (whole departments or facilities especially, but possibly also vendor-provided suites of systems) might expose business-level functionality directly at the system idealization horizon. Unlike the application horizon, which separates individual system details from the overall infrastructure, the system idealization horizon separates infrastructure details from the business functionality offered by the infrastructure. Using the unified asset search example above, the details of how many asset management systems exist in the facility and the logic necessary to manage consistency among them is the responsibility of the service domain. The business domain needs to only be concerned with the idea that an asset exists in the system and certain operations, such as search, can be carried out on the system's assets. Any system details are shrouded behind the system idealization horizon.

The system idealization horizon provides business agility to a facility. Business agility is the ability to change business processes and business rules — the way an enterprise does business — without having these changes affect the system architecture. By having the system present a palette of business services at the system idealization horizon, an enterprise is giving its workflows availability to the entire functionality of its system. Because of this, changing the workflow does not require changes to system infrastructure any more than painting a second picture would require an entirely new palette of colors different from the first one. This is the concept of business agility, and, as discussed in Section 3.2.1, it is an important (if not the most important) benefit of SOA.

The concept of these idealization horizons should become clearer as individual components of the layered SOA model are explored. It is important to note, however, that these horizons are abstract notions intended to illustrate concepts of interoperability in SOA. In real implementations, these "horizons" may be blurry, with system details leaking into the business domain where appropriate and application details leaking into the infrastructure where unavoidable. It is a significant challenge to implement perfect layers of abstraction in any sort of architecture. Always remember that the end goal of these layers is the business and technical agility required to make fast changes to systems and processes. In a perfect SOA world, a change would not leave the domain in which it was made, but even in systems with realistically "blurry" horizons, Service-Oriented Architecture limits the "ripple effect" of both technical and business changes presenting much more agility.

### 3.3.3.2 The Application Domain

There are a number of components that exist at the various levels in an SOA, starting at the bottom in the application domain. There are three important types of components that fall within the application domain and are concerned with the workings of specific systems: the application (in this model "application" can refer to any low-level component that does work in an architecture), the APIs presented by that application, and the wrappers that transform those APIs into technology-level services.

Applications and APIs should be fairly self-explanatory in this model. The application is the software package that does work, and the APIs are, as the acronym implies, the programming interfaces into the application. As has been mentioned, the application may be a portal or other thin user interface because the real component that does the work of that "application" is human. This is perfectly acceptable, and surely the majority of an enterprise's work is done by humans and not by automatic processes (at least for now). The APIs in this model, therefore, refer to the interfaces that are part of the thin or thick application — the ones that ship with the product and are there when you open the box. They are not interfaces that a systems integrator might add after deploying the application or as part of a custom solution. Anything that is custom to a specific architecture is considered a "wrapper."

Wrappers are where all the excitement happens in the application domain, or, at least, the integration-related excitement (the internal workings of applications can be pretty exciting too!). The wrapper is an "in-between" component like the "glue" of service architecture. The job of the wrapper is to take whatever APIs the application natively exposes and transform them into the technology-level services that an enterprise *wants* that application to expose. Technology-level services should represent the idealized functionality of the application, while APIs are the real-world hooks into that application. Ideally, an integrator would know the APIs that the application exposes and would have decided what technology-level services to expose before beginning to work on the wrapper. A big aspect of this is transforming the technology used at the API level to the technology chosen for the middleware layer of the SOA. Because of this, wrapper design can be anywhere from simple to very complex. Wrappers normally include data transformation and conversion (going from one representation of data to another representation of the same data), but can also include multiple API calls, polling of applications, or statefulness (where information is stored in a file or database between calls to technology-level services). Best practices surrounding wrapper design will be discussed in Section 3.3.4: Service Decomposition.

Wrappers and APIs in the application domain are "bottom-up" components. This means that they are designed around exposing an application's functionality, they are not designed to cater to individual business needs. Hopefully, there was some thought put into the business requirements when the applications to put into a facility were selected. This is not the job of the SOA integrator in this situation. The goal of the application domain is to expose the functionality that exists in an enterprise's underlying architecture. It is the goal of the upper levels of SOA to handle business requirements.

### 3.3.3.3 The Business Domain

Jumping to the other end of the SOA spectrum, the business domain at the top of our layered model includes business logic, business rules, and business processes related to the business requirements of the integrated architecture. The business domain is the area that middle management or maybe even executive management is comfortable discussing, because the rest of the architecture below it is designed so that only high-level business data is presented at this layer, not technical mumbo jumbo. Because of this, business analysts are able to orchestrate atomic business events into business processes at this layer. These atomic business events are known as business-level services.

Readers may have noticed that the word "business" was used a full twelve times in the previous paragraph. This should be a clear indicator of the purpose of this domain: to cater to the business. This is supposed to be a technical book, but one of the central benefits of SOA is its ability to turn a technical infrastructure into something that not-so-technical people can understand. Components in the business domain are "top-down" components. This means that they are designed to fulfill business requirements, but are independent from the technology that exists to meet those requirements. This is completely opposite from the goals of the application domain, and by design. Business-level services and business processes should be all about the high-level goals of the facility.

Business-level services represent fundamental business activities that the SOA can support. Depending on the needs of a facility, these can fall within a range of abstraction. In one facility, a service such as "register asset" might be considered too low-level to fall in the business domain (instead it is a technology-level service or part of the service architecture), while, in a different, more targeted facility, that service might be right at home as a business-level service. The key is to identify the right scope of business services for a given organization.

## THE DEFINITION OF A BUSINESS SERVICE

Identifying the right frame of reference is a crucial step in service design. No one wants to be creating services at the business horizon that are too low-level and technical to provide any understandable business functionality. At the same time, no one wants to be creating technology services that are just too all-encompassing, hindering reusability of those services. The tricky part is that these horizons are at different levels in every facility! A mastering facility may have business requirements that plumb the depths of technical detail, while a major network may have business goals and functions so sweeping that the technology services are wrapping whole departments. Remember that the goal of the technology-level service is to wrap a single contributing application, and the goal of the business-level service is to capture an atomic business task. A particular enterprise's definition of "contributing application" and "atomic business task" will shape its definition of technology- and business-level services.

There is a little trick that can be done to capture what level of business service is appropriate, and maybe it will help integrators to get their heads around the scope of business services in a facility. It is playfully called the "boss voice." Picture a specific person in your facility that directs business goals and functionality — the one making all the decisions about what happens and why. Not to be insulting to the VPs and Directors out there, but in the absence of a specific person, it is best to picture a loud, abrasive leader of comic proportions. It helps in this process. Once the integrator has that person in mind, he or she should realize that the business services in the enterprise should be that person's atomic tasks. So, when wondering whether a given function is an appropriate business-level service, think about if it makes sense for that person to ask for that particular function. For example, an abrasive boss might say "Schedule a studio for Thursday!" or "Pull that asset from archive!" However, he or she would never say "Configure that server for playout!" or "Log in to that system!" These tasks are too low-level for the boss and would therefore be technology services. Alternatively, he or she would never say "Produce the evening news!" This task is too high-level but the boss would want to delve into the details of *how* the evening news is produced. So maybe "produce the evening news" is a business process or something that is not in the architecture at all, but is a goal that is achieved by having people complete many independent business processes instead.

Maybe a boss in one media enterprise is at a different level than a boss in another. One boss would probably not say "Produce 1000 dubs of that asset in PAL using VTR 12!" but maybe another would. The key is to identify the right "boss voice" and use it to figure out what business services are appropriate in a given enterprise. This is not an exact science, however, little tricks like this that put integrators in the right frame of mind to produce an architecture that is useful and reusable to *them*, and that is SOA's primary goal.

Business-level services present interfaces into an entire facility. Their functionality is not limited to a single area or subsystem, but instead should be as cross-departmental as makes sense in the enterprise. Business-level services should act globally, not locally. Because of this, integrators will want to design business-level services intelligently. For example, it is probably not a good idea to expose a service called "check inventory" that only checks the inventory in a production department. Integrators should either design the check inventory service to query all departments, or have an inventory service for every department, including a "check production inventory" service.

The act of determining how to best represent business-level services is an important and challenging task. Integrators should not be misleading or short-sighted when defining services. This seems like a tall order to someone just getting adjusted to the tenets of SOA, so this chapter discusses the best practices of service exposure in the following sections.

In addition to services, the business domain also includes business processes. Business processes are just what they sound like: orchestrated workflows stringing together various services and other processes to accomplish a given business goal. Processes are the components in an SOA that are going to have the widest reach and largest aim. They are the components that will put the way an enterprise does business into its architecture. These components are so important in a media enterprise that an entire methodology known as Business Process Management (Chapter 6) has been developed to deal with them. In an SOA, business processes are the highest level components — the top of the architectural stack.

There is some gray area (not shown in this layered model) between business-level services and business processes. There is no idealization horizon between these two components, so some amount of spillover between them is perfectly acceptable. This is the world of "composite services." These are business tasks that are strung together out of fundamental business services, but are not quite complex enough to be considered a process all on their own. Good examples of such composite services are SOA components that might call a business-level service to do some amount of work (e.g., a "push episode to rough cut" service to produce an EDL) and then notify a producer that the work is being done. The notification task is an independent business-level service (because an enterprise will probably want to reuse that one in many other workflows), but the business rules of the enterprise dictate that notification should occur automatically at different points in the production chain. Therefore, a composite service is assembled to link these two business tasks.

## MASH-UPS

The Internet-savvy out there may have heard of composite services already, even though the term might be new. In fact, many have probably used composite services fairly often without realizing it. The term that kids these days are using to refer to composite services is "mash-ups." Mash-ups are globally available composite services that utilize a single user interface to access their composite functionality. Some of the most popular mash-ups combine Google's map service with another data service, such as real estate prices or classified ads, to make a specialty interactive map. Others may combine the feeds of various social networking sites to provide a single place to check up on all online contacts.

There are a million different ways that services can be combined to produce composite functionality. Mash-ups are bringing this idea to the masses. If there is no single tool that does all of the things that users want it to do, then they can roll their own! This is the lesson of composite services, and making that process easier is one of the ultimate goals of SOA.

### 3.3.3.4  The Service Domain

The SOA integrator must decide upon the right technology-level services to expose at the application idealization horizon. Realistically, there are two classes of technology-level service: application-specific services and the utility players called "infrastructure services."

This section has already mentioned application-specific technology-level services in its discussion of the application domain. These are the services that are assembled by wrapping APIs presented by applications (or, ultimately, humans). They expose the functionality of the underlying application to the rest of the SOA. Also necessary at this layer are infrastructure services, which are simple services that can be viewed as "all wrapper." They are normally written as part of the integration process and expose atomic technical tasks that can be leveraged by the service architecture to help turn application-specific services into business-level services. Good examples of infrastructure services are message encryption, name resolution, or data transformation services. When an SOA integrator needs a small component of functionality that is not available from existing applications, he or she might throw together an infrastructure service. It is a technical task (often a coding or scripting task), but a straightforward one. Together, infrastructure and application-specific services form the components at the technology level.

## THE DIFFERENCE BETWEEN INFRASTRUCTURE SERVICES AND TECHNOLOGY-LEVEL SERVICES

This section discusses two very similar types of SOA components: infrastructure services and technology-level services. Both do work in the enterprise. Both appear in the SOA model at the application idealization horizon. So what distinguishes an infrastructure service from a technology-level service and vice versa?

Technology-level services represent the functionality of underlying systems in the enterprise. Calling a technology-level service means that the enterprise is sending a message that will be transformed and delivered to an application. The application will process that message, do some work, and return a response. Infrastructure services are much simpler in scope and intent. They represent little tasks that enable complex integration, and do not make calls to underlying applications. If an integrator needs to transform drop-frame timecode to non-drop-frame timecode in an EDL, for example, he or she would write a small infrastructure service. If that integrator needs to send that EDL to a playout server to conform an asset, a technology-level service is required.

An enterprise begins any SOA integration project by wrapping applications to expose technology-level services. After beginning to integrate these services together, the enterprise may find a need for an infrastructure service and create one on the fly. They are both useful components in an SOA architecture, but they are very different types of components.

Having discussed both the business-level (top-down) and technology-level (bottom-up) components in an SOA, this chapter is left with the task of determining how to connect the two worlds. In many cases, this is the most challenging and interesting part of an SOA: taking the technology-level services exposed by the wrappers and connecting them to the business-level services needed by the workflows in an enterprise. To do this, a "glue" of system integration components must be assembled to connect the two types of interfaces. This glue is called "service architecture."

So what is service architecture? Like wrappers, service architecture is composed of "in-between" components. Unlike wrappers, service architecture does not need to deal with the technical detail of connecting to the various applications it is attempting to integrate (that was done in the wrapper). Instead, its focus is on integrating the *functionality* of the underlying technology-level services. Service architecture could be as simple as directly connecting technology-level services to business-level services, or could contain many subcomponents that group the functionality of multiple technology-level services or load balance requests among many different services in the infrastructure. The service architecture handles the system requirements of the SOA, whether they are distributing requests to multiple applications or logging all calls using a unified "activity auditing" technology-level service.

In a well-designed SOA, the service architecture will not need to worry about technical detail. Although technology-level services are ideologically quite different from the business-level services they enable, there is no reason that both types of services (and the entire service architecture in between) cannot use the same implementation technology. In fact, Web services expose infrastructure and business services in the exact same way. Also, it is the job of the middleware layer (discussed in Chapter 4) in an SOA to handle the technical detail of the service architecture by ensuring communication among components. The important difference between the two idealization horizons is not a technological one, but a theoretical one. Technology-level services present interfaces into your specific applications and contributors. Business-level services present interfaces into the architecture as a whole.

## 3.3.4 Service Decomposition

Now, all of the various components in the SOA model have been covered. Hopefully this model shows how each of these layers interacts to ultimately turn individual applications into business functionality presented to the user. What has not been discussed is how to take systems and service-orient them into such a model. This is a process known as "service decomposition."

Saying that an architect is "decomposing" services does not mean that they are dead and rotting. Instead, decomposition refers to the act of breaking down application components and identifying the important details of each service. It is a funny term to describe this process, but it makes sense, as decomposition is really breaking apart the outer shell of a proprietary application to get at the juicy bits of business functionality inside. Defining technology-level services and designing a wrapper that will turn existing APIs into those technology-level services fit service decomposition into a layered SOA model. It is a crucial step in service orientation that must be undertaken with special concern toward how these technology-level services will fit into the upper layers of an SOA.

Unfortunately (as this is a technical book attempting to provide some level of detail on implementing SOA), decomposition is partially an art form, which makes it hard to master. It is not exactly found in a manual. There are no set rules to ensure that the correct services have been exposed to the rest of your enterprise when decomposing an application. The integrator needs to have a good feel for what the application is trying to accomplish and what business value it really provides to the facility. The integrator also needs to know the ways in which the infrastructure will want to use the services. Incorrectly decomposing a service may hinder its reusability going forward. The good news is, because SOA is such an object-oriented and componentized architecture (in other words, because that application idealization horizon is in there), re-wrapping later, if needed, can be done without affecting much of the rest of the infrastructure.

What does this process of decomposition really look like? An integrator will be starting with an existing application in your facility, and the goal is to get to a series of technology-level services that the application provides. To decompose a service, there are three things an integrator needs to fully understand:

1. The application being decomposed and its hooks
2. The form the service interface should take
3. The way the completed service will participate in the overall architecture

Saying that SOA integrators need to understand the application to be exposed as a service and its hooks is certainly not stating anything revolutionary. In fact, this is mostly the same process that is gone through in a tightly coupled architecture to add a new system — talk to the end users, get the API documentation, and understand the integration points. There are a few things that will probably need to be done a little differently, however, because the application is connected to a service-oriented middleware layer and not directly to several systems.

Certainly the integrator would want to examine the APIs and hooks in the application for their ability to be wrapped. Any number of different technologies can be used to wrap an application. Remember, technology is not a part of the core SOA message. Ultimately, the integrator will have to interface to both the technology that the vendor has chosen for the application's APIs and the technology that has been chosen for the middleware layer of the SOA, so it might not be a bad idea to write the entire wrapper in one of those technologies. These issues are discussed further in Chapter 4.

Another thing to think about when examining the application is appropriately "classing" it to allow for a heterogeneous, best-of-breed architecture. As part of the integration process, the integrator should be splitting the systems in the enterprise into classes: asset management, transcoding, automation, etc. This way, if there are two vendors that both offer an editing solution, then it can be expected that they should provide the same technical-level services to the infrastructure. In other words, the integrator should determine when two different applications are providing the same technical services to his or her facility. This is at the heart of technical agility and reusability in SOA, and it can make service decomposition a little easier. For example, if a specific vendor's transcoding engine has already been wrapped to expose technology-level services, then when faced with wrapping a different vendor's transcoding engine, the integrator does not have to go through the process of determining what technology-level services to use. The "transcode asset" services (or whatever they may have been called) can simply be reused.

This ability to class applications and reuse service definitions is a huge part of the SOA message, and one of the many metrics that can be used to determine how well exposed a given application is.

# 10 QUESTIONS TO DETERMINE IF AN APPLICATION IS CORRECTLY EXPOSED AS A SERVICE

1. Are all of the operations exposed at around the same level of detail? If some services are extremely low-level and others are extremely high-level, integrators may wish to combine the functionality of the low-level operations into fewer high-level ones.

2. Would someone be able to guess the exact application underneath based solely on the operations exposed? If so, integrators may need to make the service interface more generic. No one wants to force users to think about the application. That is the whole point of wrapping.

3. Do the services exposed make sense to the people that commonly use the application? An enterprise does not want to inadvertently remove any business value from the application by wrapping it.

4. Do the services exposed make sense to the business users of the system? If not, the service will not be a useful and reusable SOA component.

5. Do the services support the business goals and requirements of the enterprise? There is no sense in wrapping applications that will not provide any business value.

6. Does the name of the service reflect something users go to that application for? There is no point in wrapping an application to do something no one would do with it anyway.

7. Is there too much business logic in the wrapper? There is always the danger of abstracting too much just to get to technology-level services. Leave most of the business logic to the service architecture connecting many services.

8. Are integrators stubbing out or finding themselves cutting corners with many of the operations the enterprise needs the application to expose? Perhaps they are trying to get the application to have functionality that it does not have. Or perhaps multiple applications are needed together to achieve some of the desired functionality.

9. Is the wrapper so simple that it is just passing through the functionality of the API? This is not always a bad thing, especially in applications with well-designed interfaces. However, one of the reasons to wrap applications is to personalize them to the needs of a facility. Rarely should integrators simply pass through an application's API.

10. Is the wrapper so complex that integrators are recreating much of the application's functionality in the wrapper? This happens often in applications that have poorly designed or unavailable APIs. An enterprise should attempt to avoid putting application functionality in the wrapper. It should find ways to leverage the functionality that already exists in the application. Don't do the application vendor's work for them!

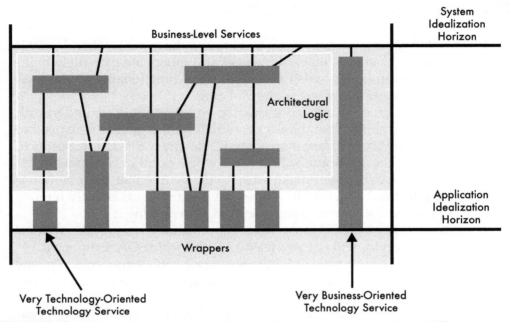

**FIGURE 3-12**   Wrappers might expose technology-level services at a number of different abstraction levels. Some well-oriented applications may even be able to be wrapped to provide business-level services directly. This often happens when the goals of the enterprise and the goals of the application are aligned.

Finally, when examining the application and its hooks, it is important to fully understand the scope of each function that the API exposes. This will allow for a correct determination of the level of service that the application exposes. As stated, the job of the wrapper is to expose technology-level services. This is correct, but it is also true that not all technology services are created equal. A complex or vertically integrated suite that handles a lot of business-level functionality might need to be wrapped. The integrator would (rightly so) not want to have to recreate that functionality in the service architecture just because a rule states that applications should expose only technology-level services. Perhaps such an application exposes both technology-level services and services that are on the same level as service architecture components or even business-level services! Don't mess with success! Determine the scope of the functionality in an application and write wrappers to that scope, as illustrated in Fig. 3-12.

Next, a service integrator needs to understand the services that an enterprise intends to expose to correctly decompose an application into a service. This goes beyond the level of simply identifying the functionality needed to integrate, which means developing the interface to call and use that functionality. Services are, after all, interfaces. The implementation of the service is beyond the application idealization horizon in both the wrappers and applications. Services, like any type of transactional interface, include operations. These operations have data that go into them and data that come out when they are completed. The act of determining service interface is therefore all about identifying transactional operations and the data that go into them.

These concepts are discussed in a technology-independent way, but when choosing the technology used to implement SOA (for example, Web services), the integrator will need to design a service interface in that specific technology. Regardless of the technology chosen, however, the specific operations used to expose must be identified. These operations should be transactional, they should be discrete, and they should be devoid of vendor-specific or proprietary concepts.

These are *custom* operations — the systems in a facility are the way the enterprise wants them to look. The integrator should not skimp and make them too similar to the APIs exposed by the application just to make wrapper design simpler. That will come back to bite him or her when the underlying systems need to be replaced or another vendor's system must be wrapped to those service interfaces. Copying the vendor API at the service interface level is simply crippling an infrastructure's reusability. That is one of the biggest mistakes integrators make when decomposing applications. Instead, service interfaces should be customized to meet the specific needs of the facility. Unfortunately, no one can dictate what that looks like except for the integrators and users in that facility. But anyone that has been in an enterprise for any length of time probably has some pretty good ideas about how this whole thing *should* work. Chapter 8 discusses some ways to get started down this design path.

## WHAT NOT TO DO: IGNORING SERVICE REUSE

As applications are decomposed into technology-level services, do not ignore the applications that have already been exposed as services. These existing services could be exactly the same as the services an enterprise needs to expose in the application currently being decomposed! Any time integrators sit down to figure out what services an application should expose, they should always look through the existing service interfaces in the enterprise first. If they see an existing interface that suits current needs, they should reuse it! An enterprise will want to take advantage of opportunities to reuse components in its SOA as much as possible. It saves work and it makes life easier for those who want to connect to these services later.

Part of this interface design is also defining the data that go into and come out of services. SOA is all about having a structured, componentized data model. The data should be defined, discrete, and focused on the business functionality of the various services. To reinforce these points, the common term used for data that services digest is "business objects." When decomposing an application, the integrator needs to determine what business objects that application requires to do its job, and what business objects it will create or provide back to the facility. Just as with operations, these business objects will be defined using the SOA technology selected with reusability as a major factor in defining these data models.

With this information, the integrator is almost ready to decompose an application. The final thing to clarify is the understanding of the service as a whole. Once the application and exposed services have been wrapped, how will it act in the overall architecture? How often is it expected to be used initially? How will other services find it and call it? What non-functional requirements (such as speed, availability, cost) does the service have? These are all important questions that need to be addressed in any integrated architecture, and SOA is no different.

One piece of advice when tackling these questions surrounding the completed service — frame them in the context of existing business requirements. Much of this chapter is spent defining these services in the abstract and how the point of technology-level services is to represent the functionality of the component systems, not to cater to the needs of the business. SOA is designed so that the integrator is able to define the functionality of these services in a vacuum, so to speak.

However, these technology-level services must be ultimately integrated together through a service architecture to expose business-level services that do have specific business requirements. Because it is very difficult for anyone to cater to all possible business requirements in service design, it is best to consider the common ways that these services will be used when determining if the service meets business needs.

Sure, the application has not been wrapped and has not exposed your service yet, but it can still be logically tested to show how that service might act in the overall SOA. A variety of different sample workflows and business processes can be developed to test how well the service would fit into an enterprise. This does not have to be done in a lab or a testing facility, it can be done on paper or a whiteboard. For example, if an enterprise is thinking of wrapping its traffic system to expose a "check for available spot" service operation, it should work out where that service call would fit in to its traffic and sales workflow. How about the cut-to-clock processes? Or the ad ingest process? As with most aspects of service design, the integrator should focus on potential areas of reusability in the service. A facility sees the most return on your investment in SOA when it is able to directly reuse components of its architecture. SOA makes this possible from a technology point of view, and SOA combined with good service design makes this possible from a business point of view.

## CASE STUDY

### Re-Wrapping Services

A major asset management vendor offers an interface via Web services that aligns nicely with the tenets of SOA. The asset management system offers multiple services, each one providing operations for a specific area such as metadata access, job monitoring, ingest, and workflow/notification. There is one WSDL per service, and the vendor ships the product with all four WSDLs, along with instructions on integration. While developing this interface, the vendor did not align the services with the major modules in its software. Instead the vendor determined the discrete business functionality that it supported and made these services.

Perhaps the end user (a media enterprise) does not envision its use of the media asset management system in terms of the four services that were identified by the vendor. Because they are Web service interfaces, the media enterprise can easily re-wrap the vendor's interface to present a service-oriented interface that more closely matches its idea of the application.

Appendix D covers, in detail, how vendors might service-orient their products more effectively.

## 3.4 WRAPPERS

This section is about one of the major components of a Service-Oriented Architecture: the application wrapper. Recall the definition of SOA from the beginning of this chapter:

SOA is an architecture of independent, wrapped services communicating via published interfaces over a common middleware layer.

Services in an SOA are wrapped. That is what makes them services. In other words, a service equals an application plus a wrapper. Wrappers expose applications as services. In the layered model of SOA components, wrappers are below the application idealization horizon, which means that they can tightly couple themselves to the application they are wrapping. Their job is to transform the application's APIs into technology-level services to be used by the rest of the facility. After an application is wrapped, there is no need to call the APIs directly.

In enterprise architectures predating SOA, wrappers may have been known as gateways, bridges, adapters, or façades. In SOA, however, they are referred to as wrappers. There may be some confusion here because an "adapter" is also a component you will see in a lot of SOA literature (this is not the same as that BNC to RCA adapter everyone is used to!). Because this is a constantly evolving field, the terminology for these components is never fixed. The term "wrapper" will be used exclusively here, but the idea of a wrapper can be easily translated into whatever the latest and greatest SOA vendor is calling it these days.

## WRAPPERS VS. ADAPTERS

Wrappers are components that transform APIs into technology-level services. The term "adapter" may also be used within the context of SOA. In most cases, SOA integrators use the term "adapter" to refer to a component in the middleware layer that transforms one standards-based method of communication to another. For example, an enterprise might have an adapter that turns RPC calls into SOAP messages (see Chapter 5), or one that turns service calls into SQL messages for a database. Adapters allow services that use different interface technologies to all connect to the same middleware layer. The middleware layer uses the adapters to convert from one technology to another, facilitating interoperability.

The main functions that the wrapper must perform are twofold. The wrapper must (1) encapsulate and abstract the application to create a service interface and (2) transform the technology used by the application to whatever is the chosen SOA standard.

Wrappers encapsulate applications surrounding and simplifying application interfaces so that only the functionality that the rest of the SOA infrastructure is interested in is exposed. Wrappers also abstract applications by presenting that functionality in a way that is not

**TABLE 3-1**

A Review of the Differences between Wrappers and Adapters

| Wrappers | Adapters |
| --- | --- |
| Considered part of the service | Considered part of the middleware layer |
| Converts data and functionality from one form to another | Converts communication technology from one form to another |
| Can be deployed as part of the application, in the middleware layer, or as a separate entity | Can only be deployed within the middleware layer |
| Always necessary in an SOA | Unnecessary in single-technology middleware layers |

application specific and is more digestible for other services in the enterprise. Encapsulation and abstraction can be accomplished by hiding, re-framing, combining, or passing through operations that the underlying application performs.

"Hiding" operations means that a wrapper can choose not to use a particular functionality of the application. Certainly no one uses every single aspect of every system that is in their facility, and an SOA integrator may therefore choose not to expose certain application functions. This is one way to simplify and encapsulate the service interface: have it do less than the application it exposes. Another possibility is that, either because it was especially well designed or because the way that particular application works is well suited to the particular enterprise, the underlying application already exposes just the right functionality. In this case the wrapper can simply "pass through" the functionality of that application without changing its scope or complexity. There is no logical change, even though the wrapper may still be performing data or technology transformations. This is sometimes the case when an application has been designed with an SOA architecture in mind.

Pass-throughs and operation hiding are obviously not common. After all, the SOA needs to idealize that application's functionality; that is why it is wrapped to begin with! Because of this, an integrator will often want to re-frame the functionality of the application to suit the needs of a facility's technology-level service(s). For example, a media movement service updates a status field that can be polled when it is finished with its transfers. The integrator wants to change that so when it is done it sends a call back to the service consumer instead. Or perhaps an asset management system returns all the results of a search in a big list, and instead it should return sets of ten entries at a time. These are both examples of re-framing application functionality, and that is the job of the wrapper. Re-framing means changing the context or logical details of the operation to meet the needs of the business. By doing those sorts of transformations in the wrapper, the integrator avoids the need to deal with them at the service level.

Wrappers may also combine many API calls into a single service operation. Perhaps it is desired that scheduling a studio should be a single technology-level service call, but it requires separate API calls to query the scheduling application for that studio's unique identifier, check its availability during that time period to prevent conflicts, and finally schedule the facility. The wrapper can hide these multiple calls behind the application idealization horizon. The APIs of two applications may need to be queried to expose a particular technology-level service! It depends on what the facility expects as technology-level services. Wrapper design should be done as intelligently and modularly as possible, but its number one goal is exposing the desired service functionality to the enterprise.

Besides encapsulation and abstraction, the other main job for a wrapper is data transformation. This may mean changing the actual data in the service inputs and outputs. For example, "firstname lastname" instead of "lastname, firstname" or "total number of frames" instead of "duration in seconds" are both data changes. These types of changes can range from the very simple to the very complex. Just as with abstraction, more than one application may need to be queried to correctly do this transformation (for example, getting a UUID for an asset out of an asset management system before using it in a transcoding engine). Good SOA design will include business data transformation tools and services in the middleware layer to assist with this.

Data transformation may also mean changing the underlying technical format of the data, for example, from Java method calls to Web service messages. A wrapper will have to do this sort of format transformation any time that the application API is implemented using a different technology than the ones supported by the SOA infrastructure (more often than anyone likes, no doubt). Thankfully, there are many tools out there to help with this technology problem. Specific technologies found in the SOA infrastructure are covered in later chapters. There are, however, some different basic architectural patterns found with wrapper construction. These are called wrapper "models."

## 3.4.1 Wrapper Models

The time has come for a media integrator to implement her first wrapper. She has followed best practices of service decomposition; she knows what she needs her wrapper to do. But what is the best way to build it? Her wrapper will be connecting an application-specific environment to an SOA middleware environment, so as far as implementation is concerned, she has three options:

1. Build the wrapper in the application using custom workflow or extensible API capabilities
2. Build the wrapper on an external wrapper platform running in a separate environment (either on the same or different physical hardware)
3. Build the wrapper in the middleware layer using SOA tools and technologies

All three of these options are not always available when building a wrapper, and an integrator may opt for one over the other, or a combination of many, given the specifics of the application to be wrapped, the services to be exposed, or both. A detailed examination of each model is needed to determine when to use which option.

First, if the option is available, an enterprise might consider actually building the wrapper using the end system that is about to be wrapped! Everyone knows that "workflow" has been the buzzword of the year for several years running, so it is very popular for media system vendors to include customizable workflow engines as part of their products. These engines can be used to build custom processes that the end system can execute. For example, a digital asset management system might allow a user to specify a workflow that automatically generates proxies and sends an e-mail when a new asset is dropped into a watch folder. It allows for the creation of compound functionality out of the existing operations in the application. This sounds exactly like what wrappers do when they encapsulate and abstract an end system! That means if the application's workflow engine is designed in an exposed and extensible way, then this in-system "development environment" can actually be used to build some or all of the wrapper!

To build all of a wrapper in an application's workflow engine as Fig. 3-13 illustrates, however, the SOA integrator must be able to expose custom interfaces using the same technology that has been chosen for the SOA. Stumbling into shared support of the same interface technology may seem like something that cannot be counted on. And, for now, it is not. No one gets the opportunity to write wrappers entirely using end-system workflow engines very often. However, as

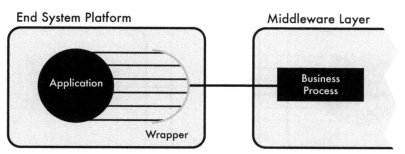

**FIGURE 3-13** A wrapper implemented in an end system application.

standardized interface technologies become more pervasive in the M&E industry, this becomes a more viable option. Web services, for example, has a high potential to be both the middleware protocol and the API implementation technology in the media enterprises of the near future (Web services are discussed in Chapter 5). But it is currently more likely that the application's custom API protocol will not match up with the technology-level service protocol. In addition to specifying custom workflow, the integrator will probably need to implement a data transformation wrapper outside of the application using one of the other two implementation models. But, much of the encapsulation and abstraction can still occur in the workflow engine.

Portions of the wrapper should be implemented inside the end system itself when the functionality offered by that end system makes it easier to build wrapper components there than in an external runtime environment. Perhaps the application provides graphical tools to drag-n-drop workflow components. Perhaps the operations to be exposed change often and a dynamic way to alter wrapper design is needed. Another good reason to expose custom application workflows as wrapper components is when the users of the application are the ones that are in charge of how the wrapper looks. They are probably already well adjusted to that application's user interface and could manage the wrapper design quite effectively.

The second wrapper implementation model to be considered implements the wrapper on a separate server or runtime environment from the application being wrapped, making it an entirely new component in the architecture. This option, shown in Fig. 3-14, is *always* open to the SOA integrator, because that individual gets to choose the nature of the

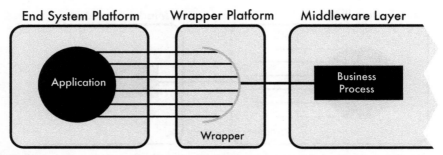

**FIGURE 3-14**  A wrapper implemented on a separate system, where it communicates independently with the API and the middleware.

platform on which the wrapper runs. The requirements of this type of wrapper design are simply that the wrapper component can call the application API and that it can expose technology-level services using the chosen SOA standard. No customizable workflow engines needed!

There are many more options open to an integrator implementing a wrapper on an external wrapper platform. There are plenty of technologies out there (such as application servers) that are ideal for this sort of wrapper hosting, and by making the wrapper independent from both the application and the middleware, the integrator ensures that it will be unaffected by failures on either side. There is just one problem with this method: it is basically full-blown programming. The integrator will be writing an application that will take in technology-level service calls and turn them into application API calls. There are no helpful environments and tools that might be found in the middleware or in the end system, so the enterprise will need to either find its own (by using an integrated development environment, or IDE) or get comfortable with writing some code. No one said this computer stuff happens without any programmers, after all! There are no popular SOA-specific wrapper development and deployment systems that would make this job easier yet, but maybe in a few years we will see some of those pop up.

Building wrappers on their own platform is the most common architecture available. An integrator would want to do this when the application to be wrapped does not allow for any customization, and the protocol it uses is not one that could be transformed to get it into the middleware layer. In other words, one would use this implementation

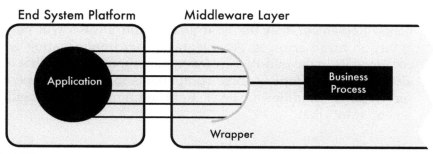

**FIGURE 3-15**   A wrapper implemented in the middleware layer.

model for the really integration-unfriendly applications — the ones that force integrators to read flat files or have highly specialized, language-specific APIs. An enterprise would also want to implement this model when wrapper design needs to be very complex; perhaps, calling the APIs of several applications or persisting information in a database between calls. After all, independently programming a wrapper gives an integrator the freedom to build it in just about any way.

The third and final implementation model for a wrapper is to put it in the middleware, as shown in Fig. 3-15. Chapter 4 discusses middleware in great detail. SOA middleware is composed of a number of different components such as enterprise service buses, messaging utilities, and data handling components. SOA integrators can take advantage of these components to do the encapsulation and data transformation they need to transform an application interface into technology-level services. For example, if the application exposes its functionality using a modern, standardized technology protocol, but not the one that has been selected for service communication, an integrator can no doubt find or build a component in the middleware layer that will do that protocol transformation. An enterprise could probably do a good deal of data transformation (reformatting the fields in the service operations) in the middleware layer as well.

An enterprise would want to implement a wrapper using middleware tools when the application to be wrapped already exposes a common interface that could be understood by enterprise IT tools, but it is just not exactly right for technology-level services. As media system vendors expose more and better interfaces, this architecture makes more sense. But a facility will want to be careful not to clog up its middleware

layer with too many custom data transformation or wrapper components! Remember that the final goal is and always will be greater
agility to make changes. As integrators are implementing wrapper
components in the middleware layer, they should ensure that they are
always loosely coupling these components to the other processes or
services in the middleware layer. Tight coupling means no agility, and
no one wants that!

Of course, an enterprise could always build wrappers using any combination of the previous three implementation models. It could implement a middleware component that does some level of data
transformation before passing off a service call to an independent
wrapper, which will split it into many calls that it makes to custom
workflows in the end system. That is one wrapper spread out over
three platforms. However, just like a middleware layer should not get
clogged up with tightly coupled wrapper components, wrapper components should not get spread all over the place, because that too may
hinder an enterprise's ability to make agile changes. Implemented
intelligently, wrappers can go in any of these places and still provide
solid technical agility. However, everyone knows that constraints of
time and budget when doing integration lead to cut corners and not-
so-intelligent implementations, so an enterprise should set itself up
for success and architect wrappers to be as straightforward as possible!

## 3.4.2 Common Wrapper Problems

There are many common mistakes that SOA integrators make when creating wrapper designs. Wrappers are often the trickiest components to
deal with in an SOA because they are the ones that have to integrate
with all manner of weird, proprietary applications. It is hard enough figuring out what functionality an enterprise wants to expose in its SOA!
But to top it all off, there are a number of tricks that end system vendors
like to pull when they are developing their applications that can really
trip up SOA integrators during wrapper design and implementation.

One of the most common problems an integrator will no doubt
encounter is the Center of the Universe (COTU) problem. The COTU
problem occurs when a vendor system must control functionality that
has wide applicability in an enterprise. There is always a way around

it, but it will oftentimes force an architecture to be far more complex than it really needs to be, with many additional components handling data consistency and transformation across big systems.

Many vendors, due to their specializations in specific areas of the media workflow, have developed pigeonholed views of the world that are all about them. Any major editing vendor is going to think of any problem as an editing problem. Any automation vendor is going to think of any problem as a control problem. In general, any major vendor defaults to the scenario where they are the only system in the facility — the Center of the Universe. They will think it is their job to handle or control all of the corollary tasks that go along with their core functionality. One common example of the COTU problem is the assignment of unique asset IDs. Every system that stores media assets in a facility — whether it be a playout system, shared production storage management, DAM, MAM, archive, etc. — will no doubt assign a so-called universally unique identifier (UUID) to each asset. The SOA solution to such a functionality would have a single "asset identification" service managing all UUIDs to ensure no overlap and assigning the same UUID to an asset in every system. However, due to its ability to affect internal consistency, many applications will not trust an external system to do this assignment. And besides, every end system has a different format UUID anyway — some with only numbers, some with numbers, characters, and dashes, etc. Every system wants to be the COTU regarding this particular functionality, and that requires an SOA integrator to build asset ID correlation services that associate the identifiers each system uses to each other.

Vendors are not wrong to consider themselves the COTU. In many facilities, that is exactly what they are, and their inability to provide certain core services would be a game-killer in the eyes of many engineers. Anyone can think of one or two vendors that truly are the COTU in a given facility, and that facility probably takes advantage of that fact to make implementation as straightforward as possible. Plus, there are always ways to work around the COTU problem. Good product design, however, would allow a component to be either the COTU or plug into an existing infrastructure. More SOA tips and tricks for vendors can be found in Appendix D.

Besides COTU, another common problem that SOA integrators face when implementing wrappers is the existence of fundamental data representation differences between applications and middleware. This does not mean the difference between "firstname lastname" and "lastname, firstname." That problem is simple to solve regardless of how a wrapper is implemented. No, these are drastic disconnects between how an application thinks about the information it needs and how middleware thinks about the information it is giving. For example, an application logs a clip's temporal metadata as a list in a text file with in and out timecodes, and the enterprise has chosen MXF as the wrapper (*media wrapper, not application wrapper!*) format for its infrastructure. The application wrapper will have to parse through the text file and insert that metadata into the MXF file, which is a very complex process. And there are other such problems that the enterprise could encounter in its SOA integration. The solution to situations like this one are always going to be case-by-case. Integrators may even come across a difference so fundamental, so deep-rooted, that they are unable to solve it. But then it could be argued that the way in which the end system is considering the problem is so disconnected from the way the enterprise is considering it (and would have forced such a change in workflow regardless of SOA integration) that the system does not actually address the functionality needed and should be replaced with a system that does.

Finally, an enterprise may encounter wrapper difficulties when it comes time to upgrade or replace its applications. Recall that the whole purpose of wrapping applications is to make them easier to upgrade or change (because you only have to change the wrapper). Still, with major upgrades, an enterprise may discover that the differences between the new and old versions are so severe that it has to practically re-write the wrapper from scratch. This will not affect other components in the architecture like a tightly coupled change would, but it is still no fun from the point of view of wrapper design.

## BACKWARD-COMPATIBLE APIS

Everyone has heard horror stories about simple upgrades breaking whole integrated systems in a facility. This is one of the problems that SOA is designed to fix. By having a single wrapper handling all API calls, integrators only have a single place to fix when an upgrade breaks the API.

Hopefully, however, they very rarely have to worry about such difficulties with upgrades. Especially with modern IT systems, vendors have been good about supporting APIs in a backward-compatible way. This means that newer versions of applications tend to support clients using them as though they were the older version. While this is obviously not always the case, the culture of integration arising out of the success of SOA is forcing more vendors to support their legacy interfaces for longer and longer periods of time. This whole culture of having an upgrade break existing interfaces is worse in the M&E industry than in most other industries today. As IT technology becomes more pervasive, so too will software upgrades become more commonplace and straightforward.

## 3.4.3 Wrapper Governance and Planning

This section has now covered, to some level of detail, the common functions, architectures, and problems surrounding wrapper design. One thing to be sure not to overlook, however, is the whole issue of managing wrapper builds and rollouts. What, in other words, makes a good wrapper strategy?

There are a couple of things to think about here. One is the idea of incremental wrapper construction. As discussed in Chapter 8, an enterprise does not have to (and in fact should not) try to boil the ocean with its SOA implementation. Do not try to get all of the functionality desired all in one project. The same goes for wrapper design. An enterprise may decide that it needs to wrap a particular application to make it into technology-level services, but that does not mean it needs to wrap the whole application all at once. It may decide to implement just a single operation or a handful of operations initially, and then go back and flesh out the wrapper to add more functionality later when there is more time and money. This is a responsible way to develop wrappers, and therefore, wrappers should be designed compartmentally to facilitate this design.

Another thing to think about is wrapper updates and reevaluation. Just as it is good practice to periodically reevaluate the systems in an enterprise to ensure that they are up-to-date and still meeting business needs, it is a great idea to reconsider wrappers and technology-level services every now and then as well. The whole goal behind building wrappers to expose technology-level services is to encapsulate applications so that they work like an enterprise wants them to work (instead of how the vendors have envisioned them working). Because how an enterprise likes to work evolves over time, technology-level services should also evolve over time. Wrapper management should be a big part of an overall SOA governance plan, which will be discussed in the next section.

## 3.5  SOA BEST PRACTICES

So far, quite a bit of information has been covered in this chapter. Those readers who came into this book unfamiliar with SOA are probably reeling at this point with all of the options open to them for integrating their enterprise systems and all of the things they have to worry about to do SOA right. This is a complex topic, and that is why it is the subject of so many IT books. There is a lot of information out there. Those looking to SOA-enable their facility (and everyone should be!) should read some of those books after finishing this one. After getting some of the central concepts down, most people find that they quickly master the art of service enablement.

SOA is an art form. Because of this, it is important to review some best practices in SOA that are often overlooked or confusing. Effective governance, data management, and use of policies are especially elusive in many SOA implementations.

### 3.5.1  Governance

SOA governance is, in a nutshell, the methods established to manage a Service-Oriented Architecture. "Governance" is an IT buzzword, to be sure, but the idea of needing effective management and oversight in large software architectures is not a passing fad. Governance is one of those points that gets stressed often in IT books on the subject, and rightly so. Many integrators' first instinct is to rush straight into an

SOA project without setting up the oversight to ensure that it succeeds. But good governance is crucial to having an SOA success. Without effective governance, an enterprise is unable to reevaluate SOA solutions and unable to help ensure reuse of components. It is unable to clearly tell if the SOA project succeeded at all! Governance is very important. But what does good SOA governance look like?

## WHAT NOT TO DO: POOR SOA GOVERNANCE

Many integrators make the dire mistake of ignoring the governance and oversight needs of an SOA project, and instead decide to jump right in and get their hands dirty. Good governance is, however, the first thing that should be set up in a facility to implement SOA!

Good governance in SOA is a full-time job. Actually, good governance in any enterprise architecture is a full-time job, but many so-called "accidental architectures" do not have good governance and therefore get more accidental as time goes on. It could be argued, really, that it does not matter what the underlying software architecture is, implementing proper governance facilitates business agility. This is very true, although using SOA makes that process much easier. SOA's horizons and levels of abstraction provide good places to draw governance boundaries: individual business units are in charge of end systems while an SOA team (like the one discussed in Chapter 8) manages the services and processes in the middleware layer.

Step one of good SOA governance is to have a plan. The end picture of SOA is hundreds upon hundreds of services orchestrated over a common middleware layer. By thinking about what that looks like in a particular facility, an integrator will ensure that every subsequent SOA project supports that end goal. A governance plan should make sure that business requirements are solidified and documented up front and followed during implementation. SOA is more top-loaded than many architectures because success depends so much on the planning done ahead of time. For example, how will a digital asset management system get wrapped effectively if no one stops to think about how it might be used in six months? In eighteen months? For service interfaces to provide agility they must be reusable, and to achieve reusability the enterprise must consider the most effective ways to implement components.

## ACTION ITEM: WRITE UP A GOVERNANCE PLAN FOR AN ORGANIZATION

Decide which business units and individuals are stakeholders in an SOA implementation, and ensure that they are involved in the right ways as the enterprise moves forward with an SOA deployment. Figure out the right types of committees to review projects, services, and business processes. Determine the best way to identify business goals and deliverables for an SOA implementation team. Even if an enterprise is looking several years in the future to its first SOA project, developing a governance plan now will make starting that project much easier

Another very important aspect of SOA governance is the reevaluation phase. At regular intervals (set up by an SOA team) the enterprise should consider all of the services in the infrastructure to ensure that they are still meeting business needs as effectively as possible. Could some services implemented long ago be replaced by reusing newer services? Could two services be combined into a single service? Could one service be split into two services to facilitate reuse? No one will catch every potential reuse point their first time through a project, so it is important to be set up for success by having many chances to make the infrastructure more efficient.

SOA governance (in the context of media systems) is discussed further in Chapter 8.

### 3.5.2  Data Management

Data management in an SOA enterprise is all about the need to understand, formalize, and log the information that flows through the middleware layer. SOA allows users to send formalized messages from service to service in an enterprise. Formalized messaging means that the data sent is universal (meeting common standards across the facility), discrete (each message serving a specific purpose), and has structure (messages composed of fields and values). This is in contrast to the current methods of many facilities, which rely on informal slips of paper, e-mails, phone calls, and hallway conversations to distribute important information. SOA will not completely get rid of these, but it will ensure that these methods of communication are backed by logged and secured formal methodologies. That is, if the SOA is designed in the right way.

It is a mistake to make these "informal" sources of data out to be the enemy of efficient workflow. Sharing work tasks and business data at the water cooler is going to happen (and also the sign of a healthy workplace)! It is just that passing information through word of mouth is unreliable and undocumented. No one can depend on informal data because that sticky note that was left on a colleague's computer monitor might fall off, the secretary might forget the details of that phone call, or that e-mail might get lost in the shuffle. There is no way to audit what happened after the fact. An enterprise can, however, depend on a work order that is posted to a portal and persisted in a database.

It is necessary and important to formalize data in an SOA. It is necessary because SOA relies upon published service interfaces to advertise functionality throughout the enterprise. These interfaces take in data the same way that a department providing a service to an enterprise might take in a form to perform work. Just as facilities implement standardized forms to reduce confusion and make the service request process more efficient, so too do SOA services rely on standardized data models to enable service calls.

Forms are a great analogy for formalized data in an SOA. The best way to turn informal data into SOA-ready formalized data is to think about it in terms of what the form would look like. Want to implement a service to reserve equipment for a field shoot? Just imagine what the requisition form for that equipment might look like, and then there is the service interface! Another thought when formalizing data is attempting to reuse the same types of data in many services. This means implementing standardized project codes and universal asset IDs throughout the enterprise and picking the same fields from service to service.

Do not have one service measure a mark-in using minutes-seconds-frames and another use total number of frames. Do that translation in the wrapper and have a consistent look across service interfaces.

### 3.5.3 Service Policies

Service policies have not been discussed much in this chapter, although they are a growing trend in the SOA world. Policies in SOA are the non-functional data that can be associated with a service interface: when is the service available, how much does it cost, how long does it take, etc. As anyone can imagine, these are important pieces of data to consider when orchestrating services. Some technologies exist to help with policy expression (Chapter 5 has more details), but all of the business tools needed to set up and enforce policies in a facility already exist in most enterprises.

Many SOA evangelists think that policies are best expressed in the service interface. Based on the understanding of SOA captured in this book, that is an accurate sentiment. A service interface knows what functional data a service uses (what operations it offers, what data it takes, etc.), so by putting policies into the interface, any user or system that calls a service will also have access to its policies. Associating policies with functionality also allows integrators to create policy subsets. In other words, different aspects of the service could have different attributes. A transcoding engine could cost more for larger jobs or only certain data access functions in an archive service could be unavailable during a maintenance window instead of the entire service.

The other option for making these policies accessible to the rest of the SOA is to implement a policy service. A policy service would be a single place that systems could query for non-functional information regarding other services in the enterprise. This model allows updates to policies independent of service interfaces, and also provides centralized management over these policies. Perhaps in the future such policy services will even be considered in the SOA middleware and be simply a part of the fabric of SOA.

Figuring out how to express policies is only half the battle, however. The integrator also needs to know what types of policies should be enforced across the facility! Engineers trying to figure out their own policies should consider the following (not very exhaustive) list of possible policies, and feel free to add their own:

- Availability of services, including peak hours and time windows allocated for specific departments or groups
- Non-functional capabilities of services, such as media formats supported
- Security models required or supported
- Expected duration of service processing, if a long-running service
- Any cost associated with calling the service
- The quality of the service performed, including third-party ratings and/or tiered groups (i.e., "fast," "medium," "best")
- Popularity of the service in the SOA

Choose policies that reflect important characteristics of the enterprise. No one wants to go through the trouble of defining and enforcing policies that do not get used, but often in a complex SOA with many services, policies can help users to make informed decisions.

## 3.5.4 When It Is Okay to Tightly Couple

It was stated earlier in this chapter that SOA is a loosely coupled, abstracted architecture, and that all communication should go across a unified middleware layer. At this point in the SOA discussion, however, a big, realistic "sort of" can be dropped in front of that sentiment. Certainly in an ideal world all SOA communication does travel over a middleware layer and all services are wrapped to a common interface technology for easy interaction. In the real world, however, there are some unavoidable situations where it is better to go ahead and tightly couple some systems and services together. Although, even in tightly coupled scenarios, the infrastructure should always be architected such that it can easily evolve into a loosely coupled SOA. This takes little to no extra effort on the integrator's part, only a commitment to leave enough hooks in the systems so that they may later be wrapped.

When is it okay to tightly couple? When loose coupling would cost too much or take too much time. Every media facility in the world would be perfect if everyone had an unlimited amount of money and time to build them. Right?! Unfortunately, no one does; so everyone has to make sacrifices to get on the air, get the movie done, or meet their budget deadline.

Cost concerns can cripple an SOA integration project. The problem with SOA as an architecture is that it costs more up front to give more savings in the long run. This is great, assuming the enterprise can take the hit up front! Everyone knows, however, that many times it just can't. When the SOA integrator is faced with the decision of how to scale back in the face of a smaller budget, the thought of taking short-cuts with the SOA deployment while keeping the scope of work the same is very tempting. This book's advice is: They shouldn't do it! The SOA backbone will need to be implemented in the facility eventually, and deploying slapdash solutions is only going to make the integrator's job harder down the line. The number one cost-consumer of SOA is going to be that middleware layer. If the enterprise cannot afford the initial buy-in of an enterprise-wide middleware layer, one or two localized middleware solutions should be implemented that can later be connected in an SOA. If the enterprise cannot afford to build wrappers for all of the applications it wants to service-enable, it should wrap one or two of them right instead of wrapping four or five of them wrong. The rest can be tightly coupled for now, and then hooked into the growing SOA when the money is available.

The same goes for those SOA projects that are up against a hard deadline. It is a time-consuming process to figure out how services should look in an ideal SOA infrastructure. In fact, the number one consumer of time in SOA projects is the up-front definition of service interfaces. Just because there is no time to do this definition right does not mean it should be done wrong. Instead, the scope of service interfaces should be scaled back and tight coupling should be used to achieve the remaining necessary functionality. For example, instead of wrapping a bunch of DAM systems poorly to get it done in a month, an enterprise can implement a basic create, read, update, and delete (CRUD) functionality via a service interface and link up the APIs directly in a point-to-point manner to handle video processing, searching, or whatever other operations it needs to expose. Later, these service interfaces can be expanded upon in a backward compatible way to ensure that the initial CRUD operations work the entire time.

Everyone will be glad the services were implemented the right way initially!

This leads to the ultimate point in SOA deployment, and one that is reiterated over and over again in Chapter 8: start small! Because SOA is such a front-loaded integration methodology, the best way to get over that initial hump of investment is to implement a series of small SOA projects. This entire chapter has discussed SOA "in the large" because those benefits of agility and visibility are much more dramatic when they are enterprise-wide. However, they are equally present, and equally important and a whole lot more achievable on a small scale. Additionally, when implementing middleware and services for the first time in a facility, integrators will find that a smaller environment helps to get the kinks worked out of an SOA deployment methodology. So, they should choose SOA for their next project or pick a proof-of-concept in a single department to try it out. No one should decide one day to forklift out their whole infrastructure and replace it with an SOA overnight as that will only lead to pain. Start small is the best advice anyone can get at the close of a chapter on SOA.

## 3.6 CONCLUSION

Service-Oriented Architecture is so much more than just the latest IT buzzword weaseling its way into the M&E industry. It is not just a passing fad. It is the culmination of decades of computer systems design and best practices. It will be with the industry in one form or another — just like computers are with the industry — for a long, long time. Perhaps as computer technology gets more pervasive in media facilities, SOA will become more ingrained in media networks and no one will notice it as much, but it will still play a vital role in day-to-day operations. It will seem unremarkable because it will be everywhere. All new technology will adhere to SOA best practices, and the enterprise will always be service-oriented.

One can only hope for such a future. In the meantime, everyone must make a conscious point to adhere to the best practices of SOA. SOA provides agility, visibility, and organizational benefits to those that take advantage of its principles. So it makes sense to learn the fundamentals of service decomposition, interface design, and SOA governance and bring those concepts into any architecture.

## WHAT TO TELL YOUR BOSS

- Do not underestimate the importance of Service-Oriented Architecture to the media industry. SOA is here to stay.
- SOA provides agility and visibility to your enterprise by exposing data and making change easier. Compare SOA to tightly coupled integration, and you will see a huge increase in value.
- Services are infrastructure components that provide business value to your organization. Creating them is as much a business analysis process as it is a technology development process.
- Setting up good governance is crucial to SOA success.

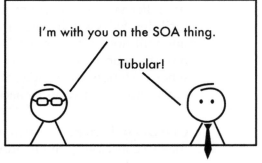

# 4

# MIDDLEWARE

The previous chapter examined the history and principles of Service-Oriented Architecture. It introduced a working definition of SOA:

> SOA is an architecture of independent, wrapped business services communicating via published interfaces over a common middleware layer.

This chapter will explore the concept of middleware — a major element of the SOA story — by looking at both the theory behind it and some specific technologies that are common in the middleware universe. By the end of this chapter, readers should be able to understand the purpose, quirks, and landscape of middleware, and be able to distinguish its various features.

## 4.1  THE DEFINITION OF MIDDLEWARE

The first and most important thing to understand about middleware is that it is not a single component in enterprise architecture. Contrary to what the marketing material of specific vendors in the middleware space seems to imply, there is no box that someone can buy off the shelf that will provide a middleware layer. It is something that an enterprise must build up and care for over time. Certainly some products may include middleware components or large pieces of an enterprise middle-ware layer, but an enterprise will probably want more than a single product in its middleware. Again, middleware is not a specific compo-nent, it is a "layer" that is found in an enterprise.

As posited in Chapter 3, these concepts do not need to be limited to the software domain — an SOA can theoretically be built out of only paper forms and people. In this case, the "middleware layer" would be a network of couriers that cart forms from place to place. However, since most of these concepts arise from the software domain, middle-ware especially, discussion will be limited to enterprise software sys-tems. Really, "middleware" as a concept does not mean much of anything outside of the world of enterprise software. But inside that world, it means a lot.

## 4.1.1 Middleware in SOA

Middleware is pervasive in enterprise software these days. While it is a crucial component of SOA, there is also plenty of middleware out-side SOA, because it encompasses so many qualities and best prac-tices that are useful when constructing software systems of any sort. Any software built on Enterprise Java, .NET, or other such "enterprise class" environments has at least some kind of middleware layer, even if it is not one as advanced as those discussed in this chapter. Middleware has applicability outside of SOA, but because of this book's focus on SOA concepts and technologies, it will focus on the middleware *inside* an SOA.

As shown in Fig. 4-1, the middleware layer serves the role of an inte-gration broker and message exchange medium inside an SOA. Systems integration is all about communication, and the middleware layer facilitates that communication in an SOA. It is the fabric that connects services, and because of that, the middleware layer is responsible for certain aspects of the communication infrastructure: security, routing, reliability, and scalability, etc.

Middleware is not a product, it is a software layer composed of many products. No one would really want a single middleware product, because part of the benefit of middleware is that it can be customized

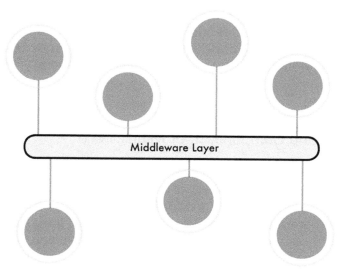

**FIGURE 4-1**   In the traditional view of SOA, the middleware layer exists, as its name implies, in the middle of all connected services, routing messages among them.

and fine-tuned to a specific facility and specific business needs. It is more like building a house. When a contractor builds a house, he or she selects different service providers for different functions, one to do electrical and wiring, one to do plumbing, etc. A contractor picks and chooses the exact features for the house based on the requirements, and those features are implemented in a distinct but coordinated way. When the contractor is done, a single house that people can move through and use has been built with components such as faucets, light switches, fireplaces, and Internet jacks that those people can use or not. It is the same way with a middleware layer. In an SOA, an enterprise wants to give its services different communication tools such as encryption, persistence, or addressing that they can use, and this is done by providing those tools in the middleware layer.

Middleware is not magic. There are no shortcuts to getting a solid middleware layer in a facility. Integrators need to think about how they want to enable the various communication qualities that the enterprise needs in that layer. Middleware is also not plug-and-play. It does not come straight out of a box requiring some customization and some integration to get right. Middleware should be configured, tested, and maintained constantly to keep up the quality of service needed in an enterprise communications infrastructure. Nothing new there — integrators are already worrying about the upkeep of their existing, non-SOA infrastructure. So, what are some of the qualities that make middleware a vast improvement over the software infrastructures of the past?

## 4.1.2  Features and Components of Middleware

Just like a house, middleware can be considered a single entity, but it is composed of many distinct components that provide unique value. Everyone has a pretty good idea of what components might go into a house because everyone knows the types of things that people will want to do in a house. So, to determine what belongs in middleware, it is important to discuss some of the things users might want to do with a middleware layer.

First, if middleware is expected to act as a communication layer between all services, than it must provide a way to send messages back and forth among services. It is the postal system in SOA — a service will drop a message onto the middleware layer, and the middleware layer will deliver messages from other services. To pull this off, the middleware layer will have to implement a number of different addressing and routing schemes sort of like an Ethernet protocol, but for business messages instead of packets of bits. This one feature (enterprise messaging) gives an enterprise the base functionality of middleware. Without messaging; an enterprise would have a hard time calling what it had a "middleware layer."

There are other important features that are common requirements for a middleware layer besides simply messaging, however. This section will enumerate a few, but one of the things that readers should learn from this chapter is that middleware is what its implementers make of it. Service-Oriented Architecture includes some best practices about the types of features middleware should have, but any implementation of SOA could use more or fewer than those. Different SOA advocates condone different flavors of middleware, so integrators should be aware that the opinion presented in this book about what is appropriate for middleware may not be universally shared.

Besides simple messaging, an enterprise may want to give its middleware layer some messaging extensions. For example, one feature common to many middleware implementations is persistence or reliability of messaging. This means that when a message is sent out, the middleware layer guarantees that it will reach its destination (even if the recipient is offline, broken, or not even created yet). This may involve attempting delivery multiple times, providing receipts, or saving the message for long periods of time. Again, the parallels to a post office are apparent.

An enterprise may want to aggregate, store, and log the data that moves through its middleware layer. One of the big benefits of middleware is that all messages travel through the same channel, so components that provide data aggregation can easily fit in to the architecture. Inversely, an enterprise may want to secure messages so that they cannot be compromised while en route to their destination. Middleware might even heavily encrypt and protect certain messages while relaying others to multiple recipients, depending on the content or context of the message.

Also, because the message sender often uses a different "language" than the message recipient is expecting, data transformation is a common middleware feature. Whether the message is sent in a different format, or the content of the message is different than required, components in the middleware should handle data transformation tasks to enable that communication to occur more seamlessly. Of course, in an SOA, most data transformation occurs in the service wrapper, as discussed in Chapter 3: Service-Oriented Architecture: Definition, Concepts, and Methodologies.

Instead of passively watching messages roll through, some middleware implementations take an active role by managing business processes that direct message flow. This is one of the most interesting use cases for a middleware layer (and one that will be discussed in detail in Chapter 6: Business Process Management: Definitions, Concepts and Methodologies). By orchestrating processes, the middleware layer can become both the technical and business center of an enterprise. It provides a common place from which to manage process instances and definitions.

Finally, one big feature for many middleware implementations is a way to view and manage the data moving through the middleware layer. When a middleware layer includes process orchestration, this data management and visibility includes not only messages and errors, but also status of business processes and outcomes of business conditions and rules. This sort of visibility may require a complex portal containing a lot of components, but would provide plenty of benefit to the implementing facility.

With this many disparate use cases, middleware may contain many small pieces, and may require some assembly. Because of this, there are many common components of middleware, and they can be used to enable many of the features previously discussed. These components are enumerated in Fig. 4-2 and depicted graphically in Fig. 4-3.

First and foremost, the middleware layer must include some data routing components (especially if it is spread across many servers in a distributed environment), and a scheme for addressing messages to other components and/or to storage and logging. These components are like routers in an Ethernet network, but for business messages. They are often implemented in software, although the concept of hardware-based, layer-seven routers is applicable here as well. Often

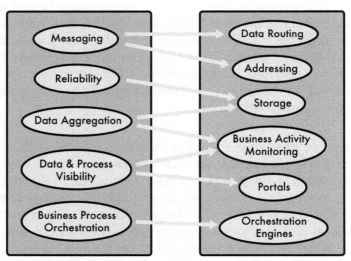

**FIGURE 4-2**   The features of middleware, mapped to the components that might be used to implement them.

at this same level are adapter components, which provide data trans-formation capabilities. If security is included in the middleware layer, it will ideally go beneath this entire messaging layer so that the mes-sages traveling over the wire cannot be tampered with. This means that the routing scheme will have to work in conjunction with the security scheme, so these are often intricately linked.

If the middleware layer needs reliability or logging/data management of any sort, then it will need to include storage components where mes-sages can be persisted and the state of the middleware can be saved. A type of software known as business activity monitoring (BAM) can help with the logging and reporting of business data, and will plug into the middleware's data storage components. In addition, an enterprise may want to include portals to provide custom views into this data.

Finally, orchestration engines are the components that enable the management of business processes in the middleware layer. Because

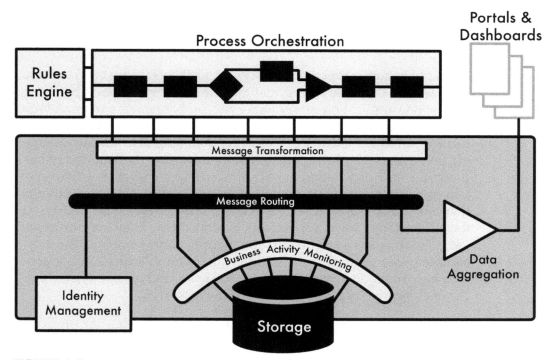

**FIGURE 4-3**  Middleware is actually a collection of disparate components that are integrated together to provide a host of services to the rest of the enterprise architecture.

effective execution of business processes often includes the checking of business conditions, an enterprise may also want to include what is known as a business rules engine to help process decisions so that its users don't have to. Again, these technologies will be discussed further in Chapter 6.

## 4.2  APPLICATION SERVERS

After a quick overview of what features a middleware layer might provide, and the components that are necessary to provide those features, it is useful to consider some specific implementations of those components, in particular, a technology that is considered the basis of all middleware: the application server. An application server is a specific type of software platform on which an enterprise can build and host applications for its users. Because it is the underlying platform, it provides many of the components that are considered part of the middleware layer. Also, the additional components that provide enhanced middleware functionality often use an application server as the place to plug into the infrastructure.

The application server is at the center of the IT industry. They are everywhere! It is guaranteed that anyone reading this book has used at least one application server today and probably many more. A Web server is one part of an app server (along with the user management, security, and load balancing that many Web sites also take advantage of), so anyone who has spent any time browsing the Web today has used one. Any distributed application such as a corporate e-mail system or payroll system sits on top of an app server. Also, some things that most people would not expect, like ATMs or the cash register at the supermarket have app servers behind them. They are pervasive today, so it makes sense to talk about application servers as the most common way to implement middleware in an enterprise. They provide base functionality to enterprise software, and are used in a number of enterprise applications, shown in Fig. 4-4.

The common application server includes some of the middleware components mentioned previously. It sits underneath enterprise applications and handles all communication to and from these applications. IT vendors have figured out this whole messaging problem

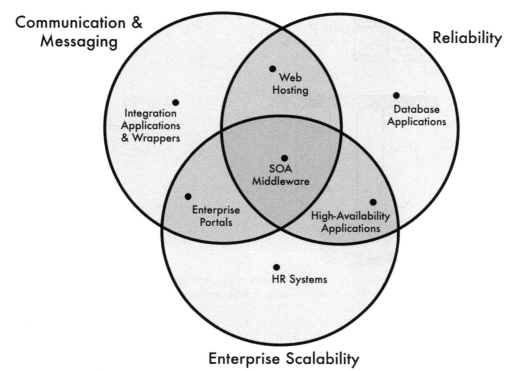

**FIGURE 4-4** The three responsibilities of the application server are to provide communication and messaging, reliability, and enterprise scalability. Some common applications of the application server make use of different aspects of these benefits.

among application servers. Application servers can handle the creation, management, and consumption of messages to the applications running on them. They will manage the communication routes into and out of enterprise systems. Application server capabilities are depicted in Fig. 4-5. Not all of the fancy routing capabilities that an enterprise could possibly want in a middleware layer are possible with an application server alone, but one of the huge benefits that the enterprise gets from an app server environment is the fact that it is a widely adopted, standards-based technology, and a number of plug-ins can be purchased to get needed functionality. In addition to messaging, however, there are a number of other middleware-related components in the average application server.

A big benefit of application servers is their reliability. It is common to have concerns about the capability of software-based tools to provide

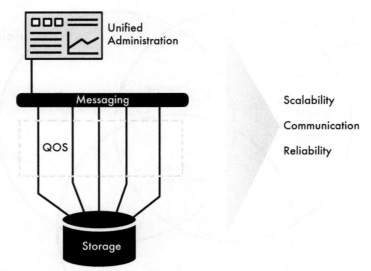

**FIGURE 4-5**   The capabilities of application servers are provided by the common components that they offer, such as storage, QoS, communication, and unified administration.

enough reliability to meet the most stringent business requirements. Especially in the Media & Entertainment (M&E) industry where reliability is a huge concern. Appendix C attempts to alleviate worry about reliability in these tools generically; however, app servers have their own ways of ensuring reliability in both performance and messaging. They plug right into a database for storage. This allows both messages and server state to be saved reliably, and provides the necessary persistence of data. Various messaging models (to be discussed in the next section) have been developed in app servers to ensure that information is accurately and reliably delivered to its recipient.

Also, app servers can be clustered across many physical devices so that a number of software programs running on many machines actually all behave as a single application server. If one machine goes down, users may notice a performance hit (depending on how many machines are clustered and how they are loaded), but they will not lose availability. This allows a single application server environment to be massively scalable to dozens or hundreds of physical boxes or locations if appropriate as shown in Fig. 4-6, allowing for many deployment options. What this really provides is a layer of abstraction away from the physical devices and applications, which is the very same technology abstraction horizon that is discussed in Chapter 3!

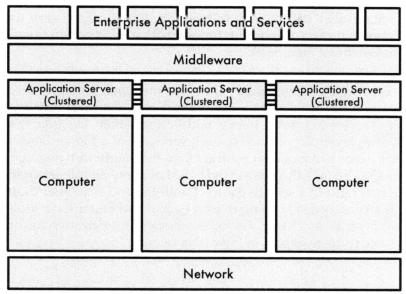

**FIGURE 4-6**   Middleware creates a layer of abstraction between the physical servers that it is installed upon and the enterprise applications that it hosts. Clustering across multiple physical processing environments creates redundancy.

Reliability and scalability are only useful if there is also some control over performance. Thankfully, application servers provide methods of managing quality-of-service (QoS) across the platform. Not QoS in the networking context (although app servers do provide some benefits there), but QoS on the business level. Recall that the application server provides a platform on which to run enterprise applications. Because it handles all of the messaging among those applications, integrators are able to set priorities and limitations so as not to overload any one system and to ensure the necessary performance.

## WHAT IS QoS?

QoS is a metric most often associated with networking. In that context, it is a guarantee established with a participant on the network that, regardless of what other traffic may be using the same network, they will see a certain performance. QoS is normally achieved through prioritization of messages and routing mechanisms that can react to heavy traffic. It can be very useful in busy networks that carry important, time-sensitive information (just like the networks in broadcast facilities!).

In an SOA context, QoS has roughly the same meaning. However, instead of the IP packets transferred over a network, it considers business messages moved from service to service over a middleware layer. The guarantee that the middleware layer can provide to each service is at a higher level as well, so it is much closer to a business contract than the bandwidth negotiations of networking QoS. In fact, there are standards that allow an integrator to establish a QoS level right in a service contract with the end system or individual. However, if an enterprise is going to tout QoS, it had better have tools in the middleware layer that achieve the same message prioritization and routing that users have come to expect in their IP networks.

> Finally, application servers provide one of the more useful features of a middleware layer: unified administration. Regardless of whether an enterprise is clustering a single app server to host many applications or communicating among many distributed app servers, the major vendors provide a way to manage the systems that have been deployed in the environment from a single place. This "enterprise console" is the basis for the portals and views of more complex middleware layers. No application server in common usage provides business activity monitoring (BAM) straight out of the box as yet, but it can provide the unified environment into which BAM can be installed. With these capabilities, application servers are a strong foundation for a middleware layer (and, indeed, for an entire SOA!).

> Application servers are a pretty interesting idea and very necessary for enterprise software integration. Even if they seem like a new concept to some, many people have heard of the two major app server implementation technologies available: Enterprise Java (or Java EE), pioneered by Sun Microsystems, and Microsoft's .NET. It is hard to be clear on which of these two technologies is more widely deployed (a safe guess would be Java EE, because many vendors provide Java EE application servers, while .NET only comes from Microsoft), but they cover over 99% of the application server marketplace between them. Any examination of

application servers, therefore, is essentially complete after looking at these two technologies and where they are headed.

## APPLICATION SERVER PROVIDERS

As mentioned previously, because the Java EE standard is an open source, there are countless implementations of the Java EE application server. Meanwhile, the .NET standard is Microsoft-specific. Some of the major vendors of application servers are listed in Table 4.1, although there are a number of free and open source implementations of the Java EE application server as well (such as JOnAS, the Java Open Application Server). Sun has developed a certification method for vendors to prove that their app server is compliant with the Java EE spec. If an enterprise is thinking of buying a Java EE application server, it should make sure that it has this certification!

The EE in Java EE is an acronym for Enterprise Edition and, much like middleware is a disparate collection of integration features, it is a varied set of Java tools and components that, together, provide application server functionality. Java itself was a programming language created by Sun in the mid-1990s, and it became very popular for Web and network application development because of its ability to generate software that ran on any computer platform. Sun made the Java language open source, which significantly increased its presence and allowed many other vendors to build their own implementations of Java. Java EE (called J2EE up until the release of version 1.5 in 2006) came along a few years later in the late 1990s as a way to combine the

**TABLE 4-1**

A List of Various Java EE and .NET Vendors

| Java EE application server vendors | .NET application server vendors |
| --- | --- |
| Sun | Microsoft |
| IBM | |
| SAP | |
| BEA | |
| Oracle | |
| Red Hat (JBoss) | |
| and many open source developers | |

Java programming language and enterprise tools and libraries to create a platform for server development, and the concept of an application server was born. Since then, many vendors have developed Java application servers of their own. These various app servers often include proprietary extensions on top of the Java EE standard for enhanced functionality. There continue to be a large number of open source or effectively "free" application servers, however, making it one of the few areas where open source technology is mainstream inside big IT enterprises. If an enterprise is looking to implement an application server platform as part of your SOA development, though, it should look at one of the major IT vendors. They are able to better provide the necessary support for their product, even though the enterprise will be paying several thousand dollars for a technology that is free on the Internet. Such is the modern world.

## COMPONENTS OF JAVA EE

Java EE application servers include a number of components that provide different functionalities to enterprise applications running within the application server. These various components are depicted in Fig. 4-7. Detailed discussion of these components is outside the scope of this book.

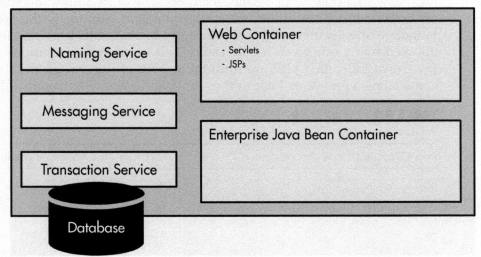

**FIGURE 4-7**   The components of Java EE have names and uses specific to the Java platform, but they provide the same generic qualities of application servers that were discussed earlier in this chapter.

For a long time, Java EE and application server were interchangeable terms, but in recent years with the explosion of the .NET platform and the increase in visibility of the application server as an enterprise component, application server has been generalized to include any enterprise server software engine. .NET came around in early 2002 as a component of Windows for hosting and supporting enterprise software, and has since positioned itself as a competitor to the Java application server. Like Java, .NET uses what it calls a "common language infrastructure" to create software that runs on any platform, which is a feature that has become a hallmark of the application server. This makes app servers ideal for the platform-independent SOA world.

Unlike Java EE, there are no open source implementations of .NET. In fact, there is really only one implementation of .NET. But this does not make it any better or worse than the Java platform at providing application server functionality. If an enterprise is implementing an SOA, it will no doubt have a mixed environment anyway. Many vendors of both SOA tools and M&E systems have chosen their side, and a media enterprise will have to use the application server that they require or ship with their software. This does not go against the SOA precepts of platform independence, though, because communication between Java EE and .NET platforms is a well-established and common component in a middleware layer (see Chapter 5 for information about Web services, one technology that provides this).

## OTHER APPLICATION SERVERS

Although the term application server originated with the Java platform, it has expanded to cover multiple implementing technologies such as .NET. Apart from these two, there are a handful of open source projects that also fill the app server role. Some, like Zope (http://www.zope.org), were built to take advantages of other programming environments to provide the same application server features. Others are simply science experiments that have gotten some steam behind them.

In reality, there is nothing to prevent a particularly inventive media company from building their own, media-specific application server. In fact, a media-centric app server might provide interesting benefits to M&E enterprises.

This concept will be examined further in Chapter 7. If an enterprise is looking to implement an app server, however, it should choose either a Java EE server based on the open standardization of Enterprise Java or a .NET server based on the support offered by Microsoft.

It is important to note that application servers are the ultimate basis of middleware. It does not matter whether an enterprise is dealing with Java EE, .NET, or both; as long as the app server has messaging, reliability, and scalability, it has the foundation for a well-implemented SOA infrastructure. On top of this foundation, an enterprise can implement all of the crazy routing, process orchestration, and BAM components that make SOA middleware truly amazing.

## 4.3  THE ENTERPRISE SERVICE BUS

When they hear the term "middleware," the hardcore IT types will probably think first of application servers. This is because the term became popular in the IT world before the dawn of the Service-Oriented Architecture age—way back in the last millennium. And they would be fairly accurate in their thinking. The application server is the basis of all middleware. But it is not the whole story.

The SOA mavens will probably think of an entirely different component: the Enterprise Service Bus (ESB). If the app server is the foundation for middleware, then the ESB is its superstructure. It is the biggest, most important part of an SOA middleware layer, and no discussion of SOA would be complete without a thorough analysis of ESBs in all of their many forms.

What is an ESB? This is surprisingly difficult to answer. The term appeared first as simply a buzzword to describe SOA middleware products that handled many aspects of message routing and transformation. These days it describes a whole class of products whose goal is to extend the simple messaging capabilities of application servers to include the kind of enterprise functionality necessary to support an SOA. One important quality of an ESB is that it is SOA-specific, whereas "middleware" in general has applications outside of the realm of a services architecture.

The contemporary understanding of an ESB is as follows: a distributed, service-oriented messaging channel that provides business communication capabilities to the heterogeneous systems attached to it. ESB is distributed, which means that it does not create a single-point-of-failure, hub-and-spoke architecture when enterprise systems are attached — it may exist on many platforms spread across many physical machines and many facilities (see Figs. 3-2 and 3-3 for a comparison of these two models). ESB also provides business-level capabilities. The communication rules and methods established in the ESB have applicability beyond the equipment room and into the board room, because they deal with the content of the messages moving across the ESB, not just the format or technology behind that content. If there is a message for scheduling, it will get treated differently than one for editorial. Messages carrying asset metadata can be transmitted one way, and control data another way. Also, ESB supports heterogeneous systems. Integrators are able to plug lots of different types of applications into a well-implemented ESB — not just applications that support a particular communication standard, not just Java EE applications, and not just .NET applications.

## THE CONTROVERSY OVER THE DEFINITION OF ESB

Of all the buzzwords and marketing terms found in this book, Enterprise Service Bus is the one that the hardcore IT folks would find the most heinous. The term arose just a few years ago as a way to encompass the middleware components needed to implement an SOA. The Gartner Group described ESBs by saying that they "act as a lightweight, ubiquitous integration backbone through which software services and application components flow." Everything about the definition of an ESB is vague and all-encompassing. This is because, like middleware and SOA, the important part of ESB is not the technologies or components, but the intention of unifying business communication.

Because this business construct was treated by many SOA vendors as a technology in its own right (although it mostly has become a technology at this point), the traditional IT community rebelled against the idea of ESB. There was nothing here, they argued, that did not already exist in the Enterprise Application Integration technologies of the late 1990s (such as application servers). They were right, but because the term Enterprise Service Bus captures the same spirit of business integration as Service-Oriented Architecture, the label has stuck, and enough enterprise IT vendors have come out with ESB products now to give this buzzword validity.

ESBs accomplish this "business communication" by implementing one or many communication models. Recall the discussion at the beginning of this chapter over the different ways that messages might be delivered from sender to recipient. An enterprise may require a way to send messages to many recipients. It may need a way to ensure the delivery of a message, even in the most extreme situations. It may want to give a level of control to the recipient about what messages it wants to receive. There are communication models, shown in Fig. 4-8, for all of these use cases. While not all ESBs support all of these models,

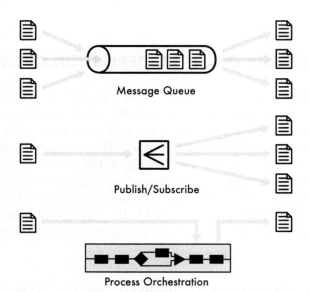

**FIGURE 4-8**   The three main types of messaging models discussed in this section include message queuing, publish/subscribe, and process orchestration.

one of the goals of the ESB is to offer a wide selection of communication options to the systems attached to it. There are, therefore, a lot of ESB products that support a whole spectrum of messaging options.

These messaging models are not new. Prior to the advent of the term Enterprise Service Bus to describe an SOA-specific middleware component that handles messaging control, there were middleware implementations known as Message-Oriented Middleware (MOM) that may implement many different models. The simplest (and oldest) model that is still in common usage today is the message queue (MQ). MQ is the bread and butter of MOM systems and still appears in many ESB implementations. The basic idea behind message queuing is that a message is placed on a "queue" in the middleware by the sender system, and it is later retrieved from that queue by the recipient system. This requires both an active sender (who can put messages on the queue) and an active recipient (who can take messages from the queue), but can use a passive middleware (the queue, after all, just sits there). MQ middleware can be made more "active" by implementing algorithms that streamline queuing orders, notify end systems, and manage old messages, but the basic idea is pretty simple. This model has the advantage of being asynchronous, which means that it does not matter if the recipient happens to be unavailable when the message is sent; the message is guaranteed to get to its destination (or sit in the queue forever if that destination no longer exists). MQs are well suited for basic messaging needs, such as sending asset metadata from one DAM system to another.

## MESSAGE-ORIENTED MIDDLEWARE AND THE HISTORY OF MIDDLEWARE MODELS

The term "middleware" itself is as old as the 1980s, when the first round of big enterprise applications were giving way to the next generation of software, and the need for significant enterprise integration arose. The idea of an asynchronous, "message-oriented" middleware layer was one of the first, and provided many of the benefits that are talked about today for middleware layers: redundancy, persistence, message transformation, etc. These first middleware models did not have a unifying standard for messaging, so integration with the layer was ad hoc and difficult to reuse. However, once a message was on the MOM, it could be stored, routed, and transformed efficiently to enable it to reach its destination.

The main things that modern middleware concepts add to MOM are a more standards-oriented implementation, componentized middleware functionality, and business-level integration tools. The middleware layers of today — whether they are ESBs, process orchestration engines, or both — provide the basis for SOA construction in a way never dreamed of by the the first vendors of message-oriented middleware.

Another communication model is known as a publish/subscribe, or pub/sub for short. Just as with MQ, the architecture of pub/sub is pretty self-explanatory. In publish/subscribe, the recipients actually make the first move by subscribing to a particular message channel or class. After they have subscribed, they will receive messages sent to that channel by the sender, or publisher. This model has more of a "mailing list" feel to it, certainly, but it can be very useful for a number of different applications. For example, non-real-time control data sent over a middleware layer may need to be "broadcast" out from the controlling system (for example, automation) to all of the recipients. A pub/sub model can accomplish this. It does not necessarily have to be synchronous communication, either. If the enterprise is especially concerned about messaging reliability (and who isn't?), it can follow a "store-and-forward" model that will persist the messages in the middleware layer before publishing them out. The middleware can then continue to try and reach subscribers that do not receive the message initially.

The third and final type of messaging model that this section will consider is process orchestration. Process orchestration is the subject of a large portion of Chapter 6: Business Process Management: Definitions, Concepts, and Methodologies. Just as MQ is the central use case of MOM, process orchestration is probably considered the central use case of ESBs. The management and execution of business processes in the middleware layer has become the "killer app" of SOA. Process orchestration as a messaging model features the most active role for the middleware layer. The basic idea behind process orchestration is that the middleware layer stores a workflow that dictates the next destination of any given message. A sender simply has to release the message to the middleware layer, and the process will determine where to send it. This is beneficial in many places within an enterprise. The more established a facility's processes are, the more benefit they feel from the process orchestration model. Again, this will be discussed further in Chapter 6.

Most ESBs provide all of these messaging models. In fact, many ESBs provide the means for an enterprise to construct a single solution from multiple messaging models (an idea worth considering). Anyone can see how these routing techniques can be a valuable asset to the messaging infrastructure of a facility. No longer will systems need to depend on point-to-point connections between systems. Their messaging can be brokered by an ESB.

Based on these capabilities, there are a number of features besides message routing that an ESB can provide to an enterprise. First of all, the ESB can provide reliable messaging thanks to persistence of messages in the middleware layer and asynchronous messaging techniques such as MQ or store-and-forward. The idea is to provide the system integrator with a messaging toolset that he or she can take advantage of when the situation demands. Reliable messaging is a very important tool to have in that set.

ESBs can also provide a load balancing capability to a middleware layer. Because the ESB is messaging-aware, it is able to determine when a system is receiving more messages than it can handle and can take steps to remedy that situation. It can load balance messages across many recipients (in the cases such as transcoding engines where it might not matter which system does the work), or simply serve as a buffer to ensure that the message recipient does not get overloaded.

The application server in middleware provides security, system reliability, and scalability. The ESB, however, provides message routing, message reliability, and load balancing features to the middleware layer. There are a number of different ESB vendors available (thanks to the popularity of SOA as an architectural model), so an enterprise can "shop around" for the specific ESB implementation that meets its needs. ESBs are arguably the most crucial component in an SOA middleware, so it is important that the ESB has the capabilities needed to integrate systems across an SOA.

## SOME ESB PRODUCTS ON THE MARKET TODAY

Because an ESB is such a desirable component for service-oriented integration these days, there are countless ESB products out there. The list below should give a taste of the marketplace, with even some open source solutions (Apache Synapse) beginning to appear. Further research is suggested for all interested in learning more:

- IBM WebSphere ESB
- Oracle Enterprise Service Bus
- Progress Sonic ESB
- BEA AquaLogic Service Bus
- TIBCO BusinessWorks
- Cape Clear ESB
- Fiorano ESB
- Apache Synapse
- Sun SeeBeyond

## 4.4 OTHER MIDDLEWARE COMPONENTS

Apart from application servers and ESBs, there are a number of miscellaneous components that may appear in a middleware layer, depending on its specific application. An application server foundation is necessary to have what is considered by contemporary thinking to be a middleware layer, and an ESB is necessary to have a middleware layer that is appropriate for a Service-Oriented Architecture. The rest of these components, highlighted in Fig. 4-9, are optional. However, they can provide specific functionality, such as message translation or decision making, that may come in handy.

An ESB has built-in message format transformation components as part of its business toolset (in other words, transformation from one

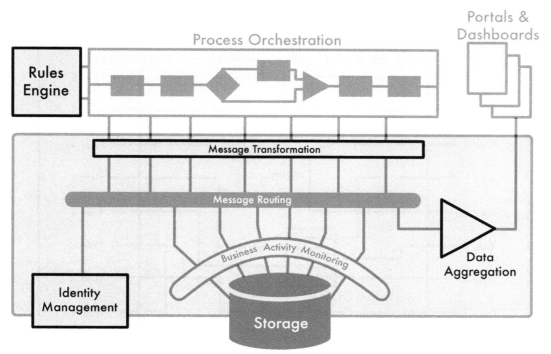

**FIGURE 4-9** There are a number of components that are common in enterprise middleware layers, but are not necessary to the support of base messaging models or the ESB concept. These components provide other functionality to the infrastructure.

message technology to another, which is a necessary feature if an enterprise is hoping to enable business-level communication). In the case of message content transformation, however, more extensive middleware components may be desired. Instead of simply copying data from one representation to another, data transformation components could actually change the business data that is transferred; for example, changing a data field from a timecode to a number of frames. Fig. 4-10 shows some possible types of transformation. These types of transformation are often necessary within an SOA, and occur in the middleware layer using data transformation components. Complex algorithms and lookup tables can be used here to ensure the business data is mapped correctly.

In an SOA, it is the job of the wrapper to do the brunt of data transformation, because it will take application-specific data and turn it into

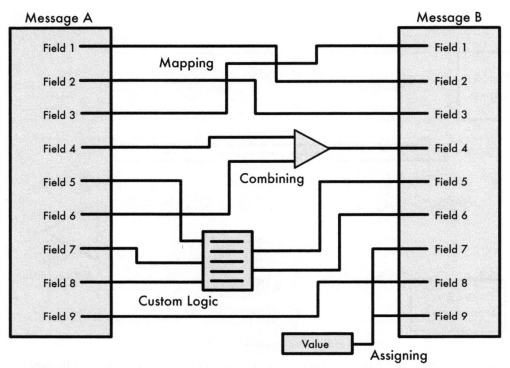

**FIGURE 4-10**   Data transformation is often required when one message must be translated to fit the schema of a different message. This is a primary responsibility of an SOA middleware layer.

data appropriate for the business (see Chapter 5 for more information on wrapper design). However, there is a regularly recurring need to have such transformation components in the middleware layer to address honest business differences in data representation. If the name of a title is one thing while it is produced and distributed internally, but an entirely different thing when discussed outside of an enterprise, then data transformation components must exist in the middleware to "sanitize" the metadata when it recognizes that the title is going to be shared outside of the facility. These are two competing business requirements that must be met simultaneously regarding data representation, and this is exactly where a middleware layer is useful.

Another optional component at the middleware layer is a repository for data aggregation. Often, the existence of an application server and ESB will also mean the existence of an enterprise database repository that could be used to store data, but without proper configuration and the right additional components, this database will not be very useful for auditing the messages passing through the middleware layer. So, if there is a desire for high visibility into the service communication in a facility (and there should be, because of the benefits that come along with such visibility), additional monitoring and storage components will be needed.

Additional storage is not a deal breaker for anyone these days, but it is an important component of the modern middleware layer, so it is necessary to mention it. Think about the amount of storage necessary in a paper-based world of forms, e-mails, and hallway conversations. Whole file cabinets in such architectures are no doubt filled with records of jobs done, bills paid, and deals closed. In the digital world, these records each take up only a few bytes, but a storage solution with the reliability of that file cabinet is needed to have the same sort of auditability in middleware.

In terms of monitoring, an enterprise will want to choose a technology that is aware of the business data that is moving through the middleware layer and can parse that data for what it is. In other words, a monitoring solution that simply stores the messages that are sent over the middleware layer and regurgitates them in a big list when viewed is not a good monitoring solution for a business-oriented SOA. The whole purpose of using a monitoring component is to implement data aggregation and increase visibility. An enterprise will want one that can present that business data in a way suitable for the business.

The benefits of business monitoring (and process monitoring) will be extensively discussed in Chapter 6. In this chapter, it is important to recognize that a good monitoring solution will entail business-aware data aggregation technology in the middleware layer and a redundant and enterprise-scale storage solution for the data aggregated.

Another popular component in many middleware layers are rules engines of some sort. Rules engine technology has taken off in recent years, especially in industries such as insurance or banking that rely on well-established, causal formulas to make business decisions. Its applicability to the world of M&E has yet to be seen, but there are no doubt some areas where they would be very useful.

A rules engine is basically a middleware component that can make business-level decisions. Business users configure the engine with the logical "rules" of the facility (such as how many hours of editing to schedule for a particular type of project or how soon before air an avail must be filled), and then services in the SOA consult the engine before performing certain business activities. The rules engine provides a unified business interface to quickly change these rules and affect the behavior of the entire facility. While many integrators are (understandably) wary of ceding any business decisions to a software component, a rules engine can potentially provide a much-needed reprieve from busy work for producers, managers, and executives. It is an optional component in the middleware layer.

## WHEN TO USE A BUSINESS RULES ENGINE

The business rules engine is one of the most misunderstood middleware components. They were invented for a particular use case: the transactional, stateless business rule. An enterprise should consider a business rules engine when it wishes to base the routing of messages across the middleware layer on transactional rules that change fairly often. For example, if different producers' jobs are sent to different transcoders, then the decision as to which transcoder a particular job is assigned is very much a business rule. However, for decisions based on what task is currently being worked on in a given process or the past history of related actions, rules engines might not be of much help. For example, if a process works differently in a breaking news scenario than it does in standard production, an enterprise will likely want to implement that through business orchestration or custom logic, not a business rules engine.

Since the majority of business decisions in the M&E industry are of the latter type, there is not a major need for business rules technology in the media industry. However, there may be some situations that it is particularly well suited for. If an enterprise does not have a solid need for business rule technology it will find rules engines to be an annoyance and an unnecessary expense.

The final middleware component that will be discussed in this chapter is identity management. Identity management is a big area of technology development in the IT space, and can be put to very good use in SOA middleware. The basic idea is this: instead of using disparate repositories and application-specific methods to authenticate users and secure systems, identity management tools allow the integrator to unify all of an enterprise under a single repository and management system of user data. This would allow easy changes to user information, or quick provisioning of new users. In an integrated SOA, identity management solutions also allow for role-based views into data, a concept that will be discussed in Chapter 6. Identity management components also make it much easier to secure services, because they can facilitate the adoption of an enterprise-wide security policy. In SOA, that means that every service can use the same method to authorize its use. These components would exist in the middleware layer where they are easily accessible by all services and processes.

While not necessary in a working middleware layer, these optional components—business data transformation, monitoring, business rules, and identity management—can provide incredibly useful enhancements to middleware functionality. Any SOA integrator would do well to look into these components to see if they could be put to use in his or her facility.

## 4.5  WHAT MIDDLEWARE IS NOT GOOD FOR

Just like all technologies, middleware has its problems. There are not as many criticisms of middleware in this book as there are of other technologies discussed, such as Web services or BPEL. This is mainly because "middleware" is such an all-encompassing term in IT; it literally means the components that sit in the middle of an architecture, regardless of what those components are. There are plenty of criticisms to throw around about specific components of middleware (identity management is over-hyped, business rules engines are not widely applicable, etc.), but a common solution to such criticism is to simply not include the offending component in your middleware implementation.

The two middleware components that were listed previously as fairly rudimentary in SOA—application servers and ESBs—are not without their faults, however. Application servers have been around for quite a long time and are therefore fairly well polished, but they are incredibly complicated beasts with many layers and even more things that can go wrong with them. Just a quick look at the sheer number of

Java libraries that are required to keep a Java EE implementation running is enough to drive any inexperienced systems administrator mad. This is not technology that can just be plugged in and immediately working; application servers need to be finely tuned and cared for. There is an argument that much of this complexity is unnecessary for providing the core functionality of the application server; therefore a number of "lean" app servers have been developed.

Unlike the well-founded application server, the concept of the ESB is a hotly contested one. Even so, the use of ESBs is often equally as complex, not to mention the fact that installing one at all adds yet another layer to the already stacked application server. However, in most SOA situations the benefits of having both an application server and an ESB in your enterprise far outweigh these costs. It just requires a whole new skill set to run correctly. Middleware makes media engineers realize what a brave new world it is, and how different this world is from the heavily deterministic, analog world that existed fifteen plus years ago.

The final criticism of middleware in general is this: it is very bad at handling media. Readers may have noticed that this entire chapter has focused solely on passing messages from place to place using middleware techniques. That is all very well and good, but in media facilities, systems also have to pass data that are a whole lot bigger than a simple message! And middleware technologies, with their caching, queuing, and routing, just are not cut out for that sort of performance. This is a huge deal for media enterprises (obviously); so much so that a large portion of Chapter 7 is devoted to discussing this very issue and ways in which SOA and middleware technology might be used to solve it. With the current IT-industry view of middleware, however, media is handled strictly "out of band" (transferred on an external bus), which is a solution that may not be acceptable to everyone.

## 4.6  MIDDLEWARE BEST PRACTICES

This chapter mentions the importance of configuring a middleware layer for both the architecture at hand and for the performance required. Because most media system integrators are not intimately familiar with the ins and outs of setting up middleware, it is worthwhile to discuss a couple of the specific areas that must be considered when planning a middleware solution. Again, middleware is not something that can simply be bought, taken out of the box, and plugged in. It must be well thought out and implemented carefully, or an enterprise may end up with a layer that does not correctly address the messaging needs of its facilities.

First, the architecture of the middleware layer must be considered. One of the features and, indeed, huge benefits of middleware is that it can be totally distributed. It provides a layer of abstraction between logical infrastructure and physical hardware. It can sit on one server, ten servers, or one hundred servers — all distributed world-wide. No single-points-of-failure here! Nearly every application server includes clustering technology to enable this scalability.

However, even with a heavily redundant physical architecture, integrators should be aware of inadvertently creating a logical hub out of their middleware layer. Technologies like MQ are great for handling messaging functionality, but if every message has to run through a single queue, the enterprise is going to face problems, even if that queue is clustered to thousands of servers. Utilize multiple messaging models, and ensure that every system has a few ways to communicate. It is great to have a single place to change business logic in an enterprise, but no one wants, for example, one typo in a business process to reroute all of a facility's control signals. It is important to strike a balance between a logical hub-and-spoke model and a totally distributed messaging bus.

Here is another important tip when rolling out middleware: have a test lab validate end systems before they go into the production environment. Because these are software systems, it is easy to set up a test environment that exactly mirrors a production environment and run middleware components through the ropes long before deployment. In fact, many SOA vendors will provide free licenses for test environments. It is so important to test and test again when dealing with so many software layers. By working all of these out in a test environment, an enterprise can ensure a smooth rollout. A sample test lab rollout is shown in Fig. 4-11.

Say an enterprise plans to have an asset management system connected to a series of other broadcast systems (automation, editing,

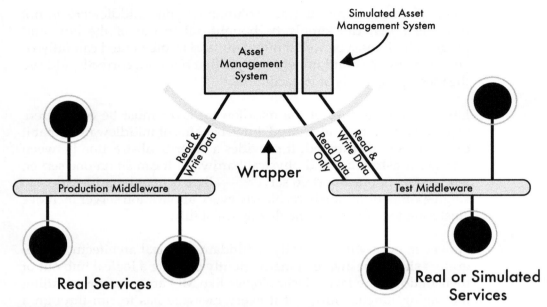

**FIGURE 4-11**   A test middleware environment might make use of a production system in a read-only fashion in order to populate test data. Otherwise, all services should be duplicated or simulated.

etc.), with control data and metadata sent over a middleware layer. In the test lab setup, integrators can exactly mirror the deployment characteristics of the middleware system by clustering the server components and even using software tools to simulate a maximum load on the network. Although determining middleware configuration is often a challenge, rolling out many copies of that configuration is not much more difficult or expensive than a single one.

Speaking of rollouts, correctly timing a middleware deployment is another important aspect of implementing an SOA. Providing ample time for training and adjustment is crucial, especially in facilities that go from a heavily manual workflow to an SOA- and middleware-centric one. An enterprise should provide at least a week or two of training for all employees that will need to use the new middleware system, and have a few months of beta testing for the kinks to get worked out of the new workflow. Some new usability issues that could be addressed might be found or (better yet) some unexpected benefits to an agile

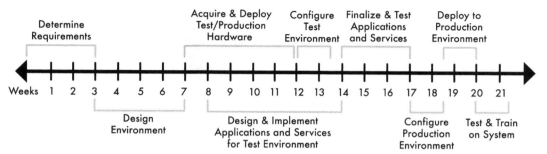

**FIGURE 4-12** A sample deployment timeline for an SOA project with test middleware environment.

messaging infrastructure might be discovered. A timeline like the one in Fig. 4-12 should be developed for all major deployments. Do not rush middleware deployment. It is important to do it right, because once an enterprise has middleware in place, future changes will be made easier.

One other best practice to make mention of is the concept of synchronous vs. asynchronous messaging. This concept is discussed in Chapter 3: Service-Oriented Architecture: Definitions, Concepts, and Methodologies, but because middleware is not necessarily tied to SOA, it is important to revisit this discussion in the context of this chapter. The basic premise is this: synchronous communication is a model wherein both parties engage in dedicated conversation with each other; asynchronous communication works more like a bulletin board or e-mail, with each party sending messages that the other party can pick up later. Fig. 4-13 shows the difference between these.

SOA focuses on the positive aspects of asynchronous communication. A service requester does not have to wait for a response to continue to work; the other party could be bogged down or offline and messages would still get through. However, there are also benefits to synchronous communication. The requester gets immediate confirmation that the message was received, which gives more information about what is going on in other systems and can therefore reduce the complexity of business logic (fewer exception cases to account for). Also, an enterprise is able to trade more and more immediately relevant information

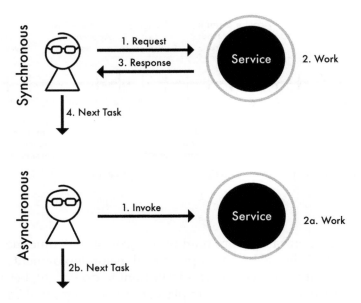

**FIGURE 4-13** Synchronous communication requires that the invoker wait for a response before continuing with its workflow, while asynchronous communication does not have this restriction. This is the same as the concept of transactional vs. fire-and-forget services in SOA.

between parties (have more of a conversation and less of a game of "phone tag") when communicating synchronously.

An enterprise is going to want the benefits of asynchronous messaging when communicating among end systems hanging off of a middleware layer. In fact, many of the messaging models discussed in this chapter facilitate this sort of asynchronous communication among systems. An enterprise is also going to want the benefits of synchronous communication for the little things like message confirmation and working out technical details; in other words, the things that the middleware layer handles. Therefore, the best way to set up messaging in an enterprise is to have synchronous communication between the system and the middleware, and have the middleware facilitate asynchronous communication from system to system.

This is exactly the space in which Business Process Management (BPM) occurs. By having business logic in the form of processes at the middleware layer, the middleware is providing the best of both worlds. BPM is discussed extensively in Chapter 6. BPM and middleware work extremely well together because middleware can help to facilitate many of the best practices of BPM.

## 4.7 CONCLUSION

There are whole technical levels to middleware whose surfaces are only grazed in this chapter. If readers are interested in learning more, they should begin by learning a little of the history of the application server and what types of computing it was designed to accomplish. By now, the concept of middleware has grown out of its humble beginnings and takes its place at the center of modern enterprise communication. Middleware offers many features to the systems integrator, and has therefore become an invaluable resource. It can provide reliable messaging and translation capabilities to enterprise systems, especially in the context of an overarching SOA.

Right now middleware can be a little inaccessible to those without a certain level of enterprise computing experience. However, it is getting easier and easier to implement a middleware layer in a facility. As enterprise computing becomes easier, middleware will take an even more established role in the facility. In fact, middleware will be so common and necessary, that most integrators will take it for granted. It will just be there, like Ethernet is just there today, providing its services to all. And that is not a bad thing.

## WHAT TO TELL YOUR BOSS

- A middleware layer is a unified communications infrastructure that transmits messages from system to system in an enterprise.
- Middleware is not a single product, it is a set of components. And an enterprise has to pick the right components for the task at hand, otherwise the middleware layer will not be the solution for its messaging requirements.
- Middleware has uses outside of SOA. However, an enterprise will need a well-architected middleware layer to implement SOA.

- Middleware technologies are constantly evolving. Right now there are many great SOA-specific components that can enhance a more traditional messaging infrastructure. These are worth looking into.

# 5

# WEB SERVICES

Service-Oriented Architecture is discussed quite a bit in this book. However, SOA is no more than a design methodology for combining loosely coupled systems into a unified, services-based infrastructure. For the most part, all that it can provide are best practices around decomposing services, organizing middleware, providing good governance, etc. It is an idea (a very good idea, but still just an idea) about how systems should communicate. To make the promise of SOA a reality, specific technologies are still needed to *implement* SOA systems. Specific technologies to implement middleware systems are needed as well as specific technologies to wrap and expose end systems as encapsulated services with published interfaces. In this chapter, wrapper and service exposure technology is explored. Specifically, it is a detailed look at Web services, the most widely used technology for implementing SOA within an enterprise.

## 5.1  WHY WEB SERVICES?

Web services is an XML-based communication protocol for exchanging messages between loosely coupled systems. Many have heard of Web services before as an equivalent concept to SOA; in truth, the two are often confused. Integrators should remember throughout this chapter that talking about Web services means discussing a specific technology capable of realizing the design principles of SOA. Web services is a technology; SOA is a design theory. They are two distinct concepts. One of the more common mistakes seen in marketing material and vendor discussions surrounding SOA is the constant confusion between SOA and Web services—the most popular SOA implementation technology. These two are separate concepts and understanding this appropriately prepares the reader for the rest of this chapter, which is a technical discussion of Web services and its associated standards.

To enable service exposure and messaging, an SOA technology must both represent service interfaces and present a way for two services to communicate. This is exactly what Web services is—a method of system communication. In Fig. 5-1, Web services provides the technology to define service interfaces, send out service messages, and receive and parse responses. The middleware in an SOA is the medium across which Web services messages travel. It is a communication technology just like all of the many other communication technologies in the Media & Entertainment (M&E) industry (such as the ones discussed in Chapter 2).

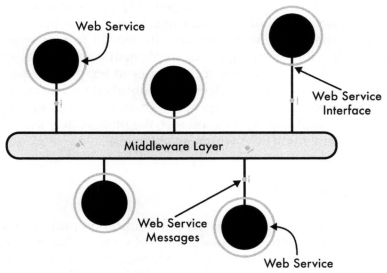

**FIGURE 5-1**   Web services fills an important role in an SOA at both end services and in the middleware layer.

## 5.1.1  A Media Engineer's Perspective

As part of an examination of the details of Web services, integrators should review what is important to engineers of media systems so that they can see where Web services makes sense or where it may fall short.

As mentioned in Chapter 3, Service-Oriented Architecture is completely technology independent. An enterprise could implement an SOA using people as services and paper forms as messages moving among them. It then goes without saying that any sufficiently standardized computer communication technology that is message-based and platform-independent can be used to implement an SOA as well. So why focus on Web services?

## STATISTICS OF WEB SERVICES

The main reason to focus on Web services technologies in this book instead of the myriad other ways to enable Service-Oriented Architecture is simply because Web services is the most widely adopted SOA technology out there. The Web services industry is a multi-billion dollar software industry, expected by IDC in a 2004 report to top 11 billion dollars in 2008. Sure, M&E companies have always worked a little bit differently than the GMs, Microsofts, and Wal-Marts of the world, but the fact that Web services is such a large player in the IT integration world is why it is the main focus of exploration of such technologies.

Web services was designed from the ground up to leverage the benefits of XML to create a loosely coupled technology capable of handling the demands of an SOA. Web services and most of its associated technologies were standardized by the Web Services Activity group within the World Wide Web Consortium (W3C), and the Organization for the Advancement of Structured Information Standards (OASIS), starting in early 2002. Since then, Web services has skyrocketed to the top of the SOA world in terms of its adoption by IT enterprises and support from SOA vendors and evangelists. At this point, mentioning SOA without mentioning Web services would be telling an incomplete story, as Web services has realized many of the promises of a service-oriented enterprise. Much of this success has to do with the Web services' ability to be secure, reliable, and responsive, but it is also because Web services is presented as an open standard using an already well-founded technology: XML. Obviously it is important to media systems designers that the communication methodology used is standardized to ensure the greatest interoperability.

## WHAT IS THE W3C?

The World Wide Web Consortium was founded in 1994 to develop and promote new standards for the then-developing World Wide Web. Their most notable standard is the Hypertext Markup Language (HTML), but they are also responsible for CSS and XML. The W3C developed the WSDL and SOAP standards that are discussed in Section 5.4.

For more information, see their Web site at http://www.w3.org.

### 5.1.2  Important Characteristics

Any communications technology adopted in M&E must be capable of carrying the messages that need to be sent. Web services meets these needs by providing an extensible message format that can carry any payload needed for almost any application.

As can be seen in Fig. 5-2, the most important aspect of any technology in media is its reliability. Media integrators often say that they cannot afford one frame of downtime; therefore systems that use Web services must be designed in appropriate ways to maintain that level of reliability within enterprise media systems as a whole. However, even though integrators may not use Web services in every area of a system, they need to be assured that the messages sent over these interfaces are delivered accurately. There are ways to build systems using Web services that are at least as reliable as any other technology used in media systems today. Like a good "Ack/Nak" mechanism, media architectures need to guarantee that messages successfully arrive at their destination.

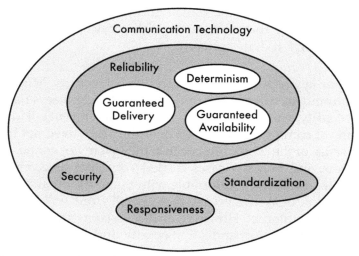

**FIGURE 5-2**   Important qualities of communication protocols for media engineers.

Another characteristic of communications familiar to many students of serial control protocols and others is flow control. Integrators need to be assured when sending a Web services message that it is sent to a destination that exists and is able to process the request in a timely fashion. A means of notification is also necessary if the receiving service is not capable of handling the request, as is an intelligent way of handling such situations.

It is important in media communications that the means of communication be deterministic. The meaning of this will vary widely from one part of a system to another, but it generally means that the media enterprise can count on the transmit-to-receive time of the communications to be timely within a reasonable bound of variability. Web services (and many other protocols) are not timely enough to be appropriate in real-time, frame accurate applications. They can, however, be used appropriately in conjunction with technologies that do meet those requirements successfully.

If Web services is used in a production environment, integrators will need it to be responsive. Nothing annoys an operator more than pressing the "play" button and waiting a second or two for the image to start. Systems using Web services have to be designed to address this by ensuring that the transit and processing time for messages is appropriate for the application. Web services can be designed to be very "timely" if done correctly.

Another key aspect of communications is security. Much of the thinking around security in the minds of media engineers has been driven by security concerns in and around the Internet. However, many means of communication used over the years have not been secure in any sense of the word, but because they were not connected to outside systems, and in many cases carried very little data, media engineers and integrators felt comfortable with them. Automatically, when engineers think of Web services, that "Web" word will likely make them think of the Internet. However, as discussed in Section 5.4.2.1 on SOAP security (and in Appendix C: Security and Reliability), Web services can be made extremely secure, and there is no more an inherent reason to connect Web services enabled systems to the outside world as there was with any other technology used in the past. Even when these systems are connected to outside entities there are many standards and methodologies to make such connections secure. Web services are used in high-value, high-security banking transactions as well as many other highly secure applications. Done right, Web services can be as secure as it gets in communications.

To a large extent, the technologies and standards supporting Web services are what provide this reliability, timeliness, and security. So, as part of the exploration of Web services technology, this chapter examines IT standards such as XML underneath Web services.

## 5.2 XML: EXTENSIBLE MARKUP LANGUAGE

Web services is an XML-based communication technology. A Web services interface passes XML documents back and forth. XML, as a standard, has a very buzz-worthy feel to it, and rightly so. Take a look at any server-based enterprise IT technology—from wikis to identity management—and XML will likely be right at its heart. Even in the M&E industry, many vendors or organizations like the Society of Motion Picture and Television Engineers (SMPTE) have begun to adopt XML as a primary means of engaging in inter-system communication.

Media integrators of all stripes have no doubt encountered XML schemas or APIs just by doing routine product research.

XML was standardized by the W3C in early 1998 as an outgrowth of the Standard Generalized Markup Language (SGML). As the acronym suggests, XML—like SGML before it and its prettier, more popular cousin HTML—is a markup language, which means that an XML document consists entirely of data marked up by descriptive tags. These tags can provide additional information about what these data are and how they should be used or interpreted. IT and M&E vendors alike are finding this additional information to be incredibly useful in expressing many types of data, from system commands to feature film descriptions. So XML is, for all practical purposes, here to stay. Although XML seems to many like a cluster of greater than signs, colons, and backslashes, media engineers should not worry; it is not that scary, and there is more there than meets the eye. XML is everywhere, and before going any further, it is important to stop and think about just what that means.

## 5.2.1 The Benefits of Using XML

When deciding upon data representation for APIs or interfaces, integrators have a few options. They could use comma-separated values (CSV) and cram all the data together on one line with a comma or other character as a delimiter, like this:

```
0000-3BAB-9352-0000-G-0000-0000-Q, Attack of the Giant
Sandwich, 01:30:00:00, Pastrami Production, 111 Rye St.,
Hollywood, CA
```

This certainly saves a lot of space, but, being so compact, it makes it difficult to determine what these data mean and what relationships exist among them. To address some of these issues, integrators could encapsulate these data into a formal structure, like in object-oriented programming languages:

```
Movie {
  ISAN = 0000-3BAB-9352-0000-G-0000-0000-Q
  Title = Attack of the Giant Sandwich
  Duration = 01:30:00:00
  Owner = Pastrami Production
}
```

```
Company {
    Name = Pastrami Production
    Street = 111 Rye St
    City = Hollywood
    State = CA
}
```

This format provides more information about what the data represent. Readers can see now that these data are referring to a movie, and that the long string of digits is an ISAN number. However, this type of representation leaves integrators with no good way to show the various hierarchical relationships or associations between values that might exist. Besides, there is no consistent way to package these data for delivery to another system — Java does it differently than C++, which does it differently than C#, and so on. So, XML can be used:

```
<movie ISAN="0000-3BAB-9352-0000-G-0000-0000-Q">
    <title>Attack of the Giant Sandwich</title>
    <duration>01:30:00:00</duration>
    <owner>
        <name>Pastrami Production</name>
        <street>111 Rye St</street>
        <city>Hollywood</city>
        <state>CA</state>
    </owner>
</movie>
```

Now the document has structure, hierarchy, and human readability. No data in an XML document stand alone. Tags are used to sort, classify, and describe values so that in an XML document integrators are never left with that integer at the end and no idea what it means. These data have context.

## DECONSTRUCTING AN XML FILE

One of the main benefits of XML should be obvious: XML is a structured representation of data. Tags can contain character data, specific enumerated values, or more tags. A schema file is used to specify what information can go into an

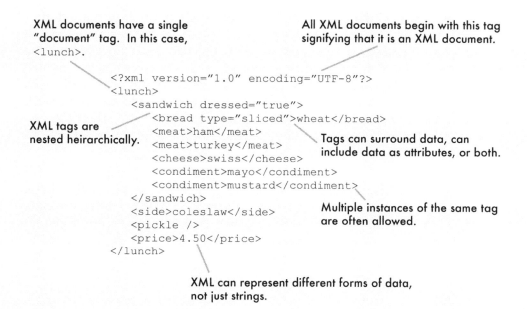

XML documents have a single "document" tag. In this case, <lunch>.

All XML documents begin with this tag signifying that it is an XML document.

```
<?xml version="1.0" encoding="UTF-8"?>
<lunch>
    <sandwich dressed="true">
        <bread type="sliced">wheat</bread>
        <meat>ham</meat>
        <meat>turkey</meat>
        <cheese>swiss</cheese>
        <condiment>mayo</condiment>
        <condiment>mustard</condiment>
    </sandwich>
    <side>coleslaw</side>
    <pickle />
    <price>4.50</price>
</lunch>
```

XML tags are nested heirarchically.

Tags can surround data, can include data as attributes, or both.

Multiple instances of the same tag are often allowed.

XML can represent different forms of data, not just strings.

XML message, and in what hierarchy. In the previous example, it can be specified that the <owner> tag only contains specific tags such as <name> and <street>, or it can be specified that the <state> tag contains one of the fifty U.S. states, or it could be specified that the content of the <duration> tag be formatted as four sets of two digits separated by colons. A document that does not meet these specifications will be considered invalid and rejected by any XML parser that meets the W3C standard. In this way, system vendors can enforce data integrity in any XML-based interface.

## XML SCHEMA

XML schema is the standard that is used to define what data goes into an XML document. Because XML can represent arbitrary data, any XML document attempting to communicate information will need to have an associated schema describing the form that information will take. One schema can provide the

structure for many XML documents, however. A schema will provide definitions such as "the element called rundown will have sub-elements called
date, clip, and producer." A schema can also define restrictions: "the
transcodeJob element must include one and only one fps attribute, which
must be a number." When a system receives an XML document, it will check
it against its schema for validity. If the XML document is not valid (for example, if you put in "thirty" for the fps attribute instead of "30"), then the system will reject the document. Having and conforming to a schema is
everything in the XML world.

Getting into the XML schema standard is beyond the scope of this book
(there are many XML books out there for the curious). It is enough to note
that XML documents have associated schemas, and that any technology that
deals with XML (such as Web services) will also have to deal with XML
schemas.

The hierarchical nature of the XML schema allows for easy representation of complex objects. In the real world, data often exist hierarchi-
cally—a sequence has subclips, which have frames that have
attributes such as resolution and aspect ratio. XML is great at handling this type of data. It was because of complex data such as the
information contained in these examples that XML was invented.
Hierarchy also increases the human readability of documents
(another main reason for the XML specification).

An XML document covered in acronyms and complex tags is not the
simplest poetry. In fact, sometimes it can get quite cumbersome.
However, when the other options are comma-delimited files or binary
encoded data, integrators are glad to get something that at least contains whole words. And even if documents are too complex for direct
human browsing, many tools out there, such as every major Web
browser, include XML display capabilities. In addition, parsing XML
using standards like Extensible Stylesheet Language Transformation
(XSLT) can provide useful, understandable information out of even

the most complex XML documents, and so the goal of human readability is still achieved, more or less.

## XSLT

In addition to schemas, there are many other XML-related standards out there to leverage the benefits of extensible markup. One of the more interesting is XSLT. This language allows integrators to take the data in one XML schema and transform it into another XML schema. One area where this is especially useful is making XML documents into HTML files (recall that, because XML is an arbitrary markup language, HTML can be considered XML following the HTML schema) for display in a Web browser. XSLT is also at the core of the data transformation technologies that are discussed in Chapter 4.

Other associated XML technologies include XPath for identifying specific elements in an XML document, XForms to define a way to input XML data, or XLink to create hyperlinks to specific XML elements.

Some of the crustier engineers out there may ask: "What is the value of human readability in the first place?" Going through the trouble of individually identifying all data values in a document is time-consuming, space consuming, and probably unnecessary. Certainly, if these engineers' processors are having difficulty handling XML parsing (if, for example, they were still using their trusty Amiga 1000) and would do noticeably better with some native binary, by all means they should use a more concise messaging method. However, this is probably not the case. XML's standardized hierarchy of name-value pairs gives integrators one major advantage that cannot be achieved with any of the other messaging formats discussed: it allows systems to trade information without knowing many details about each other. A J2EE-based system can just as easily trade XML with a .NET system as it can any number of other proprietary architectures. XML is an open standard that basically describes itself, and so two systems need only the scantest of information to start talking to each other.

In fact, two systems can have slightly different ideas about what sort of data to expect, and still be able to communicate effectively. This is called extensibility, and it is this important benefit that puts the X in XML.

## WHAT IS EXTENSIBILITY?

The "X" in XML stands for "eXtensible" (in that cute way that acronym makers have of lopping off the leading "e" to get more Xs into daily conversation). But what does extensibility mean? A simple example may help explain the concept.

```
<asset>
    <name>New Hamburger Commercial</name>
    <duration>00:00:30:00</duration>
</asset>
```

The above XML document snippet is valid for the following schema: an asset has a name and a duration. But, because XML is extensible, the previous example could also be valid for an even simpler schema—an asset has a name. Notice that this asset does in fact have a name. Just because it also has a duration does not mean that a system only interested in the name would turn away the above message. It would be able to grab the name out of the document and ignore the duration.

Extensibility works the other way, too. For a system with a more complicated definition—an asset can have a name, duration, category, and producer, for example—the above message is still valid, and any XML parser will let it through (assuming the category and producer are optional metadata). In this situation, the complex system may not get enough of the information it needs to handle the request out of this message, so setting required and optional fields in XML schema is important. This extensibility means that two systems that speak *almost* the same language can communicate, although in one direction of the communication, information that the second system cannot use will probably be passed over. XML does not remove the need to have systems that produce the required information. It only allows integrators to transition to them more easily.

To demonstrate the value of extensibility in enterprise communication, two systems can be envisioned (for example, scheduling and ingest) that trade XML messages to confirm schedules. A sample message from System A to System B might look like this:

```
<schedule>
  <event date-time="2008-05-01-22:00:00">
      <name>The 3(rd) Annual Culinary Awards</name>
      <duration>01:00:00:00</duration>
      <channel>1</channel>
  </event>
</schedule>
```

Both systems have ways to deal with this data, so when System B receives the message, it knows to block off 10:00–11:00 p.m. for the Culinary Awards on Channel 1. Now let's say that we upgrade System A to a fancier, newer model scheduling system that includes the concept of event priority. The Culinary Awards, a relatively important ingest, gets a "high" priority. Now when System A sends a message to System B, it looks like this:

```
<schedule>
  <event date-time="2008-05-01-22:00:00">
      <name> The 3(rd) Annual Culinary Awards</name>
      <duration>01:00:00:00</duration>
      <channel>1</channel>
      <priority>high</priority>
  </event>
</schedule>
```

However, System B is still the older system and does not have the concept of priority. When its XML parser receives the message, it does not understand what the <priority> tag means. XML is extensible, but this just means that System B ignores the unknown tag and schedules the Culinary Awards for 10:00 p.m. anyway. System A could send out these XML schedules to a dozen other systems for different purposes, and the ones that used priorities would pick up the tag while the others would simply look past it. In this case, XML extensibility is allowing a media enterprise to upgrade its systems one at a time without needing to worry about breaking existing communication paths.

With the many benefits XML gives, it is no wonder that the programming world sees uses for XML above and beyond simple messages like the ones seen previously. Additions to XML such as signatures and encryption have led to its use as a security and authentication mechanism. Also, since approximately 2001, database vendors have been introducing native XML databases (NXDs) that actually use XML for data storage. And, of course, XML has been the focus of countless data standardization efforts, such as Web services.

## 5.2.2 XML in Web Services

XML is a perfect match for Web services. To work as a method of system communication in M&E (or any other industry), Web services needs to be standardized, reliable, secure, and responsive. XML, as the underlying enabler of Web services, does not innately provide all of those things to the standard (for example, extensions such as XML encryption are required to support most security models), but, as shown in Fig. 5-3, the qualities of XML lay a solid foundation on which Web services build.

The messages that move among Web services are modular. In fact, as can be seen in the discussion of the WSDL standard in Section 5.4, a single service provides several discrete operations. These operations

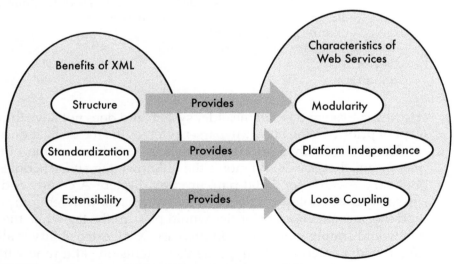

**FIGURE 5-3** The benefits of XML and how these support Web services.

can have complex data in their input and output messages. For example, a getMetadata operation might take in a single asset identifier, but output a structured, hierarchical representation of that asset's metadata. An authorizeUser operation might require simple user identification data and return a complex, structured representation of that user's access. The structure of the data in XML enables these types of operations without the use of complex programming of the interfaces.

In addition, the fact that every modern platform, computer language, and programming environment out there has an XML parser means that Web services can be truly platform-independent. Many platforms even have Web services tools or libraries, but even those can at least leverage the XML standard to easily read and write messages in a Web services network.

The largest and most difficult challenge Web services in an SOA environment poses to the underlying messaging architecture is the need for loose coupling. XML delivers on this brilliantly. Loose coupling, with its black-boxed view of the world, requires that any interface point in no way reflects the underlying implementation of the system. XML's extensibility makes this ideal much more achievable by allowing system implementations to selectively choose bits and pieces from the interface. If an ingest system does not know how to deal with priorities, it does not have to broadcast this embarrassing fact to the rest of the network; it just lets the priorities roll in and promptly ignores them and does its job as it always did until it also can get upgraded! No one is the wiser and nothing breaks. The media enterprise has achieved independence between the interface (the elegant face that the whole world sees) and the implementation (with all its warts)! XML and Web services are truly a match made in heaven.

## 5.3 WEB SERVICES ROLES

Roles in Web services examine what it looks like for two systems to communicate in a Web services world. Even apart from the liberal use of the word "services," anyone could begin to see similarities between the characteristics of Web services technologies and the characteristics of a Service-Oriented Architecture. There is a reason that Web services is the technology of choice for SOA proponents: it was designed with

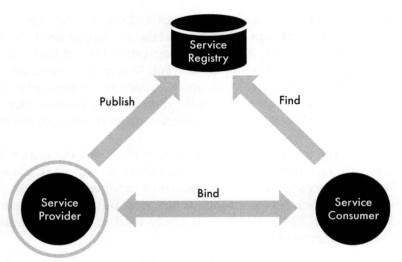

**FIGURE 5-4**   The three roles in Web services communication and how they communicate with each other.

service orientation in mind. In that vein, this section takes a closer look at the Web services message exchange protocol and begins to dig deeper into what makes SOA work.

As shown in Fig. 5-4, there are three roles in Web services communication: the service provider, the service consumer, and the service registry. In essence, this means the system offering a service, the system that needs the service, and the system that enables and "brokers" that exchange, respectively. The service provider publishes information about its interface to the service registry. The service consumer then finds the interface in the registry and binds directly to the service provider. The presence of a third party in what would otherwise be a two-way conversation may seem a little bizarre, and, in fact, the role of the registry is a hotly contested one among the big players in SOA. There are benefits and shortcomings to this type of communication. Each of the three roles has its own responsibilities and constraints.

## 5.3.1 The Service Provider

The service provider is the system that offers a service to the rest of the Web services network. If an integrator is looking at Web services as just a technology used by computers to talk to each other (a perfectly valid outlook), then the service provider would be the application that has a Web services interface. If that integrator considers the Web services network to be an SOA filled with business services, the provider could be an individual, business unit, or entire facility. Sure, it all ultimately boils down to applications sending bits over a network, but if the applications in question are portal servers, service gateways, or dedicated tools (such as editing stations or newsroom computer systems) that package the information and give it to a human to do work, it can be considered just as valid to view the people that perform the actual work as service providers. In fact, it often helps when envisioning an SOA to picture these roles filled by the humans doing the work instead of the applications that they use. Since the technical requirements of Web services communication are described here, however, the focus will be on the provider as application.

The service provider has an interface that it presents to its consumers. It also has an implementation that fulfills that interface. Recall, however, that it is not important *how* the provider does its work, only what it offers to do. That interface must describe everything that the consumer needs to locate and use the services offered by the provider.

Everyone spends a good portion of their lives dealing with service providers, whether that is giving shirts to a dry cleaner and expecting to get them back laundered or giving a budget to producers and expecting to get back completed TV shows. People are able to do this because they know a thing or two about their service providers. They know where the dry cleaners is, and they (hopefully) have a pretty good idea how much money is needed for a given show to be produced. At a high level, there are a number of things that any consumer of services has to know about the provider before he, she, or it can use the provider's services. These include:

- What specific services the provider offers
- What these services accomplish
- What information these services require
- What information these services provide back
- How to request these services
- How the services provide a response
- Where the provider is located
- What is the availability, reliability, and quality of the provider

Some of the needs listed above can be assumed if not provided. For example, a service consumer could assume that the provider is constantly available (never down) or it could implement other methods for determining availability. A service consumer also could assume that an operation that takes in a username and returns a first name, last name, and address is returning the information about the user the consumer submits. Some of these needs cannot be assumed, however, such as the location of the provider, or what information the provider needs to perform a service. Basically, the more information a provider gives, the easier it is for a service consumer to use the services offered by the provider.

The above provider information can be specified using Web services standards such as the Web Services Description Language (WSDL). A service provider is expected not only to present this information in a way that the consumer can understand (hence the many standards), but also to deliver what the service promises. Providers' responsibilities are therefore twofold: they must publish their interface to any and all consumers, and they must implement the services specified in the interface. Again, the details of implementation do not matter here — everything is loosely coupled, after all! One side effect of loose coupling (in both Web services and SOA), however, is that services are expected to be independent. A service provider should not expect to trade twenty messages with the consumer before providing the service; it receives a message, performs the service, and then sends a response.

A classic example of a service provider is a credit card authentication service. If a credit card provider decides to begin authenticating credit card purchases via Web services, they would prepare an interface document that would provide anyone who wished to use the service all the information needed. An online retailer could then send credit card information to the provider as specified and get back an authentication message indicating whether or not the credit card went through. The service provided is discrete, transactional, and hidden from the consumer (loosely coupled).

## 5.3.2 The Service Consumer

The same transaction looks very different from the point of view of the service consumer. Service consumers have two responsibilities as well: they must acquire and understand the service provider's interface (the what, where, and how of the service) and they must be able to generate messages that conform to that interface. If people wish to use the services of a dry cleaners, they have to know the cost and how long it will take, and they have to be able to provide the cleaner with money and clothing to be cleaned. No self-respecting dry cleaner would deal with a customer that asked it to wash a dog—a service consumer should not expect a service provider to do anything except what is in its interface.

It may seem as though a large onus is put on the consumer to be able to communicate effectively with the provider. The truth is, it is also the responsibility of the service providers to make themselves accessible. If dry cleaners charged $100 to launder a shirt, they would not get very many customers. In the same vein, if a service provider required that consumers submit an XML document that contains a list of every employee's social security number to request a service, it is understandable if a consumer cannot deliver. The use of messaging standards (both technology-wide like SOAP and industry-specific like BXF in M&E) is very helpful, because conforming to standards helps to equalize expectations on both sides of the transaction.

Just as with the service provider, the implementation of the service consumer of course does not matter, with one major difference: the consumer does not need to present an interface itself. A consumer application could be entirely written in Java or .NET with no concern for what the provider is using as there is no standards-based interface required in Web services for the consumer. In other words, all of the work to loosely couple this transaction rests with the service provider. The service provider's implementation must conform to its published interface. Assuming the consumer can format XML messages to send to the provider based on the provider's interface, it can use any method to process its data.

It is easy to see how a service provider in a Web services infrastructure fits in to the SOA message: the business services in a Service-Oriented Architecture are Web services providers. It is, however, not as straightforward to determine where service consumers fit in. The use of the word "service" here is also no doubt confusing, as it is used to refer to both an endpoint in Web services communication and an entity in a Service-Oriented Architecture. They are nearly analogous, but not quite.

In reality, service consumers and service providers exist both as end services and as processes in the middleware. Fig. 5-5 shows an example architecture where this is the case. A service consumer is any system that uses a service. In tightly coupled systems, services directly call each other, so each service is both a provider and a consumer. In the loosely coupled SOA world, processes in the middleware layer orchestrate most of the service calls, making the middleware layer itself the main service consumer. Also, as mentioned in the discussion of Business Process Management in Chapter 6, the processes in the middleware layer also can act as service providers! Every business service in an SOA is either a service consumer or a service provider, and many are both.

The service registry fits into SOA as well, right in the middleware layer. This component of the Web services protocol is discussed next.

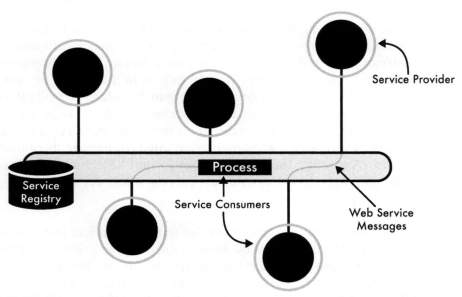

**FIGURE 5-5**   An example of how each Web services role might fit into a Service-Oriented Architecture.

### 5.3.3 The Service Registry

The service registry is an unnecessary (but helpful) participant in the Web services publish-find-bind handshake. With it, service providers have a single place to put their interface information, and service consumers have a single place to locate information about service providers. Without it, service providers must distribute their information to all consumers, and consumers must keep information about service providers on hand instead of locating a provider when one is needed. There are strengths and weaknesses to both models.

Without a service registry, a service consumer must get the interface documentation directly from the provider. This could be done either formally or informally. If the provider has a published standard interface (a WSDL file), then the file could be sent. If there is no standardized documentation, the details of the interface would have to be codified into some sort of informal documentation that could be read by a human and hard-coded into the service consumer. For example, if the service provider is an accounting portal for timesheet submission, the accounting department could e-mail information out to all other departments about how to connect with the timesheet service, and then each department could design a service consumer around that information. This makes it more of a challenge to design a Web services infrastructure as an SOA, because even if it is a dynamic process that is calling each service instead of an end-system application, all of the information about service interaction is still hard-coded into the process and therefore much more difficult to change. Not to mention that each service provider has the added responsibility of distributing its interface to every possible consumer; this is no small task.

If a service registry is present, however, then service consumers can find services that are available when they need one, and updating service interfaces becomes a much easier task. While there is a Web services standard for service registries (Universal Description Discovery and Integration; UDDI), a service registry could also be a much less formal entity such as a database of services sitting on a server or even an employee in charge of cataloging enterprise-wide service interfaces.

The following scenario illustrates how service registries fit into Web services communication. An operations line manager in a large media enterprise buys a new transcoder. He will be using it for four hours a day during the week, but wants to make it generally available to the rest of the enterprise at a specific rate when he is not using it so that he can recover the cost of buying it (for the sake of the story, everything in the enterprise works on a Web services based SOA). The line manager publishes the transcoder's service interface to the service registry, along with the times it is available and the rate that his department is charging for its use. See Fig. 5-6 for a diagram of this scenario.

A producer in the same media enterprise needs a transcoder for two hours a day over the course of the next two weeks to make preview copies of an upcoming television special. She queries the service registry and finds six transcoders available at the times she needs them. She selects one and creates a business process that will push assets from her shared storage into the transcoder and reflect the charge on her budget. Because the communication was brokered through the service registry, the producer and the line manager never had to meet to do business together, and both parties benefited from the transaction.

If the producer wanted to get fancy, she could also design her process to query the registry when there was an asset that needed transcoding,

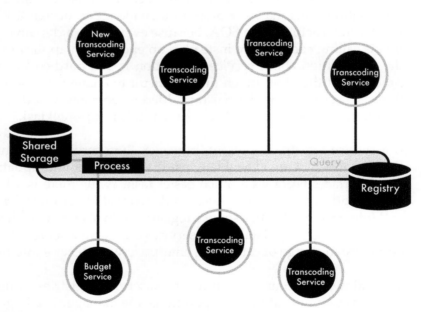

**FIGURE 5-6**  An illustration of the example scenario, using a registry.

and then select the cheapest transcoder available. This potentially could save her a little bit of money, though there may be a certain point at which the media enterprise does not want business decisions like this to be made automatically. In that case, the options could be presented to a user through a portal to make the right choice.

A service registry like this can work in both tightly coupled and SOA environments. In point-to-point Web services architectures, a registry may be the only system that has knowledge of every service in the enterprise (although, considering how accidental architectures arise, it is more likely that the enterprise will end up with multiple registries, each of which have partial views of the infrastructure). In an SOA, however, this sort of service query is exactly the type of thing that a middleware layer is supposed to offer to its component services. This is why many SOA vendors will include Web services registries in their middleware suites. Integrators can, of course, opt to avoid a registry altogether regardless of their architecture, but having a registry can help organize and streamline service design and messaging.

## 5.4 WEB SERVICES STANDARDS

If implementing Web services was as easy as sending any XML messages back and forth, then every media facility in the world would have them overnight and you could pick up six at the corner grocery for a dollar. Unfortunately, the role-based view of Web services (with service providers, service registries, etc.), and indeed the entire concept of loose coupling, requires strict adherence to some pretty interesting standards.

Web services is a brokered communication methodology. Because of that, three standards are necessary to allow Web services to be universally digestible: a well-documented way to describe a service provider's interface, an optional published registry methodology, and an accepted XML messaging format. The W3C and OASIS have defined specific ways to represent each of these. Only these three are needed, all other necessary standards are extensions to these three. In other words, by understanding these three standards, a service has all the information it needs to communicate with other services. The "big three" standards are individually called out on Fig. 5-7, and each are specific XML schema to enable and support Web services communication.

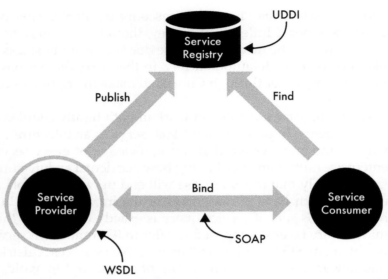

**FIGURE 5-7**   The major standards in Web services and where these fit in with Web services roles.

## WHAT IS OASIS?

The Organization for the Advancement of Structured Information Standards (OASIS) is the other major standards body in the Web services world (with the W3C). It was initially formed in 1993 to address possible uses of SGML (a precursor to XML) in the IT industry, but since the advent of XML it has generalized its work to include many Web-based information technologies.

In addition to UDDI and BPEL (to be discussed in Chapter 6), OASIS is working on a number of very interesting Web services related efforts including many of the WS-* standards discussed in this chapter and Web Services Distributed Management (WSDM), which would provide a way to manage all Web services in an enterprise in a unified manner.

Their Web site is http://www.oasis-open.org.

## 5.4.1   WSDL

The most important of the "big three" standards is the service interface standard: WSDL (pronounced whiz-dull). WSDL is the most important of the three because it has the job of communicating all of the critical information. Messaging standards are discussed later, but it is important to note that a service's WSDL document specifies which messaging standard will be used for service communication. Also, because service registries are optional in Web services communication (and they refer to WSDL files anyway), virtually everything important anyone needs to know about Web services begins and ends with WSDL.

WSDL is designed to communicate information about how to connect with and use the service it describes. Information a consumer might need to use a service provider includes:

- What specific services the provider offers
- What these services accomplish
- What information these services require
- What information these services provide back
- How to request these services
- How the services provide a response
- Where the provider is located
- What is the availability, reliability, and other quality-of-service (QoS) characteristics of the provider

WSDL does not address all of these points. To fully describe a service provider (including semantics about the available services and non-functional requirements such as availability), integrators need to pair WSDL up with other Web services standards, such as WS-Policy or Semantic Annotations for WSDL. These miscellaneous standards are important if they intend to design a secure and reliable infrastructure (and who doesn't?). Some of these standards are discussed in Section 5.4.4 below. Here the focus is on the specific subset of the above list that WSDL provides. A WSDL document (on its own, with no semantics, policies, etc.) is designed to provide what is minimally necessary for service communication. This is:

- The operations available in a service
- What data these operations require
- What data these operations return
- Where and how to connect to the service provider

# DECONSTRUCTING A WSDL FILE

```
<?xml version="1.0" encoding="UTF-8"?>
<wsdl:definitions xmlns:wsdl="http://schemas.xmlsoap.org/wsdl/"
   xmlns:soap="http://schemas.xmlsoap.org/wsdl/soap/">

   <wsdl:types>
      <xsd:schema xmlns:xsd="http://www.w3.org/1999/XMLSchema">
         <xsd:complexType name="sandwichType">
            <xsd:sequence>
               <xsd:element name="meat"
                  type="xsd:string" />
               <xsd:element name="cheese"
                  type="xsd:string" />
               <xsd:element name="condiment"
                  type="xsd:string" />
            </xsd:sequence>
         </xsd:complexType>
         <xsd:element name="sandwichElement"
            type="sandwichType" />
      </xsd:schema>
   </wsdl:types>

   <wsdl:interface name="orderInterface">
      <wsdl:operation name="orderSandwich">
         <wsdl:input messageLabel="sandwichType"
            element="xsd:string" />
         <wsdl:output messageLabel="sandwich"
            element="sandwichElement" />
      </wsdl:operation>
      <wsdl:operation name="orderDrink">
         <wsdl:input messageLabel="drinkSize"
            element="xsd:string" />
         <wsdl:output messageLabel="drink"
            element="xsd:string" />
      </wsdl:operation>
   </wsdl:interface>

   <wsdl:binding name="orderSOAPBinding"
      interface="orderInterface"
      type="http://www.w3.org/2004/08/wsdl/soap12">
      <wsdl:operation ref="orderSandwich" />
      <wsdl:operation ref="orderDrink" />
   </wsdl:binding>

   <wsdl:service name="orderService"
      interface="orderInterface">
      <wsdl:endpoint name="orderEndpoint"
         binding="orderSOAPBinding"
         address="http://www.sandwich.com/orderService" />
   </wsdl:service>

</wsdl:definitions>
```

Types use XML schema to describe XML tags that can be used in the interface.

Interfaces describe service operations and the messages associated with those actions.

Bindings describe the technical details of the service call.

Service tags give the service's location.

WSDL files have specific elements that communicate all of this information. Unfortunately, there are multiple versions of the WSDL specification. For the sake of explanation, this book uses the WSDL 2.0 terminology, but the WSDL 1.1 terms are identified below just in case because most Web services software packages are still solidly in 1.1 territory. The four main WSDL 2.0 elements are:

1. Types
2. Interface (called message and port type in WSDL 1.1)
3. Binding
4. Service

Types in a WSDL file are chunks of XML schema that describe the data the service takes in and out. For example, a service may provide a getAsset operation that returns asset metadata looking like this:

```
<asset uuid="a00012038" format="mxf">
    <duration>00:00:30:00</duration>
    <title>Big Sandwich Restaurant Commercial Spot</title>
    <dept>sales</dept>
</asset>
```

The exact hierarchical format that these data take will be described in WSDL types so that the service consumer can parse and understand the information.

WSDL interfaces associate specific data types with operations that the service offers. Using the above example, a WSDL interface element might define the getAsset operation, and dictate that it takes in an asset identifier and returns an asset element (defined in the types section, of course). Web services operations can also error out, returning fault messages that must be handled on the service consumer side (although good service design will minimize possible faults). Common fault situations occur when input data are improperly formatted or if required elements are missing. Some service providers choose to represent business conditions as WSDL faults as well (for example, having getAsset return a fault if no assets matching the request are found). This is certainly not a bad idea, but it is up to the media enterprise to determine what is the best practice for its classes of services.

Bindings in a WSDL document describe what specific messaging formats the service expects and how those messages are transported. If requests are to be sent as document-literal SOAP messages, for example, this element will say so (message formats are discussed in the next section; phrases like "document-literal SOAP messages" will be rolling off media integrators' tongues in no time!). Finally, services describe where the service provider is located (using a URL and a binding as defined earlier in the WSDL document). Together, all of these elements provide the framework for Web services communication.

### 5.4.1.1 Ways to Use WSDL

The basic structure of WSDL as described above may suit the needs of a majority of service providers. There are a handful of situations that may require a different basic take on the idea of service invocation, however, and there are advantages and disadvantages to the different ways in which WSDL can handle these corner cases. For example, let's say that an integrator wants to use a transcoding service to prepare a low-resolution version of an asset for offline edit. Various transcoders in the facility are busy at random intervals, so the integrator decides that the service consumer should choose a transcoding service provider at runtime. This example highlights a complication with the standard in the way it was initially conceived: WSDL documents are static — they are tightly coupled to a specific endpoint location! With the WSDL standard's fixed service elements, integrators have to specify a hard-coded URL to the interface, giving the consumer one or more fixed locations to choose from at runtime (see Fig. 5-8).

The endpoint decision process can be pushed further up the chain when routing is to be done based on content. For example, if all assets with a <dept>sales</dept> tag go to the sales department's asset management system while all assets with the <dept>prod</dept> tag go to the production department's asset management system, a business process can be used to select the correct static WSDL for each message. When service selection is instead a question of availability, capacity, or changing location, endpoint discovery should probably be handled at the WSDL level. Assuming there is no need to depend

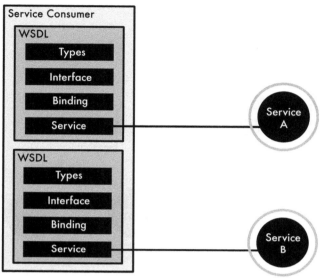

**FIGURE 5-8** In static WSDL service invocation, the WSDL document contains both operations and endpoints, giving each service a fixed endpoint.

on a proprietary WSDL extension hocked by a middleware vendor, a dynamic service interface is the best solution.

There are three ways to tackle this problem. The first is to create a transcoding "gateway" that will present a WSDL document to any consumer who needs to transcode an asset and forward their messages to whichever transcoder is currently available. The gateway would keep a collection of transcoder WSDLs and use service calls or other standards like WS-Policy to determine availability behind the scenes. This solution, shown in Fig. 5-9, has the advantage of total independence (read: loosely coupled) from both the service providers (all of the different transcoders) and the service consumer. Neither one needs to know that a gateway is being used; they can each assume they are providing or requesting a static service from a fixed endpoint. Gateways are a popular solution to the dynamic service problem, but may not be ideal for everyone (such as business units who do not have the authority to deploy service gateways or SOA ideologues who hope to avoid real programming at all costs in favor of fancy XML trickery).

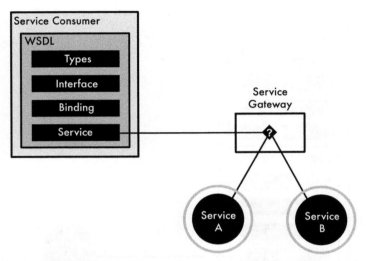

**FIGURE 5-9**   In service gateway-based invocation, a gateway is used as the service endpoint, allowing the logic of service selection to be abstracted to the external gateway.

An Enterprise Service Bus (ESB), like the ones discussed in Chapter 4, could fill the role of such a service gateway.

The second option to achieve dynamism can be considered more of a hack, certainly, but one that solves the problem entirely from the service consumer's point of view. This makes it a useful solution when the service provider is unable to change (if it is, for example, hosted by a different enterprise). Consumers need the first part of the WSDL document to design service calls (how can a request for an asset be written if the consumer does not know what the format of the request is?), but the end of the WSDL document, the service element, tightly couples that WSDL file with its endpoint. The solution here is to split the WSDL into two parts: one that contains all the XML necessary to code the service consumer and one that simply contains the endpoint location, as seen in Fig. 5-10. If there are five separate transcoders that all present the same interface, instead of having five independent WSDL files, the service consumer can cut up the WSDL files to produce one WSDL with all the operational data, and five endpoint files that reference that WSDL. Cutting up a WSDL file on the consumer end is perfectly fine. As long as the service provider receives XML messages that do not conflict with the original WSDL document, the consumer

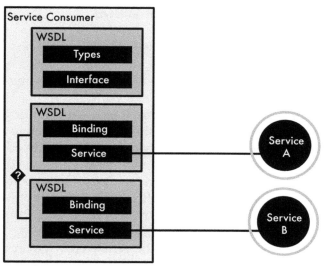

**FIGURE 5-10** Another option for managing multiple service endpoints is to split the WSDL file so that one set of operations refers to multiple services. In this method, the service consumer contains service selection logic.

can have any view of the provider's interface it likes! The consumer can then compose messages to the base WSDL file and choose a specific endpoint right before invoking the service. This is the approach commonly taken by BPEL implementations, as discussed in Chapter 6.

The third option for dynamic invocation involves querying a service registry at runtime. This is a preferred method, because it is the only one that allows service providers to change their location without having to redistribute endpoint references to all service consumers or gateways. This methodology will be discussed with UDDI (the registry standard) later in this section.

It is important to discuss the workarounds done to use WSDL in the real world. Certainly, no standard is perfect (not even Time Code!), and, should an integrator design a service consumer, he or she will no doubt have to muck around with the WSDL file to get it to work properly. The realistic goal of both Web services and SOA is not to completely eliminate integration woes (that would instead be SOA's idealistic goal, perhaps), but instead to reduce them as much as possible. WSDL, for all its faults, is a step in the right direction.

### 5.4.1.2 Future Directions of WSDL

M&E people are certainly not new to the complications of making spec-ifications. They have had a much longer, more storied history of techni-cal standards than the IT folks. One thing that everyone can agree about standards, though, is that they are a pain to improve. It is much more likely that newer and better technologies with newer and better stan-dards will come along to replace the current ones before the current ones are able to experience a single revision. WSDL is already on its 2.0 ver-sion, which is more of a foothold than most standards seem to get these days. The 2.0 version is mostly a fix for the problems and inconsistencies in 1.x WSDL (which was not officially endorsed by the W3C). Still, it seems that WSDL does not have many places to go from here.

The more likely candidates for the WSDL crown over the next several years as Web services hit their middle age years in IT departments (and teenage years in M&E) are the seemingly endless WS-* stan-dards. These are discussed in Section 5.4.4, but provide advantages over simple WSDL because they offer a cafeteria menu of functional-ity and specification to service providers.

This is not to say that WSDL should be avoided. On the contrary, WSDL is the absolute way to go when doing service design, and will be for quite some time. Unlike some of the other standards discussed (UDDI, for example), WSDL is not a specification in flux; IT integra-tors today are simply asking the standards bodies for more function-ality on top of WSDL. In other words, no one will ever get fired for using WSDL. And certainly no one will ever get fired for choosing Web services to integrate software systems.

With WSDL in hand, integrators can take advantage of the fundamen-tal benefits of Web services to enable an agile SOA. It is the most established and the most important of the "big three" standards. WSDL is the reason Web services work.

## 5.4.2  SOAP

Another major standard that is often discussed in the same breath as Web services is SOAP, an XML messaging standard. "SOAP" looks a lot like "SOA," and readers may be juggling quite a few acronyms in their heads at this point in the book, but it is important not to get these two confused. SOAP is a protocol for representing the Web services messages that go back and forth in a Web services based SOA. At the time of its inception, SOAP was the acronym for the Simple Object Access Protocol, but now, amusingly, it stands for absolutely nothing. The W3C, which maintains the standard, decided that the acronym was inaccurate and dropped it for version 1.2. After all, the protocol focuses on the transmission of messages and not on access. Also, objects represented in the standard do not have to be simple, they can be of any level of complexity that XML allows. Two out of four ain't bad, though.

SOAP's purpose is to take XML messages intended for service endpoints and represent them in a way suitable for sending out. Besides the actual XML content of the Web services message, there are a number of things consumers might want to include in any communiqué that they send to or from a service:

- Who sent the message
- Who the message is intended for
- A unique message identifier
- A message timestamp
- Message security

SOAP facilitates all of these. It is not the only option for Web services messaging, certainly as WSDL outright supports both SOAP and traditional HTTP for message transport, and WSDL 2.0 even includes provisions to extensibly refer to arbitrary binding protocols. This basically means that any messaging standard is supported for the industrious integrator willing to define one. SOAP binding can provide all of the aspects of messaging listed previously, and is often the de facto pick for Web services.

SOAP documents are organized in a very simple manner. They contain an envelope (as the root element), which includes both a header and a body. This makes them very similar to HTML documents to those familiar with them. As in HTML (and as in the real-world object to which both SOAP and HTML are an homage to: the old-fashioned letter), the SOAP header contains message metadata and identification, while the body contains the message itself.

## DECONSTRUCTING A SOAP DOCUMENT

SOAP messages include an envelope,
header, and body.

```
<?xml version="1.0" encoding="UTF-8"?>
<soap:Envelope xmlns:soap="http://www.w3.org/2001/12/soap-envelope"
soap:encoding="http://www.w3.org/2001/12/soap-encoding">
   <soap:Header>
      <seller soap:actor="http://www.sandwich.com/vendor">
         Mom's Deli</seller>
      <buyer soap:actor="http://www.sandwich.com/purchaser">
         John Footen</buyer>
   </soap:Header>
   <soap:Body>
      <sandwich dressed="true">
         <meat>turkey</meat>
         <cheese>muenster</cheese>
         <condiment>mayo</condiment>
      </sandwich>
   </soap:Body>
</soap:Envelope>
```

SOAP headers can contain any information
you want, but the standard also defines some
default header parameters.

SOAP bodies contain the actual
message being sent.

The SOAP header, like all of XML, is extensible, and can contain whatever information is needed, such as a timestamp or unique message identifier. End nodes can be designed to parse specific information contained in the header; many middleware vendors include their own extensions to SOAP messages. Because of extensibility, any extensions not understood by the receiver are simply ignored!

There are also certain ways in which the SOAP specification suggests that the header be used (ways that any consumer or provider that supports the SOAP standard will know about). For example, SOAP 1.2 includes the concept of a "role" (called an "actor" in version 1.1) that can specify what type of endpoint or service should process the message. For example, if a service provider receives a message with the role specified as "executive" but it only holds the role "operations," it may opt to forward the message along or ignore it instead of processing it. This type of architecture is very useful when dealing with service gateways, because SOAP messages can be tagged with "gateway" and "destination" roles to inform the gateway whether or not it needs to route the message.

SOAP messages can either travel over an HTTP connection (creatively called "SOAP over HTTP") or as a language-specific remote procedure call (SOAP RPC). In the "document-style" HTTP case (as opposed to RPC; document-style appears more often even though HTTP also supports RPC calls), the body of the SOAP envelope will contain an XML document that matches up with an input specified by an operation in the service provider's WSDL file. This document will represent some hierarchical object in XML such as an asset, user, or collection of strings. In the RPC case, however, the SOAP body contains a function call of sorts, and can be used to refer to a specific function written in Java, C#, etc. The RPC case, as one might surmise, is not very SOA-friendly, as it discourages a loose coupling between the interface of a service and its implementation. The rest of this chapter will focus on SOAP over HTTP with document-style encoding.

Because of SOAP's header vs. body structure, there are a number of best practices and additional standards surrounding the use of SOAP documents in real-world applications.

### 5.4.2.1 SOAP Additions

The message to be sent between services is not as straightforward as simply structured data with an XML representation. It could be a security key or even a .JPG image. For this purpose, the W3C (always eager to make a new standard), specified a way to represent SOAP with attachments. This protocol uses headers to associate another file (theoretically sent along with the SOAP document) with a specific message. The common use case envisioned is the transmission of image data, which crops up from time to time in the IT world (sending a headshot along with user info, for example). The mind of a media system integrator immediately jumps to much more ambitious attachments. These should be cautioned against. Further discussion of media movement in an SOA appears in Chapter 7 of this book, but, for now, suffice it to say that SOAP with attachments should be used sparingly, if at all.

## WHAT NOT TO DO: LARGE ATTACHMENTS

Just because the SOAP standard allows integrators to attach additional files to a SOAP message does not mean that they should make extensive use of this capability. The SOAP stack is a tall one and includes XML parsing and TCP handshakes, among other things. Especially when middleware is introduced into the equation, a single SOAP message could go through many iterations of processing to route and deliver it. Keeping messages short helps to keep a SOAP-based infrastructure manageable. One way to deal with large files for transfer is to do so "out-of-band," such as including in the SOAP message details required to get the file via FTP, Samba, MDP, or some other standard designed specifically around the movement of large files.

The other two most common additions to the SOAP standard are security related. Security at the message level is often a good idea inside an enterprise (but not always necessary). Large IT corporations that transfer social security numbers, medical records, financials, and all sorts of other heavily regulated data have demanded the sort of security SOAP provides, and have made heavy use of message encryption and signatures. Media enterprises may not face as many regulations as medical or financial companies, but it is common to encounter a media facility that will treat its data with equal care for fear of leaks or piracy that will affect the bottom line. So here, too, message security finds a home.

SOAP does not include a method to encrypt messages. That is handled at the XML level by the XML Encryption standard. In SOAP messages, it makes a lot of sense to encrypt the body while leaving the header (and any routing information) plaintext, so XML Encryption gets a lot of use with SOAP. For example, schedule data for an automation system could be encrypted over the wire in its entirety:

```
<env:Envelope xmlns:env="http://www.w3.org/2003/05/soap-envelope">
    <env:Header>
        <to>automation-5.facility.com/schedulingService</to>
        <from>scheduling.facility.com</from>
    </env:Header>
    <env:Body>
```

```
              <EncryptedData xmlns="http://www.w3.org/2001/04/
              xmlenc#aes128-cbc" MimeType="text/xml">
                     <CipherData>
                            <CipherValue>1183BA ... </CipherValue>
                     </CipherData>
              </EncryptedData>
       </env:Body>
</env:Envelope>
```

Encryption is also done at the XML element level, so a service provider/consumer could choose to encrypt selectively at the sub-message level. Using the previous example, the scheduling service could have business rules stating that only asset metadata gets encrypted to prevent listeners from getting schedule information before it is published:

```
<env:Envelope xmlns:env="http://www.w3.org/2003/05/soap-envelope">
       <env:Header>
              <to>automation-5.facility.com/schedulingService</to>
              <from>scheduling.facility.com</from>
       </env:Header>
       <env:Body>
              <entry uid="00014238901">
                     <window date="20080101" time="14:00:00"
                     duration="00:30:00" />
                     <asset>
                            <EncryptedData xmlns="http://www.w3.org/2001/04/
                            xmlenc#aes128-cbc" MimeType="text/xml">
                                   <CipherData>
                                          <CipherValue>8E898A ... </CipherValue>
                                   </CipherData>
                            </EncryptedData>
                     </asset>
              </entry>
       </env:Body>
</env:Envelope>
```

The standard defines a number of supported encryption formats, each of which has its own unique identifier (the examples above use 128-bit AES encryption, as can be seen in the xmlns attribute). The XML encryption standard also includes methods for transmitting keys for PKI encryption. Further research on encryption techniques can be done with other sources, but suffice it to say that XML Encryption includes the standard bag of tricks in use today to ensure safe and secure messaging.

The XML Signature standard also helps to secure messaging infrastructure, because it can be used to authenticate a message from a service provider. Again, this standard is not SOAP specific, but because SOAP messages use a header, they have the perfect location for an XML Signature built in. An XML Signature consists of an encrypted signature element and a key to authenticate the signature. It supports a number of encryption standards (though a smaller batch than XML Encryption), and, just like XML Encryption, can authenticate an entire message or a message subset.

The use of these security methods in Web services communication has been codified into a set of best practices called WS-Security. WS-Security is one of the WS-* standards discussed in the next section. It is also important to reiterate that these security methods are currently used in industries with extreme security concerns (equal to or, perhaps, *greater* than M&E). These tools are up to the task of securing a media infrastructure. An example scenario, shown in Fig. 5-11, gives some idea of the range of SOAP security.

In this example, asset metadata from five distributed asset management systems are sent using SOAP messages to a remote cataloger for metadata entry. The cataloger adds metadata, and then sends a SOAP message back with the entire, updated record. The cataloging facility uses a service gateway as an entry point for federated communication with the asset management systems' facilities. Messages sent to this gateway are routed through the public Internet. The media enterprise in this example does not want its asset data logged outside of its facilities. Service gateways will probably store messages to ensure delivery, and who knows what happens out there on the Internet! Because of this, each asset message is encrypted using XML encryption and only decrypted at the cataloging station or at the originating asset management system. A key is distributed beforehand to ensure this.

In addition, because the cataloging facility wishes to distinguish between asset management systems and only wants to catalog data from these five systems, each asset management system includes a

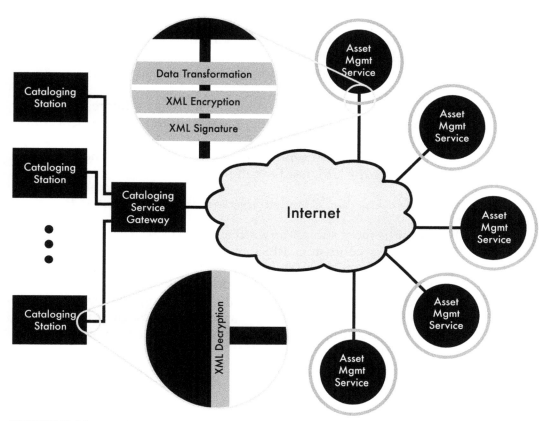

**FIGURE 5-11**  An illustration of the example scenario, showing wrapper details and how XML standards are used to provide security.

unique XML Signature for authorization. This also ensures that the service gateway will return the asset to the correct system after cataloging.

As this example shows, encryption and signatures provide for a secure messaging infrastructure, even over the wild and woolly Internet.

### 5.4.2.2  Shortcomings and Potential Solutions of SOAP

SOAP messaging, while very useful, is not without its faults. For example, SOAP is not a lightweight messaging standard. This allows it to work well in heavy-duty architectures that require encryption, gateways, and attachments; but in simpler architectures this can become cumbersome. Making a simple service request that perhaps requires only a single piece of data still entails the construction of a SOAP envelope and reference to the correct bindings (when perhaps all that is needed is to send a single, unencrypted asset ID!).

For this reason, a competing standard known as Representational State Transfer (REST) is gaining popularity in the Web services community. REST uses common HTTP GET and POST functions (already built in to browsers) to send Web services messages. These can be built right in to the URL used to call the service:

```
http://service.facility.com/myService?uuid=000138751
```

REST is a little more straightforward to use than SOAP and even looks a little bit less confusing. REST and SOAP can certainly be used together in harmony, though many Web services programming tools do not yet fully support REST. In addition, REST brings with it an entire architecture that many consider to be competitive with SOA! Expect SOAP to share the spotlight with other messaging protocols as Web services tools improve and standards continue to evolve.

### 5.4.3 UDDI

The last of the "big three" standards describes a way to implement a service registry in a Web services infrastructure. UDDI is an XML standard sponsored by OASIS. It is designed to allow service providers to publish their interfaces to a service registry and have service consumers find them. UDDI, in true service-oriented form, only specifies the interface to the registry, not the implementation of the registry itself. The full range of UDDI interface options are depicted in Fig. 5-12. Different vendors of registry software implement UDDI in different ways and most middleware vendors include a UDDI registry running on the application server as part of their middleware solution. UDDI also works in a stand-alone, point-to-point environment as a "service" unto itself. Either way, though, UDDI has not turned out to be the standard its inventors originally intended.

The initial vision of UDDI (and of the Web services registry in general) when it was conceived in 2000 was twofold: first, to serve as an

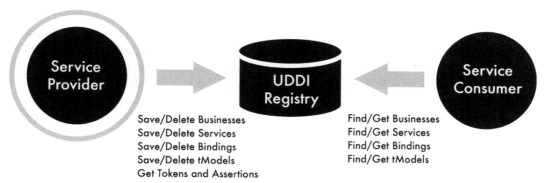

**FIGURE 5-12**   A summary of the possible ways to use a UDDI registry. Both service providers and consumers call the registry.

intra-enterprise registry of Web services for different business units to access and use (focusing on "discovery" of new Web services and the SOA ideal of broad reuse including the repurposing of services beyond the original intentions of their creators); and second, to serve as a *global* Web services registry that an enterprise could query to find services out there on the Internet. It is interesting to note that the latter purpose was always held forefront in the mind of UDDI's advocates, and so shaped its development quite a bit. Needless to say, this idyllic version of a future where everyone can find services in one place has not come to pass. Services (and registries) continue to be spread all over the place, with no one yet able to really organize the chaos.

Before criticizing the naiveté of OASIS for thinking that a global registry of Web services would take off, media enterprises should picture some of the benefits that such a service directory would bring. From a consumer point of view, decisions about who to choose to provide a given service could be informed and easily made. Right now, if consumers want some selection in what services they consume, they can use specific tools (if someone has gone through the trouble of making them) such as a search engine that compares prices at select online retailers. With a global registry, such tools could be constructed easily for any available service, from doctor's appointments to credit checks. They would not be limited to select service providers but automatically be up-to-date with all providers listed in the registry, since any such tool would query the constantly updated global registry. Inside the M&E industry specifically, a global registry could be especially useful given the large amount of outsourced and freelance services that are used. A studio could use such a registry to search for, negotiate with, and provide media to a post house for creation of dailies, and theoretically use a different post house for every job based on price and availability. Having formalized, published interfaces for services makes it easy to request a service from both a business and technical perspective.

The IT industry seems to have decided, however, that UDDI is not the standard to provide this utopia to the world. A quick look at how UDDI works, and the types of things it is especially well-suited for, helps integrators to understand why.

### 5.4.3.1 UDDI Data Types

UDDI is a searchable directory of service interfaces and descriptive information about those interfaces. It receives SOAP messages from both service providers looking to publish their interfaces and service consumers querying the directory for an interface to call. To facilitate effective interface searching and browsing, UDDI organizes directory information in a hierarchical way (a "taxonomy," so to speak), shown in Fig. 5-13.

The top-level concept in a UDDI registry is that of a business entity. This is anyone who publishes a group of services (i.e., a service provider). In a media enterprise offering services to the rest of the

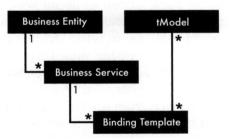

**FIGURE 5-13**  The data types contained within a UDDI registry. Business entities contain one or more services, which contain one or more endpoints (bindings). Bindings and tModels have a many-to-many relationship.

industry in a global registry, the business entity is the media enterprise. As an engineer offering technical services to the rest of the enterprise via an internal UDDI registry, the business entity could be a department. The business entity represents the "author" of the published services, so that a user could query the UDDI registry and ask for all of the services provided by the archive department, by the accounting department, or by the post house across town that they are thinking of using.

Underneath the business entity is a collection of business services. These records in a UDDI registry provide descriptive information about the services offered by the service provider (business entity). Service providers could associate one or more names with any service if they wanted (for example, if they wanted to call a service operation both "Schedule Production Switcher Operator" and "Schedule Vision Mixer Operator" are interchangeable to allow for both US and UK users). By having a descriptive business service entry in the registry, the UDDI standard solves the problem created by the overly technical WSDL standard by giving service interfaces a human face.

Most integrators may not be able to deal with the fact that the service fnp_02_httpSOAP takes in a voloc and a fnpcutlist, but when they search for "finalize news package," they should get the fnp_02_ httpSOAP service back with a description: "this service will finalize a news package if provided with a voice-over location and rough cut list." They would also want some data on supported formats, instruction information needed, and who is doing the final edit; at least enough information to follow up with this enterprise or department about the service they offer. This type of basic semantic integration is discussed as a WSDL extension, but it is absolutely necessary in a searchable registry and has been a part of UDDI since the beginning.

Business services have one or more binding templates underneath them that provide service locations and access information at a technical level. Binding templates also have what UDDI refers to as "tModels" associated with them that describe what specific technical operations and XML data are part of the service. It is interesting to note that UDDI does not store WSDL files directly as its intention was to be independent from the WSDL standard. To get a WSDL document for a service posted in a UDDI registry, the service provider has to include the WSDL location in the service's binding. So if a service provider wants to publish to a UDDI registry and have people access its WSDL, it will also have to host the WSDL document in an accessible location that the registry can point to. This is not totally inconvenient, because if the provider wanted to change a small WSDL detail, it could just do it without having to republish to any registries.

### 5.4.3.2 UDDI Publishing and Discovery

So now that the sort of data lives in a UDDI registry has been covered, the next topic is how to use a registry. The UDDI standard includes a number of WSDL files that describe ways in which it can be used. A UDDI registry is, therefore, a service itself that can receive SOAP messages to save information to it or get information from it. Publishing to UDDI is fairly simple: a business entity simply gathers the information that they want available in the registry, organizes it in the fashion called for in the WSDL document, and sends a service call out to the registry. Querying the registry for a service is slightly more interesting.

There are two methodologies for querying a registry for service information: design-time and dynamic. Some might argue that, based on the UDDI specification and the various ways that UDDI allows for service discovery, its definers had design-time queries in mind as the primary way to find a service. But, really, dynamic discovery is where this whole thing gets interesting.

A service consumer writing a business process that needs to call a service can query a UDDI registry to find an appropriate service. This can happen by searching for a specific business entity (that post house that you know does what you need, for example) and browsing through all the services they offer, or by searching for a specific service description (like "scan film"). Because UDDI offers a hierarchical data model, users can "drill down" to find exactly what they need. For example, if they ask the registry to return all the services that post house offers, they can then select one specific service description and find out all of the different ways and locations they can access that service. Then they can select a method that meets their needs and get a WSDL file. Once a user has the WSDL file, he or she can write the service consumer process around it, and the process will bind directly

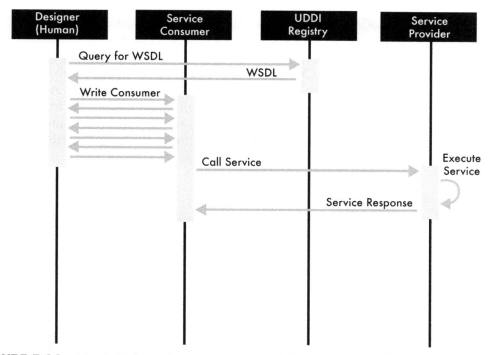

**FIGURE 5-14** A UML diagram showing the steps in design-time service discovery.

to the service provider and call the service. This is called design-time discovery, and it is shown in Fig. 5-14.

## tMODELS

It is obvious the IT community came up with this word. Just look at it: it is camel-cased and is not self-explanatory in the least! Even so, when using a UDDI registry, integrators will find tModels ("technical models") to be very useful. A tModel is a way to represent a generic service in a UDDI registry. The idea here is that a single tModel would describe a class of services in a technical enough way for users to write calls to this type of service; however, the tModel would still be generic enough that many service types and versions could still conform to it. This would allow integrators to write a service consumer without knowing the exact nature of any service providers.

So what does a tModel look like? The short answer is: just about anything! OASIS left the requirements for tModels pretty loose when they published the UDDI specification. As long as the provider gives its tModel a unique name, it can describe it in any way. One common way for a tModel to generically describe a service is for it to include the first half of its WSDL document — the data types and operations the service offers — without including any information on how to connect with that service. This provides a service consumer with enough information to form service calls without losing the flexibility of dynamic service discovery.

Integrators can also leverage the technical information available in a UDDI registry to enable dynamic discovery of services. Dynamic discovery, shown in Fig. 5-15, takes advantage of the tModels used to represent service operations and data. When writing a process that

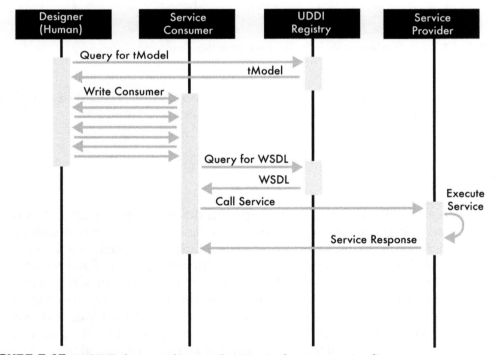

**FIGURE 5-15**   A UML diagram showing the steps in dynamic service discovery.

consumes a service, at some point the specific service operations are needed to finish the consumer. Even in an SOA, where a process may be wrapped, integrators still need to write that wrapper to the specific service operations. A service consumer, wrapper and all, cannot be deployed until it has knowledge of the type of data the service requires. However, assuming the process or wrapper is written to account for dynamic discovery, the physical location of the service and specifics of service binding do not have to be known until the service is called (long after the integrator has gone home to bed). Using UDDI, integrators can write to a class of technical services and put off the discovery of a specific service until the moment that service is needed.

The key to achieving dynamic discovery is that tModel. When planning to write a dynamic service consumer, integrators will query the UDDI registry for a specific service, get its tModel and the first part of its WSDL document, and write their consumers to those specifications. With that information, they will know that the service provider has an operation called fnp_02_httpSOAP and it takes a voloc and fnpcutlist, and they will be able to write all the data transformation they need into that process or wrapper. Then, when the service consumer is ready to send its service call out, it will query the UDDI registry for the service provider tModel. Any binding templates that get returned will provide a specific location where it can send its service call and get a response. The service consumer can even use the rest of the details included with the business service to decide which binding template to choose (based on cost, time, or other service "categories"). The service called dynamically might not even have existed when the service consumer was written, but because it adhered to the same interface standard (and published the same tModel), the consumer is able to use it anyway.

Dynamic service discovery is a little confusing to everyone, especially to someone who has spent little time in the Web services world. The important facts to know about the service are that it requires a service registry (like UDDI) so that the service consumer can query for providers at runtime, that it leverages the technical descriptions found in WSDL and tModels at design time, and that it is not easy to achieve. The huge benefit from dynamic discovery, though, is not being tied to a specific service. Without dynamic discovery, every time a service goes down, the integration staff will have to fix the business process that calls it. With dynamic discovery, processes react to changes in the service architecture without any input from humans. That is achieving real agility!

### 5.4.3.3 The Catch-22 of UDDI

UDDI is not all a bowl of cherries, however. Even in the preceding (mostly positive) description of the standard, readers may have seen a few holes. For example, the business-oriented nature of UDDI data may not be appropriate for all situations where a registry might be desired. What about registries deployed within an enterprise or business unit? If all of the services in a registry belong to the same business entity, what good is having a business entity "layer" in the registry? It could be argued that in these situations, a registry is not necessary at all, especially when looking at IT's underwhelming use of the UDDI standard (when compared to WSDL and SOAP).

Whereas SOA describes an architecture that can be built up slowly over time in such a way that participants feel business value at each step, UDDI describes a component that becomes most useful once it has been massively adopted. What good, after all, is a registry with no or few entries? And if there are no registry entries, what motivation is there to keep people publishing to the registry so that one day it might have enough entries to provide significant benefit to an enterprise? This fact alone is often cited for UDDI's failure as a global registry — the reason there are no Web services brokers scattered throughout the Internet right now providing services for all. The services (at least in the IT industry) are out there. There is just no one-stop shop for them.

## CRITICISMS OF UDDI

There are varying opinions about the UDDI standard. One of the more interesting criticisms of the current standard is the fact that UDDI is a service registry, and not a service repository. This means that UDDI describes the services in an enterprise and how to find them, but does not store the WSDLs. Instead, it points any service consumers to where the service provider has published its WSDL document. To the service consumer, this distinction is relatively meaningless, but to the service provider it means that a WSDL must be made available to consumers at all times, even when the service itself is not available! Many people feel that it should be the responsibility of some central entity, such as a service repository, to provide WSDL files to everyone, and UDDI just does not have that capability.

Another criticism of UDDI is its lack of good semantics. Web services stored in a UDDI registry have some amount of metadata associated with them—names, owners, descriptions, etc.—but there is no good way in UDDI to make a service easy to search for. In fact, there is no good way to search for Web services period! In this modern age, with Internet powerhouses like Google telling us that search is the future, having a hierarchical registry with no semantic search capability seems a little outdated.

Even with these criticisms, UDDI is the only game in town. No other standards-based service registry exists today. Many large IT vendors have proprietary versions of the registry that add some additional functionality, but for true interoperability, it is UDDI or bust.

Is the problem with the UDDI spec? Could a better designed technical solution cause people in various industries to begin to publish services to global repositories? Some people think so, and so more standards like the Web Ontology Language (OWL), are popping up to fill apparent needs in expressing services descriptively for people to query. But still many others feel that UDDI is a solution looking for a problem: people don't yet need service registries in their lives. While this may be true on a global level, it is certainly not true on an enterprise scale. Many facilities have implemented service registries to great success, and in the media industry, this success can be duplicated.

## DYNAMIC SERVICE DISCOVERY

While the media industry is only beginning to see the use of dynamic service discovery in production environments, it is commonly used by IT departments in large media enterprises. A major motion picture studio determines which is the best method for shipping all shipments, including media, via dynamic service discovery. They use business rules to determine the service with optimal cost and speed and then dynamically initiate the shipment via that carrier by binding to the correct shipper's WSDL and making Web services calls. This provides excellent flexibility by hiding the underlying details of which carrier will be called for a particular shipment from the higher level business process.

The moment a department or project team discovers a service out in the enterprise they did not know existed, using a registry like UDDI is the moment that the service registry has begun to provide business value. Reaching the critical mass of broad reuse is when service registries really shine. The IT pundits are correct when they say that a service registry is not appropriate for all situations; enterprises that still have few services or have a controlled service library run by a strict service oversight team will probably receive little benefit from UDDI. But they will also never reach one of the critical goals of SOA — broad service reuse.

The catch-22 of service registries on an enterprise scale is that they are really most useful once there is an infrastructure of services from all areas of business, available for consumption by the entire enterprise; conversely, the best way to get to the point of critical mass where service development is done across the enterprise is to have a registry available. With careful planning and a well thought out SOA roadmap, a registry can be put to great use in a facility. But until an organization is willing to put that same kind of planning into service-enabling the global community, there probably will not be any UDDI registries out there on the Internet to help people find a good deal on a mortgage!

## 5.4.4 Other Standards

Throughout the discussion of WSDL, SOAP, and UDDI, this book has pointed out some of the little problems that have cropped up over the years since these standards have been in widespread use: WSDL does not represent policies very well, WSDL does not include semantics, SOAP is not a lightweight messaging standard, and UDDI does not have advanced search capabilities. Web services are an incredibly useful method of communication, but there are certainly many who see the frayed edges of the core set of standards. The IT industry has been adding to and refining Web services standards since their inception, and by now they have quite a menagerie to choose from that can do everything from interface security to atomic transactions.

Coming from the media world, an engineer's first thought may be, "So many additions and changes to the standards? By now they are probably completely unusable, because who knows which version your system supports!" Well, this is where the extensibility of XML comes to the rescue. By starting with the "base" standards of WSDL, SOAP, and UDDI and adding extensions on top of that, any system that supports Web services will ignore any fields or directions they do not understand and still get the core Web services message. More standards allow integrators to take advantage of those systems that support and benefit from additional information while not requiring them to shut out any legacy systems that don't! Extensibility provides the best of both worlds.

The first thing that people noticed about creating a Web services infrastructure that needed addressing was the lack of unified best practices in service design and consumption. Sure, the *technology* has existed to send Web services messages back and forth since the inception of WSDL and SOAP, but few people were clear on what they were doing. If, for example, a reader were to simply read this chapter and then go out and attempt to build a Service-Oriented Media Enterprise, they run the risk of doing so in a way that is cumbersome and difficult for others to use. Thankfully (for these readers), this book has endeavored to include a unique take on SOA best practices so that readers can design an elegant and effective SOA, and thankfully (for everyone), a group called the Web Services Interoperability Organization (WS-I) was started to promote common practices among Web services developers and users.

The WS-I's goals are far-reaching. They aim to promote Web services interoperability in all senses of the phrase, whether that be through standardizing common messages, creating useful tools, or simply educating users. Their most notable work to date has been the creation of the WS-I Basic Profile, a specification that dictates best practices around SOAP messaging, WSDL documentation, service discovery, and much more. Part of the specification is a tag that can be inserted into messages and interfaces to inform participants that a service conforms to the Basic Profile. If this tag appears in a service call, the service consumer can make all sorts of assumptions about how that service is implemented. The work that the WS-I has done is really very good, and after readers have finished reading this book and telling all of their friends about it, they should look at the Basic Profile to understand more about best practices on Web services implementations.

Apart from WS-I, the vast majority of additional Web services standards all fall into the same category and cut a wide swath of functionality that is otherwise missing from the Web Services world. These standards are called the WS-* (read: "W-S-Star") standards because they all begin with a WS- signifying Web services. The complete list of these standards is shown in Table 5-1. They have all arrived on the scene in the last few years and come from the efforts of several large IT companies such as Microsoft, IBM, BEA, Oracle, and Sun. They are now mostly W3C or OASIS standards or working groups looking to become W3C or OASIS standards. The WS-* batch of standards provides a whole range of additional functionality to Web services. A few major ones are notable and will be mentioned, but for any Web services need you may have, there is probably a WS-* standard to deal with it.

The WS-Policy standard stands out as one of the more interesting of this bunch. When selecting a service provider, integrators will want to consider a number of factors, including non-functional requirements such as availability and QoS. The WSDL specification alone does not account for any such non-functional requirements, instead it sticks to the purely functional ones (what operations the service offers, what data it takes, etc.). The goal of the WS-Policy framework is to provide

**TABLE 5-1**

WS-* Standards (in alphabetical order)

| | | |
|---|---|---|
| WS-Addressing | WS-Discovery | WS-Provisioning |
| WS-AtomicTransaction | WS-Eventing | WS-Reliability |
| WS-BaseNotification | WS-Federation | WS-ReliableMessaging |
| WS-BrokeredNotification | WS-Inspection | WS-SecureConversation |
| WS-BusinessActivity | WS-Management | WS-Security |
| WS-CAF (Composite | WS-MetadataExchange | WS-SecurityPolicy |
| Application Framework) | WS-Notification | WS-Topics |
| WS-CDL (Choreography | WS-Policy | WS-Trust |
| Description Language) | WS-PolicyAssertions | |
| WS-Coordination | WS-PolicyAttachment | |

a way to assert these NFRs right in the service interface, allowing service consumers to make better decisions about which service to use. The framework provides a way to make assertions on how a service must be used (many common assertions are defined in other standards such as WS-PolicyAssertion and WS-SecurityPolicy). Possible policies include encryption and security requirements, service expiration, or even any custom policies desired. Service providers can even host your policy assertions themselves and have the WSDL link to them (allowing change without needing to redistribute WSDLs to all consumers or WSDL repositories).

Another (related) WS-* standard that is very popular among Web services integrators is the WS-Security standard. WS-Security provides a method for leveraging XML encryption and signatures to include security tokens in SOAP messages. While the XML standards discussed elsewhere in this book go a long way for securing individual messages in a Web services infrastructure, WS-Security provides additional functionality and a greater range of security options. It is also the best way to use XML encryption and XML signatures with Web services. Considering the security needs of the M&E industry, this specification is a welcome addition! WS-Security is also notable for another reason: unlike other WS-* standards that provide functionality that can be easily ignored by consumers that do not support the standards, WS-Security must be supported on all sides of the interaction (otherwise the consumer will not be able to decrypt the provider's message or accept its security token)! This is of course for the best, because no one would want a security policy that is rendered meaningless through ignorance of the policy; however, it is something to keep in mind when using WS-Security in Web services. Consumers (or intermediaries in the middleware) will have to support it as well. If security is crucial in a service, though, WS-Security is the way to go!

Another major concern that many M&E integrators have regarding Web Services architecture is the reliability of the infrastructure. One good thing about the hardware-based networks of many media facilities is that reliable messaging is simply a question of physics — if the cable is the right length and connected on both ends, then the control signal is going to get there on time. Once a TCP stack and Ethernet routing is inserted into the picture, things get more complicated. Thankfully, reliable messaging can still be achieved, and the appropriately named WS-ReliableMessaging standard provides that in Web services at the level that media engineers have come to expect. WS-ReliableMessaging uses the same sort of logic that TCP uses (acknowledgments, message numbering, and other fun techniques) to create a messaging infrastructure where even the most severe of network failures will not cause a message to get dropped. The standard also encompasses service providers that will continue to send messages until the consumer acknowledges. In situations where critical Web services messages have to go over unreliable networks, WS-ReliableMessaging is the right tool for the job.

The last WS-* standard to be discussed here is the WS-Federation standard. The concept of federation, which is simply the interaction of systems managed by different entities, is covered in detail in Appendix E, but it is important to note that the Web services standards bodies have been considering federation as well, and have solved many of the problems associated with federating services. The standard describes a way to broker information exchange between federated domains in a secure and authorized way.

There are other efforts out there besides simply the WS-* and WS-I standards to extend the capabilities of Web services. One of the more important standards in the Web services world discussed in Chapter 6 is BPEL (see Section 6.3.4.2). There are also standards that exist to dictate how Web services interact with portals, how Web services can be implemented in various programming languages, and many more.

# THE JAVA COMMUNITY PROCESS

Lots of organizations, not just the W3C and OASIS, have put some thought into Web services technology. One method some grassroots-style contributors have used to advance Web services is the Java Community Process (JCP). This is the primary way that the open source community contributes to the Java programming language and, because Java is integrally associated with many enterprise computer technologies, a whole range of related topics (including Web services). Contributors create Java Specification Requests (JSRs) that are reviewed and voted upon. Some of these JSRs are Web services related specifications such as JSR 224, the Java API for XML Web services. Other non-Web Services related JSRs may be of interest to media professionals.

One notable spec to come out of the JCP is JSR 168, the Java portlet specification. This document specifies a way to define portal elements using Java, and was a major influence on the development of the associated Web Services for Remote Portlets (WSRP) specification. Another popular JSR is 170, the specification for a Java-based content repository.

It is important to note that Web services technologies are, by definition, language independent, while the JSRs are obviously Java-specific. Realize, though, that development is being done in all areas of enterprise computer technology to enhance the world of Web services.

One trend that has been seen as Web services standards have developed, and that has hopefully come across in our discussion, is the increasing focus on enhanced dynamism and reusability of services. The WS-* standards, as shown in Fig. 5-16, have helped this trend along. Standards like WS-Policy make dynamic service discovery easier and more useful; WS-Federation and others allow services to be available to a wider range of consumers. Web services have become indistinguishable from SOA to many people (hopefully not readers that have gotten this far!), and this is because the goals of Web services are becoming more and more aligned with many of the goals of SOA: agility in service communication and visibility into policies and service availability. Web services and SOA are a well-matched pair.

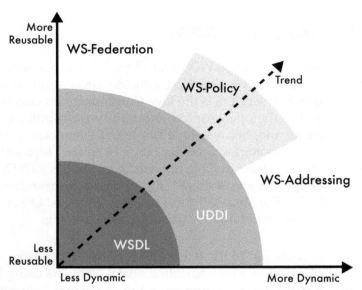

**FIGURE 5-16**  Web services extensions such as WS-Policy, WS-Federation, and WS-Addressing provide additional functionality to services based on WSDL and UDDI. As more extensions are developed, the goals of reusability and dynamism are becoming more and more achievable.

## 5.5  WEB SERVICES CONSIDERATIONS

Even understanding everything there is to know about Web services, WSDL, SOAP, and UDDI, the skeptical media engineer in everyone may still be rolling his or her eyes. This is a standard based on XML, after all. It is bulky! It is slow! It is no match to good ol' reliable coax cable strung between two boxes! Well, that crusty, embittered techie everyone has inside is not completely wrong. Web services are good for many things, both within an SOA and without; but Web services are not good for everything.

Web services, based on XML standards, are slower than most dedicated systems communication environments. This is mostly because of the number of steps necessary to package a message to send out. Business data to be sent to a service provider need to get placed into an XML message, that message needs to get wrapped in a SOAP envelope, then that SOAP document will get sent over TCP in packets (and everyone knows how many layers the TCP stack has!). On the other end, the service provider will receive the message, encode it as XML,

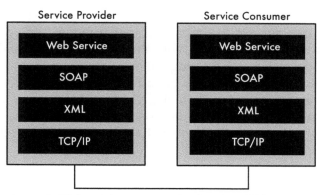

**FIGURE 5-17** The layers in Web services communication. Any Web services message goes through this stack on both the provider and consumer side.

validate the XML, then strip the message of its SOAP envelope, parse the message, and present the business data to the service. These layers can be seen in Fig. 5-17. As anyone can see, Web services transactions do tend to have many steps because they sit on top of all of these layered standards.

Also, as mentioned, XML documents are slightly longer and slower to deal with because of their human readability and extensibility. Every data field has a tag associated with it, and the SOAP envelope of a message adds quite a few more tags into the mix. Compared to comma-delimited files and other space-savers (binary-encoded, anyone?), XML is a hefty medium for messages. Add to that the fact that XML readers will parse through and validate any XML message they receive (checking for completeness and validity) before delivering it to the user, and there is a recipe for still more small delays in the messaging cycle.

In addition to being slower than some, Web services are also less deterministic than some of the messaging technologies that the media industry has grown accustomed to. After all, Web services messages are sent over IP, a technology that accepts some degree of packet loss, in a reliable way. But to ensure reliability, TCP will resend packets until receiving acknowledgment for each packet, and WS-Reliability will resend whole messages until receiving acknowledgment for each message! So users cannot depend on a certain response time in milliseconds from a Web services call. It could take a mere fraction of a second to send a

SOAP message and have the service provider send a response, or it could take several seconds. And that response time could vary from message to message, even with the same service provider. There is no deterministic way of figuring out exact response times in such an infrastructure. So, can a system get a response from service within a fixed number of video frames? Maybe. Maybe not. An upper limit of response time could be determined in most cases, but response times will vary more widely than with some of the more traditional media communication protocols.

In addition, Web services messages are not good at moving large amounts of data from place to place. SOAP with attachments could be used, but there is little true support for it as yet and putting large files through service wrappers is not the best idea. Integrators will probably want to find some other way of transferring large files between systems.

What does this mean for the media integrator? Basically, it means that Web services are not appropriate for every situation. Namely, real-time applications or situations where exact, deterministic timing is critical to messaging success are not good places to stick a Web services stack. In addition, communication scenarios that are not easily compartmentalized into discrete messages (such as streaming applications) would not do well in a Web services infrastructure. These things can still be SOA-enabled (though sticking real-time messaging over middleware technologies is also probably a bad idea; see Chapter 7 for more details), but use of a different messaging technology than Web services is suggested or required. An example where Web services may not be appropriate (and how to work around them in the context of a Web Services infrastructure) follows.

In the situation where a media enterprise has a traffic system, an automation system, clip storage, and a playout server integrated together to play out programs, there are a few different types of data that are needed to be moved around. Schedules and asset metadata need to get between traffic and automation well before air. This would be a good use of Web services because the information can take advantage of structured, extensible XML for representation. To move an asset from clip storage to the playout server, integrators will not want to use Web services for the file transfer, although the automation

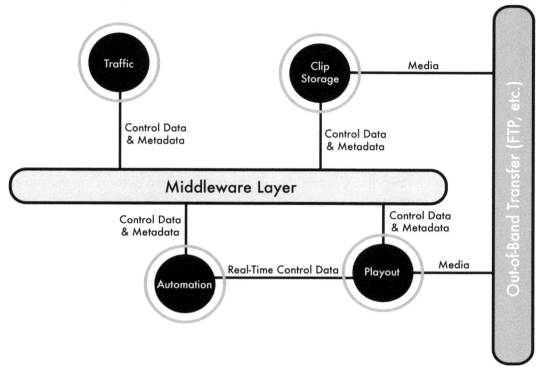

**FIGURE 5-18** An illustration of the use of out-of-band transfers and real-time communication in a Web services infrastructure.

system could use Web services calls to trigger the out-of-band transfer. Real-time control data going from the automation system to the playout server should also not be done with Web services. A depiction of this architecture appears in Fig. 5-18. To put this setup in the context of an SOA, integrators would want Web services coming into this entire integrated system to schedule the "playout service," for example, although the details of how assets are played out (via real-time control protocols) are beyond the service boundary.

## ACTION ITEM

Determine where Web services are appropriate in the enterprise, keeping in mind the strengths and limitations of Web services communication.

## 5.6  HOW WEB SERVICES ARE BETTER THAN OTHER COMMUNICATION METHODS

The previous section discussed situations (such as frame-accurate communication) where Web services are inappropriate. This section discusses situations for which they are especially well suited. Any data produced by multiple systems in a facility that may be needed by those multiple systems or may be subject to representational differences from system to system are good choices for Web services. Web services are ideal for control data, business data, and metadata in a media enterprise. Control data — instructions to a system for the purposes of configuration or triggering an action (remember though, not in real time!) — are good choices for Web services because often a single system will receive control information from multiple sources and these sources will all have different ways of representing these data. If an engineer thinks about how many different services may send information to an automation system, they will have a good idea of why control data benefit from Web services' features. Business data — user information, finance information, or scheduling information — require security and extensibility. Web services provides these benefits, and so, as the IT industry has discovered, they are a good match for such business data. Also, metadata, with its myriad standards and pervasiveness throughout many media systems in an enterprise, provide an excellent venue for Web services to show value.

Web services are well suited for a number of industry tasks because they are extensible, dynamic, dispersible, maintainable, secure, and supported. XML, the basis of Web services, allows for extensible tags (that may be understood only by a subset of systems or just the originator of the message) to be included in messages without affecting behavior among non-compliant systems. This allows services to communicate with other services that share only subsets of their functionality. Extensibility means that Web services are good choices in mixed environments where systems may be of different versions or brands. Extensibility is also a good thing to have in situations where communication standards among systems change often. Extensibility allows integrators to make changes in a backward compatible way, but always supporting existing interfaces. This means that upgrades can be done with minimal impact to other systems and processes. In any scenario where this might otherwise be an issue, an enterprise should consider Web services.

Web services are dynamic. By using techniques such as splitting the WSDL file or implementing a UDDI registry, a Web services infrastructure can be made that determines the final location of any service only at the moment it is needed. In architectures where systems and services move or change often, this dynamism provides valuable benefit. For example, in mobile production teams that may or may not have a given system available to them depending on the location or configuration of their current setup, implementing dynamic service calls and resilient processes using Web services is a very good idea. In addition, scenarios where the number of systems available to perform a given service fluctuates often (due to spotty network availability or shifting organizational boundaries), the ability to dynamically discover services available to do a task allows integrators to take the most advantage of the systems available at any given moment. Dynamic services are nearly impossible to create using tightly coupled or proprietary communication standards, but for Web services moving across an enterprise network, it is part of the design.

In addition to being dynamic and extensible (as shown in Fig. 5-19), Web services are a standardized addition to the TCP stack, and that means it works over everything from dedicated, carrier-class networks to theoretically dial-up connections. No special infrastructure is needed to support the bulk of an enterprise's Web services needs. Using the right level of messaging security, Web services calls could travel over

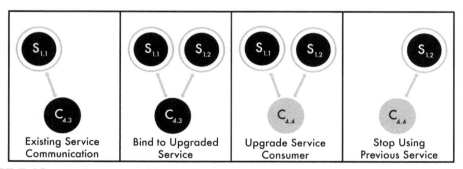

**FIGURE 5-19**   An illustration of how Web services is extensible and dynamic.

the public Internet with the same level of reliability that they travel within an enterprise. This means that geographically dispersed facilities benefit from using Web services as a communication protocol. Even in situations where the physical separation between two services might not be much but their organizational separation prevents the establishment of a dedicated communication channel, Web services can come to the rescue. Using extensions such as WS-Addressing, WS-Reliability, or WS-Security allows you to send messages over unreliable or insecure networks as though they were dedicated links.

Due to all of this resiliency and extensibility, Web services end up a little bit easier to maintain than most communication standards. Certainly, if an enterprise is on top of its game, it is able to maintain a communication infrastructure regardless of its implementation, but in many cases, pristine architectures fall prey to the wear and tear of everyday use — routers begin to get overloaded and patch bays fill up or slowly devolve their normals into a spaghetti of tangled wires. With a Web services infrastructure, especially paired with a unified middleware layer, maintenance is a matter of ensuring reliable enough connectivity to the central network. Web Services calls do not rely on exact timing nor do they require unique connectors. All that a service requires to communicate is a connection to the rest of the enterprise network. They can, therefore, be distributed across a large infrastructure, as shown in Fig. 5-20.

And yet, at the same time as they are able to move across enterprise-wide networks and the Internet, Web services also includes more security provisions than many other communication standards. Sure, a poorly designed Web services infrastructure presents no security benefit over existing methods (and may actually be less secure due to XML's human readability), but when security is taken seriously as a design consideration, Web services allows for complex security models that can meet a variety of unique needs. With the ability to encrypt and digitally sign individual messages (as well as the ability to set up secure channels using extensions such as WS-SecureConversation), Web services is a good choice for important business data moving across insecure networks. This level of security comes in handy when transferring metadata or business information to third-party enterprises or when your systems handle large amounts of data with varying security levels. Web services is good for creating this kind of complex messaging environment.

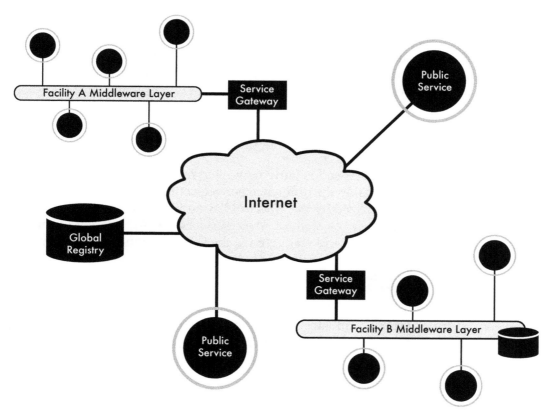

**FIGURE 5-20**  An illustration of how Web services may be distributed across facilities and enterprises.

Web services are also better than many other communication methods because it enables loosely coupled architectures. As this book focuses on SOA, quite a bit of space has been given to the subject of loose coupling and the benefits it brings (agility, visibility, productivity, etc.). These are benefits that many different types of enterprises need. Infrastructures that see a lot of system upheaval such as theaters or studios that serve many purposes throughout the year and companies focused on new media and cutting-edge technology all could benefit from greater business agility. Not every communication protocol can be used to provide this sort of agility. A tightly coupled architecture is only remotely agile if the new systems support the exact same standards as the old systems, and even then configuration differences will trip integrators up. Web services allows the integrator to separate interface from implementation, and this enables the construction of SOA and all its benefits. This is basically the ultimate reason that Web services is a great communication standard: it works with SOA, and SOA is a great architecture.

## A BRIEF HISTORY OF WEB SERVICES

Much of the technology discussed is fairly new, even from an IT point of view, where just a few months makes the difference between cutting-edge and out-of-date. XML 1.0 was standardized by the W3C in 1998, and by 2000, many IT vendors were publishing their version of Web services. SOAP arose out of Microsoft's COM technologies and was given to the W3C for standardization in May of 2000. WSDL came as a joint effort between IBM and Microsoft in March of 2001. After this, the parallel growth of both SOA and Web services (both contributing to each other's popularity) took several years, and it has only been in the past few years that Web services has been a buzz-worthy topic. This is more than enough time for the IT industry to develop several major implementations of the technology and really prove its mettle, however.

There is one more reason why Web services is better than other communication methods; Web services, unlike many of the media standards that media engineers have known and loved in the past, has the weight of the entire IT industry behind it. The M&E industry relies on vendors to support the standards it uses to integrate its systems, and Web services already has the support of a large fraction of vendors that are used in the industry. But it is not only the automation system vendors or editing system vendors that are offering Web services support, it is also the business and IT systems, HR, finance, security and authentication, shipping, and so on. And these business systems are supporting Web services in a big way. Media enterprises may see greater adoption percentages for many of the largest M&E data communication standards (such as SDI) in the industry, but M&E standards have seen very little adoption outside of the media industry because they are designed to have very little purpose outside of this arena. Try finding a banking system that supports MOS—it is not going to happen, of course! And never forget the sheer size of the IT industry compared to M&E. On pure volume, Web services has major momentum.

IT support of Web services is a major benefit to the media engineer because the future of media integration, like it or not, involves these IT systems in a big way. Integrators need to connect with their HR and their accounting systems to provide for end-to-end process management in the enterprise. Just because these services do not handle media does not mean that they are unimportant to M&E workflows. They are very important, but in a totally different way than most of the system's integrators are used to. As more and more IT systems (content management systems, Web servers, etc.) are repurposed into the media operations space, integration using Web services makes more and more sense.

## 5.7  CONCLUSION

Hopefully, this exploration of Web services technology has shown that the best practices and ideals of SOA are a little bit more realistically achievable than they may seem at first glance. Using XML, WSDL, UDDI, and SOAP, integrators are able to get their systems to expose business service functionality to the rest of the enterprise, and this helps to push the media enterprise into the elusive world of loose coupling, where the SOA benefits of agility and visibility are felt. Knowing how it works also allows integrators to focus on the more important question: What do we do with it? This question is addressed in Chapter 6: Business Process Management: Definitions, Concepts, and Methodologies, but just looking at some of the benefits of Web services answers that question for many. This is technology that is very applicable to the needs of the M&E industry.

Web services works for a number of applications in M&E. The key to leveraging the benefits of Web services is to know where they are most useful, and where it is better to use a more traditional communication standard. The reason that Web services is so valuable is because it works where traditional communication standards *don't* offer many good, interoperable solutions (although many have tried). Areas like metadata exchange, multi-system work order management, or integration with IT and business systems are the best examples of this. Even in the absence of an overarching SOA architecture, Web services works well for these applications. Of course, in the context of an SOA, Web services provides so much more. Getting started now with a Web services infrastructure, even if there is no budget or support to adopt SOA, will help media enterprises move toward an SOA in the future (see Chapter 8). This scenario has already played itself out many times in large IT enterprises, where Web services is far more pervasive and important than in M&E (for now). This has been mentioned before, but this is the strongest reason to move toward Web services integration: IT is already there.

Do not downplay the influence that the IT industry has in M&E. In a world where more and more of our systems are created and supported by major IT vendors, the role of IT in media standards uptake is growing. This may not seem all that important to that crusty media engineer inside everyone, because the M&E industry has come so far without being big on the IT radar, but IT will play a much more crucial role in M&E going forward. Web services, having come initially from the IT side of the fence, gives enterprises an edge when dealing with the increasingly commoditized systems of the future: Web services already speaks the language of IT. More and more media companies are adopting Web services as a communication protocol, but it is largely already there in IT. This means that business applications (like PeopleSoft and SAP systems) already support Web services. Right now. When integrators are faced with the challenge of building new media functionality into their facilities, they will be thankful that all of those business systems already have Web services support.

There is also a general trend in the M&E industry over the last couple of decades as the IT and computing industries have risen in size and importance: standards, technologies, and best practices of these industries, invariably, wind up here in M&E. Many traditional media engineers are loath to admit it, but like it or not, what IT is supporting will affect what M&E will support. And IT is supporting the tenets of SOA and Web services standards. All users would do well to pay attention.

And it is already happening. Media vendors of all sorts have been, over the last several years, adopting Web services as a supported communications methodology. Fewer have adopted the tenets of SOA to guide their service exposure, but offering Web services interfaces is still a strong step in the right direction. Some of the more common areas to service enable (probably due to their nature as oft-integrated systems) are transcoding, digital asset management, and scheduling systems. A vendor looking for some advice on how to correctly service-enable your media products should take a look at Appendix D. A media enterprise looking for Web services enabled vendors and products should see Chapter 7 for an in-depth look at the unique challenges that M&E vendors and enterprises face when service-orienting their facilities using Web services. If they are not exposing Web services interfaces already, integrators should be challenging your system providers now to enhance their products and provide better interfaces like Web services to facilitate next-generation integrated networks. There is a good chance, however, that many of them are already exposing Web services as part of their product. This chapter has discussed ways to wrap applications so that they present Web services interfaces (the common case for the near future), but if a system already offers a Web services interface, even if it is not the same one that it should ultimately present, the act of wrapping and integrating that system becomes much easier.

## ACTION ITEM: VENDOR SUPPORT

Talk to representatives from your vendors about their current or planned support for Web services standards. Many M&E vendors currently support Web services standards and will support users as they move toward SOA. Others are more behind the times. Knowing where vendors fall on this continuum will help to predict how big a task becoming a Service-Oriented Media Enterprise will be.

Web services adoption in the M&E industry, therefore, is not a question of "if," it is a question of "when." Web services are the future of enterprise computing communication, and as the future of the media industry looks like it will heavily involve enterprise computing, the industry will be unable to avoid Web services. Thankfully, Web services offers a number of benefits over the way things are currently done such as extensibility, security, and loose coupling. Web services is not a panacea; it does not solve all problems in M&E, but it is a great start. And a Web services architecture is one that can form the basis of a solid enterprise communications infrastructure that meets the criteria of a Service-Oriented Architecture and takes into account all of the quirks of media movement, storage, and playout. Web services, in other words, is the future.

## WHAT TO TELL YOUR BOSS

- Web services hits a sweet spot in M&E with metadata, business data, and non-real-time control data. Do not start implementing Web services at every integration point in your fa cility. Be smart.
- Web services is based on well-founded IT standards, so the support, adoption, and momentum is already there. Take advantage of it.
- There are extensions to the core Web services standards to provide all kinds of additional functionality such as security, routing, and semantics. And more to come!

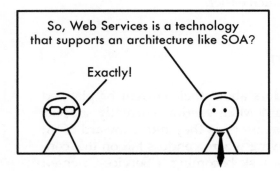

# 6

# BUSINESS PROCESS MANAGEMENT: DEFINITIONS, CONCEPTS, AND METHODOLOGIES

Many integrators, especially those in the media space, choose to focus primarily on the technological aspects of integration (in other words, the "what"), often at the expense of the business and logistical aspects of integration (the "why" and "how"). It is not obvious why this is; perhaps because those who deal primarily with systems find their jobs easier when the users of those systems are not in the picture. Much to these integrators' chagrin, modern practice in systems integration — the same modern practice that has brought SOA and Web services — dictates that the business and workflow issues of integration are equally as if not more important than the implementing architectures and technologies. Integration is a two-sided coin, with the systems integrated on one side, and the people requiring what integration provides on the other. One cannot exist without the other.

If Service-Oriented Architecture is mostly the systems side of the coin, then Business Process Management (BPM) is mainly the human side. SOA considers the services that the system offers, the interfaces for those services, and the communication between them. But an effective integrated solution requires so much more than just these three things. It requires, just to name a few, a methodology for using the solution, a way to design the solution based on clear business and workflow requirements, and a rationale behind each technology choice made in the solution. This is the realm of BPM, which concerns itself with processes, organizations, and models.

Business Process Management is a term that, like SOA, does not have clear-cut boundary lines defining what it is and what it is not. BPM arguably got its start in the late 1980s when it was first discovered that the world of workflow and engineering management could be combined with the world of Enterprise Application Integration (EAI) to mutual benefit. By managing processes and ensuring that those processes matched up with the architecture that enables them in the most efficient way possible, integrators realized they could save countless hours of wading through a morass of non-intuitive integration. It involved a style of development that started with the process, not with the technology!

With the advent of process automation technologies, BPM has become very popular, especially in process-driven areas such as the manufacturing or service industries. Thanks to these technologies, having a well thought out process means that an enterprise can save time and money directly and automatically, not just by giving workers the opportunity for efficiency. Since BPM concerns itself with both the development of business processes and the links that those business processes have with the underlying system, it is really a larger concept than SOA, which considers mainly the architecture and technology itself. In many ways, SOA could be considered a part of BPM!

BPM all comes down to the business process. An example process appears in Fig. 6-1. Just as the service is the fundamental building block of SOA, the business process is the fundamental building block of BPM. A process can be of many scopes — short ones that may run for a few seconds to distribute completed work all the way to long ones that may run for several years as a major business goal is realized. In Media & Entertainment (M&E), the word "workflow," which bears some relationship to the concept of a business process, has been bandied about for many years now. The main difference between a workflow as it is thought of by media vendors and a business process in the world of BPM is this: a workflow almost always focuses on a vertical silo of functionality such as editing or asset management while a business process should include horizontally integrated tasks that cross departmental and system boundaries. A business process should not be limited by technological or organizational lines but should represent as well as possible the way that business is really done in a facility.

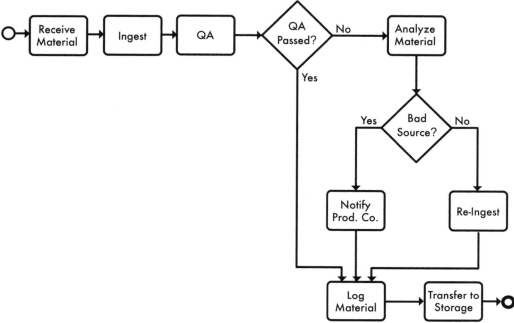

**FIGURE 6-1**    A business process is a sequence of tasks that extends across the entire enterprise. This simple example shows the process used to ingest new material in a particular facility.

## WHAT IS A BUSINESS PROCESS IN THE MEDIA & ENTERTAINMENT INDUSTRY?

Every individual facility may have a different idea of what its business processes are. They are, in a nutshell, the steps that an enterprise goes through to meet its business goals. This may mean any number of processes at many levels of detail:

- Post-production
- Ingesting assets from tape
- Preparing assets for playout
- Storage and maintenance checkups
- Commercial sales
- Cataloguing
- Control room configuration and setup

So how does BPM affect the model of Service-Oriented Architecture that is presented in previous chapters of this book? Well, in truth, BPM has a complex and many-layered relationship with SOA. As stated previously, many consider SOA to be simply a subset of BPM, which looks at not only system architecture, but also the business processes needed to take advantage of it. The simpler answer is this: BPM gives SOA meaning. And SOA gives BPM a blank canvas on which to develop integrated, process-oriented solutions. While it is basically an abstract philosophy on how integrated enterprises should work, BPM affects an SOA project in two very concrete ways: by directing the methodologies used to develop and implement an SOA solution, and by providing business processes that can be exposed as services and run in the middleware layer of an SOA.

The metaphysical aspect of BPM's involvement in SOA is that BPM turns the development of an SOA solution into a managed business process itself! BPM dictates that any integration project (especially one on the scope of an enterprise-wide SOA rollout) should begin with a consideration of the business processes to be used. In other words, start with business processes, and then allow service interfaces and technologies to fall out of that analysis. Sometimes this is not possible on its own (such as when a project is constrained by specific, already-purchased technologies), and that is where SOA tricks such as wrapping and data transformation come to the rescue. In this way, SOA enables BPM while BPM is enabling SOA — a symbiotic relationship that brings a lot of benefit to the enterprise implementing these best practices!

The other major area where BPM affects an SOA integration project is by providing the business processes that exist in the middleware layer and by helping to direct traffic from one service to another. This architecture is shown in Fig. 6-2. This is classic BPM as envisioned by the EAI pioneers many years ago: taking a business process and realizing it within an integrated solution.

Even though it may live in a process orchestration engine on the middleware layer, a business process in an SOA is a service. It can present an interface and be called by various clients attached to the SOA. Even though its main work is routing communication to other services based on business goals, the process can provide its services via an interface to users or other processes. It only makes sense, of course: a producer may want to fire off a process that will initiate and manage the production of a television show while providing constant feedback to all those involved. He or she should be able to simply call a

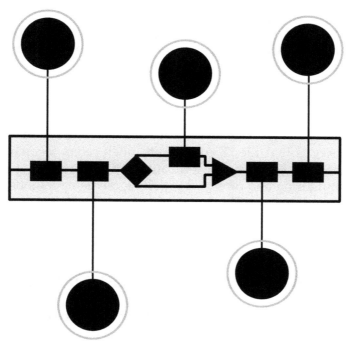

**FIGURE 6-2**   A business process in an SOA environment will live in the middleware layer, perhaps in a process orchestration engine, and can provide information about how service communication is to be routed and managed.

service interface to accomplish this. This is exactly the type of thing that a business process in an SOA environment can do.

Media & Entertainment, after all, is no stranger to world of Business Process Management. In fact, because of the need to produce content at a rapid pace (such as in news organizations), media enterprises have had to streamline their operations. The M&E industry does not currently distinguish between their version of BPM and the generic concept of "workflow," however. Media workflow solutions fall all over the place — from specific product uses that would not be considered part of BPM to actual BPM solutions. There may be some areas of BPM innovation occurring in the M&E industry, but there is no discipline to guide and foster that innovation.

For example, one area that is very well developed in M&E and often confused with BPM is automation. Because of a need to get content on the air in a frame-accurate, hands-off way, automation systems have had "workflow engines" in them for a long time that will schedule file transfers and push media out without human intervention. But automation is not Business Process Management. The media industry has not yet seen a widespread acceptance of BPM or process orchestration, but with the advent of SOA in media enterprises, BPM is not far behind.

## IMPORTANT NOTE

Process orchestration is not automation. The source of much of this confusion in the M&E industry is that the IT community often refers to orchestration as "process automation." However, the term automation has a very specific meaning in M&E: configuring and directly controlling media operations and equipment like ingest and playout. This is not what is meant. In fact, as discussed in Chapter 7, these BPM and SOA technologies are not a good substitute for tried and true automation systems.

## 6.1  THE BENEFITS OF BUSINESS PROCESS MANAGEMENT

BPM, much like SOA, is often sold as a panacea for any enterprise-wide problem by IT hucksters the world over. It is important to consider the true benefits that BPM brings to a facility, and not to assume that it can address all challenges that a company could face. These benefits will seem very familiar to those that have already been discussed in Chapter 3: Service-Oriented Architecture: Definition, Concepts, and Methodologies, because they are the same core abstract benefits that SOA provides to a facility — agility and visibility!

Because BPM deals with the business processes that are occurring across an enterprise rather than the systems used to implement certain steps in these processes, the details of how agility and visibility are achieved are of course very different in BPM than in SOA. One should ask the question: how can formalized business processes increase an infrastructure's ability to react to change? To provide useful information to its users? There are a number of possibilities.

### 6.1.1  Agility

Even without process orchestration of any sort in place, BPM brings agility into an organization. Formalization of workflows and processes alone makes changing those processes easier simply because the current processes are now documented. If an enterprise realizes that a change to workflow is needed, no one should have to go through and figure out what is currently being done in a facility as that information will already be available to the team responsible for changing the process. Anyone who has ever been on such a team knows that the upfront organizational work is half of the challenge! Having a methodology in place to formalize processes, a standardized way to document them, and an excuse to keep them up to date is a lifesaver in these situations.

However, if process orchestration (or at least some method of active process tracking) is in place, then there are other agility-related benefits. Agility is all about implementing change in an enterprise quickly and effectively. Process orchestration technology can help with that by versioning processes and managing their lifecycle. An enterprise can have many variations of a single process in place simultaneously and running at once. This is how it is in many facilities when change is implemented: one or two groups test out a new process or workflow while the bulk of the participants continue to use the existing, tried-and-true process. Once the new methodology has been working successfully for a fixed period of time, it can be rolled out enterprise-wide. Most BPM technologies are capable of managing different versions of processes almost seamlessly to facilitate this type of deployment plan.

As shown in Fig. 6-3, a facility can manually manage multiple versions of a workflow, having some users follow a new plan while the rest do what they have always done. However, if an enterprise formalizes these processes and puts them into a workflow engine, then the system architecture that everyone is using can also manage these multiple versions. Information can be routed to different places depending on which version of the process the users are using. All of this happens automatically, so that users only have to worry about the human tasks and not all of the corollary logistic detail.

This brings up another aspect of agility provided by BPM (in an SOA architecture) — a focus on process outside of any technology enhances the agility benefits of SOA immensely. This is what BPM (and also SOA) teaches: that the business processes in an enterprise do not depend on the systems that implement them, but solely on the business goals they are trying to achieve. A "tight coupling" of processes

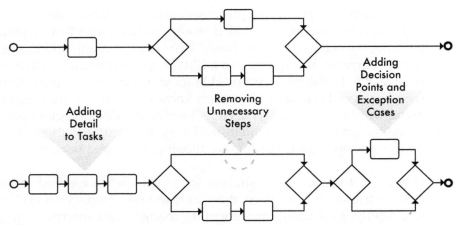

**FIGURE 6-3**  Change often comes in the form of a process variation. Using BPM techniques and technologies, an enterprise can implement two or more versions of a business process and seamlessly transition between them.

to technologies tends to occur naturally in a facility (much like SOA's accidental architecture), so implementing BPM best practices means keeping processes agile and vendor-neutral (see Fig. 6-4). A workflow is less useful if it only works for a particular vendor's product, which means that a facility cannot switch vendors without drastically affecting their business processes.

Implementing vendor-neutral processes not only means that an integrator can change technology without drastically affecting process, it also means that he or she can change processes without drastically affecting technology. If an enterprise succeeds in keeping the business data that flows through its processes technology-independent, then these processes can be re-engineered without spurring change in the underlying technology. BPM can leverage the layer of abstraction provided by a Service-Oriented Architecture to help achieve business agility.

## CASE STUDY

### Process Agility

A small post-production house re-engineers its entire enterprise infrastructure to align with the precepts of BPM and SOA. All of its editors are given enterprise portal pages that are exposed as editor services, and its scheduling system is wrapped to present a service interface as well. In addition, there are transcoding services and services that present proxy assets for review. The processes of allocating a new editing job, editing and review, and finalizing a completed product are formalized and put inside an orchestration engine.

This works well for the facility for about a year, but clients begin to ask for an additional approval step between the rough cut and online edit. The post house changes its formalized editing and review process to include this step, which simply leverages the existing review service. The new process is online within an hour of the business change being approved, and all incoming edit jobs that request this new process begin to be funneled through it. The post house has demonstrated its process agility.

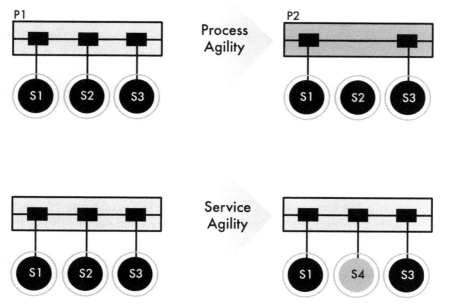

**FIGURE 6-4**   Process agility and service agility are similar, but not identical. In a facility implementing the best practices of both BPM and SOA, these two types of agility complement each other.

## 6.1.2  Visibility

BPM and its technology also provide the benefits of increased visibility to implementing enterprises. This visibility takes a variety of forms, from a general increase in workflow awareness to specific available products that track process status and statistics. This is the area of BPM that has been most explored in recent years by IT vendors, and is also one of the most exciting parts. However, just as with BPM's agility benefits, visibility is even felt in the enterprise just by formalizing business processes, before all of the fancy technology is purchased.

By capturing the way things are currently done in a facility and properly documenting those processes, a systems analyst gives the enterprise the gift of process awareness, which is a type of visibility. Suddenly, it is possible for everyone to be on the same page regarding what participants in the process are doing. Formalizing processes is a way of weeding out misconceptions about what is going on in a facility, which can work wonders for increasing effective communication and process efficiency on its own.

Communication is increased when processes are formalized because each participant in the process now has situational awareness of what is going on around him or her. An assistant producer now knows that the editors take advantage of logging notes in a particular way, so that AP will endeavor to capture the most useful information for them. A colorist now knows how finished material is catalogued, and can appropriately adjust metadata provided at his stage in the process. Process awareness removes ignorance as an excuse for miscommunication, allowing a facility to focus on streamlining instead of simply following its processes.

Having formalized processes also helps to streamline the bottlenecks and easy areas for increased efficiency can be recognized and amended quickly. If a tape operator is dubbing ten tapes of every broadcast, and it is determined that only five of them are used for anything, the operator can cut his or her output in half without affecting the rest of the process. If all producers use a single, backlogged transcoder because it comes up as default, this work can be load balanced better across all of the transcoders in the facility. These sorts of quick fixes do not require any technology or integration, just process visibility. They are the first way that an enterprise will benefit from BPM.

There are other, more technical visibility benefits to BPM as well; benefits that are felt not through governance and best practices, but through implementation of a specific product or use of process orchestration within an enterprise. Such technology can provide immediate feedback on business initiatives and detailed statistics of past performance. For example, a producer could have a portal page giving her up-to-date information on average asset completion time, facility load, and any particular jobs that are nearing or past deadline. These types of process metrics in the world of BPM are called Key Performance Indicators (KPIs).

KPIs, as their name would suggest, measure the performance of a particular process or facility. Although a set of KPIs might include data that comes from a single system (such as average length of time spent at an editing workstation), it is more common that a KPI is generated based on information coming from many systems and aggregated in one place (such as an SOA middleware layer). They are commonly presented to the user in a single location: an enterprise dashboard. This is often a Web site served by whatever system is aggregating data. KPIs are one of the key visibility benefits of BPM.

## KEY PERFORMANCE INDICATORS

The following are a few examples of KPIs that might be found in a media facility. While these may inspire a business analyst, KPIs are not general-purpose. A facility's KPIs should be dictated by the unique business requirements of the enterprise:

- Percent utilization of edit bays
- Average duration of asset production
- Daily consumption of tape
- Maximum and minimum equipment usage in a month
- Number of production projects behind schedule
- Average number of assets per video server

KPIs are distinct from the type of systemic visibility granted by product-specific views or standards like SNMP. They do not measure technical status, they measure *business success*. To effectively do that, they must be endowed with the business intelligence necessary to determine success in a particular enterprise goal. A KPI that measures an inane or vastly varying statistic like number of times "play" is pressed versus "fast forward" is of no use to anyone.

Providing the business intelligence needed to drive useful KPIs is the job of the business analyst driving BPM in an enterprise. It is not always an easy or straightforward task. With the right BPM tools, however, the job of drawing the data necessary to inform those KPIs is straightforward, making the identification of KPIs the hardest part of the process. Some best practices to help with KPI identification are explored in Section 6.2.2 as part of the "Ten Commandments of Workflow Analysis."

The class of IT tools that deals with KPIs and BPM visibility is known as business monitoring. Again, the aspect of business monitoring that distinguishes it from other monitoring solutions is that it deals in business-level information, not technical data. Readers may be noticing a pattern at this point with both BPM and SOA: a solid focus on the business, and not on the underlying technology. Modern software architectures want to measure business-level events, not the bits on the wire. Gathering of these business events can be done in a number of ways. SOA technologies such as Web services can be used to put business event generation and communication on the same technical level as business messaging in an enterprise, or some vendors have put out their own technologies that transmit business events at a different layer than the one traditionally used by SOA services (although often using many of the same middleware solutions). The point is, the technology to measure such business data is out there, and the challenge then becomes what to do with it.

Dashboards and portals are common uses of KPIs and other visibility metrics provided by BPM technologies. The term "dashboard," for those unfamiliar to it, refers to a user interface that presents large amounts of data, aggregated from many places, in a single view. An example dashboard is shown in Fig. 6-5. Often, these dashboards are graphical in nature and easy to navigate. They might present green and red lights to represent the current state of a facility's KPIs, or they might feature gauges to represent moving averages. Many IT vendors produce dashboard products, or one could be custom-built for an enterprise, if desired.

There are also other ways to take advantage of BPM visibility. For example, one simple but very useful application is to give everyone in

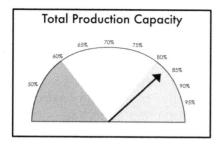

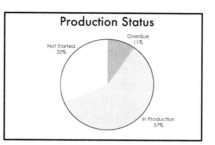

**Service Status**

| | | |
|---|---|---|
| ● Ingest A | ○ System Status | ○ Playout Prep |
| ○ Ingest B | ○ Transcoding A | ○ Scheduling |
| ○ Ingest C | ○ Transcoding B | ◐ Editing A |
| ○ Ingest D | ○ Transcoding C | ○ Editing B |
| ◐ Logging A | ○ Transcoding D | ○ Editing C |
| ○ Logging B | ○ Transcoding E | ○ Playout A |
| ○ Cataloging | ○ Library A | ○ Playout B |
| ○ Storage Mgmt | ◐ Library B | ○ Playout C |
| ○ Sales | ○ Support Svcs | ○ Playout D |
| ○ Finance | ○ Feeds | More... |

**Notifications**

[1 APR 08 12:55:57 PM] Editing A OFFLINE
[1 APR 08 12:40:02 PM] Production "Newsforce 0427" marked COMPLETE
[1 APR 08 10:17:12 AM] Production "Newsforce 0401" marked OVERDUE
[1 APR 08 12:00:01 AM] Regularly scheduled service check COMPLETE
[30 MAR 08 6:30:00 PM] Library A ONLINE
◉ [30 MAR 08 6:27:45 PM] Library B OFFLINE - No library services online
[30 MAR 08 4:13:14 PM] Cataloging job #13485 COMPLETE
[30 MAR 08 2:01:58 PM] System capacity at GOOD levels
[30 MAR 08 1:50:28 PM] Storage Management: 10 TB free
◉ [30 MAR 08 12:48:06 PM] Transcoding C at 90% capacity
[30 MAR 08 10:30:17 AM] Production "Newsforce 0330" marked COMPLETE

More...

**FIGURE 6-5**  An example of an enterprise dashboard. Important data is presented in a graphical, easy-to-understand way to provide a valuable overview of current business status.

an enterprise a Web-based to-do list, using the current state of processes and business tasks in the facility to populate it. A user can log on in the morning to see what tasks await him or her, and, as those tasks are completed, the task list will be dynamically updated based on business events moving throughout the integrated facility and the output of those tasks automatically moved downstream in the process. A task list is also useful for managing human-only tasks that may otherwise have no computerized feedback to a process orchestration engine. These types of tasks are still common in the M&E industry due to the craft-based nature of its work and the late arrival of digital technology. Users can complete their tasks, and then click a button on the task list reporting that completion to the rest of the infrastructure thereby updating everyone's task list.

This leads to a basic but pervasive concept that has been central to BPM's usefulness inside the IT industry, and will be central to making it work inside the media industry as well: role-based views. In an enterprise architecture with plenty of visibility (such as the one promised by BPM), no one wants too much information going to any one place or any one user. For both security reasons and because of the sheer overwhelming nature of too much data, giving a single user a dashboard with everything on it is a bad idea. Most BPM tools can easily split this data up by role, so that producers get a different view of things then writers, editors get a different view then colorists, and engineers get a different view then archivists. This may even stretch so far as generating completely different KPIs from the same base data. The executive producer might be interested in average project throughput, while an editor is concerned with average media storage throughput, and a system administrator might be more concerned with peak media storage utilization. Role-based views ensure that everyone gets access to the data they need. Certain users, such as producers or managers, can have multiple "roles" and see multiple views of the enterprise data. Presenting data in a role-based way is a major boon for those implementing BPM solutions.

## 6.1.3 Organizational Benefits of BPM

Although agility and visibility are the main selling points of BPM, there are a few important ancillary benefits that should be covered as well. Because BPM is a set of best practices that informs enterprise integration, it requires a certain level of commitment from members of an enterprise to be successful. But, if the commitment is there, BPM will pay an enterprise back tenfold in increased efficiency. BPM creates both better communication among business groups and more efficient processes to streamline the output of those groups.

Even in the formalization of processes (and not the automated execution of processes), there are many communication benefits. Having a fixed process allows participants — whether those participants are users, teams, or whole departments — to see their touch-points, or where important data move in or out of their hands. Everyone knows what information they need to do their jobs, and what information they need to give to others so that those participants can do their jobs. This has an overall effect of increasing useful interdepartmental communication.

In addition, formalizing processes reduces the number of informal processes that exist in an enterprise. Every media facility has a number of informal processes that have developed organically over the years to meet various unspoken business needs. Perhaps a particular server has a quirk that only a handful of engineers know. Workarounds are developed and passed orally from one user to the next, never written down anywhere for posterity. Every few months someone new asks how to get around that particular problem. Anyone who has spent any time in a media facility knows all about these little shortcuts and quick fixes. They are easy to develop, but they are also difficult to maintain and dangerous to have around. What happens if the server crashes the day that the one person who knows all the little secrets is on vacation? It is a much better practice to formalize important processes and distribute that information to all involved. That way, there are no misunderstandings about how things are done.

## ACTION ITEM: INFORMAL PROCESSES

Ask workflow participants about their informal processes. In every facility, no matter how small, there are workarounds to common problems and undocumented procedures to deal with exception cases. Any business analyst eliciting the common workflow should also discuss their uncommon and informal workflows with process participants. The types of steps that many media workers take in their day-to-day actions can often be a surprise!

BPM helps to reduce these informal processes by providing users with the right way to do a particular business task. Perhaps the organically developed workaround *should* be the formal process to handle that situation! But it should definitely be captured and available as a resource for all those who participate in the process, and not left up to hearsay and water-cooler talk.

If an enterprise does decide to implement process orchestration to streamline the execution of processes (and every enterprise should at the very least consider implementing it), then that business "automation" can bring about its own efficiencies. Processes will run more smoothly if no participant in the process has to worry about what happens next in the process and a software version of the process running on a middleware layer routes all of the important data to the next stage automatically. Orchestration engines can pull data from any point in the process and provide it for later steps. If this is done then users do not have perform unnecessary steps such as gathering data from different sources or distributing it to all of the other members of a team or department — the software architecture can do that automatically.

## WHAT NOT TO DO: APPLY AUTOMATION EVERYWHERE

Automation cannot be applied everywhere. The worst-case scenario is a world where users are trapped in the processes that were initially set up, with no leeway to make ad hoc changes or to address exception cases. It should be obvious to all that the benefits of BPM are felt most when they are applied to all places where they are needed, and *only* to the places where they are needed. There is no sense in "fixing" processes using process orchestration and automation where the process is not broken and enough visibility exists.

Finally, having formalized and well-defined processes in an enterprise is useful when considering expansion or re-engineering of the underlying system. Why? Because a formalized process is basically an established use case of the system! It describes exactly how users take advantage of a system's functionality and how the system is expected to react in different scenarios. Having a set of formalized processes around an integrated architecture gives the integrator a huge jumpstart in development or the creation of RFP's for vendors. Media enterprises should be looking for ways to formalize their processes up front for exactly these reasons. BPM envisions a world in which requests for proposed work contain pages and pages of process diagrams that dictate how the system is to be used. With some of the process representation standards discussed in Section 6.3.4.1 (such as BPMN), these diagrams could even provide executable logic for development or testing!

## 6.2 WORKFLOW ANALYSIS

The benefits of BPM are not fully realized without effective analysis of what actually goes on (and what should go on) in a facility. After all, the "B" in BPM stands for "business"! So, the best place to begin an in-depth look at Business Process Management is by discussing the first step in the BPM cycle: analysis of workflow and business processes.

There is no real way for a business analyst hoping to create an effective BPM solution to do so without first talking to the ultimate users of that solution. This may take some time to do (which initially bothers many enterprises that are looking for a fast turnaround), but is incredibly important, and the time spent on business analysis will be returned with interest through the efficiencies gained. BPM, like SOA, is a top-loaded methodology that requires a lot of work up front before much benefit is felt, but will bring more benefit to an enterprise later than more evenly distributed methodologies. An enterprise should commit to a certain amount of elicitation and planning to ensure an effective solution.

The first step in business process analysis is choosing the right stakeholders to drive business detail into the workflow. This book does not delve deeply into the ins and outs of making that choice, but there are countless business books out there that do. The short reason is that much of the detail of who to talk to and what to talk about is specific to the enterprise in question. A much more interesting and generally applicable question is: Once processes are elicited, how can they be captured and analyzed? There are BPM tools that provide modeling and simulation capabilities for just this reason!

## 6.2.1 Business Modeling and Simulation

When an end user is describing his or her workflow to a business analyst, how does that really look on paper? Everyone has seen process models in an industrial engineering textbook as a way to explain the flow of computer code, a script for a telemarketer, perhaps even as a description of workflow in the M&E industry! These models have tasks, links between the tasks that give them an order and causality, decision points that may change the flow of the tasks, and maybe even other features and callouts.

There are other features to process models that the best practices of BPM would have an enterprise consider. For example, swimlanes are a way to easily capture roles and responsibilities in a process. They also serve to highlight the all-important points of trade off in a process; for example, when the production department is done with a media asset and hands it off to post-production for processing. Swimlanes are especially useful during this first elicitation phase of a BPM project, because they allow end users to easily see what their responsibility is when providing the business analyst with real-time feedback on the accuracy of the process models as they are built. Swimlanes also "force" an enterprise to consider whose responsibility a given task is. After all, that task has got to go in *one* of the swimlanes. If a department or user is unsure about the delegation of responsibility for a given task, that is a red flag that signals the need for process formalization and perhaps even change. A swimlane example is shown in Fig. 6-6.

One could use a simple presentational program like Microsoft Visio™ to capture this sort of data in an enterprise. Everyone has seen the capabilities of such a program and the types of documents that can be produced. These types of programs are useful for conveying information to users (for example, if it was desired to post one on the wall of a facility to inform employees of what they should be doing), but they do not include any analysis tools and they do not create processes that can be understood and run by BPM process orchestration engines. There are other, BPM-specific modeling tools out there that can do these things, and most feature all sorts of additional bells and whistles to add to a process analyst's toolbox.

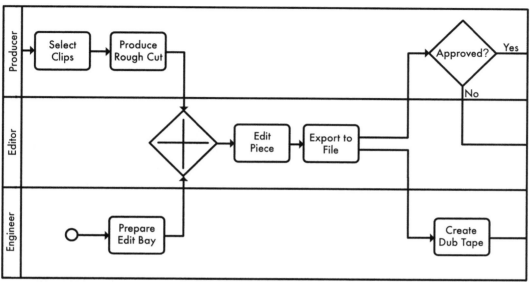

**FIGURE 6-6** A simple process model featuring tasks, links, decisions, and swimlanes. Swimlanes highlight divisions of responsibility in a process, whether they are between the user, department, or facility.

One thing that these tools capture very well is the non-process-related metadata in a workflow. Simply drawing labeled boxes and lines on a piece of paper does not easily leave an analyst with any way to capture durations, costs, or other restrictions. In much the same way as many project management tools do, process modeling programs feature ways to dive into particular tasks and provide that additional detail; a detail that is very useful in process analysis. The types of data that might be captured in such a way include:

- Temporal data — task durations, timeframes, business hours
- Resource data — what is needed for each task, man-hours of work, utilization
- Cost data — task cost, resource costs, process expenses and revenues
- Business classifications — organizational groupings of resources, task and process distinctions (e.g., jurisdictional)
- Exception cases — points where a process often encounters breaks, methods to undo a given task
- Miscellaneous restrictions — things to consider for each task and resource

## CASE STUDY

### Using BPM for Technology Selection

A network affiliate wishes to design and implement a tapeless workflow for the production of a new local program. The station begins not by choosing technology, but by doing a business process analysis of how they want to produce the show. Business analysts sit down with different stakeholders at all levels of the process to determine the optimal workflow in each department and at each level. Because this is a new (or "to be") process, there is no existing process with which to compare, so the business analysts are able to combine the information elicited into the ideal workflow for that station. The business process is again presented back to the affiliate, whose feedback further refines the final product.

After the business process is completed, the station uses the use cases contained therein to select the technology that best suits their needs. They decide on the right type of acquisition equipment and a collaborative editing and asset management solution that will allow them to most closely follow their ideal processes. The new show is a success!

Besides process representation, another area where business process modeling tools provide a lot of value to an enterprise is process analysis. Many tools feature ways to statically analyze a process (e.g., number of man-hours allocated to a specific resource), and many feature ways to dynamically analyze a process; that is, simulate it. Simulation can be a perfect way to determine whether or not a process change will work in the context of an enterprise's existing processes. By setting up initial conditions and accurately capturing the workflow as it is carried out in a facility, a simulation tool can provide information about what the state of the facility will be like in a day, a week, a month, or a year. It is a valuable tool for a process analyst to have in his or her belt. It is also really cool. However, simulation is not appropriate for every process analysis situation.

The use of simulation tools is most appropriate in scenarios with fixed boundaries and established business goals. A perfect example of this is the "what if" situation. If a facility has a set of established and formalized business processes in place and a set of fixed business goals (such as a budget to remain under or a fixed time frame to accomplish work within), a simulation tool can be used to determine the effect that a process or system change would have on the status quo. For example, how much faster could a facility publish media to a Web site if they purchased an extra transcoding engine? How much money is saved by outsourcing a particular task instead of doing it in-house? How much faster can the assets get out the door if the executive producer's approval is only required for flagged material as opposed to all material? These sorts of questions can be answered by altering the process and running a simulation. Simulation, therefore, is well suited to a trial-and-error method of solution development.

Simulation is *not* useful in scenarios that are open-ended or ill-defined. In other words, simulation cannot be used to discover business goals in a facility. A business analyst, for example, could not use simulation tools (as they exist today) to determine the cheapest way for a news organization to produce the news given a set of restrictions. Trial-and-error might be used to find the cheapest of a set of alternatives, but no tool in existence today allows a user to click a button and have the process self-optimize. While this would be a neat trick, the moral of the story here is that the enterprise itself has the best idea of what makes a process better; simulation cannot provide that idea to the enterprise. Luckily, in most cases, the players in an enterprise often already have ideas about how to approach improvement that simply need some testing through simulation.

## CASE STUDY

### Using Simulation to Improve Processes

The graphics department of a major cable network is unsure about the best ways to add efficiency into their processes. They decide to commission a workflow analysis that will determine the best places for improvement. Business analysts sit down with stakeholders from within and outside the department to elicit the existing graphics process (the "as is" process). This information is confirmed with the network, and then used as the basis for a number of "what if" simulations.

Each simulation tests a specific condition that might improve the processes at the network. Three simulations are found to have a positive impact, so they are tested on the elicited process at once. The results are shared with the network, which decides to implement all three improvements over the course of the next year.

What follows is a handful of business process modeling tools at the time of publication that provide all or most of the capability described in this section. The IT industry, like the M&E industry, is an ephemeral beast, so any thorough exploration of process modeling tools should be conducted anew. Simply putting "BPM modeling tool" into a search window should return ample list of results. The list in Table 6-1, however, is a good start.

## 6.2.2  The Ten Commandments of Workflow Analysis

Even with a fancy BPM modeling tool, business process analysis is not simply about plugging data into a computer and getting an answer out the other side. Acquiring the proper modeling tools and knowing how to use them is only half the battle. Having a successful BPM project also means understanding the business processes being managed, effectively using the tools to capture and formalize these processes, and knowing what to do with the processes after they have been captured. Much like effective SOA development, BPM is as much of an art form as it is a science. However, in what may possibly

**TABLE 6-1**

A Partial List of Available BPM Business Modeling and Simulation Tools

TIBCO Business Studio

IBM WebSphere Business Process Modeler

Savvion Process Modeler

Oracle Business Process Simulator

BEA AquaLogic BPM

EMC Documentum Process Simulator

SAP NetWeaver

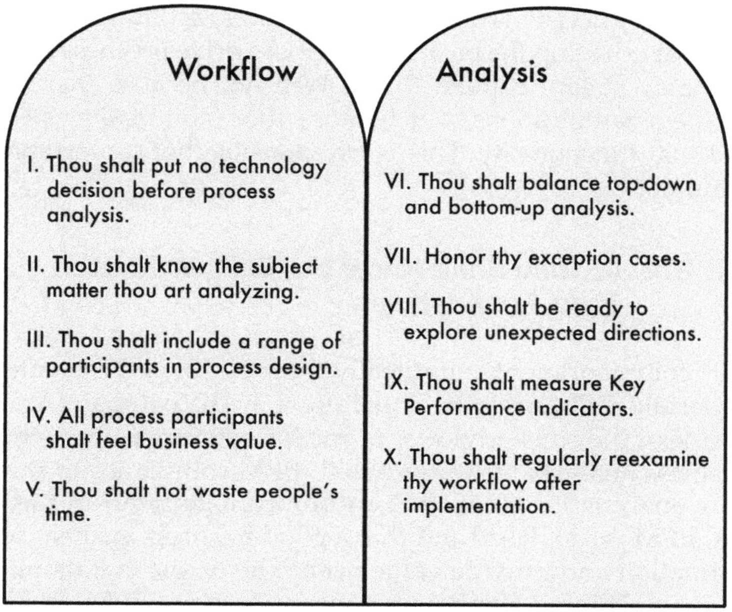

**FIGURE 6-7**  The ten commandments of workflow analysis.

be the most straightforward advice in this entire book, this section presents ten "commandments" of process modeling and analysis, shown in Fig. 6-7, that *all* media enterprises should follow when undertaking a BPM initiative. Business analysts and managers alike should learn and follow these best practices, because failure to do so will likely lead to BPM disaster.

### 6.2.2.1  I. Thou Shalt Put No Technology Decision before Process Analysis

The biggest message of BPM (and of SOA) is clear: the business comes first. Making technology decisions based on features, prices, or vendor relationships is a surefire way to end up mired in a workflow spider web. This lesson has been talked about in recent years with the explosion of workflow-related tools in the media industry, but it is the first lesson of BPM and should not be overlooked.

Business goals (what an enterprise wants to do) drive business processes (how the enterprise wants to do it), which drives technology decisions (what works in the way the enterprise wants to work). Having technology decisions drive business processes puts an enterprise in danger of also having the business processes drive business goals. A TV station may stream content to the Web not because they analyzed the business ramifications, but because their automation system already had that functionality. This is irresponsible but, unfortunately, far too common.

### 6.2.2.2 II. Thou Shalt Know the Subject Matter Thou Art Analyzing

This commandment is not really directed toward the enterprises that undertake BPM projects; hopefully a media company knows its own business. No, this advice is to media enterprises that choose to hire business analysts or contract with BPM companies to provide workflow analysis for them. It is an unfortunate trend in the IT industry that BPM is a skill set, and that a good business analyst can come into a situation and provide value even if he or she is unfamiliar with the territory. This is a dangerous concept, because BPM should be driven by those that drive the business itself.

Horror stories of IT analysts coming into a media enterprise and getting the business process wrong are far too common. Common symptoms of a process design that breaks this commandment are mixed levels of detail (having a highly technical, detailed step immediately followed by a wide-reaching task encompassing multiple users), forced process formalization (in areas where processes are more fluid and organic), and ignored exception cases (see Commandment VII). Media enterprises should do themselves a favor and ensure that process analysis is done by media professionals that know and understand at least the basics of BPM.

### 6.2.2.3 III. Thou Shalt Include a Range of Participants in Process Design

Business processes are best when they are cross-departmental and cover many areas of concern. They should represent the holistic view of the enterprise, unhindered by any particular technology, silo, or perspective. This is why it is so important to include every type of process participant when eliciting and analyzing workflow. When documenting a mastering process, a business analyst should be sure to ask each class of contributor — producers, color correctors, telecine operators, storage administrators, etc. — what their role in the process is and how they view the process as a whole.

This is not to say that every last participant needs to be interrogated, but that a thorough process analysis covers all bases. There may be organically developed, undocumented workarounds at the lowest levels of a process that are the key to process efficiency on the highest levels. If a business analyst only talks to the managers of a given department or organization, these crucial details are easily missed. This means more time spent in process elicitation, but with greater payback.

### 6.2.2.4  IV. All Process Participants Shalt Feel Business Value

This commandment is arguably the most difficult of all of the best practices in this section. It is clear that the types of business processes that are most likely to succeed when implemented in a given facility are those that help everyone. The number one reason that formalized processes fail in an enterprise is simple: people just do not follow them. This is often because the individual contributors to a process are not given enough impetus to contribute. If a process dictates that an editor will export completed projects to two different folders and log metadata inside a Web-based form when done with a session, it better be easy for that editor to do those things and he or she should feel some business value from these actions. For example, perhaps the Web-based form has information about upcoming tasks, and by logging specific metadata, that editor can see relevant, up-to-date statistics about work being completed. If it just feels like busy work, it will not get done.

Many times it is simply impossible to provide enhanced business value across the board. For example, if a redesigned ingest process requires that a shipping department fill out additional details upon receiving a new batch of tapes to provide later workers with more effective information about their workload, there is very little that can be done to get the shipping department to care about those additional details. In cases where busy work is unavoidable, good BPM dictates that the busy work should not be necessary for process success. Business analysts should ensure that the data necessary to complete a task is available in multiple locations, just in case someone neglects to fill out a form in a portal. As long as everything possible is done to streamline the flow of information, the process will succeed.

### 6.2.2.5  V. Thou Shalt Not Waste People's Time

This commandment is a strong message to those business analysts out there who have fully embraced the fact that BPM is a front-loaded methodology that requires a commitment to process elicitation: Do not unnecessarily drag out this process! BPM initiatives are only tactical goals of an organization in the most dire of circumstances. More often than not, they are implemented to address a long-term strategic goal of increasing workflow efficiency. This means that all of those process participants included in process design have daily workloads to get to. Regardless of the current state of the business processes in an enterprise, the people most crucial to changing that state are the ones knee-deep in the processes every day, and that fact should be respected by business analysts that hope to elicit useful information out of process participants.

### 6.2.2.6  VI. Thou Shalt Balance Top-Down and Bottom-Up Analysis

Top-down analysis is starting with the high-level business goals and, from there, deriving lower-level processes. Bottom-up analysis is starting with the desk procedures carried out by individual process participants and, from there, deriving higher level processes. These two are shown in Fig. 6-8. Saying that a good analysis balances both top-down and bottom-up process development is not contradicting Commandment I (business comes before technology) because low-level processes are not technology driven. They are user driven. They represent the way that the individual users want to do their work. This is an important perspective that should be considered during process design.

A good workflow analysis process is more "outside-in." It starts by examining the high-level business goals of the workflow thereby identifying the highest level processes. But, before getting mired in the middle processes that may or may not be the right way to achieve those high-level goals, a business analyst should also examine the best and most efficient way that individual contributors do their work. If a

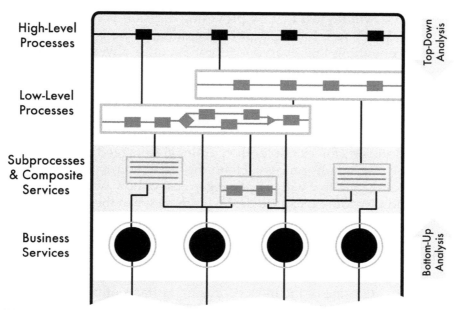

**FIGURE 6-8**   A balance of top-down and bottom-up process analysis is important to fully capture the entire spectrum of what goes on in a facility. Ignoring one or the other will lead to a set of one-sided processes that will either not accomplish the goals of the enterprise or not describe an achievable workflow.

line manager knows the best way that his or her department gets its job done, that point of view should not get superseded by what gets filtered down from above.

### 6.2.2.7  VII. Honor Thy Exception Cases

No process, no matter how well thought out, is perfect. There will always be some unknown that must get worked into the design, or some unforeseen circumstance that causes participants to develop a workaround. Exception cases are unavoidable. Formalized processes are much better at dealing with day-to-day workflow than informal processes mostly because informal processes treat every day like an exception case. At least by formalizing a process the enterprise gets the bulk of the use cases out of the way, leaving only a few straggling situations as exception cases.

While it is impossible to capture every single exception case in a process model, it is possible to capture the bulk of them. A good business analyst will do just that by providing decision points and additional task details to inform exception handling. There is, however, always that one thing that everyone forgot about. It always happens that, a few months after implementing a new process in an organization, someone discovers some use case that was left out. The key to designing a process that deals with these unknowns is to make sure there are always multiple ways to achieve any business goal. If a process only facilitates task completion by scanning a media asset tag barcode at a workstation, for example, then a single untagged asset could bring down the whole process! Honoring exception cases means understanding that they will happen regardless of how water-tight a process is and providing means to deal with them when they do.

## CLASSIFYING EXCEPTION CASES

Exception cases are some of the most confusing artifacts of process analysis. They will crop up in nearly any process, and, if not handled properly, could cause a great deal of grief. Even though each individual exception case is unique to a given process, there are still general classes of exception cases that can be defined to provide scope to a business analyst's quest to ensure minimal impact of exceptions on processes. These categories are:

- Technical problems — failure of a technology component in the process
- Missing data — the absence of one or more prerequisite pieces of information into the process
- Time crunch — the process is not provided ample time to complete
- Resource crunch — the process is not provided ample resources to complete
- New business requirements — the process that must be completed to meet business goals is different or altered from the one defined

A good business analyst will consider all five categories of exception cases when designing a new business process for implementation in an enterprise.

### 6.2.2.8 VIII. Thou Shalt be Ready to Explore Unexpected Directions

The lesson of this commandment is that an enterprise should not take anything for granted when considering new business processes. If a facility has worked one way for 20 years and is looking for ways to increase efficiency, the stakeholders in that process should be willing to sacrifice the way it has always been done to facilitate the necessary changes. This best practice especially applies to those enterprises or managers that create unnecessary and conflicting business goals for a workflow analysis initiative. For example, by saying "We have to reduce costs around here as much as possible, but we cannot touch the shared storage system because everyone already knows how to use it," a manager is not considering all business process options. Perhaps there is a way to replace the storage technology, train the users, and still cut costs more effectively than keeping it. By setting arbitrary rules and conditions, an enterprise is not open-minded to change and therefore will not be prepared for necessary change.

### 6.2.2.9  IX. Thou Shalt Measure KPIs

One of BPM's big selling points is visibility into a facility's inner workings, and one of the main ways in which that visibility is achieved is through the use of KPIs. KPIs are discussed in detail in the previous section, but they are also included here to make the point that KPIs are always a good idea. Even if the BPM technology necessary to automatically measure KPIs is in place in an enterprise, the work done to identify them and associate business goals with real, quantitative numbers is not wasted work. Defining and measuring (manually, if necessary) KPIs allows a facility to know when it is meeting its business goals. Every business process that is defined in an enterprise should also include the KPIs that indicate that the process is healthy and working. Without KPIs, no one is able to tell whether a BPM initiative is a success or a failure, so no one will know whether it was money wasted or a process to be repeated. KPIs provide irrefutable facts around the quality of a business process, and should be a part of every business process analysis.

### 6.2.2.10  X. Thou Shalt Regularly Reexamine Thy Workflow after Implementation

This final commandment is, to a certain extent, the most important of all. Enterprises change and evolve as business goals and external influences change. Using a formalized but outdated business process to accomplish the work of a facility is worse than using an informal process, because it forces users to work against the goals of an enterprise instead of, at the

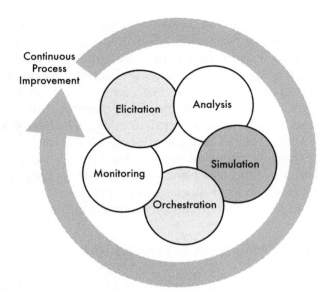

**FIGURE 6-9** Continuous Process Improvement is a cycle of process analysis that ensures that the business processes executed in a facility are always germane to the business goals of that facility. It is a cyclical methodology that requires the establishment of a permanent CPI team in an enterprise.

very least, organically responding to them. However, far more effective than either of these is an up-to-date formalized process. Therefore, a business process should not exist in a vacuum. It should be a part of a comprehensive BPM program that dictates regular reconsideration of workflow and a policy of Continuous Process Improvement (CPI).

CPI is depicted in Fig. 6-9. It is a term heard often as part of the BPM message. It is a methodology that forces an enterprise to reconsider its processes on a regular basis to ensure that they always remain applicable to the business goals of the enterprise. To work, CPI requires the establishment of a permanent team to kick off process analysis. The logistics behind building and maintaining a CPI policy in a media enterprise are more thoroughly considered in Chapter 8.

## 6.3 PROCESS ORCHESTRATION

After an enterprise formalizes their processes, there is the question of what to do with them. Certainly, one option is "nothing"; simply documenting the processes in a manner available to all process participants and referring users to that documentation would go far to increase efficiency and reduce confusion. BPM best practices, however, call for so much more than this.

The other end of the spectrum is to put all of these processes into a process orchestration engine, running on top of an SOA, and have a middleware layer that routes all messages automatically and calls services, many of which carry out tasks without human intervention. This is an ideal, but it may be a bit unrealistic for many areas of the M&E industry, especially as media requires so much human craftwork. The best solution for a particular media enterprise is somewhere in between, and each enterprise may be ready for more or less process orchestration. However, if the transition to digital has taught the media industry anything at all, it is that all media facilities could use at least some orchestration.

## 6.3.1 The Process Layer

This section looks at the BPM technologies that enable process orchestration in a facility. This is an area in BPM that has become somewhat inseparably linked with SOA technology, because the best way to orchestrate processes is on top of an SOA middleware layer. In fact, the SOA layered architecture discussed in Chapter 3 shows business processes in a layer by themselves — a process layer (see Fig. 6-10). These processes exist as software constructs within a process orchestration engine that is part of the SOA middleware layer, but the process layer is a logical division between the services that do the work and the workflows that arrange these services. In an SOA, it is possible to change processes without changing services, and possible to change services without changing processes. That interface point — where the process calls the interface presented by the service — is the only thing that affects both layers.

The process layer in an enterprise SOA architecture may be logically independent from other layers in the architecture, but it cannot exist on its own. It is intimately linked to the lower layers in the sense that these layers must provide an environment in which business processes can run. The SOA middleware layer provides that environment through the inclusion of process orchestration engines. These engines may run in an application server environment or may simply communicate directly with the more traditional middleware components (middleware is explained thoroughly in Chapter 4).

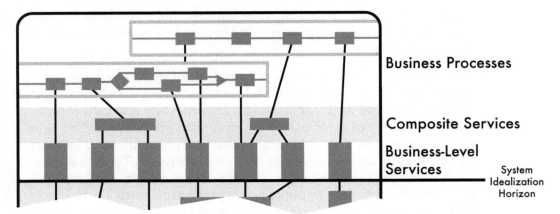

**Business Processes**

**Composite Services**

**Business-Level
Services**                              System
                                     Idealization
                                     Horizon

**FIGURE 6-10**   The layered model of Service-Oriented Architecture features a process layer at the
very top. Business processes are the ultimate business abstraction in SOA, providing users with the
maximum amount of freedom to describe their real workflows, independent from underlying
technology.

This does not mean, however, that the processes themselves are just
another middleware construct. They are at a much more business-
centric level than the communication-focused middleware layer. Some
SOA theorists even consider process orchestration to be another type
of service that hangs off of middleware and gets quite a few messages
delivered to it (since services use the process to determine where messages go next). For the purposes of this explanation, it is enough to
consider process orchestration as occurring at the very core of the middleware, such that every message is routed through a process before
reaching its destination. This vision of process orchestration stays true
to the idea that the businesspeople in an enterprise have control —
through processes — of how communication flows in a facility.

The relationship that business processes have with SOA services is
much less complex than the relationship they have with a middleware
layer. Because processes link and orchestrate business tasks, it is easy
to envision a world where every task in a process corresponds to a
service operation at the business service layer. This is nearly accurate,
and is only complicated by the fact that processes *themselves* may have
service interfaces and present themselves as services to be orchestrated by other processes! This is the idea of a subprocess, and it is one
that is crucial to process reusability in an enterprise. A process integrator might define a batch of processes that are used by many higher

level processes. These subprocesses then run in a process orchestration engine and become highly reusable assets for a facility.

## 6.3.2  Architectural Considerations for Processes

So, tasks in a process might be implemented by business services directly, or they might be implemented by subprocesses that orchestrate other services and processes. This is not the only concern an integrator has when implementing process orchestration in a facility, however. There is also the big question of whether to implement a task automatically or through human intervention, as well as how to configure processes and services to take full advantage of the features of a process orchestration engine.

Full automated orchestration of all business processes in a facility is rarely condoned, and does not make much sense in the common case. There must be some breakdown between those tasks in a process that are procedural (that is, automated or carried out by services) and human tasks. Chapter 3 discusses this same dichotomy regarding service design, and in fact the two decisions overlap quite a bit in enterprise architecture design. Process orchestration adds a quirk, however, in that many process orchestration engines (because they provide visibility) will have some method of directly interacting with users through notifications or portals. These routes can be considered for human tasks that are basic and may not need the benefit of a full business service interface (such as decision approvals). All procedural tasks and the rest of the human tasks should go through service interfaces to implementations at the application layer. For human tasks, it is best to provide the user with as much process context as possible so that he or she may work in full knowledge of process state. This context should be worked into the interface of all human tasks presented as business services.

## HUMAN VS. PROCEDURAL TASKS

It is important to classify tasks in a process appropriately. Tasks that are rote and unchanging are effective to automate procedurally, while tasks that require some level of craft or organic response should be handled by human participants. Table 6-2 shows some examples of each. When in doubt, make the task a human task.

**TABLE 6-2**
Examples of Human and Procedural Tasks

| Examples of human tasks | Examples of procedural tasks |
| --- | --- |
| • Edit an asset | • Transcode an asset |
| • Write a script | • Determine the availability of a resource |
| • Color correct a clip | • Ingest a media file |
| • Approve a rundown | • Distribute a rundown |
| • Enter descriptive asset metadata | • Populate asset metadata from an external source |

Another major architectural consideration for process integrators is the timeliness of a given business process. As discussed in Section 6.3.4, the major process orchestration technologies are able to provide different types of functionality for different types of processes. One factor is how long an enterprise expects a process to take. In the case that a process is short-running (such as a completed edit session checking off an item in a checklist and sending out a round of notifications), then it can be streamlined so that it leaves a smaller "footprint" in the SOA middleware. This has performance benefits for a facility, but also probably means that there is no access to particular functionality; namely process state visibility, but also (in many cases) process persistence. This means that if there is a system failure, that process could be dropped entirely. As mentioned, this type of configuration is best for short-running or highly componentized processes.

The long-running process is another category of business process to consider. A long-running process traditionally represents workflow that is heavily human-driven or extended over many hours, days, or months. A good example of a long-running process is the production of a news program or the ingest of a shipment of tapes. These processes will need the extra functionality provided by many process orchestration engines such as process state visibility and process persistence. These are the processes that managers are going to want to check up on to see how they are progressing, and so having a portal page that provides that functionality is incredibly beneficial to an enterprise (and reduces the number of phone calls from managers to their teams). Most enterprises find that the vast majority of business processes orchestrated are long-running processes. Short-running processes only come into play in highly transactional or subprocess situations. Long-running processes tend to better represent the workflows as envisioned by the users, although short-running processes have their place as well.

## LONG-RUNNING VS. SHORT-RUNNING PROCESSES

In process orchestration terms, a "long-running" process means one that conserves state and can be paused for long periods of time. A "short-running" process is one that must complete after it begins with no downtime. This is a technical distinction for process orchestration engines. Some examples of each are provided in Table 6-3. When in doubt, implement a process as long-running to ensure that no delays will cause the process to fail.

**TABLE 6-3**
Examples of Short- and Long-Running Processes

| Examples of long-running processes | Examples of short-running processes |
| --- | --- |
| • Ingest an asset | • Transfer a file |
| • Generate show schedule | • Prepare schedule for distribution |
| • Post-production | • Distribute color-corrected asset |
| • Pre-production | • Notify producers |

The discussion of long-running processes (especially regarding process persistence) brings up another important process orchestration consideration: managing process instances. A facility must manage running processes in two ways. First, after a process has been defined and implemented in a process orchestration engine, a facility must be able to inspect, start, and stop every single instance of that process. This means having both an administrative view into process orchestration and a manager's portal for process visibility. However, the other major process management issue in BPM is the management of process templates as they are rolled out and upgraded. When a new version of a process is developed and implemented, the last thing an enterprise wants is to cut off all running processes mid-stream to push this new version to the facility. No, the process orchestration engine must be able to handle tiered deployments of processes, allowing all running processes to complete using an older version of the process while all new processes make use of the new version. Those implementing process orchestration should choose an engine that facilitates this easy rollout of process upgrades.

The final architectural consideration for process orchestration is how a facility will connect and expose its systems to processes for orchestration. Obviously, the strong preference of the authors of this book is to expose systems as services using SOA technology, so Chapter 5 covers many ways to go about defining services that can be utilized by business processes. One of the big discussions in SOA, though, is how best to expose the business functionality of applications as services. Specifically (with regards to BPM), when an enterprise application has some amount of workflow orchestration already built in — a number of media vendors are providing workflow tools in their applications — how do those workflow engines interact with external business process orchestration?

The best answer to this question is that external process orchestration handles business workflow whenever possible. By using built-in workflow tools to "pass-through" base functionality to an application interface (shown in Fig. 6-11), an enterprise can externalize workflow orchestration out of an enterprise application and into a BPM process layer. Many times this will make workflow changes much easier to implement and much more visible to the rest of the enterprise. However, like most things in SOA and BPM, passing through workflow has its benefits and negatives.

Passing through functionality is especially good to do when an enterprise wants or needs to swap out components in the workflow with those not provided by the implementing application or add new components not provided. It is much easier to plug service calls into a process orchestration engine than it is to custom integrate into an application's workflow orchestration engine. Also, passing through makes sense when the core functionality provided by the enterprise app is already fairly business-oriented and could be orchestrated by

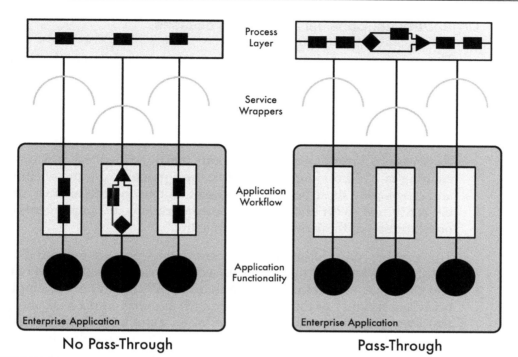

**FIGURE 6-11**  "Pass-through" workflow in enterprise applications can be used to externalize the business process capabilities of an application into a BPM process layer. This should be done on business processes where an enterprise wishes to use other services not provided by the application or on business processes that experience a high amount of change.

business-level processes without needing re-wrapping or further abstraction. If the core functionality is instead fairly low-level, perhaps the application workflow solution could be used to present higher level functionality to a process orchestration engine instead of just blindly passing that functionality through. Section 3.4 further details the ins and outs of wrapping enterprise applications like this.

Passing through application functionality is bad, however, when any one use of that particular application would require multiple calls to those functions. The idea with BPM process orchestration is to orchestrate business workflows, not simply to put low-level technical workflows into a fancy, expensive engine. Listen to SOA: leave the technical details behind the service interface. If technical details are slipping into business processes, it is a red flag to an organization that the services and processes used were not designed effectively.

### 6.3.3  Organizational Considerations in Processes

The architecture of a business process solution is only half of the story, of course. Just as SOA brings business focus through standardized interfaces and service layers, BPM is an attempt to bring focus to the business issues in an enterprise by allowing business processes to direct technical communication. Therefore, even if a BPM architecture is implemented in the best way possible for a facility, it is still useless (or worse, counterproductive) without the right business processes running in it. Section 6.2 discussed the best practices around eliciting and developing these business processes, but an enterprise must also be concerned with the business considerations of implementing orchestration of these processes in a facility.

The number one question when considering process orchestration should be: Where is it needed? This section has discussed the benefits and challenges associated with an automated BPM solution, but simply because a facility has the capacity for such automation does not mean that every single process should run in an automated fashion. First, automated orchestration amplifies the effects of poorly designed processes, such that even the smallest incorrect detail in a workflow becomes a major headache when it happens every single time that particular workflow is executed. Even in a facility with perfectly designed business processes that accurately reflect workflow and successfully capture all exception cases (a pipe dream, to be sure!), implementing automated process orchestration across the board may cause resistance to change or dissatisfaction with existing processes. The worst feeling a media worker can have is feeling constrained by the systems and processes used. A BPM solution should enable functionality, not disable it. A process integrator should never impose unnecessary structure where none is needed.

## WHAT NOT TO DO: RIGID PROCESSES

Do not create unnecessary rigidity in business processes. Every business process has exception cases to it. Even business processes that account for most exception cases will miss a few. The perfect business process is one that is flexible enough to respond to both the common exception cases (through explicit fault workflows and procedures) and the uncommon ones (through the use of human intervention and "sanity checks").

Automated process orchestration is good in many situations, however. Short-running processes especially benefit from this. Situations where a single event should cause a number of steps to be taken call for such orchestration. On top of that, long-running processes that have fixed structures for a reason — strict industry or corporate oversight, products that can be easily ruined by incorrect processing, or heavy interaction with outside parties — could be orchestrated in an automated fashion to enforce the policies of the enterprise. Full process orchestration can be a very useful tool when it prevents mistakes without also preventing workarounds.

The most common case, however, is a hybrid of orchestrated and non-orchestrated processes. This situation would occur when a long-running process, expertly designed, is simplified by the removal of detail or the lumping together of several steps into an "orchestratable" process to be run in BPM process orchestration software. This way, humans have more control over the natural flow of the process, because sections that are heavily human-driven remain so. But, the orchestratable process still contains enough detail to provide visibility to producers, managers, etc., and the automated processing of messages allows the information and media hand-offs that occur between process participants to happen in the background. A business analyst should still capture these business processes in detail, but a process integrator should consider creating a new version of the process to smooth orchestration.

Another case to consider is the specific situation where a facility has two very similar processes running in slightly different contexts. For example, ingesting tapes that come in from the field at the beginning of the day may be nearly identical to ingesting commercials coming in on tapes in the middle of the day, with a few notable differences. Similar processes may be running on different services or systems, in different departments, or just for different reasons. The best practice for an enterprise to follow here is to reuse whenever possible. If two similar processes can be broken down into a series of identical subprocesses with some differences in integration, those subprocesses can be reused wholesale. If this is not possible, then an enterprise should attempt to make the interfaces to these processes as close to identical as possible to facilitate agile substitution if desired later.

These and other solutions require solid enterprise governance. If departments are constantly squabbling over whose responsibility a particular process is, a truly horizontally integrated solution is difficult if not impossible. Good governance is the subject of Chapter 8.

## 6.3.4 Standards

An exploration of any new media or IT trend would not be complete without an in-depth discussion of the standards efforts moving forward in the area. BPM is no different, as there are two major standards that have been put forth to describe and orchestrate business processes. One, Business Process Execution Language (BPEL) is an effective and widespread way to capture and orchestrate processes, while the other, Business Process Modeling Notation (BPMN), really represents the future of BPM. BPM is unlike SOA in the fact that there are not a plethora of competing standards, and the ones that do exist are seeing widespread adoption with only a few vendor-specific quirks. Any thorough study of BPM requires in-depth knowledge of both of these standards.

### 6.3.4.1 BPMN

BPMN will seem the more familiar standard to most, so it will be discussed first. It provides a palette of standardized icons that describe a process in a graphical way. BPMN is incredibly useful to process analysts and integrators alike because it presents a business process in such a way that it is easily understandable by process participants unfamiliar with the standard, but also includes restrictions on process design to ensure consistency across different processes. It is the *lingua franca* of process modeling, and many BPM tools out there today support it.

BPMN is currently in the hands of the Object Management Group (http://www.omg.org), the same group that pioneered the CORBA standard discussed in Chapter 3. It is used to capture the flow of tasks in a process, including decisions, branches, and (to a certain extent) stakeholders. It makes heavy use of swimlanes to denote task responsibility, and may even be used to document how messages move from system to system. The various BPMN elements are shown in Fig. 6-12.

A typical BPMN process begins with one or more "start" nodes and ends on one or more "end" nodes. In between, process flow can flow

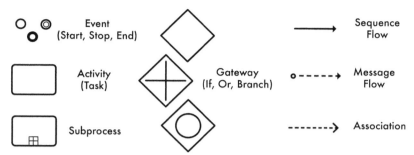

**FIGURE 6-12**  BPMN includes elements representing various aspects of business processes.

linearly or branch through decision blocks at points where the work-flow may change. Some common extensions to BPMN can even be used to represent exception cases or time-out situations. As this standard grows and evolves, there is the potential for creating very expressive processes that capture complex information in an enterprise.

### 6.3.4.2  BPEL

The other major process standard in the BPM space is BPEL. This standard is very different from BPMN and has been around a good deal longer. Even though they both capture business processes, BPEL attempts to accomplish a very different process than BPMN. While BPMN attempts to document processes in a human-digestible, easy-to-communicate way, BPEL documents processes in a programmatic, XML-based way so that they might be executed inside a process orchestration engine. A BPEL file is not a graphical depiction of tasks and process flow; it is many lines of task identifiers, links, and conditions, one after the other. BPEL is not pretty to look at, but it is effective at what it does: executing processes.

BPEL files are managed by process orchestration engines. A single file represents a process template from which many process instances can be created. A process instance may spin off messages to services or other middleware components, each of which is correlated to a particular point in the process of a particular image by the process orchestration engine. Its use of XML allows BPEL to be exchangeable between orchestration engines.

# DECONSTRUCTING A BPEL FILE

```
<?xml version="1.0" encoding="UTF-8"?>
<bpel:process name="sandwichProcess"
  targetNamespace="http://www.example.tv/sandwichProcess"
  xmlns:srv="http://www.example.tv/sandwichService"
  xmlns:bpel="http://schemas.xmlsoap.org/ws/2003/
     03/business-process/" />

<bpel:partnerLinks>
  <bpel:partnerLink name="sandwichService"
    partnerLinkType="srv:sandwichLT" />
  <bpel:partnerLink name="personService"
    partnerLinkType="srv:personLT" />
</bpel:partnerLinks>
```

Partner links identify services that can be called within the process.

```
<bpel:variables>
  <bpel:variable name="money" messageType="srv:moneyObj" />
  <bpel:variable name="newSandwich"
    messageType="srv:sandwichObj" />
  <bpel:variable name="boughtSandwich"
    messageType="srv:sandwichObj" />
  <bpel:variable name="satisfaction" messageType="srv:emotionObj" />
</bpel:variables>
```

Variables store business data to pass between steps.

```
<bpel:sequence>
  <bpel:receive partnerLink="personService"
    portType="srv:personPort"
    operation="srv:getSandwich"
    variable="money" />
  <bpel:flow>
    <bpel:invoke partnerLink="sandwichService"
      portType="srv:sandwichPort"
      operation="srv:selectSandwich"
      inputVariable="money"
      outputVariable="newSandwich" />
    <bpel:invoke partnerLink="sandwichService"
      portType="srv:sandwichPort"
      operation="srv:buySandwich"
      inputVariable="newSandwich"
      outputVariable="boughtSandwich" />
```

The invoke component calls a service synchronously.

```
    <bpel:invoke partnerLink="sandwichService"
      portType="srv:sandwichPort"
      operation="srv:eatSandwich"
      inputVariable="boughtSandwich"
      outputVariable="satisfaction" />
  </bpel:flow>
  <bpel:receive partnerLink="personService"
    portType="srv:personPort"
    operation="srv:getSandwich"
    variable="satisfaction" />
</bpel:sequence>
```

Process steps are arranged in a flow and called sequentially, although links can also be used to associate steps.

```
</bpel:process>
```

BPEL does require the use of other standards in an infrastructure to be put to use; namely, BPEL is dependent upon the WSDL standard discussed in Chapter 5 to identify service partners and send messages. The standard was originally submitted to OASIS in 2003 with the intention that it would support a Web services infrastructure and that is essentially how it exists today. However, some contemporary process orchestration engines essentially "wrap" BPEL processes to allow non-Web services communication in and out of the business process. Web services is the primary SOA standard, but even if it weren't, BPEL's dependence on WSDL would make a strong case for a Web services infrastructure.

Just as in BPMN, BPEL features a number of process components (listed in Table 6-4) to route and automate business processes. There are two "camps" of process components: those that are part of the OASIS standard (now at version 2.0 as of March 2008) and those that are common proprietary extensions by major vendors to flesh out the functionality of the BPEL language. The BPEL standard includes an ample amount of functionality, but many vendors have found that additional components help integrators when they are going for particular types of processes or process patterns. The danger here of course is that any deviation from the standard set renders a process incompatible with other vendors'

**TABLE 6-4**

A List of Standard and Common Proprietary BPEL Process Components

| Standard BPEL components | Common proprietary BPEL components |
| --- | --- |
| • Sequence | • Human task |
| • If | • Custom code |
| • While | • Notify |
| • Repeat until | • Subprocess |
| • For each | • Timeouts |
| • Assign | • Documentation |
| • Invoke | • Expiration or time scoping |
| • Receive | • Atomic transactions |
| • Reply | |
| • Wait | |
| • Fault | |
| • Compensate | |

orchestration engines and therefore less agile. This concern must be weighed against the benefit that any proprietary extensions might bring, but integrators should err on the side of standardization.

The standard process components in BPEL mirror those available in BPMN. Components in BPEL are referred to as "activities," and can represent almost any sequence of tasks. The main components are "invoke" activities, which send out a service call and await a response. Such calls can also be placed asynchronously using "receive" and "reply" activities. These three are the workhorses of BPEL, and any actual business processing that occurs in a business process happens using them. In addition, there are a number of ways to adjust the process flow using "if," "while," and "forEach" components. BPEL processes utilize variables to store XML values sent and received from tasks, so there are also components to assign and manage these variables.

Of course, any sufficiently popular standard will have a whole bevy of proprietary extensions that vendors create in the name of enhanced functionality. BPEL is no different. If anything, BPEL is worse than many standards because of its direct appeal to business users (aka the ones writing the checks), and so it is actually quite difficult to find a process orchestration vendor that does *not* include BPEL extensions. These various products all tend to offer similar extensions, however, which actually points to missing components in the BPEL standard. Additional functionality may be included in the next revision of the standard, but everyone knows how slow such processes are.

Human tasks or notifications are popular extensions. These will often interact with an e-mail client, portal, or task management system to get a process instance directly in front of a user's eyes. Direct adapters into business rules engines are also popular because many process orchestration vendors also offer business rules functionality whose use they want to encourage. Finally, many orchestration engines will feature some way to include small executable blocks of code in a BPEL process. These components allow integrators to put arbitrary functionality into their processes, which many consider to be a very good thing.

Service calls in BPEL processes are accomplished by defining partner links to Web services. These partners can be assigned to various tasks in the process, and the orchestration engine will make a service call to that partner when the task comes up in the sequence. As mentioned previously, these partner links must be to Web service enabled end-points; a dependency of BPEL. As a general rule, all work done in a BPEL process is through Web services, but the process just organizes and routes the message flow.

Many orchestration engines provide a way to use business rules to direct the flow of processes, even though these are proprietary extensions to the BPEL standard. This can be very useful, however, especially when particular decisions change based on the current state of the enterprise. For example, a business rule might dictate that all tapes flowing into a facility are QC'd and then approved by a producer. However, at a certain point, there might be too many tapes for the producer to review individually, creating a bottleneck. So, a process is designed with a decision point for whether or not the producer approval is required. The high water mark after which tapes are only QC'd once should be a tunable metric. With business rules in an orchestration engine, it is!

## IMPORTANT NOTE

The main difference between business rules engines and orchestration engines is this: business rules engines are heavily transactional in nature while orchestration engines are process driven. A business rules engine will take in information and provide back information immediately, while orchestration engines may take some time and use several services possibly with complex logic to gather the information to provide back.

There are a number of shortcomings to BPEL, to be sure. Certainly, useful components such as business rules, human tasks, and code snippets might improve the standard, and its reliance on the WSDL standard is also limiting. However, more generally, it is found that the structure of BPEL is just too convoluted for those users that need to understand it most — the business users. In reality, writing out a BPEL process is too detailed a task for a business analyst, but designing a BPEL process is too business-oriented a task for a programmer. It is a puzzling catch-22 for advocates of BPM — how to get the runtime reliability of an orchestration engine while still approachable to business users.

There must be another logical layer in place here or a way to go from the business concept to the process execution without having both in the same place. The solution here is possibly to move past BPEL as a standard at all! BPM is about the business, after all, not the technology. The rest of the IT industry seems to be starting to think this way as well. BPM evangelists are already flocking in droves to the newest and greatest of the business process standards: BPMN! Instead of writing out in an executable way all process details, BPMN is able to capture many important facets of a business process in an easily digestible format. This is preferable to the business users because they are able to make changes to processes quickly without having to think about the medium in which the process is represented as they design it.

Moving toward BPMN and away from BPEL as the primary BPM standard is also preferable to the programmers out there as well. BPMN is robust enough to capture many process details. It can then be transformed into whatever executable format an enterprise chooses! If a business prefers Enterprise Java classes, then the business process can be transformed into a Java framework for process execution. If a facility's middleware layer instead includes a BPEL orchestration engine, the BPMN model can be transformed into an executable BPEL process and orchestrated. BPEL then becomes just one option out of many, and the various IT vendors can have a field day providing proprietary extensions that are unique to their environment. No longer does the BPEL process need to be standardized and agile; that is now the role of the BPMN model.

Because of this movement toward BPMN, there have been a number of efforts to find a good way to import and export BPMN models from one enterprise to another. Perhaps the most promising at the time of this writing is the XML Process Definition Language (XPDL), which is an XML-based way to represent a BPMN process. That definition may seem very similar to the definition of BPEL, but instead of focusing on execution and service partners, XPDL simply focuses on turning a graphical representation of a process into exchangeable text. It is much simpler and more focused than BPEL, and can perfectly describe a BPMN model.

## 6.4 CONCLUSION

Business Process Management, like Service-Oriented Architecture, is an ethereal thing. BPM is not a comfortable space to traditional media engineers, who are much more at home when discussing specific technologies. Instead, BPM is the realm of the business user — someone who does not care as much about what is doing the work as about what work is done. However, it is increasingly important in today's world, as the focus of integration shifts to the business or process layer and not the application layer. BPM advocates a new way of thinking and a new way of integrating systems and (more important) people.

This chapter discussed both the BPM best practices that business analysts should follow when eliciting and designing business processes, and also the best practices and technologies that integrators should consider when implementing those processes in a realistic way within an enterprise. BPM is only as good as an organization makes it, but if ample time and interest is spent, then the results of a BPM effort will really pay for themselves and then some!

The future of BPM is hazy; perhaps the efforts of BPM advocates will create a whole new science of integration that launches a thousand different product lines and technologies. However, it is much more likely that the best practices of BPM will become so widespread and atomic that they will simply blend with the whole concept of "integration." The term "Business Process Management" may become passé, but the ideas will certainly live on in all enterprise integration projects.

## WHAT TO TELL YOUR BOSS

- BPM is a burgeoning field that helps to define and orchestrate business processes and workflows in an enterprise.
- BPM is heavily associated with SOA in common understanding, and many BPM tools use SOA technologies to enable their functionality.
- BPM provides agility and visibility to an organization through business process analysis techniques and orchestration technologies.
- There are a handful of popular BPM standards out there such as BPEL and BPMN.

Boss, did you buy this crazy coffee maker?

It has a portal that shows me peak performance and average cups consumed per hour!

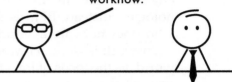

You've really taken to this whole BPM thing! But, our time and energy should be spent on the areas where BPM does the most good, like our production workflow.

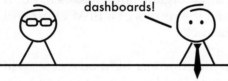

We'll get to that too. First, I've implemented a BPM dashboard that shows me the success rate and KPIs around all of our BPM projects... and then I'll make a dashboard of dashboards!

Slow down there, Cowboy.

# 7

# WHAT IS THE SERVICE-ORIENTED MEDIA ENTERPRISE?

The last few chapters of this book cover cutting-edge software architectural concepts concerning Service-Oriented Architecture (SOA) and Business Process Management (BPM). These concepts — however important to the Media & Entertainment (M&E) industry they may be — are generic enough to apply equally to a wide range of industries and applications. In other words, there is nothing particularly media-specific about SOA and BPM. While this book attempts to present these ideas from a media perspective, they are the same ideas that have been important to the IT industry over the past several years.

These ideas are important because the media industry faces many of the same challenges as the IT industry. The world of media, however, is distinctly separate from the world of IT. For every challenge and opportunity the two industries share, there are an equal number of challenges and opportunities unique to the M&E industry. There is certainly a great deal of overlap between the two (especially since the advent of digital production and distribution), which is why the concepts of SOA and BPM have such appeal to media professionals right out of the box. But there are also many differences.

Differences in culture, differences in schedule, even differences in the simple concept of time, all highlight the reasons that the M&E industry has remained consistent while the thriving IT industry has solved many of the long-standing problems of many other industries.

## CASE STUDY

### The Differences between IT and Ops/Engineering

One of the key issues that the media industry is facing today, particularly in broadcasting, is the lack of fresh engineering personnel joining organizations directly out of college. This, combined with a shifting skill set caused by more and more file-based technology adoption, means that a dramatic skills shortage is in the making. A major national broadcaster in Europe decided to proactively attempt to address this issue.

One solution examined was the possibility of using IT personnel to shift into engineering disciplines. Success in initial attempts at these transfers was hit and miss so it was decided to do a study to determine why this was the case.

Twenty-five people were transferred from engineering to IT and twenty-five were also transferred from IT to engineering. These staff were monitored over a year for key factors such as job performance and job satisfaction.

The results of the study were actually quite fascinating. Only a small number of staff (approximately 25%) were able to make the shift successfully between the two positions despite similarities in technical skill sets. This was true regardless of whether the person was originally from IT or from engineering.

There was a common trait seen in those who failed to make the switch. They were people who were really only comfortable with one paradigm of how to troubleshoot. Successful IT personnel took the time to examine methodically the root causes of the technical problems they faced and would work to try to ensure that the problems were not repeated. Successful engineering personnel were comfortable with quickly determining a workaround to keep a system functional and only secondarily attempted to ensure that the problem would not recur. They focused on keeping the system "on-air" using any means necessary.

Those that could work with either paradigm could switch between both roles more easily. The broadcaster ensured that future recruiting efforts would take into account these personality factors in addition to the technical ones.

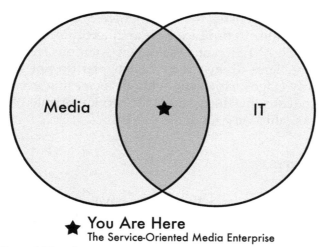

★ **You Are Here**
The Service-Oriented Media Enterprise

**FIGURE 7-1**   Media and IT each present their own unique challenges, but there is an area of synthesis addressed by the tenets of the Service-Oriented Media Enterprise.

Even looking at the concept of services in an SOA, one can see that many services necessary for basic functionality in an M&E enterprise have no use outside of one. Services such as transcoding, distribution, traffic, and even more generally applicable concepts like asset management all have media-specific details that are complex and crucial. The best practices and technologies advocated by the IT industry regarding service design and implementation are still applicable here (they are perhaps even more important than usual thanks to stringent response and reliability requirements), but they must be enhanced to account for the ways in which media affect the equation.

What is needed, therefore, is a new software architecture that combines the best parts of media and IT. What is needed is a service model that takes into account the problems associated with large media files, a strict focus on timing, and a unique industry culture. What is needed is a synthesis of the IT-born architectural concepts of SOA and BPM and the solutions developed by media professionals over the years to solve the unique challenges of the M&E industry.

A media enterprise that leverages the best practices of these methodologies will truly be able to address both its existing challenges with greater efficiency and the new challenges that current methods do not yet address. This type of organization is service-focused, but it is still industry specific. It is a Service-Oriented Media Enterprise.

This chapter discusses the areas where SOA and BPM interact with media solutions to produce new architectures for the M&E industry, shown in Fig. 7-1. In many cases, new solutions are required. Many of the technologies discussed in this chapter do not yet exist or are in their early stages. However, with an increasing need for SOA in the media industry, the full extent of the Service-Oriented Media Enterprise will be a reality very soon.

## IMPORTANT NOTE

The central tenets of SOA and BPM were covered in earlier chapters to give unfamiliar readers a crash course on current IT thinking in software integration — knowledge that can be found in many books on the topic. Hopefully this has been presented in a uniquely fun and engaging way! This chapter focuses on the specific ways in which that current thinking can be applied to the M&E industry, which is a topic that has not yet been fully explored by other authors and integrators. The content of this chapter cannot be found by simply asking an SOA expert from another field.

This is, in other words, the part of the book that really matters.

## 7.1  MEDIA CHALLENGES AND WAYS TO DEAL WITH THEM

SOA is well-suited for asynchronous, message-based system communication. It was conceived to handle integration to legacy applications and to work over unreliable networks such as the Internet. Media is often — but not always — far removed from these situations, because media enterprises set up and depend upon fast, reliable connections. So, if SOA cannot solve every problem in the M&E industry (and no single technology or architecture can), then what are the challenges in media that are not covered by generic SOA solutions?

This section identifies a number of media-specific challenges that separate the M&E industry from other industries where SOA and BPM may exist unaltered. These are listed below.

- Media culture
- The size of media

- Managing time-based content
- An abundance of legacy systems
- Codecs and transcoding
- Media metadata
- Reliability needs
- Security needs
- An abundance of exception cases

Each of these will be considered in turn.

## 7.1.1  Media Culture

One of the most elusive aspects of the media industry — one that is hardly ever mentioned outright but is felt by all newcomers — is its unique culture. Media organizations are craft-oriented, heavily collaborative, widely dispersed, and full of people that have been doing things a certain way for a very long time. This presents a challenge for service-oriented design methodologies simply because of the assumptions often made by IT integrators. Any media engineer who has had to deal with IT consultants unfamiliar with M&E is aware of the difficulties that arise from implementing IT solutions while ignoring media culture.

A media enterprise is a craft-oriented business. Those on the outside of the industry have a hard time getting their heads around the concept of "craft," or the fact that a certain amount of creativity and uniqueness needs to go into every asset produced by a media facility. Media production is not entirely an assembly line process. There are certainly large areas of production that can benefit from heavy business process orchestration and formalized rules. But there is also a little bit of reinventing the wheel that must be done every single time, simply because creativity is involved. No one wants to make the exact same movie twice.

This means that in the Service-Oriented Media Enterprise, integrators leverage formalized business processes whenever possible, but account for the myriad exception cases that will crop up. There is no excessive automation because there cannot be too much automation without having the product suffer. Regardless of how many process definition meetings an enterprise has, there will still be large chunks of the production process that are human-led.

In addition, an M&E systems integrator does not have the same luxury of commoditization that an IT systems integrator enjoys. For media professionals, it *does* matter which transcoding service is called, it *does* matter who is editing the news story, and it *does* matter how long it takes to pull an asset from archive. The truth of the situation is that a certain amount of the implementation detail must be communicated for a realistic media service infrastructure to work. In SOA, the goal is to separate interface from implementation, so by identifying what aspects of implementation are actually non-functional requirements of the service, an integrator can push these details into the interface and keep service definitions abstracted.

A media enterprise also features a much more collaborative environment than many traditional IT companies. Media is the work of many people, some only working on a few seconds of the duration of an entire finished product. A single asset will need to be accessed by many individuals, sometimes for an extended period of time, and each may require a different portion of that asset or a different view into a particular production.

In the Service-Oriented Media Enterprise, an SOA integrator must ensure that service interfaces are designed appropriately for collaborative work. For example, an integrator will not find the same need for atomic transactions in a media enterprise that he or she would find in banking or insurance. Also, simply beginning service design with collaboration in mind will affect how services are exposed. Instead of service operations that complete work tasks like editing or mastering, there may be service operations that allow service consumers to *contribute* to these tasks. Because collaborative service behavior depends on who else is using the service, it may be difficult to make certain media services completely stateless and transactional (as is the SOA ideal).

A media enterprise is often more dispersed than those of many other industries. Participants in M&E business processes can be found all over the world working from home, studios, on-site, etc. Many of these participants work on a freelance or project-to-project basis, and many production companies will move from location to location with each

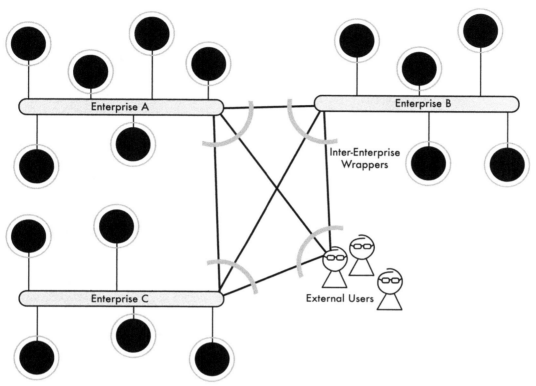

**FIGURE 7-2**   A federated infrastructure features peer architectural domains that interact in established ways to allow for collaboration and communication among each other.

new project (or sometimes many times within a single project)! The distributed nature of most media processes is the reason that companies that make media transfer software or specialize in the delivery of in-production assets have flourished. An SOA can absolutely handle such an environment, but certain details must be taken into consideration.

One such consideration is the need for a secure, federated infrastructure when dealing with distributed services. Traditional software architectures feature a single managing authority — one entity that can serve as a resource regarding who is authorized to participate, what services are available, and other details. In a federated architecture, there are multiple domains on equal footing with each other that must work together to provide this information to those that need it. An example of a federated architecture appears in Fig. 7-2. Federation is not an easy task to accomplish, and has been the subject of many technologies and standardization efforts. Federation is covered in detail in Appendix E.

Service design is also a challenge when dealing with remote or partially disconnected teams. Middleware is designed to be able to deal with service providers and service consumers that have spotty availability. Integrators must ensure that when a producer accesses her media management services on a WiFi network in a coffee shop that her service is executed or at least correctly compensated for if her connection is dropped mid-request. There must be a focus on data synchronization and on service integrity when dealing with remote teams as so often is the case in M&E.

Also, process design must take into account the correct distributed workflow in media processes that use remote production or post-production teams. Integrators and process modelers should look for opportunities to take advantage of BPM and SOA to assist the distributed workflow. For example, if a single media asset is worked on many times in its production cycle across a handful of locations, the business process describing that cycle should be configured to minimize the amount of time that asset spends in transit from location to location or may consider multiple copies of an asset with final conformance.

Traditional IT processes do deal with distributed services. In fact, SOA was originally designed to handle an Internet-wide service model fairly well. The Service-Oriented Media Enterprise, therefore, has a need to stick to the original tenets of SOA — avoiding conversational and inefficient service interfaces is a must!

A final aspect of media culture to be contended with is also the most ephemeral: its people. Media is filled with the some of the most traditional, and change-resistant engineers out there. "But it's always been done that way," is a phrase not alien to the modern media integrator. In other words, the people in a potential Service-Oriented Media Enterprise must be handled with care. For example, in media facilities, there are often two technology-focused groups to contend with: a business-focused IT group and an operations-focused engineering group.

SOA is about breaking down silos like these and horizontally integrating, but, in this case, there are a few good reasons to recognize some divide. Because of the need for extreme reliability and responsiveness, a media engineering group will often run its own segregated, controlled production network. This idea does not mesh well with the SOA concept of a single, unified middleware layer. Some planning must go into getting services on the IT network (such as billing or scheduling) to communicate effectively with services on the production network (such as playout).

In addition, using a single SOA governance team that regulates service design and deployment is a heavily touted method of implementing service orientation in pure IT organizations. Difficulties among business groups are worked out by involving the highest levels of management in an SOA initiative. In media organizations, however, these business group divides can often extend to the highest levels of management! Asking IT and operations to work together on something as crucial to both groups as service design may be asking for a few gray hairs.

A cultural problem can have a cultural abatement, though. What is needed is a new style of SOA governance. Chapter 8: Moving toward the Service-Oriented Media Enterprise explores ways to implement an effective SOA governance team in a traditional media organization.

The old-fashioned media engineer also has very specific opinions on what it means to archive a media asset. With regards to saving material for posterity, the media industry thinks extremely long-term (as in decades and hundreds of years). This means that, unlike traditional IT systems, the media integrator must design a Service-Oriented Media Enterprise (both its systems and its data) for the duration. For example, choosing a metadata schema is an incredibly challenging exercise in media that many have spent years exploring in books and on standards bodies. The heavy up-front commitment of SOA is therefore often compounded by the need in media to think with a longer term view.

Another quirk of the media industry's unique sense of time is that, instead of using middleware persistence or server-based storage as a permanent repository of data as many modern companies do, a media facility has an entire archive service that involves hierarchical storage management and (probably) a temperature-controlled vault somewhere that is earthquake-proof. This is a need pretty unique to M&E,

and therefore a challenge to the media integrator: do not consider the middleware to be a critical location for data persistence in a process, make use of an archive service.

## THE GREAT DEBATE: FILM VS. DIGITAL STORAGE

One of the issues that garners much debate among the engineering types in the media space is how to best store media assets for the long term. The media industry has a medium that has served it well thus far for the long-term — film — but is it practical for the future?

Those who remain proponents point to an excellent life span for film when stored well, as is done by many film studios. With the exception of nitrate-based stocks, which have presented an element of danger given their unstable (explosive!) nature when stored for some time, film has been shown to maintain a reasonable quality, stability, and replay-ability for 50 or 100 years after it was produced.

On the other hand, many point to problems they have had with analog or digital electronic media. Every broadcaster who has been around for a while has "lost" tapes forever because they cannot be replayed. Equally scary is the story that many a crusty engineer can tell of data formats that became unreadable over time due to media degradation, software obsolescence, or the unavailability of a device to even insert it into!

But there is a problem with film. It is clear at this point that it will eventually go away or become too expensive as demand for it dramatically decreases. The percentage of materials that are "born digital" are quickly on the rise and digital cinema is gaining wider acceptance. Film cannot be the answer for any or certainly most assets if the long term is truly considered.

This is where a Service-Oriented Media Enterprise has the potential to come to the rescue! The keys to making digital archives work are clear, well-defined processes that help ensure an organization avoids some of the pitfalls that have plagued electronic or digital storage in the past. By applying process orchestration and metrics to the archival process it is possible to help maintain a regimen of copying data on a regular basis so that existing media are refreshed and migrated to new media. It also helps to assure regular QA and, if necessary, data format translation so that software remains capable of understanding and playing back the data.

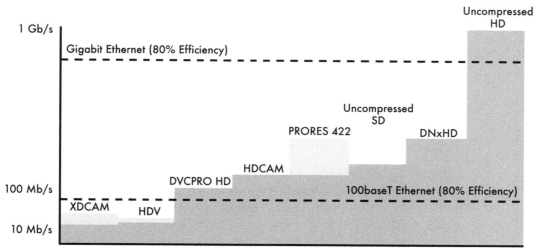

**FIGURE 7-3**  A depiction of popular media formats, ordered by bandwidth size. For real-time media transfer of a single file, the available bandwidth must be guaranteed equal to or greater than these figures. Larger bandwidth means a larger file, although storage of the media file is obviously also dependent on the length of the media asset.

## 7.1.2  The Size of Media

Speaking of archive and media persistence, the management of media is a huge area where the M&E industry has unique challenges. "Of course managing media is unique to the media industry," one might think; "That's what makes it the media industry!" However, now that digital media has become pervasive, the IT mavens out there might make the exact opposite argument: "Media is just files, and can be managed just like the IT industry has been managing files for decades."

This is only partially true. It may be the case that video servers and IP-based broadcast equipment have reduced non-archival media to bits on a computer disk, but that does not make this media the same thing as a company's e-mails or Word documents. Media is much larger than the files that traditional IT, and therefore the standard use case of SOA, is used to dealing with. Instead of simple messages needing to move from service to service, there is a need for entire media assets to move through the software infrastructure. A comparison of the bandwidth necessary to manage various formats of media is shown in Fig. 7-3. With such large (and sometimes streaming!) files comes a number of unique challenges with regard to storage, transfer, and capacity.

With so many media files needed in a functioning media enterprise, meeting storage requirements is crucial. Whereas in most traditional SOA implementations, a relational database attached to the middleware layer is ample to capture and persist important service communication, network-attached storage (NAS) or storage-area network (SAN) solutions are required to hold the large media files of the Service-Oriented Media Enterprise. This is not a book about such storage solutions, but their implementation has been a subject of many books in the media industry.

Perhaps the whole idea of media in an SOA is a bad one to begin with. After all, the point was made in Chapter 4 that the middleware layer as it is commonly implemented is an inappropriate place to store media at all! Middleware is a messaging layer, and media is significantly more cumbersome than simple messages. Indeed, for near-term solutions, it *is* inappropriate to move media across an SOA fabric. Large media files can clog up middleware, and technologies such as SOAP and Web services do not yet have good ways to deal with media.

In the long term, however, this will need to change. It is unavoidable that the services in a Service-Oriented Media Enterprise will need to exchange media assets; that is what makes them media services in the first place! Thoughts on the future of media in middleware appear at the end of this chapter, in Section 7.2.2, but for now, the best practice is to avoid storing media in middleware. Instead take advantage of a storage service that can be implemented using SAN or NAS.

Also, lest the integrator forget, media metadata is a crucial source of information in an SOA as well, and must be considered when designing a middleware layer. It is appropriate to store metadata in the middleware layer, as many services will need to take advantage of a common repository of asset information. Regarding the Service-Oriented Media Enterprise, the focus is on sizing middleware repositories appropriately to handle the amount of metadata that will need to be stored. In some facilities, an SOA will need to manage hundreds of thousands to millions of assets (if each new version of a product gets its own asset ID and record), and care must be taken to ensure that these metadata are online and accessible.

Regarding bandwidth and throughput of media, there are a number of areas where the principles of SOA must evolve to tackle the evolving

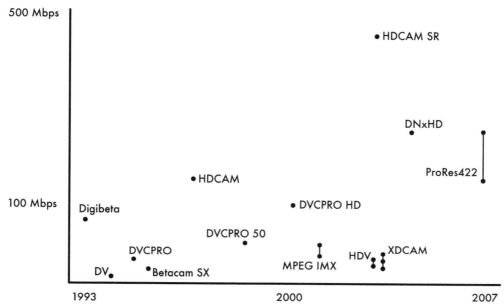

**FIGURE 7-4** This graph shows the evolution of digital media data rates over the past several years. The trend is clear: media is not getting any smaller, so software architectures that support media must expand to handle these data rates.

needs of the media industry. For example, while the transfer of a record from one bank to another (or one hospital to another, etc.) can be considered a trivial task if both ends of the transfer are available at the time, the transfer of media assets from one place to another is significantly more difficult. And, as time goes on, media formats get more and more difficult to transfer, as shown in Fig. 7-4! A single 4 K asset can take hours and hours to transfer over a standard Ethernet connection, and the transfer cannot just be initiated and then forgotten. Media file transfers must be *managed*.

Many vendors in the M&E industry have made fortunes producing products that will speed up or monitor the transfer of media assets. It is expected that, in the Service-Oriented Media Enterprise, the functionality to monitor and manage media transfers will exist as well. This can be accomplished through well-planned service design. Integrators must ensure that any services that transfer media have ways of reporting the status of these transfers. Process designers should assume that media transfers take extended periods of time, and poll for completion, independently wait for a response from the service indicating completion, or assume that the transfer is incomplete and continue with the process. They should not set up a media transfer as a synchronous activity in a business process as this is asking for a stalled or frozen process.

Again, the point was made in Chapter 4 that media moving across an SOA should actually be avoided at all costs. Current SOA technology is inappropriate for tackling the high bandwidths required, and the levels of abstraction involved in transmitting across a middleware layer would cause any sufficiently sized media asset to be broken up into message-sized chunks and reassembled at its destination. This is already happening at the IP layer, and it should be avoided at the business layer.

So how does media move through the Service-Oriented Media Enterprise? In the absence of a media layer (discussed later), media movement should be handled out-of-band. File transfer and transfer management services should be called when media movement is required. Integrators should implement business processes monitoring and managing current transfers, and have formalized ways to deal with the exception cases when transfers fail or are interrupted. Media movement in a contemporary SOA is a *service*.

## 7.1.3  Time

Inside the world of media, the concept of time has all sorts of connotations that do not exist outside the world of media. If Amazon or Google's servers go down for one second during their busiest time of the year, everyone using them waits a little longer for their page to load, and then continues with what they were doing. The consumers don't notice (that much), and no real money is lost. However, if the servers at a major television network go down for one second during the Super Bowl, that network can lose millions of dollars in ad revenue and half a dozen people probably lose their jobs. It is a very, very big deal. So when applying the precepts of SOA (which can handle those Web servers just fine) to highly sensitive broadcast equipment, one must tread carefully.

The difference in the meaning of the phrase "real-time" is exemplary of the fundamental disconnect between media time and IT time.

In the M&E industry, real-time means that the information in one frame of media is transmitted in the time it would take a viewer to watch that one frame (1/30th of a second, for example). Real-time for SOA technologies, however, probably means that the information is delivered within an acceptable reaction time for a human user. This could be sub-second, or it could be several seconds. Integrators hoping to use SOA technologies to transmit messages in "media real-time" should be wary of anything on the market today that promises that level of performance. It simply is not there yet.

So how is real-time performance achieved in the Service-Oriented Media Enterprise? Exactly the way it is achieved today! Today media enterprises use automation and air-chain-ready systems to transmit media around a facility in real-time. Introducing SOA into that facility should not change this air chain. SOA and BPM do not take the place of automation in a media facility. Integrators should use automation for what it is good for: real-time media operations. In the Service-Oriented Media Enterprise, automation is a service.

Another way that the management of time rears its ugly head in the media industry is through the content itself. Media assets — regardless of their quality, completeness, or intended recipients — all have a duration. This means that media assets have a temporal context: once a piece of media starts playing, the audience will get confused should it end prematurely. Media also may have temporal metadata associated with it such as scene labels, dialog and closed captioning, or mark-in and mark-out points. Unlike the stateless information that flows through other industries' infrastructures, media is time-based.

## THE ASSUMPTIONS THAT COME WITH TIME-BASED CONTENT

- It can only be consumed properly at a fixed rate and in a fixed amount of time.
- It often does not make sense when viewed partially, interrupted, or in the wrong order.
- It must ultimately be streamed to the user (although that streaming may occur on the client).
- It must ultimately be decrypted and undigitized to be used (a fact commonly known as the "analog hole").

Time-based content complicates business processes and service design. For example, unlike the insurance industry, which might have highly transactional, stateless business rules (that the rules engines discussed in Chapter 4 handle well), the media industry has time-sensitive rules. A local television station might not be able to play two fast-food commercials within five minutes of each other, or an airline ad during the commercial break of an action movie featuring a plane crash. These rules require time-sensitive metadata, and can be a challenge to stateless SOA and BPM tools.

Service design is also complicated by time-sensitive media. For example, an asset management service might store an entire media asset for use by the rest of the enterprise. An editing service, however, may only need five minutes of media located halfway through the file. SOA tools cannot handle this type of a situation on their own. An Enterprise Service Bus (ESB) may be able to translate messages from one form to another, but no ESB on the market today can create subclips!

These situations are why a well-implemented Service-Oriented Media Enterprise contains many media-specific infrastructure services. When dealing with time-based content, a little bit of code goes a long way. A subclipping service or a time-based rules engine can be a highly reusable component in an SOA. Integrators should look for opportunities to create small utility services to ease the process of working with media in a software architecture.

One final aspect of media that complicates facility design and drives software architects up the wall is live production. Media engineers have developed all sorts of clever tools and tricks to deal with this very unique architectural challenge: streaming images across an enterprise as they occur. Live production is difficult because of its extreme unpredictability. If the talent makes a mistake or an unexpected event occurs on camera, the production team (and therefore the systems they are using) must be able to react. In live production no one can afford to wait for a sluggish service response, and no one can be forced into using a formalized business process when there are so many exception cases to be dealt with.

This is not to say that the tenets of SOA and BPM are not of use in live production. If anything, having a more agile infrastructure is a great benefit. It is important, however, to focus on creating flexible processes and services when dealing with live productions. If a process analyst misses an important exception case, there is no time to work around it; it is crucial to use the tenets of good process design. With versatile services and open, user-driven processes, however, SOA and BPM can make live production easier to set up, take down, and execute.

## 7.1.4 Legacy Systems in Media

It is commonplace for engineers and technicians of one field to look at the engineers and technicians of another field and think, "It is so much harder for me than for you!" M&E is no exception. Media engineers take a special delight in proving how difficult it is to integrate with the convoluted legacy systems out there that SOA is theoretically so good at wrapping. Security concerns mean that many legacy systems of the last twenty years do not have good network access. A blurring of preparatory control (which can easily be SOA-driven) and real-time control (which cannot) interfaces, among other things, have caused vendors over the years to make systems that are incredibly difficult to use in any way other than exactly the one intended. In other words: an integrator's nightmare.

IT firms, may have to deal with old terminal-based servers, but at least these have a network port and a command line. The situation in media is often worse, which media engineers will be quick to admit. This manner of sadistic bragging on the part of the media engineer is a concern for media integrators, both because of the truth of the situation and because of the culture created that thinks that legacy media systems are impervious to effective integration. The best way to address both concerns is by developing SOA proofs-of-concept that tackle the most difficult integration challenges right off the bat. Chapter 8 contains more information on this subject.

The other piece of advice regarding legacy systems in M&E is to pay attention to the best practices contained throughout this book. If the only way for an enterprise to gain access to the functionality of one particularly ornery legacy system is to provide a full-time user with a portal interface to carry out tasks manually, and it makes sense, then so be it! Integrators should not let the details of the implementation affect the business-oriented nature of the interface. That is the whole idea behind SOA: the interface is independent from the implementation. There are always ways around difficult integration challenges, although some may be cost- or time-prohibitive. As long as smart decisions are made, any integration will be beneficial to the enterprise at large.

### 7.1.5 Codecs and Transcoding

The media information that moves throughout the Service-Oriented Media Enterprise is unique not only because it is large and time sensitive, but also because it is quality sensitive. Media quality is important. It is not sufficient to have the wrong media at the right place at the right time. The media must be at the right resolution and in the right format to be used effectively. An integrator that ignores resolution, bit-rate, or compression artifacts in media has obviously never had to deal with trying to edit a 4 K video clip on a laptop computer or answering the calls of angry advertisers whose television ad quality is awful.

When money is processed in a bank, it does not lose some of its worth at each step — the amount remains consistent throughout any given business process no matter how it is split up or distributed. That is actually the whole point of banking in the first place. With media, however, this is not the case. Data loss is an acceptable aspect of the normal course of business in the M&E industry. Each processing step in media requires a specific quality and format of media, and there are many actions such as transcoding that intend to affect the quality of the media that passes through it. Sometimes these processing steps have the unfortunate side effect of lowering the overall possible quality of that media through the introduction of compression or processing artifacts. This means that the more steps that a single media asset goes through, the worse it will look. This is known as generational loss.

## WHAT GENERATIONAL LOSS REALLY LOOKS LIKE

Uninitiated engineers in the M&E industry may doubt the significant effect that generational loss has on a single piece of media. However, depending on

the type and amount of processing done, the effects of generational loss can be severe. The top image is an original image from a video clip prior to processing. On the bottom is an image only five generations later. This means that it was put through some sort of video processing five times. Artifacts can be seen around many of the block edges; the processed image is of a reduced quality. A good integrator will ensure that the consumer never sees an image like the one on the right by parallelizing media processing as much as possible.

The allowance of generational loss in the media industry (and its overall focus on media quality) means that an integrator cannot just design processes that always pull the closest available media for the job. Just because the correct media asset was identified does not mean that it is available in the correct version or in a high enough quality to generate the correct version. So how does one deal with the whole issue of production media quality in the Service-Oriented Media Enterprise?

First, many production services such as editing or logging are usually not quality dependent and can work just as well with a low-resolution proxy version of a media asset as they can with the full-resolution asset. In fact, some services may work better with a low-res proxy because the smaller asset size will allow for processing on slower computers and transfers over more restricted networks (like the ever unstable Internet). A best practice when dealing with such services is to use a proxy whenever possible. The idea is that the proxy is linked to the full-resolution asset, so that business decisions made on the proxy (such as the generation of an edit decision list) can be easily transferred to the full-resolution asset. Proxy assets are much easier to move or stream around a facility infrastructure (although probably not small enough to move quickly through a middleware layer like traditional SOA messages). Business processes that make use of a proxy until it is absolutely necessary to bring in the full-resolution asset (for online editing and playout, for example) will be making effective use of their media assets.

Unfortunately, the media integrator cannot follow the best practices of SOA in their entirety when passing media from service to service as opposed to messages. Since the quality of the media must be taken into account, services must have ways to identify not only the specific media asset required, but also its quality. This is a major design consideration when building service interfaces. Also, the media integrator cannot just create a business process that takes the media from one service and delivers it to the next service in line, running it through a transcoder if it needs to be of a different quality. That is a surefire recipe for excessive generation loss and many complaints. Instead, one should consider passing the "youngest" and highest quality asset possible into a given service to allow for the highest quality output of that service. This means that some form of asset management must take place in the middleware layer!

This would need to be done either virtually through direct access to the central storage or physical copies. This type of architecture would drastically affect process design because every other step in a media process would have to be to the central repository service in the form of a "check out" and "check in" type of mechanism. However, it would solve the quality issue discussed. This type of centralized asset management is one of the most common media architectures in modern media facilities today. It is not ideal for the Service-Oriented

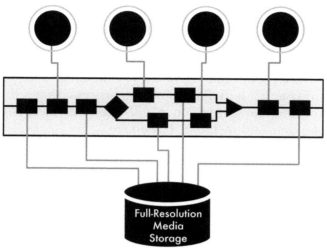

**FIGURE 7-5**  Centralized media transport, transcoding, and storage is a good solution for the issue of service media quality, because the best possible media can be delivered to any service in the infrastructure. However, it complicates process design by forcing many calls to the media repository service.

Media Enterprise of the future because it complicates process design without enhancing the business goals of those processes. Media access should be completely abstracted from the process so that these steps would be completely hidden. To do otherwise would go against the precepts of BPM. However, this type of architecture, shown in Fig. 7-5, is a good solution in the near-term to handle the business needs of the M&E industry given the realities of today's technologies.

One final impact of media quality on the architecture of the Service-Oriented Media Enterprise is the media quality needs in multi-platform distribution. In this kind of distribution the media integrator is often starting with a single asset version and spinning off multiple new versions: one for HD television, one for SD television, one for Internet distribution, one for DVD, and so on. Suddenly the media enterprise must juggle many different media files, all that represent the exact same asset, just at different qualities. In reality, this may be done in some form many times throughout the production process, but at distribution there is often an explosion of new files. Each specific file must be identified as a particular asset, and there must be some way to semantically link all of these files together to make a single, composite picture of one piece of media. It is a challenge for the media integrator.

Thankfully, media asset management (as a service) can handle many of these woes, making it perhaps the most important service of the burgeoning Service-Oriented Media Enterprise. However, just as when implementing a centralized storage and media transport solution, the design of an asset management system must take into account the ways in which it will affect business process design through its interface and the ways in which it will affect service design through the business data and metadata it manages.

## 7.1.6 Metadata

Metadata semantics and management are areas that traditional IT types may typically gloss over in their integration (although this tide is changing with the explosion of Web 2.0 technologies and metadata on the Internet). However, this is a crucial area of concern for a media facility. The question of what to call things only seems trivial to the inexperienced. Committees are formed within media enterprises to tackle this very issue! It is no easy task.

Recent years have seen the M&E industry get a real grasp on the importance of metadata, though. "Metadata" is always one of the most popular topics of discussion at NAB, IBC, or SMPTE, and shows no sign of waning in its relevancy. In the Service-Oriented Media Enterprise, this issue is not any less important. If anything, metadata is much more important, because SOA best practices entail a consistent view of a facility's data. If every service is using a different metadata standard, then there must be a way to translate between the different metadata standards used. This takes more than just a metadata schema — it takes a whole ontology of terms, meanings, and the links between them.

Metadata management is complicated. For example, the previous section discusses the importance of including media quality considerations in service design, which means that each service must identify what specific format of media it requires, what resolution, what frame rate, what bit depth, any wrappers that are necessary, and a couple hundred other things that may crop up. And each service must identify these things in such a way as to be understood by the business process calling it and any other service to which it must pass information. This can easily get out of control.

## WHAT ARE SEMANTICS?

Semantics are, by definition, the meanings that people attribute to particular words or phrases. These meanings may be definitional or relational (in other words, how a particular term is related to other terms). A metadata field such as "title" or "duration" gives media a definition, while a field such as "source material," "quality," or "ISAN number" relates that media to other media assets or to external systems of understanding.

The study of semantics is a big area in this Internet age, and not just in media. It is often difficult to determine what metadata means. For example, are the two title fields "2008-04-01 News Block A" and "Segment 1 News TUES" describing the same media asset? Is a best-light transfer quality of "4" good or bad? Is providing a five-digit asset ID ample for the number of assets expected? To thrive, the Service-Oriented Media Enterprise must be able to answer these and other questions. However, SOA technologies do not provide a working semantic system to an enterprise, but they help to implement a well-thought-out semantic system successfully.

The best way to deal with an explosion of metadata in a media enterprise is to leverage standards wherever possible. This aligns nicely with the precepts of SOA and is simply a good idea. Hard work has been done out there to generate standards such as MXF, AAF, MPEG-7, and others. Many of these standards are actually used by media vendors and can easily get folded into wrapper design of common media services. The other main benefit of leveraging metadata standards in the Service-Oriented Media Enterprise is simply a logistical one: by using an already-written standard, the enterprise does not have to take the time to write their own standard and conform everything to that new in-house standard.

Of course, there are always areas where the base set of metadata standards do not cut it in a given enterprise. Every media facility does things slightly differently — it is a craft-based industry after all. A good course of action here is to start with a standard and extend it to meet the business needs at hand. Many of the relevant standards have a mechanism for doing this. The most important goal in the Service-Oriented Media Enterprise is that each internal service reflects what is really done in the facility and is able to communicate effectively. A secondary goal is the exposure of services and functionality to federated entities (other business units and third parties). It would be ideal to be able to use the same metadata standard inside a facility as outside, but this is also an unrealistic goal. The integrator should select or extend a metadata standard that meets the needs of the first goal, and then use data transformation or gateway services to make a subset of that metadata available in a generally consumable format.

Finally, when dealing with a metadata explosion in a media enterprise, it is important to do data transformation in the right place. It may be unrealistic to expect that every service in a facility will use the same metadata standard. One of the benefits of SOA, after all, is its ability to deal with heterogeneous environments. Data transformation of the type discussed in Chapter 3 can be leveraged to allow for many metadata schemas in a single enterprise, but, if used incorrectly, this type of data transformation could also explode exponentially against the number of metadata standards used. Leveraging an enterprise-wide schema or an "infrastructure standard" with smaller pockets of other formats of metadata is the best way to deal with this situation.

## 7.1.7 Reliability

The need for utmost reliability in the M&E industry goes hand-in-hand with the time-focused nature of both media and media culture. Especially in television or other broadcast media, consumer expectations regarding reliability are severe. The old adage about losing a second of the Super Bowl, mentioned previously in this chapter, is no hyperbole. Even in methods of distribution such as feature films that are not as time sensitive (in other words, are not broadcasting, but instead getting put to film or video and sent out physically), reliability is still a huge concern. Regardless of the manner of distribution, the acquisition of media is always going to be time sensitive. No matter how good the director may be, if the system drops three frames of footage on acquisition, that one-tenth of a second will never occur again. No one dies (as can happen if some computer systems go down these days; for example, life support or military communication), but it is not the office e-mail server, either. The M&E industry takes reliability very seriously, and that means that media integrators must, too.

## THE COST OF AIRTIME

One thing is very clear about television: it has the unarguable characteristic of real-time consumption. At the end of the day, the point is to display a program to a viewer. That viewer cannot accept watching that program at 2× real time, nor will he or she accept a program that comes in slower than real time. Unfortunately, humans can only consume these programs at one speed!

Humans also have a nasty habit of getting bothered or even annoyed when their program is interrupted, even briefly. Whether it be a drop of audio, unexpected black, a freeze frame, or picture distortion, too much of it and people simply change the channel.

And that presents a problem for a broadcaster. What they really sell is eye-balls on advertising. If the viewers turn away, then they will simply make less on each ad or have to do more "make goods" (replaying the ad and taking away from other ad space that can be sold). Now what can that mean in terms of money? Sometimes it is not too bad — some ad space can go for as little $100 for a single spot in the United States.

The worst case scenario is much more fun to consider, though: the Super Bowl. In 2007, it was reported that the cost of airing a Super Bowl commercial was $2.6 million! That dollar amount does not even include the costs of pro-ducing the ad.

So what does this mean in terms of cost for time? Each second costs more than $86,000! How about a single frame of the media (Super Bowl ads are 30 frames per second)? Putting up a single frame of the commercial costs more than $2800! But what it would really cost, if a broadcaster lost a few frames or a second of that commercial, would be the full $2.6 million, because the loss of even a part of the ad is considered a full loss.

As anyone can see, this is just part of the reason that broadcast engineers can be so focused on zero downtime with their systems. If an e-mail is delayed a few seconds, nobody will probably notice. Somebody will notice even less than a second of black screen, and that means lost revenue. In this business, time really is money!

There are two general ways to factor in media reliability in the Service-Oriented Media Enterprise: design service-oriented systems reliably, and isolate critical air-chain systems from the rest of the infrastructure.

Reliability requirements should not ever be ignored, even in the earliest stages of system design. Integrators should design both middleware and end service systems to be as reliable as possible. This almost always means clustering application servers, implementing a reliable network with plenty of failover, not ever introducing a single point of failure into the design, and building in lots of backups and redundancy. The same techniques used in the world of traditional hardware media systems integration can be put to good effect here. When designing a service model or middleware layer, integrators should include detailed information about redundancy, clustering, and procedures for recovering from backup states.

As mentioned earlier in this chapter, SOA has yet to replace the reliability of the traditional media air chain. SOA is not a substitute for traditional automation. In the Service-Oriented Media Enterprise, however, an SOA solution is integrally linked to the critical air chain in a number of places (such as loading files on playout servers ahead of schedule, sending non-real-time control data, and collecting statistics and business metrics of the entire process). Integrators must think carefully about how their critical systems fit in with an overall SOA strategy. They must strike a balance between a completely integrated system that introduces layers of abstraction that may interfere with their reliable systems and a completely isolated system that does not get any of the SOA benefits of agility and visibility. The best way to do this is to involve SOA solutions in all non-real-time activity and leave the real-time critical path to traditional technologies that are monitored and supervised by an SOA solution.

## 7.1.8 Security

Another area where the media industry has unique challenges is the realm of content security. Media is not alone in having security concerns. No one would want their bank to leave account information unprotected, and there are certainly some defense or government data that are a lot more valuable than the latest Spider Man movie. However, the M&E industry faces some unique security challenges and has the opportunity to implement some unique security methods and solutions. The modern Service-Oriented Media Enterprise is positioned to take advantage of some of these methods.

One major concern of studios is the constant threat of media piracy or content theft. Many security holes are immediately opened when information is the primary asset to secure. Measures must be taken to protect media throughout its production cycle by preventing anyone from copying five episodes of the latest hit TV series to a flash drive from an editing workstation and walking out the building with no one the wiser. At the same time, media must be protected after its production cycle to prevent a consumer from ripping a DVD and distributing it via BitTorrent. Much high-profile work has been done in this area, and the tenets of SOA and BPM can help.

One major difference between the two scenarios described above is the state of the media needing to be secured. In one situation, during production, the media may be unfinished and *need* to be accessed by many people as part of the standard production life cycle. Media enterprises often outsource much of their work by sending dailies to post houses or external color correction facilities, and perhaps even going so far as to outsource media storage! Therefore, it is a kind of "B2B" security that is needed — security that focuses on watermarking assets, forensics, and keeping track of what is going on inside and outside a facility regarding a particular media project.

When dealing with consumers ("B2C" security), the focus is on preventative measures and Digital Rights Management (DRM). SOA and BPM do not offer a particular solution in either of these areas because they are simply a set of software architectural best practices. However, there is quite a bit of work being done in the area of media security and forensics, and SOA/BPM can help an integrator take advantage of these technologies and put them to maximum effect.

One way to do this is to use BPM software and watermarking services to set up an automated watermarking chain within a facility. It has become possible in production facilities where security is a strong concern to uniquely watermark assets at each stage of the production cycle. This way, if content is leaked and distributed prematurely, the studio can determine where in the workflow the security breach occurred. If it is the copy given to a particular post house, for example, one could bet that the studio will not work with that post house ever again. Right now this is often done manually; for example, an editor will watermark a piece he or she has just finished before sending it to a producer for review. However, with the use of an orchestration engine and a watermarking service exposed to a middleware layer, this procedure could happen automatically at the end of each task. Even in a heavily human-driven production workflow, BPM engines can track where an asset is in its life cycle and ensure that assets are watermarked in an appropriate way to facilitate accurate forensics.

## WATERMARKING TECHNIQUES AND TECHNOLOGIES

Digital watermarking is an effective way to track a media asset even if it gets wrapped and unwrapped through various formats and standards. Watermarks change an asset by embedding additional information, often without affecting (or at least drastically affecting) the experience of the consumer. They are commonly used to communicate copyright or ownership information, but can also carry more detailed information, such as the exact position in the workflow that a media asset was generated. The watermark is gathered forensically, so this technique can only be used to audit a breach in security, not prevent it.

There are essentially two different types of watermark: visible and invisible. A form of visible watermarks is seen every day on television when a network or local affiliate plasters its logo on the bottom corner of the screen. They might also be seen in copyrighted images found online. These types of watermarks are often intrusive and obvious, so they are, in most cases, inappropriate as a method of forensically marking media. However, they can also be subtle, such as a computer-generated reflection or light in the background of an image. By giving different versions of the media different sets of these visible watermarks, media enterprises can go back and determine from which version a particular asset originated.

Invisible watermarks insert information via subtle change to the media (such as encoding a message on the least significant bits of the pixels in a video) that can be extracted by computer analysis. Invisible watermarks have improved dramatically over the past several years, and many watermarking technologies are totally imperceptible to the eye, but can be interpreted by a computer even after the asset moves through the "analog hole." The watermark can be recovered even if it is filmed on a camcorder from the back row of a movie theater.

Another technology that benefits from SOA is Digital Rights Management. This type of content security is typically placed onto media assets before they go out the door to the consumer, hopefully protecting the asset from tampering and unsupported use. In the Service-Oriented Media Enterprise, DRM is a service that, just like watermarking, can be called upon at the appropriate point in the production workflow. Assuming that both of these services have a way (out-of-band) to access the media in question and deliver it to the next service in the workflow, either task can be completely automated so that none of the managers in a facility need to worry about the correct watermark or whether a particular asset has been wrapped with DRM — it will happen as the business rules dictate.

## DRM TECHNOLOGIES

Digital Rights Management technologies protect a media asset through preventative measures such as encryption. These technologies are constantly evolving due to the fact that their usefulness is negated when techniques are developed that allow circumvention.

One of the earliest successful DRM technologies was the CSS standard used to encrypt the content on DVDs. Since that time, the number and complexity of these schemes have exploded. With countless distribution channels and formats popping up online, there are many different types of DRM technologies in use today.

When security services are combined with a centralized media storage and management solution as described in Section 7.1.5, business processes begin to get a little bit complicated. The media business analyst will have to insert multiple logistic steps such as watermarking and transcoding in between each major production task, when really, all anyone wants to concentrate on are the major production tasks. This shows the need for a unified media layer such as the one discussed later in Section 7.2.

### 7.1.9 Exception Cases that Affect Integration

Every industry has its exception cases. The media industry, especially in areas such as news production and feature production, is, appropriately, no exception. As discussed in Chapter 6, these exception cases can be dealt with through BPM techniques and technologies. However, BPM tools were built with IT and non-media exception cases in mind, such as a user canceling her order before hitting "confirm." How are media exception cases different, and what types of tools are needed to deal with them?

One major area chock full of exception cases is news production. The whole concept of "breaking news" feels like, in reality, one huge exception case. When the aliens land on the front lawn of the White House to make first contact, a news producer is not going to have time to re-engineer her processes to account for the extra footage in the system or a new timetable: she is going to have to get some cameras out there to capture this historic moment! Every day in a newsroom is like this, too. Perhaps nothing gets quite so important in a given day as aliens landing, but when major news breaks, there is no time to plan or think. The services and processes that are in place in a news facility must be able to accommodate such situations.

The key here is process and interface flexibility. Whereas many IT firms see benefit from forcing their users in to a specific business process (to ensure compliance or consistency), in media this is not the case. Integrators should design processes to facilitate the maximum amount of flexibility while maintaining a kind of consistency and improving visibility. They should never lock users in to a particular process and they should never, ever force users to use the services provided in order for later services or systems to work properly. The system should allow users to circumvent it and, if needed, "synchronize" afterward to account for any disconnects. Of course, having users working against the system should not be the goal of any integration effort, but without flexible processes, users will be forced to find ways to get their jobs done when their jobs don't mesh up exactly with what the integrated system *thinks* their jobs are and may even cease to use the system altogether.

## CASE STUDY

### Breaking News

An enterprise-scale news operation recently decided to take a look at process flows in many areas of their organization. The goal was to examine with an open mind how work was done and seek efficiencies. There was no real attempt in this project to seek specific opportunities for orchestration, but rather to examine whether technological or operational changes could result in improvements in capital or operational budgets or in better product going to air.

One of the interesting questions posed at the beginning of the project was whether any efficiencies or changes could be found in the most chaotic area that this organization dealt with on a daily basis: breaking news. It is common knowledge that breaking news is an extremely dynamic condition that would be difficult to document, let alone find opportunities for process improvement.

An interesting finding came out of the study. There was actually little in the way of major differences between the breaking and normal news workflows. The real differences from a process perspective had to do with the speed and intensity with which everyone executed the same process as well as the skipping of approvals and checks that otherwise would have been sought. In every other respect, the breaking and non-breaking workflows looked very similar.

While this was surprising to some of the management who had sponsored the project, it actually came as no surprise to those who dealt with actually getting breaking news to air on a daily basis. During an elicitation meeting when incredulity was expressed at the similarity, one producer said, "You should have expected this. While it may look like chaos on a certain level, it is *controlled* chaos. It is much like an emergency room in that doctors may also appear to be in chaos in a trauma situation, but actually follow a pretty structured path."

The lesson here is important. Workflow is not always what everyone expects. It is important to talk to the people who really do the work to get a clear understanding of potential exception cases. They are the ones who have the clearest vision of what actually happens. Similarities can sometimes be found even in apparently disparate workflows. This helps the integrator when seeking to identify services and common subprocesses.

Another area of media production that demands flexibility is a situation where something has to happen once and only once. For example, a big scene in a summer blockbuster may require location shooting in South America with specific software tools for special effects, which means a big, complex field setup of computers and equipment that will run for two weeks out in the middle of the rainforest somewhere and then dismantled and never used in that configuration again. SOA will not help to protect these machines from the harsh jungle elements, but it can help to provide the maximum amount of agility regarding ad hoc and constantly evolving infrastructures.

One suggested way of establishing good agility to deal with one-off processes is to develop a reusable library of composite services. Composite services are shown in Fig. 7-6. They take advantage of a handful of lower level business services to create a combined functionality, such as creating an asset record in a DAM system, generating a new to-do list item for asset catalogers, and e-mailing a producer. While business processes may last days, weeks, or months and be composed of hundreds of steps or layers of subprocesses, composite services are designed to be transactional and quick. They are the medium-sized building blocks of the Service-Oriented Media Enterprise; large enough to simplify certain complex tasks but small enough to be reusable in many situations. One way to think of a composite service is like a macro in a computer program such as Microsoft Word — it combines a few lower level tasks into a single event making that event more repeatable and reusable.

Composite services can be very useful in situations such as location shooting (whether in the previously mentioned rainforest or somewhere

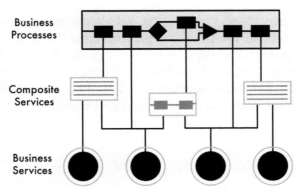

**FIGURE 7-6**   A composite service combines the functionality of multiple business services in a highly reusable way. Composite services are more complex than business services, but simpler than business processes.

much more civilized, such as the summer Olympics) where a workflow must get assembled on the fly. What is especially helpful in situations like these is a tool that can assemble business services into composite services or composite services into more complex services and processes and get these services exposed quickly. Many SOA vendors are beginning to experiment with such products, and in a few years, these SOA "macro tools" will become commonplace.

Combining this idea of composite services with the need for various out-of-band media tasks such as transfer, transcoding, or watermarking makes for a series of highly reusable "composite media services." For example, a single call at the end of a major production task could watermark an asset appropriately, move the completed asset to central storage, store its metadata in an asset management system, and update a project schedule. Composite services are very useful in M&E, and will continue to get more important as larger, course-grained chunks of functionality are required in new situations.

The media industry certainly does have a number of one-off processes that make no sense to capture in a process orchestration or BPM engine. However, inside the M&E industry there is clearly the feeling that many more of these processes exist than actually do. News and feature production, for example, both encounter new situations with every subsequent project. However, there are large portions of workflow in both cases that remain the same (with different content) every time, and can be captured and, in some cases, automated to streamline production.

The key here is to generalize a workflow to the extent needed, but still leverage some specificity to formalize and capture processes. For example, having a "football news production" process may be too specific, but having a "news production" process may be too general. Centering on something like "sports news production" allows for a useful level of abstraction and processes that will actually repeat with each broadcast. As mentioned elsewhere in the book, the point of BPM and process orchestration is to help with the execution of workflow. A media integrator should not formalize processes to such an extent that they become a hindrance to the enterprise, but at the same time, he or she should take advantage of formalized processes where they make sense.

## WHAT NOT TO DO: FERVENTLY AVOID ORCHESTRATION

Many media professionals (especially those who have been around since the days of incredibly unreliable digital technologies) look with a wary eye upon business orchestration, rules, and BPM tools. After all, it is dangerous to leave it up to a *computer* to make business decisions! However, simply dismissing these technologies completely is ignoring the opportunity for huge efficiency increases. Even in a facility that wishes to decide what comes next manually at every step of the way, business orchestration and business rules can still be used to deliver all of the relevant information to the users to allow them to make a better decision. Processes do not have to be long-running to be successfully orchestrated! In fact, the shorter, more tactical processes are the ones that often make the best automatic processes, because they are able to accomplish a single business goal in a streamlined, reusable way.

One should not, therefore, avoid orchestration out of unbridled conservatism.

## 7.2  THE MEDIA LAYER

Most of these unique problems and unique solutions in the M&E industry center on one thing: the media itself. In addition to the craft nature of many processes, dealing with media is what makes M&E so unique. There are ways to account for this in SOA or BPM design, but in many cases, these can be considered workarounds. Implementing a media movement service, a transcoding service, or an asset management service all seem unnatural to media professionals. After all, the point of integration in the first place is to make dealing with the media easier, not more difficult! And the point of SOA is to make the steps needed for effective integration business steps that align with the goals and needs of the business, not technology steps that force engineers into thinking a particular way that requires a steep learning curve. In many ways, media seems forced into the concept of SOA.

Still, the media industry needs the tenets of SOA. Right now, media integrators face business problems, technology problems, and media problems. SOA aims to turn technology problems into business problems (of course in reality, it cannot completely rid an enterprise of

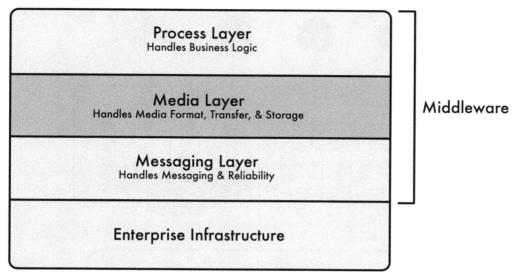

**FIGURE 7-7**   A media layer sits "above" the middleware layer and handles aspects of dealing with media files that a traditional middleware layer cannot. To the services accessing the infrastructure, no difference is apparent.

technology problems, but it is better than any other method out there currently). And, by doing that, SOA brings significant benefit to the media enterprises that implement it. However, SOA does nothing for the media problems in a facility. It is hard enough solving the business challenges that arise; media integrators need a way to solely focus on business challenges in the same way that an IT integrator can when implementing SOA. In other words, the benefit that SOA brings to a media facility could be so much greater if an effective way to deal with media in a service-oriented way is found.

What is needed is a way to abstract the media in the same way that SOA abstracts the technology — a "media aware" SOA. This is the real innovation of the Service-Oriented Media Enterprise: a media layer that handles aspects of media format, location, and quality and makes these facets of integration completely independent from the decisions of workflow and business service. Such a thing does not yet exist in a realistic, reliable way anywhere, but is a necessary development if the M&E industry hopes to see the same rate of return from service orientation that other industries have seen. Fig. 7-7 shows the position of the media layer amid the other, traditional SOA layers.

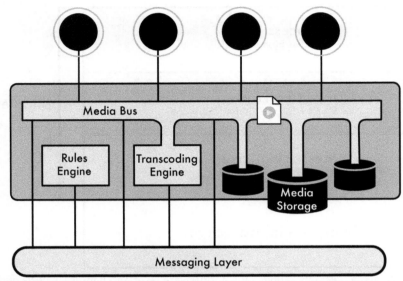

**FIGURE 7-8**   A media layer as envisioned in this book features the following components: a business rules engine, a media bus, media storage, and a transcoding engine.

## 7.2.1 Necessary Components of a Media Layer

A media layer would be integrated in with a traditional middleware layer and would handle many functions that, due to restrictions in SOA technology, are currently handled by services. The goal is to take as much media-handling responsibility as possible out of the hands of services so that these components can focus on the business goals of the enterprise. The question then arises: What functionality is appropriate to push to a media layer?

To effectively handle media, a media layer would need access to the media itself, knowledge of what media needs to go where and in what format, and the means to deliver it. In terms of layer components, this means business rules regarding media, a media transport mechanism, media storage, and media format conversion and transcoding. These components are shown in Fig. 7-8.

### 7.2.1.1 Business Rules

When envisioning a so-called media layer, a business rules engine of any sort would not be the first thing an engineer thinks of. These sorts

**TABLE 7-1**

A List of the Types of Rules that Might Be Found in a Media Layer and Why They Are Useful to the Media Enterprise

| | |
|---|---|
| Rules regarding media format and source | Minimizes transcoding and generational loss in a facility |
| Rules regarding transfer management | Transfers can be made as efficient as possible |
| Rules regarding media location and storage | Users would not have to worry about where to put an asset |
| Rules regarding security | Responsibility for security can be out of the hands of fallible users |

of things are more common in traditional middleware layers and, at first glance, have little to do with media. But dealing with media inside a facility is all about business rules! From the type and quality of media that is necessary at each stage of the production process to the best way to go from MPEG-2 to VC-1, business rules are everywhere in the media layer. Including some way to programmatically determine the correct course of action for a given media-related situation is a primary need for a media layer, otherwise this layer will be unqualified to take any media management responsibility out of the hands of engineers; no one would trust the media layer to treat the media correctly. Some examples of these business rules appear in Table 7-1.

One of the classes of business rules that belong in a media layer  refer to transcoding and where to draw source material. As important as the transcoding of media is to the production process, it is an area dictated by easily formalized rules. For example, by specifying which files represent original media assets and which represent proxies or lower resolution copies (as many asset management systems do), a media integrator could configure a business rules engine to always draw media from the original whenever it is needed by a service. The service interface would only have to specify the asset identifier, not the specific file. The media layer would take care of resolving that identifier and picking the right version of the file.

Another aspect of transcoding that business rules in the media layer could handle is the choice of an appropriate transcoding engine (also "hidden" behind the media layer of abstraction) for the given media asset. All experienced media engineers know that no two transcoders from different manufacturers operate exactly alike. Every facility has a specific (but probably oral and undocumented) set of rules that they follow when selecting a transcoder for maximum efficiency and quality: only send MPEG-4 jobs to transcoder 5, load balance by which department is requesting the transcode, etc. These business rules belong in the media layer so that it can route transcoding jobs automatically, letting users worry solely about what asset they need to pick, not what version or how to get it to the correct format.

Timeliness is another area where business rules in the media layer would come in handy. If a business rules engine has knowledge about how long given systems and services take to carry out tasks based on the length of media (a functionality sorely missing from common middleware layers today), then messages could be routed to ensure that deadlines are met the best they can be. This would involve having service interfaces that include deadlines or priorities that service consumers could set, and then offering tools at the media layer for processes to make decisions based on that deadline/priority. In such a system, if two requesters submit media for processing, and the media layer has knowledge of which of the two processing services is faster, it can route the message with the nearer deadline to the faster service. A useful functionality, to be sure!

Timeliness also comes into play regarding transfer times. Current SOA technologies that are highly transactional and expecting small messages, do not provide a good way to offer visibility into an in-process transfer. A media layer, since it would include a media transfer bus implemented using media-specific movement technology, could offer hooks into transfer times for services or other middleware components to take advantage of. Business rules using these might send e-mails if transfers are delayed, paused, or completed; pick the best method of transfer for a given need; and warn users of scheduling transfers that might extend beyond specified deadlines.

Business rules regarding media storage are also a necessity at the media layer. Not only are rules surrounding the load balancing of hard drives or tape storage to provide enough free space (HSM) necessary, but also the location of media files in storage. To effectively abstract the movement and management of media away from the service interface, the media layer must include storage and have some control over the various media storage locations that services can access. The goal with media storage business rules is never to have a service consumer or provider worry about *where* the right media is. If a consumer has media on a SAN and requests processing of that media from a service located in another facility, business rules in the media layer should recognize the need to move the media, initiate the transfer, and confirm that the transfer is complete (or complete enough to begin work) before sending the message along to the service to begin processing. All of this would be transparent to both the consumer and provider, allowing both to focus on the business goals of the exchange instead of the logistics.

Finally, business rules at the media layer should cover aspects of media security. Earlier in the chapter, it was mentioned that implementing a watermarking chain using a traditional middleware layer meant designing convoluted processes that called a watermarking service every other step. In a media layer, that could be specified at a level below the process, so that business rules could dictate that every time media changes hands, it is watermarked (or encrypted, or any other security need) in a specific way before sending it along. Since the media layer has control over media storage and transfer, it can handle many such aspects of security. After setting such a rule, the media integrator would then only have to use the service interfaces, certain that media sent to them was meeting security requirements.

The main idea behind including a business rules engine as part of an ideal "media layer" is to create a method for engineers, producers, or editors to manage media through changing rules rather than directly working with the media files. It is a new way to think about it, more like adjusting the flow of a stream of media rather than individually moving tapes from place to place. But it is a more efficient way of handling what is otherwise a fairly mindless task of media management. It is important to get media management right in a facility, certainly, but once it is right, it will not change often.

### 7.2.1.2 The Media Bus

Without the ability to move media from place to place inside or outside a facility, a media layer would be unable to shield the users of the

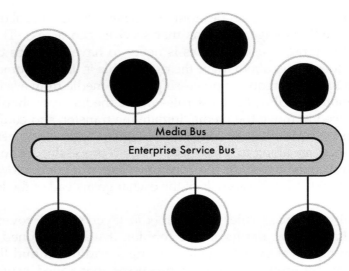

**FIGURE 7-9**   In the Service-Oriented Media Enterprise, a media bus can be used on top of an ESB to give the appearance of moving media "in-band."

infrastructure from the logistics of media. When implementing a traditional SOA, a media integrator should follow the best practice of moving media out-of-band of the middleware layer using media movement services or shared storage. However, this solution can only go so far, especially in enterprises with a lot of media movement (such as those distributed to many locations)! Just as a traditional middleware layer can offer the increasingly popular ESB technology as a way to abstract message movement and routing, so too does the media layer need a "media bus" to abstract media movement in a reliable and timely way.  In a sense, the media layer extends the traditional ESB, as shown in Fig. 7-9.

Software to expedite media movement is big business in the M&E industry. A media bus is not a replacement for these technologies. The Service-Oriented Media Enterprise, with its media layer, would leverage existing products and standards to implement a media bus. Technically, the media bus would still be out-of-band from the middleware layer and the routes through which SOA messages pass, but its location in the media layer would abstract the details of media movement away from services using the bus. Out-of-band, in other words, does not mean out-of-control. What is needed for a successful media bus is a way to manage transfers inside the context of an SOA. A standard in this space would allow many vendors to put their "secret sauce" media movement technologies to work inside the media layer!

A media bus would have to include hooks for two separate functionalities: transfer negotiation and status visibility. The media bus would have to provide the means for two services to negotiate a media transfer that both can agree on (much the same way that TCP does over IP) in either a manual or automated way. Since all media enterprises share the same business goal of wanting media transfers to occur as fast as possible, this negotiation has the strong potential to be completely automated and under the covers of the media layer. It would allow two services to decide upon a method of transfer (FTP?, MDP?, etc.), a bandwidth allocated for the transfer, the starting and ending file names and locations, etc. This sort of a handshaking is necessary for a successful transfer, so a media bus would have to discover or give services tools to publish what methods various service endpoints support, their maximum number of simultaneous transfers, and so on.

## MDP: A MEDIA BUS STANDARD?

The Pro-MPEG Forum started a working group in 2003 known as the Media Dispatch Group with the intention of developing a vendor-neutral way to exchange media files across an IP network. The standard they developed became known as the Media Dispatch Protocol (MDP).

MDP does for media what an application server does for messages: it creates a layer of abstraction to handle the logistical details of a file transfer. An MDP "agent" coordinates a transfer with another agent, figuring out available bandwidth, transport protocol, security needs, etc. — all automatically. If two endpoints in a media layer speak MDP, then the details of how a media transfer might occur can be left out of the interface details of those endpoints. It could handle the things that a media layer must handle.

The best part about the MDP? It is based on XML, just like the common SOA Web service standards. At the time of this writing, MDP has recently undergone SMPTE standardization, and very few implementations have seen the light of day. However, time may prove that MDP is a real contender for enabling a pervasive media transfer infrastructure.

A media bus would have to provide visibility into the transfer in-progress to allow other media/middleware layer components (such as business rules engines or portals) to manage or report transfer status. This is an important aspect of the media layer for the same reasons laid out in the section above on business rules — media transfers are not like the traditional IT transfers of a number of smaller documents — they take a long time, and a media-aware SOA must account for this.

### 7.2.1.3 Storage

Storage is yet another potential component in the media layer to abstract media management away from the services in a Service-Oriented Media Enterprise. Certainly various end systems that would be exposed as services in an SOA will have storage associated with them, and some, such as archive services, may have storage as their primary business function! There are options here, and the jury is still out on whether or not media storage is *needed* to effectively imple-ment a media layer, or if it is just one style of doing so. Like so many things in SOA, the answer is enterprise specific.

In a facility or department that focuses on media storage as a primary business goal (such as an archive or a near-line storage rental house), it is imperative to not put storage behind the veil of service abstrac-tion. Storage *is* the business in these situations, so it is appropriate for storage to also be the business services. In these cases, it is not neces-sary to implement a storage solution inside the media layer. If any-thing, it will only confuse the true business of these facilities. Facilities that provide storage solutions to third parties, however, would have good business if they are able to *be* the storage inside a media layer!

There are many other types of enterprises where media storage is con-sidered a part of the underlying infrastructure, and in these situations, it makes sense to take that worry away from users of the system. A stor-age solution inside the media layer must be able to plug into a media bus (so that media can flow into or out of it), and in general be able to be managed programmatically by business rules or other such control software. Many shared storage solutions on the market are able to do just that (although often in a proprietary way), and perhaps all that is needed are programmatic hooks into an existing collaboration suite sit-ting on top of a SAN to make storage in the media layer a reality.

### 7.2.1.4 Transcoding

The final major component of the media layer is a transcoding service. In Chapter 3, it was mentioned that transcoding makes a perfect business service in a traditional SOA: it is transactional, business-level, and part of many crucial M&E processes. Business rules in a media layer could make this service available to all, without having to worry about media transfer. It could be as easy as including a transcoding step in a business process.

One can also see that a transcoding service is crucial to the goals of the media layer: to abstract the media away from the business services. If transcoding is implemented wisely, with access to the right transcoders given to the right services, then business processes or business rules in the middleware could easily take advantage of transcoding as a service to ensure the media is delivered in the right format in a timely manner.

## 7.2.2  A Service-Oriented Media Utopia

This vision of the ideal media infrastructure, built with SOA best practices and media technologies, is now possible. All of the necessary components exist and, with enough elbow grease, can be made to interoperate in such a way to provide users with an agile set of business-oriented services built on top of a reliable, standardized media layer. But it is not easy. Chapter 8 focuses on ways to make this vision more achievable. In many ways, though, the vision does not go far enough. Why have a media layer separate from a middleware layer, even if they are integrated and beyond the concern of the business services? Why keep transcoding, archive, or other parts of a standard media infrastructure as business services? The business should care about creating and distributing new media, not storing and managing it! There are areas of the ideal Service-Oriented Media Enterprise that are not realistic today, but hopefully, one day, the SOA promises of agility and visibility will be perfectly aligned with the media needs of media quality and reliability. One day a facility will be able to change everything about the way it does business without having to change a single thing in the infrastructure.

One major development that will make this goal possible is the development of a high-bandwidth, high-reliability ESB (an Enterprise *Media Service Bus*, so to speak) as shown in Fig. 7-10. The main concern with

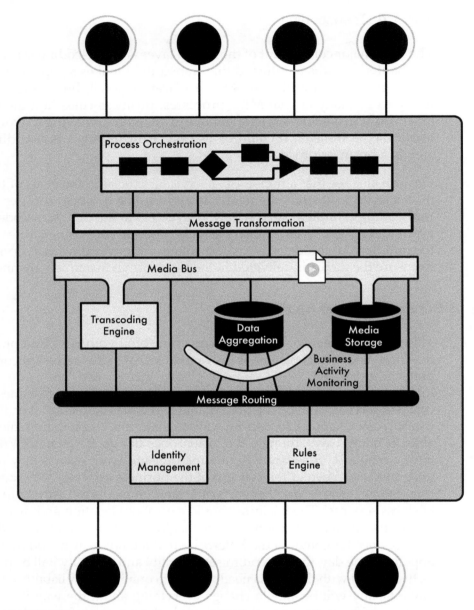

**FIGURE 7-10**   In the Service-Oriented Media Enterprise of the near future, an "evolved" middleware layer will be able to handle the demands of heavy media traffic, and the media architecture will look more like the Service-Oriented Architecture that currently handles traditional IT infrastructures.

ESBs and with middleware layers in general is their inability to handle large media files "in-band," requiring instead media transfer services or a parallel media bus to fill this requirement. If, however, the open standards used to route messages in an ESB can evolve to be able to handle large media files in a reliable, efficient, and high-bandwidth way, then there is no need for a separate media bus! The media and the messages can move together across the same network. No standards body has considered how middleware standards might be expanded to meet the needs of media, but many, such as the Advanced Media Workflow Association (AMWA), are beginning to explore this area.

When discussing an integrated media and messaging bus, one can take the unification of the middleware layer a step farther. Just as messages have transformational components in the middleware layer to change map one message standard to another, so too can media! The equivalent technology to message transformation in media is transcoding. Transcoding is such a crucial element to media management that it should become part of the media management fabric in an enterprise — part of the media middleware layer.

In a Service-Oriented Media Enterprise, a transcoding server or multiple transcoding servers could be made available as part of the middleware layer. Then, when a service consumer requests some work from a business service, business rules would determine that media need to get moved and transcoded, the transcoding server would get alerted to transcode the media, and then the bus would negotiate a transfer to the destination. All of this is done without involving either the service or the consumer of the service (or even, for that matter, any business processes designed by analysts — no need to involve them in the logistics of media management!). It does not get coded into processes or services, it just happens.

## 7.3  CONCLUSION

The utopian vision of users that do not worry about media format, formalized business processes that automatically send notifications and route media, and transcoding that just happens without anyone thinking about it is not as far off as people think. To get there, the media industry must be willing to put more effort into the standardization of technologies and interfaces to technologies that will facilitate interoperability in this space. The Service-Oriented Media Enterprise is a necessary evolution of the tenets of SOA put to use in the M&E industry. The sooner the industry gets to the point where a truly integrated media and middleware layer is possible, the better off it will be.

This chapter has covered the major differences between the enterprises that Service-Oriented Architecture was meant for and the realistic enterprises in the media industry. It also suggests some ways to work around these differences in the near term. By implementing specific types of services and specific middleware layer components, an integrator can create a "media layer" that will help to smooth over the challenges of media management in an SOA.

Ultimately, however, for the true goals of service orientation to be 100% reached in the M&E industry, work must be done to resolve the differences between SOA/BPM technology and media technology. This work is well on its way, and much is achievable now. All that remains is the standardization and wide acceptance necessary to create critical mass. In the near future, the truly Service-Oriented Media Enterprise will be a reality.

## WHAT TO TELL YOUR BOSS

- While SOA and BPM solve many of the problems currently faced by media professionals, the M&E industry has many unique challenges that are not effectively covered by current SOA technology.
- No good way to incorporate media into a modern middleware layer currently exists.
- The Service-Oriented Media Enterprise of the near future will employ a "media layer" that handles many aspects of media management for the services plugged into it.
- An effective media layer includes business rules, media transfer, media storage, and transcoding services.

# 8

# MOVING TOWARD A SERVICE-ORIENTED MEDIA ENTERPRISE

Thus far, this book has focused on the specific technologies and architectures that enable a modern media infrastructure. However, the reader hoping to use this information to enable change in his or her enterprise in the short term may be thinking, "That's great, but how do I get there today?" The last thing anyone wants to do is a complete overhaul of a facility's infrastructure, regardless of the benefits promised by the new architecture. To make Service-Oriented Architecture and Business Process Management realistic and achievable, an integrator must develop a transition plan to get from the current state of the media enterprise to the Service-Oriented Media Enterprise.

SOA installations and BPM-oriented enterprises do not pop up overnight. Even in the IT industry, where companies might be a little more willing to switch over to the latest and greatest software architectures, SOA did not come in as a whirlwind and change everything immediately. The evolution of SOA and BPM in other industries has been steady and deliberate, with smaller projects slowly building into a service-oriented enterprise. SOA is not a bleeding-edge technology that makes or breaks a new company. It is a set of best practices that is appropriate in many different business situations and technical infrastructures. In media, there is no difference — a slow and steady adoption of

SOA and BPM is the only way to build up capability in an enterprise. The Service-Oriented Media Enterprise, like Rome, is not built in a day.

## CASE STUDY

### Phased SOA Implementation

The credit arm of a major financial firm decides to begin the process of SOA-enabling their business. They decide on a multi-phase approach that steadily builds their SOA infrastructure instead of forklifting out entire server rooms at once.

The first phase of the project is focused on service enabling a few of their applications and getting a customer-facing Web site online to make use of these services. Their initial middleware layer is not complex; it simply manages communication to and from the Web server. All services are hard wired; they did not use dynamic service discovery or service registries/repositories initially. The later phases of the project added more and complex services to handle greater amounts of functionality, and additional middleware components, including different messaging models and a service registry. The success of the initial Web site was such that they were able to move on to later phases sooner than expected, thus illustrating that a gradually built SOA (assuming business value at every step) gives time for enterprise buy-in and ample resources.

At the same time, this means that the Service-Oriented Media Enterprise is a major investment for M&E companies looking to adopt its principles. An enterprise looking into SOA should be prepared for a long-term commitment. It will not be a painful commitment. There are ways to make even the most difficult SOA projects affordable and doable, but it will take time and require significant effort. SOA and BPM inform all areas of the business. If a media company does not want SOA to ever touch certain areas of its workflow, it probably does not actually want SOA. This is not to scare perspective implementers from the idea of the Service-Oriented Media Enterprise, but only to prepare them for the significance of the undertaking.

There are many reasons to move toward the Service-Oriented Media Enterprise. A number of these reasons are covered in the previous chapter, but perhaps the most compelling reason for an enterprise to take this step *now*, as opposed to in five years when the precepts of SOA and BPM are pervasive and accepted in M&E, is that it provides a media enterprise with an edge. The SOA/BPM "edge" is simply this: the greater agility provided by these best practices means that an adopting enterprise is able to react to changes faster than its competitors. This has the side effect of compounding on top of itself. Starting SOA and BPM projects now means that an enterprise will be more agile when it comes time to expand upon those installations later. Each subsequent project will come easier than the next; the competition will never be able to keep up in theory! The myriad benefits of early adoption of SOA and BPM are shown in Fig. 8-1.

Recall that SOA (and BPM, for that matter) is a top-loaded investment. This means that the majority of the time and money spent on SOA projects is up-front time and up-front money (a possible timeline

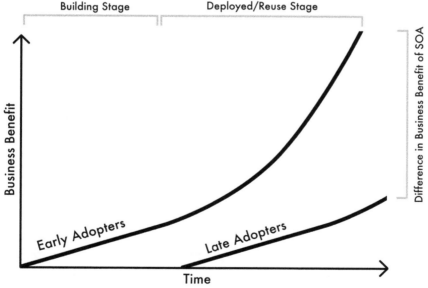

**FIGURE 8-1**  This chart shows the benefits of early adoption of SOA and BPM. Business analysts agree that the earlier an enterprise gets into an agility-producing architecture such as SOA, the better off that enterprise will be.

of SOA investment is shown in Fig. 8-2). This is dangerous in certain situations, because it means that a majority of the investment is spent before any business value is felt from the project. This can be a bad thing when a business unit needs to justify its costs to the rest of the enterprise. Each subsequent project is easier, but that does not help to convince skeptics of the value of the architecture. There are ways to circumvent this difficulty that will be covered in this chapter. The bottom line is: integrators should be realistic about the time, cost, and effort of SOA and BPM projects, but they should also not ignore the importance of showing business value quickly.

So, it may be a challenging road, but the rewards of the Service-Oriented Media Enterprise are great. And it is a very doable thing. There are necessary steps at every phase of the project life cycle to effectively accomplish the goals of the Service-Oriented Media Enterprise. The rest of this chapter walks the reader through each of these phases and discusses how even the most conservative media enterprises can begin down the path to service orientation!

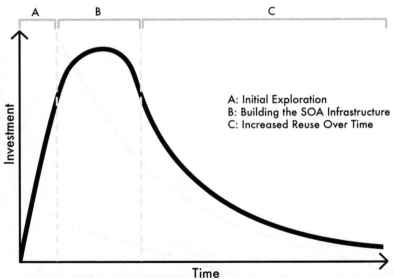

**FIGURE 8-2**   SOA and BPM are top-loaded investments. This chart shows the investment that a media company might make in SOA over the course of three years and the amount of return that company can expect. This chapter will cover methods by which an enterprise can balance this graph.

## 8.1 BEFORE BEGINNING

Hopefully the concepts of SOA and BPM are so exciting that integrators want to begin right away to implement such projects in their facilities. However, there are a couple of tasks that must be considered before implementing development. As mentioned above, both SOA and BPM are top-loaded architectures, and they will impact many areas of the business. It is not advisable to jump right in without testing the water first!

Unless it is the CEO of a media enterprise that is considering the move to service-orientation (not unheard of!), then the clear first task of any service-oriented integration project is to get buy-in from the upper management of the enterprise. Without support from the highest levels of management, any major SOA initiative will fail. The reason for this is simple: SOA and BPM affect many areas of the business. Any major development or integration project requires buy-in from department heads including engineering management. SOA projects, however, affect nearly every area of the business — engineering, operations, IT, production, even HR and finance — so the lowest common denominator across all of those departments is fairly high up in the food chain. Ideally, SOA/BPM projects should get the sign-off of a CIO or CTO, and this really means getting the thumbs up from all of the individual departments affected.

### WHAT NOT TO DO: NEGLECTING BUY-IN

Never neglect to get the buy-in of upper management! SOA and BPM initiatives are long term and wide reaching. To ensure the success of the initiative as a whole, the Service-Oriented Media Enterprise advocates within the enterprise must get their executives not only on-board with the initiative, but excited about it! When the goals of SOA and BPM stretch all the way up the ladder, there is no end to the benefits that can be achieved!

Any project that requires this much involvement is bound to be a political challenge. It is hard enough for most IT and operations departments to agree on anything, much less collaborate on a joint integration effort. Thankfully, SOA and BPM were made to live with these sorts of politics. Service boundaries and process definitions actually help to split the project along business lines instead of technical lines. This means that each individual department involved will be able to concentrate on the functionality it needs to provide to the overall effort, instead of having to administer someone else's server just because it happens to be in a certain equipment room (or some other equally arbitrary assignment). This can have the pleasing effect of abating the political turmoil around an integration project; something any integrator is sure to be thankful for!

The other major aspect to consider before starting an SOA/BPM project in earnest is to ensure that business value will be felt at *every* stage of the project. It is especially difficult with these particular architectures to get into a mode where all work done is preparatory toward some ideal future — installing middleware layers, wrapping services without regard to how they might be immediately used, etc. This is a mistake; integrators should promise to all project stakeholders that every move toward the Service-Oriented Media Enterprise is one designed to provide participants with measurable value. Without this, all of the managers and users who do not see all of the cool work done wrapping and integrating will quickly lose patience with the questions, time, and budget of an SOA project. Before going into requirements definition or even forming a Service-Oriented Media Enterprise team, the enterprise must make the commitment to provide project participants with business value.

## IMPORTANT NOTE

It is so important when starting an SOA/BPM initiative in a media enterprise to make a strong commitment to establishing business value at every step of the way. It may seem to engineers or integrators that a project done simply for the sake of expanding an enterprise's infrastructure is a good idea, but the end users of that infrastructure will resist any change that does not provide them with some benefit. Both SOA and BPM can provide valuable business functionality with every addition if they are managed correctly. The Service-Oriented Media Enterprise team must ensure that this occurs.

## 8.2 THE BIG PICTURE

Many enterprises begin their journey toward service orientation with a very strong end goal in mind. Perhaps this goal is an ideal facility where no users need to worry about video and audio format or where their assets are getting distributed. Perhaps this end goal is a production house that can turn around its entire operations in a day and be totally prepared to work on the next project. Perhaps the goal is simply a more efficient version of what is being done currently. An enterprise does not have to have a big picture in mind to get started on an SOA project; it could simply pick an area of the business that has new requirements and implement those requirements using the tenets of SOA and BPM. However, if integrators are only moving tactically from project to project without some higher level mission, they are not enjoying one of the greatest parts about the journey to service orientation, and will no doubt miss out on countless opportunities for additional efficiency through the synthesis of disparate services and projects.

Every enterprise should have a bigger goal in mind when beginning SOA integration. This allows integrators to make strategic choices about which projects to tackle and which areas of the business to service-orient for maximum effectiveness. An SOA roadmap is a crucial piece of this whole puzzle. While it is possible to develop real SOA functionality without such a roadmap, it is not the best way to go. Especially for a Service-Oriented Media Enterprise, which may include requirements around media movement and management that the traditional best practices of SOA do not directly address, having a holistic SOA integration goal is of supreme importance. It does not matter what this goal is; it could be related to functionality desired in the ideal infrastructure or efficiency of work in an ideal facility. No truly interesting functionality (such as the abstraction of media movement using a media layer) will come out of simply moving from project to project aimlessly. An enterprise has to have a direction. Better yet, an enterprise should have a specific architecture (such as the one discussed in this book) as its end goal, as shown in Fig. 8-3.

### 8.2.1 Forming the Service-Oriented Media Enterprise Team

And now: the starting pistol! It is time to begin working toward the goal of service orientation in the enterprise. The first major task that

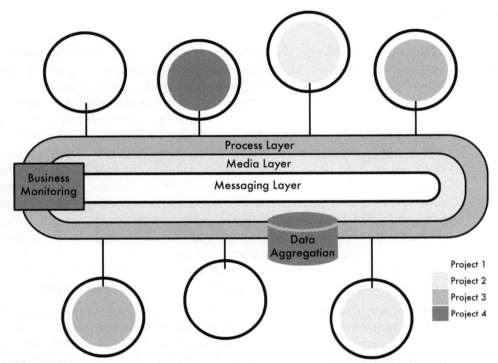

**FIGURE 8-3** Having a big picture for SOA integration allows an enterprise to choose projects that build to support this goal. Each project should provide business value to stakeholders while working toward an ideal infrastructure for the facility.

an enterprise is faced with, right out of the gate, is ensuring proper governance and responsibilities as the SOA/BPM initiative moves forward. That means putting a specific team together to tackle the planning and execution of SOA projects. All SOA experts suggest forming a single group that will persist across all SOA projects — a core team of SOA and BPM proficiency and responsibility. If the enterprise opts for many teams, one for each project undertaken, then there is no continuity among projects, and there is no clear responsibility for overall planning and direction. A single SOA team is the way to go, and it should be the first thing created as part of an SOA initiative!

### 8.2.1.1 Responsibilities of the Team

The responsibilities of such a team are varied, but all are extremely important to the success of the overall Service-Oriented Media Enterprise initiative. It is important that these responsibilities exist together, because they complement each other and are most efficient when executed in tandem. Neglecting any of these responsibilities (a common mistake) is a dangerous thing to do, and, while it may not cause failure of any single SOA or BPM project, it will lead to disorganization in the overall initiative.

The major responsibilities of the Service-Oriented Media Enterprise team are

- Creating and maintaining a roadmap
- Enterprise SOA and BPM governance
- Project oversight

Just as it is important to have an end goal in an SOA/BPM initiative, it is equally important to create an initiative roadmap that shows how to get from the current state of the enterprise to that end goal. This roadmap is the first responsibility of the SOA/BPM team. By starting with the ideal goal of the SOA/BPM initiative, the team should determine tangible steps necessary to achieve that goal. They should evaluate various end solutions and break the chosen one into disparate short-term projects, each of which provide solid business value to the enterprise. This roadmap will dictate which SOA projects must be done and it what order to achieve maximum return on investment.

Once project work has begun, it is not enough to simply follow the roadmap from start to completion. After every major task, the SOA/BPM team should reevaluate where they are on the roadmap, reassess the enterprise goals, and confirm the next step along the route. This continuous reevaluation ensures that as business requirements and goals change, the service-oriented initiative will evolve to serve the needs of the enterprise. In many ways, this means that there is no true end to the road. As the goals of a business are constantly evolving, therefore, this team's work will remain relevant.

A second responsibility of the SOA/BPM team is enterprise governance. This means that the team must define and delegate responsibility for various projects and development efforts, catalog and manage the specific architectures created, and look for ways to achieve synergy in these architectures. One facet of this governance is the high-level definition of services and processes in an SOA. The team should provide this direction to the development and integration groups that it has delegated to build these services. Also, their responsibility over SOA governance also means that the team is responsible for finding opportunities for reuse in services and processes. They must keep track of the architecture created and ensure that it is used to its fullest potential.

## WHAT IS GOVERNANCE?

The term "governance," when used in reference to Service-Oriented Architecture, has a specific meaning. It is similar to the concept of IT governance, which deals with setting goals, structure, and accountability to technical projects and departments to ensure that they are successful. SOA governance takes that one step farther by considering service monitoring, policies/contracts, and reuse. Implementing good SOA governance means making sure that all services deployed in an enterprise meet quality standards, that they are all effectively managed and documented, and that, when changed, these services meet set change management and reuse policies. Implementing good SOA governance means setting the law of the land, and then making sure that all enterprise teams follow that law.

The third and final responsibility of the SOA/BPM team is project oversight. This does not mean project control or management as those responsibilities are better delegated to specific teams or departments for the execution of particular tasks in the overall initiative. Project oversight is really the coordination between projects. The SOA/BPM team must ensure that individual projects are executed in the right order and time frame, and that resources are used as effectively as possible. They are ultimately responsible for the success or failure of the entire enterprise-wide SOA initiative, so it only makes sense that the team should have some visibility into how various component projects and efforts are progressing.

### 8.2.1.2 Composition of the Team

Picking the right individuals to make up a Service-Oriented Media Enterprise team is a challenge, to be sure. The composition of this team is also very important, for in many SOA or BPM projects, this team has to serve both as primary executor of SOA and BPM development and as main cheerleader of the initiative to the rest of the enterprise. Half-hearted or non-invested participants can easily derail the entire effort! A great deal of thought should go into the composition of the team, and, once decided, this composition should change as little as possible. There is no point in having a single team to ensure continuity if the members of the team change every few weeks!

The primary point to make about the members of the SOA/BPM team is this: it is not a technology committee. One common misconception about both SOA and BPM (corrected many times throughout this book) is that they are specific technologies that can be learned and mastered. They are not; they are sets of best practices and concepts to be followed. Because of this, there is surprisingly little technological expertise required on the SOA/BPM team. It may help to have someone who has mastered Web services or BPEL, because this often means that they have SOA or BPM experience elsewhere. However, this knowledge may also derail the team from its necessary area of expertise: the business. An enterprise certainly does not want a team that suggests cutting-edge technologies without thinking of the specific business needs being fulfilled. In other words, while technology knowledge is a part of a service-oriented initiative, it never defines the primary goals.

It is more important to have representatives from every major group of stakeholders on the SOA/BPM team including every business unit involved, and maybe even representatives from different levels of the business. It may be very useful to have a line manager to give the perspective of individual workers while also having an SVP to give the perspective of the entire enterprise. This would certainly facilitate the "outside-in" style of analysis discussed in Chapter 6. The major advocates of SOA in the enterprise should also be involved to provide inspiration and direction. However, an enterprise should avoid creating a team that will spend so much time fighting for individual pet projects that they do not work cohesively toward an enterprise goal. Depending on the size of the enterprise, the team should be from 5–20 people. However, it is more important that all business groups be represented on the SOA/BPM team than that it stays above or below a particular size.

## CASE STUDY

### Forming the Team

One major studio decides that they will form a Service-Oriented Media Enterprise team to explore and plan SOA/BPM initiatives in the organization. The major advocate for SOA in the enterprise is a director of technology. He discusses the idea with a VP of technology, and they select team members. The VP serves as the team leader, running meetings and monitoring progress. The director and several other directors of various technology departments make up the bulk of the team. In addition, there are a couple of project managers and facility managers on the team to provide leadership over the expected SOA/BPM projects and insight into the existing infrastructure, respectively. The CTO of the studio is also a member of the team, but is not expected to attend meetings regularly.

The team decides to meet once every week, interviewing stakeholders or reviewing plans, until after the first project kickoff and then once a month after that. The director and VP will accomplish or delegate additional tasks in between. In one month they expect to have an initial roadmap, and their first project kicking off a month after that.

## 8.2.2 Developing a Roadmap

The first responsibility of the Service-Oriented Media Enterprise team is the development of an initial roadmap of projects that will achieve the business goals of the SOA/BPM initiative. This is essentially a requirements definition effort, because the team will need to assess all of the various functional and non-functional goals of the completed integration effort and also determine their relative importance to each other and to individual stakeholders in the effort. This information can be used to create a battle plan that addresses the most important areas of development and integration first, and logically moves from project to project to maximize SOA reuse and business value.

Really, the only way for the team to acquire this information is to talk to each of the stakeholders in the initiative (or at least enough of them to identify all requirements). The first part of this task, then, is identifying all of the right people to interview. These are the individuals that will be the source of all of the requirements definition for the initiative, so it cannot be just anyone. Unlike process analysis, which works best when speaking with participants at every level, requirements elicitation should focus on the business stakeholders and those who have a wide-reaching view of the enterprise. The team should schedule a few hours with each to discuss the ways in which SOA and BPM can benefit that person's particular department or goals. For some stakeholders, this may mean explaining the core concepts of SOA and BPM so that they understand where the initiative is headed.

## IMPORTANT NOTE

The SOA/BPM team can tell it is interviewing the right stakeholders when the people brought in both have personal knowledge of the systemic problems to be solved and can understand and get behind the idea of solving these problems using SOA. The ideal stakeholder is someone who could participate on an SOA/BPM project team defining processes and service interfaces, even if he or she does not have the time or the enterprise ultimately decides to outsource that work.

The goal of this elicitation is not only to identify the major SOA and BPM business goals, but also to determine which are the most important. As the team speaks with various stakeholders, it should focus on the identification of particular pain points — areas that are really frustrating to someone. These pain points should then be ranked in order of importance. This ranking can be determined by comparing a rough order-of-magnitude benefit of alleviating each point, and a rough order-of-magnitude difficulty of doing so. The team should focus on the easiest goals that bring the most value, and move toward the harder goals that have little value associated with them (if it is decided to tackle those at all!). In this way, the roadmap of SOA/BPM projects is established.

# RANKING BUSINESS GOALS

When determining the best SOA/BPM projects to choose as part of an enterprise roadmap, the team should develop a ranking system that balances the importance of the business goals of the project against the resources required to complete the project. An example of this ranking is shown in Table 8.1.

**TABLE 8-1**

Ranking of Pain Points Based on Rough Order-Of-Magnitude Difficulty

| Description of pain point | Enterprise need | Difficulty | Team ranking |
| --- | --- | --- | --- |
| Scheduling errors made several times a week | 9 | 4 | 1 |
| Producers constantly e-mailing for status updates | 6 | 2 | 2 |
| Manual work order entry required every time | 4 | 3 | 3 |
| Pre-production process takes too long | 7 | 7 | 4 |
| Post houses ship tapes back through mail, requiring ingest | 2 | 8 | 5 |

The values are on a scale from one to ten.

Throughout this process, the team should remember another goal of an SOA or BPM initiative: to implement a high-level architectural solution that addresses many business requirements. The team should take the ranked list of goals/pain points and identify holistic SOA architectural solutions that might address groups of these goals. What sort of middleware layer is needed? How might the services be organized? These sorts of questions are the ones the SOA/BPM team needs to ask to maximize reusability in the solution architecture. If each goal is addressed separately, the team is missing the whole point of placing these business goals under the umbrella of an SOA initiative: to unify the solution architecture.

The next step is to organize the roadmap around what particular project should be attacked first and how. This requires an analysis of the overall goals of the SOA/BPM initiative. If, based on a difficulty/ benefit analysis, the first project is determined to be automatic notification upon successful ingest and playout, for example, then the next step is to determine what about this project will define success. Obviously, getting the functionality required is a necessary component of a successful first project, but there should also be corollary goals related to the overall SOA/BPM effort. Perhaps the first project needs to provide a specific ROI to validate the choice of SOA and BPM. Perhaps it should be designed such that it can be used to demonstrate the benefits of SOA to a larger audience within the enterprise. Perhaps it should focus on building up as much of the middleware layer as possible to support later projects. These additional goals keep the entire initiative on track and have the potential to affect which project is chosen to be first. Projects should be weighted and ranked appropriately with regards to these goals, as shown in Fig. 8-4.

At this point, the team can proceed to define the rest of their initial roadmap. Each business goal addressed should include some level of detail about the solution suggested and the SOA components necessary to achieve that solution. Each project should add to the overall SOA architecture in some way so that the complete architecture is slowly built up over the course of several projects.

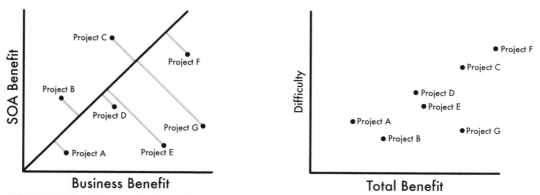

**FIGURE 8-4** This graph shows the ranking of business goals/project ideas by difficulty and benefit. Projects are additionally weighted based on their ability to provide corollary SOA/BPM initiative goals.

In addition, the team should ensure that each project contributes to the overall agility of the completed infrastructure. This means that solutions should reuse components whenever possible, and components designed in an early project should be designed to the greatest extent possible with later projects in mind. If that notification service in the first project is needed in the third and fifth projects as well, but with additional parameters, the service should be initially implemented in such a way so that addition of those parameters later is a straightforward task.

The team should also ensure that every project provides business value to the participants. If possible, each step should provide business value that provides a key benefit that users would not see in the "non-SOA" version of the project (such as increased visibility). If one step in the overall SOA/BPM initiative does not provide an improvement to the regular workflow, but takes up many people's time with elicitation and requirements definition, then the enterprise will not react well to the completed project. Project stakeholders need to see the benefits that they are paying for with time, effort, or budget money.

At this point, the initial roadmap is complete. The SOA/BPM team never really puts this document to bed until the end of the entire SOA initiative, however. It is a living document. At the end of each project, the team should reevaluate the roadmap and determine if it needs to be altered to more clearly reflect the current state of the enterprise (whether that be through changing business goals or conforming proposed solutions to unexpected changes in the infrastructure). Continuous reevaluation is necessary to keep the SOA/BPM initiative streamlined and relevant.

## SAMPLE ROADMAP

The roadmap generated by the Service-Oriented Media Enterprise team will differ from enterprise to enterprise based on the specific SOA and BPM needs. The sample table of contents below represents one possible enterprise roadmap.

1. Overall Goals of SOA/BPM Initiative
   a) Composure and Mission of Team
2. Results of Elicitation Effort
   a) Organizational Structure as It Relates to the Initiative
   b) Pain Points
   c) Desired Functionality
3. Projects
   a) Executive Summary of Planned Projects
      • Ranking and Justification
      • Final Architecture
      • Overall Timeline and Budget
   b) Project 1
      • Goals
      • Project Limitations
      • Possible Components and Solutions
      • Timeline and Budget
   c) Project 2
      • Goals
   d) Project 3
      • Goals
   e) Project 4
      • Goals
4. Conclusion
   a) Roadmap Reevaluation Procedure

## 8.2.3  Types of Projects

After establishing an initial roadmap, the Service-Oriented Media Enterprise team can focus on kicking off SOA and BPM projects to accomplish their specific goals. Depending on the current state of a facility's architecture and the position of the enterprise, these projects can take a few different forms. Different types of projects can have different challenges and different timelines. An SOA team should correctly assess each project type separately to determine not only the largest challenges and opportunities, but also the best way to address them. A single SOA roadmap may have many different types of projects in it.

The types of SOA/BPM projects that will be considered in this chapter are:

- SOA from scratch (a "greenfield" scenario)
- Opportunistic integration
- Proof-of-concept projects
- Passive, or read-only integration

### 8.2.3.1 SOA from Scratch

The first type of SOA/BPM project to consider is also the rarest: building new functionality where none existed previously. This sort of "SOA from scratch" is rare because an enterprise that has been around for any amount of time will have existing systems and infrastructure to contend with, not to mention the workflows that have been established (either formally or organically) around how to use these systems to accomplish the business goals. A pure greenfield situation in SOA and BPM has no existing systems to integrate with and no preconceived notions about how the system should be used. An integrator that is given the opportunity to build an SOA from scratch is lucky indeed! An example of this type of architecture appears in Fig. 8-5. It is as close to the SOA ideal as one will find in realistic architectures.

Even though this type of project is rare, it is worthwhile to consider because it informs projects in existing facilities that are either breaking new ground in terms of functionality or given leeway to completely overhaul certain aspects of the business and essentially start from scratch, if needed. Greenfield projects represent the ideal. In this case, a greenfield SOA project means that integrators can define services that represent the way they do business (as should happen in all SOA projects) and then also choose technology that makes service implementation as straightforward as possible. This is a luxury that integrators retrofitting existing infrastructures with SOA architecture do not get!

To a certain extent, SOA from scratch represents true service enablement. Even in the most dedicated SOA teams, certain service interface sacrifices will be made in the name of implementing services only with available technology and/or keeping service implementation costs cheap. When there is no available technology with which to

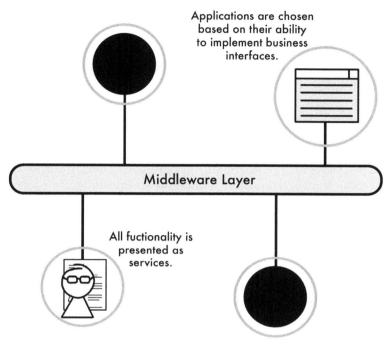

Applications are chosen based on their ability to implement business interfaces.

Middleware Layer

All fuctionality is presented as services.

**FIGURE 8-5**  A sample greenfield SOA architecture demonstrates how technology can be chosen based on its resemblance to business-oriented services, instead of vice versa. This type of architecture minimizes integration complexity.

implement services, the implementation team has free reign to define interfaces totally from the point of view of the business process. True service enablement means 100% process over technology. In many realistic scenarios, that is only possible in a new facility.

In addition, SOA from scratch allows integrators to take full advantage of a pillar of BPM: completely horizontally integrated workflow. In existing facilities, the fact that established departments and teams have been there for years imposes political boundaries that hamper technology integration. Perhaps the system that one group loves is disliked by another. Perhaps the budgetary cycles of various departments are out of sync, forcing single departments to implement new functionality without the support of the rest of the enterprise. Regardless of the reason, political boundaries often force compromise in SOA. But in new facilities, there are no existing silos; an enterprise can take full advantage of the tenets of BPM and involve all departments equally in service development and deployment.

Existing facilities must also deal with legacy systems and the barriers they impose upon integration. SOA is all about the repurposing of legacy systems to meet contemporary business needs; however, it does not completely solve the legacy system problem. Even with all the right tools, it is still difficult to get new functionality out of old systems. When an enterprise is building from scratch, these constraints are not present. There are strong benefits to beginning with the wrapper design and, from there, choosing an implementing technology.

An enterprise that goes into product selection with SOA in mind can plan ahead of time how various systems might best implement given business functionality. A service interface describes the use cases of the underlying service. These use cases can be developed prior to technology selection and compared to the use cases put forward by various technology vendors. This significantly reduces the sense of urgency associated with getting what is there to work how people want to use it.

Because many existing systems in facilities are there as the pet project of some director or VP, greenfield projects also have significantly fewer political issues to contend with. A new SOA/BPM project can provide the right boundaries to systems for various stakeholders to make their own, because the technology abstraction layer separates the functionality of a service from whatever vendor the CTO really likes. And the best part of this is that by starting out in an agile SOA, an enterprise can cater their architecture specifically to a constantly evolving infrastructure. Even after the adoption of SOA principles, many facilities find those legacy systems worming their way into the implementation of many services. A new SOA installation can get a lot closer to the "one application, one service" point, which enhances agility and reusability.

One thing for enterprises to watch out for in greenfield SOA/BPM projects is the use of SOA and BPM best practices as a panacea to make up for the fact that no one has thought about the true business requirements, opportunities, and challenges of the system. Just deciding to build a new facility using the tenets of SOA does not automatically make it well designed. Much thought has to go into service design and implementation and process design and deployment for the benefits of SOA and BPM to be felt, even in a new facility. No enterprise can simply implement a new SOA without putting in the work to fully analyze its business and workflow. Once an enterprise takes the time to do this analysis, however, an "SOA from scratch" architecture is often easier to build than one repurposing legacy equipment. As mentioned previously, though, it is rare to find this situation in practice.

### 8.2.3.2 Opportunistic Integration

Arguably, the approach to SOA and BPM integration that is most realistic is an opportunistic one. "Opportunistic" in this context means that the SOA and BPM projects that the Service-Oriented Media Enterprise team selects and initiates are projects that would have to occur regardless of the architecture used. Then, instead of taking a traditional approach to the execution of that project, SOA best practices are used. For example, if it is decided that Web distribution is a new business goal for the enterprise, and the asset management and transcoding systems must be upgraded and/or changed to achieve this functionality, an SOA approach can be taken instead of a more traditional integration methodology. In addition to achieving the functionality required, the enterprise will gain a foothold into the world of SOA and BPM. An example of this type of architecture is shown in Fig. 8-6.

Because the project provides necessary functionality for the enterprise, these opportunistic projects will garner the support even of potential SOA detractors in the enterprise. In addition, these types of projects will typically have a slightly larger budget available than greenfield projects or proofs-of-concept because the enterprise funds regular upgrades and replacements as part of the cost of doing business. If it is SOA/BPM evangelists within the enterprise that are managing the opportunistic project, then this type of project is a good way to introduce an enterprise to the concepts of SOA and BPM without asking a lot of people for funding or support.

At the same time, the project selected must be appropriate for a first SOA integration attempt. The SOA/BPM team should not select a

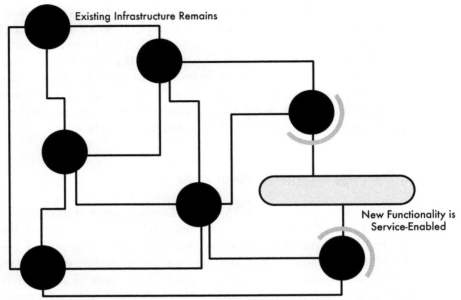

Existing Infrastructure Remains

New Functionality is
Service-Enabled

**FIGURE 8-6**   Opportunistic integration is new functionality, but in the context of an existing system. This example diagram shows a potential opportunistic architecture. The SOA environment created is not the primary environment, but it is designed for expansion.

project that has a particular time crunch associated with it, or a project that is of a sensitive nature. In other words, although unlikely, the integrators should be able to re-work the project after an initial attempt and still achieve success. After all, this would be the first venture into SOA for the enterprise, and there is the danger that the SOA learning curve will impact the project itself. This is another facet of opportunistic SOA/BPM integration: SOA and BPM are not the primary goals of the project.

In this sense, opportunistic integration is almost a "stealth" approach to SOA. SOA and BPM best practices are snuck in as corollary goals to the project — the project sell is the intended functionality, SOA and BPM are simply a means to an end. If, at the end of the project, the enterprise has a good aftertaste from the methods used, then the Service-Oriented Media Enterprise team has succeeded in its goal. However, there is a danger to this as well: the first priority is unarguably the immediate goal of the project. If the enterprise gets into the unfortunate situation where it must choose the success of the project or the use of SOA methodologies, it will almost always choose the success of the project. This is an especially unfortunate situation because then SOA and BPM are given the stigma of "the techniques that almost derailed the business." This is why it is so important to select the right type of project as a first go at SOA and BPM.

### 8.2.3.3 Proof-of-Concept

A third way for the Service-Oriented Media Enterprise team to introduce the concepts of SOA and BPM to an enterprise is through the use of a methodology-led candidate project; in other words, a proof-of-concept. This type of project would be designed simply to show off the tenets of SOA and BPM. The end functionality of the system created should be useful to the enterprise, but certainly not critically necessary. It is an SOA/BPM sales tactic for an organization that needs proof of the benefits of the architecture. An example of this type of architecture is shown in Fig. 8-7.

While they are excellent for introducing SOA and BPM to an enterprise, proof-of-concept projects are appropriate only in very specific situations. They have a tendency to get expensive, both because they are not achieving any necessary functionality so any money spent on them is a difficult expense, and also because the need to show off SOA and BPM at their best often leads to the creation of large systems with complex middleware layers (all the bells and whistles, as it were). Because of this, an enterprise should only consider a proof-of-concept when it can afford both the time and expense of one. Even if the project is a hands-down success in terms of functionality, if management is upset about the resources used then the goals of the project will not be achieved.

The key to building a successful methodology-led project is choosing the right functional requirements. The completed project should highlight the strengths of SOA and BPM — agility, visibility, accessibility, and enhanced productivity. The completed project should be a shining star in the enterprise and show people what SOA and BPM can really do. The primary goal of the initiative is to impress, and so choosing functional requirements that are not impressive is setting the project up for failure.

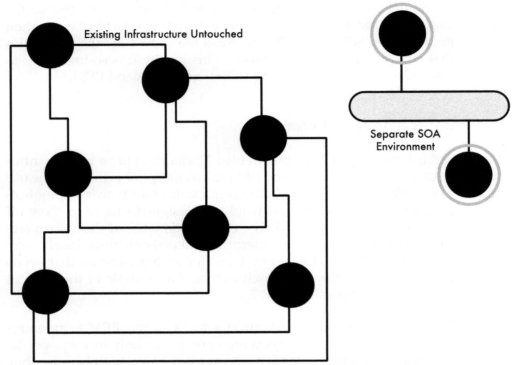

Existing Infrastructure Untouched

Separate SOA
Environment

**FIGURE 8-7**  A proof-of-concept SOA/BPM project would be initially created separately from the rest of the (traditionally integrated) infrastructure. Only after proving its worth would the system be worked in to the facility at large.

After all, SOA and BPM are the whole point of a proof-of-concept project. If the Service-Oriented Media Enterprise team chooses this type of project as a way to introduce these new techniques to an enterprise, they must succeed. It is often hard enough to convince a company to pay for an initial technology proof-of-concept, but convincing them to pay for a second if the first does not correctly achieve its goals is practically downright impossible! However, if the right functionality is chosen and the tenets of SOA and BPM are embraced and followed, then this type of project is a great way to introduce these concepts to an enterprise.

### 8.2.3.4 Passive Integration

The final type of project that a Service-Oriented Media Enterprise team might choose as part of an enterprise SOA/BPM roadmap is a

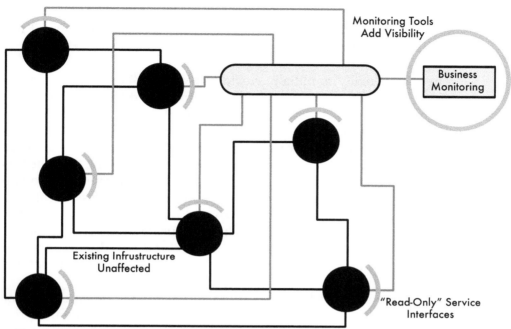

Monitoring Tools
Add Visibility

Business
Monitoring

Existing Infrustructure
Unaffected

"Read-Only" Service
Interfaces

**FIGURE 8-8** Passive integration does not provide additional functionality to end users, but will show the benefits of SOA.

passive integration project. Passive integration is like a proof-of-concept because it is extraneous to the necessary functionality of an enterprise. At the same time, however, passive integration is similar to opportunistic integration because the project itself is heavily ingrained and integrated with existing functionality. The idea is this: an SOA project that does not actively affect the functionality of the system but instead "monitors" what is currently going on showcases the visibility benefits of the architecture and can provide an SOA foothold in the infrastructure. An example of this type of architecture is shown in Fig. 8-8.

In especially conservative or technology-sensitive enterprises where, due to the nature of the work done, it is difficult to suggest changes to the infrastructure, passive integration may be just what the doctor ordered. It is appropriate for scenarios where there is a strong need for SOA integration in production, but there is either no money for replacing full sections of the system (not that a full overhaul is ever a good idea) or little buy-in from the important stakeholders. Passive integration allows an enterprise to see the benefits of SOA (and BPM, through the use of KPIs and dashboards) without feeling that it has made a commitment to it or "wasted" much effort on it.

The idea is really to initially create a "read-only" type SOA environment. A middleware layer can be put into place that gets information from various production end systems but does not affect their functionality or the way in which they communicate and work with each other. This information can then be delivered to managers or other stakeholders to show a visible, horizontal workflow. The focus here is on monitoring and showing that SOA and BPM more easily provide access to data than traditional integration techniques. Passive integration is a project style unique to SOA and BPM. It is difficult, in other words, to show off a particular technology using these techniques, but because SOA and BPM represent architectural paradigms, they can prove their worth (and safety) without affecting the regular workflow.

The main goal of such a project is to garner trust in an enterprise for SOA and BPM techniques. The Service-Oriented Media Enterprise team should really want to move on to actual projects and get real SOA functionality in a facility, so a passive integration project should only be considered when it is necessary to overcome a political barrier to SOA and BPM. Passive integration can help to get buy-in from doubtful executives, and can help to sell the concept to managers across the entire enterprise. One thing that this type of project does not do is introduce the regular process participants to the concepts of SOA and BPM, because nothing really appears to change after the introduction of passive SOA/BPM integration. Still, these projects may be worth considering in certain situations.

## 8.2.4 Benefits That Grow Over Time

After an initial project, run by a project team but overseen by the Service-Oriented Media Enterprise team as step one of its roadmap, the enterprise can move on to additional SOA and BPM projects and watch its architecture grow. Later projects are not the same as this first project because certain qualities of an infrastructure change with the amount of SOA integration in the enterprise. These benefits, shown in Fig. 8-9, make additional projects easier and more achievable, both

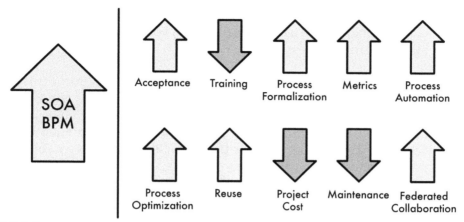

**FIGURE 8-9**  The benefits of an SOA/BPM architecture grow quickly over time. These qualities make each additional SOA/BPM project easier than the last as the entire architecture builds up speed toward the ultimate goal of the Service-Oriented Media Enterprise.

from a political and technological standpoint. SOA and BPM are both heavily top-loaded concepts. This means that after the initial hurdle, SOA and BPM quickly become second nature.

One of the major hurdles an initial SOA project faces is acceptance from the organization at large. SOA projects often need to prove their worth. However, after an initial project, acceptance of SOA and support for SOA within the enterprise grows. In-house integrators that may have been untrained in techniques such as wrapping or middleware messaging require less training and education with each project and quickly become masters of SOA techniques. Managers that had to be taught the basics of service exposure and definition are prepared for the next project. BPM interviews require less explanation, and there is less adjustment necessary in the way all stakeholders have to think about their systems. In other words, after the initial project, the enterprise begins to get over the learning curve.

From a BPM standpoint as well, subsequent projects are easier. The first time through, nearly every process in the enterprise will be undocumented or informal. This may require a lot of business analysis to get an initial batch of workflows formalized and potentially orchestrated. However, when it comes time to attack the next set of functionality, the facility will already have some formalized workflows to start from. As more projects are completed, the enterprise gets closer and closer to the ideal of a completely managed set of processes describing all aspects of business.

In addition, the more business process monitoring put in place, the easier it is to both determine business needs for future projects and to identify further areas where business monitoring might be useful. The collection of metrics in a BPM environment is a cumulative act. With each new batch of services or processes, there are yet more business metrics and KPIs available for viewing. This allows managers and integrators to fine-tune their dashboard views of the enterprise and get better information from their systems. Also, having a certain set of KPIs in practice for a given period of time will help business analysts identify more KPIs for the enterprise. This might arise because new KPIs will naturally fall out of existing KPIs (average terabytes of digital media storage used per month follows naturally from average number of tapes used per month) or will come directly from system users after they get a taste of what is possible (the dub operator asks for a fulfillment time gauge so he or she can keep an eye on due dates easily). Metrics are a big area where SOA and BPM best practices make things easier over time.

Automation of business processes will naturally increase as SOA/BPM projects get completed. Even in facilities where human workflow prevails and automation takes a back seat, if the technology is there, the enterprise will slowly begin to adopt automation in the places where it is appropriate. In addition to helping the enterprise work more efficiently, this helps integrators and business process analysts by providing a process "palette" on which they can build. If switching to backup systems and notifying producers when something goes wrong gets automated in an early SOA/BPM project, that same process can be used to deal with exception cases in later projects!

This brings up another important point about both SOA and BPM over time: reuse of services and processes will drastically increase as the adoption of SOA and BPM increases in the enterprise. This only makes sense, because each subsequent project will create more services and processes in the enterprise, so there is a greater chance that any given set of business requirements will depend upon already developed functionality. This also has the beneficial side effect of decreasing cost with each additional project. SOA and BPM get cheaper as they go, which means the initial investment into the architecture will better pay for itself the more invested an enterprise becomes. Reuse is one of the central tenets of SOA; making use of that reuse should be a goal for any enterprise.

SOA and BPM architectures have a habit of self-optimizing themselves as well. Self-optimization, in this context, means that integrators will tend to use the most efficient means available to them to accomplish a given business requirement. As more business requirements are fulfilled by SOA systems, services and processes will get shuffled around and aligned in an efficient way to suit those needs. For example, an infrastructure service to delete an asset record might be created for one project. The next project may require a methodology to delete an asset from storage. These two can easily be combined into a unified "delete asset" business service. The more functionality in the infrastructure, the better it aligns itself with business goals and needs. This is a difference from more tightly coupled architectures, which actually complicate themselves as business functionality increases.

The maintainability of an SOA system increases as it grows as well. As more applications in the enterprise become service-oriented and unify themselves into a common middleware layer, it becomes easier to centrally manage and administer the infrastructure as a whole. As logic gets externalized out of end systems and into a business process layer, it becomes easier to manage these processes as they grow and change. SOA and BPM are about unifying architecture and workflow horizontally across the entire enterprise; there are fewer silos to manage and fewer different concepts of workflow to balance. This also reduces total cost to maintain the systems, because more administrative functionality can be centralized and less time is spent figuring out where any problems or changes lie. These benefits are felt daily by those who use the integrated systems, which may explain why acceptance and support of SOA and BPM grow as they permeate throughout the enterprise.

Finally, one often-overlooked benefit of a steadily increasing SOA/BPM infrastructure is the increasing ease of opening up that infrastructure to other facilities or organizations. Many media enterprises are becoming more and more open to federation and collaboration with other enterprises as business requirements evolve to compensate for the social networks and integrated offerings of the modern age. SOA and BPM can provide that federation. A whole book in itself could be written on the political challenges and opportunities of this sort of open enterprise, but, needless to say, the technical challenges can be best addressed through a service-oriented infrastructure and solid, publicly exposed service interfaces.

All of these benefits are felt as SOA and BPM adoption in an enterprise grows. The Service-Oriented Media Enterprise team is responsible for harnessing these benefits as opportunities for expansion. This is why the enterprise roadmap designed by this team must undergo constant reevaluation and revision. The enterprise is constantly evolving; SOA and BPM simply help it to evolve in the right ways.

## 8.3 THE SERVICE-ORIENTED MEDIA ENTERPRISE PROJECT CYCLE

Business Process Management dictates specific ways in which the project life cycle can be improved to better reflect and support the processes of the enterprise. In addition, Service-Oriented Architecture best practices provide suggestions to an implementing organization on how best to develop services as part of an SOA initiative. The concept of the Service-Oriented Media Enterprise would certainly be lacking if it did not also include insight on the project life cycle of SOA/BPM projects in M&E! This life cycle is shown in Fig. 8-10.

The SOA/BPM team in an enterprise should set up a project team to tackle each individual project. This team is responsible for executing the project from start to finish. The Service-Oriented Media Enterprise team should oversee the project, but the project team should be the one doing the work (even if the two teams share many members!). This ensures that the SOA/BPM team stays wide reaching and forward looking.

The steps in an SOA/BPM project's life cycle are as follows:

- Analysis: a BPM-led effort to identify and define requirements and processes for the project functionality

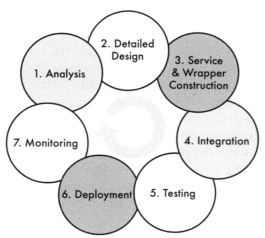

**FIGURE 8-10**  The Service-Oriented Media Enterprise project cycle summarizes the best practices of both SOA and BPM. It is intended to support the BPM concept of continuous process improvement.

- Design: technology- and process-specific planning for project execution
- Service and Wrapper Construction: an SOA-specific development task encompassing all new functionality in the system
- Integration: tying together the new and reused services with the detailed business processes
- Testing: deployment of the services and processes in a controlled environment to ensure that requirements are met
- Deployment: steps taken to put the completed system into production
- Monitoring: the project phase that includes evaluation of project success through monitoring of business metrics and planning for future projects

Each of these steps will be considered in turn. At the end of the project life cycle, the project team should cede responsibility back to the Service-Oriented Media Enterprise team, who can determine when it is best to reconsider specific project requirements for continuous process improvement. Basically, with this project life cycle, all of the SOA and BPM best practices are combined to guide the project team to service-oriented success.

## 8.3.1 Analysis

The first phase of an SOA/BPM project life cycle is arguably the most crucial phase in terms of overall project success: the analysis. SOA and BPM are both top-loaded architectures, which means that the more time spent doing initial elicitation and requirements definition, the better off the project as a whole will be. Successful SOA/BPM projects do not begin by simply diving into the work and starting to integrate systems; they are methodical and detailed, preferably leaving no stone unturned in the planning stages. The goals of this analysis phase are the same as in any type of project: business requirements, constraints, and timelines. However, the means by which these goals are achieved is different.

The key to good project analysis is that it be driven by the best practices of Business Process Management. BPM helps define the best ways to analyze the workflow in an enterprise (as discussed in Chapter 6), and this type of analysis is entirely appropriate for an SOA project, especially one that will include process orchestration as part of its set of functional requirements. A project team should elicit workflow from all stakeholders — making sure to stay true to the ten commandments of workflow analysis — and develop a comprehensive view of the way things are currently done in a facility and the ways in which the project would affect that workflow.

Modeling tools are a good way to capture this information. Business process models are also a good way to elicit feedback from process stakeholders on the quality of the analysis. If a project team misunderstands the desired workflow, that disconnect will come out through a representational model and be resolved well before the design phase begins. In addition, the business process models serve as a welcome method of documentation for project requirements that is easily understood and useful once the system is in place for training or orientation purposes.

Models can also be used to perform what-if workflow analysis as discussed in Chapter 6. In cases where there is some uncertainty around how an enterprise wishes to do its work in the context of the new system, business process simulation can be a useful tool to crystallize business requirements. This simulation must be done in the analysis phase of the project, because once a design or a test system is in place it becomes too difficult to make fundamental changes to the proposed system. In addition, using simulation tools ensures that the project team has considered as many options as possible when designing the proposed workflow and system. The goal of BPM and SOA is to allow organizations to work in the way that they want to work, but when an enterprise does not know how it wants to work, simulation tools can help a team to make suggestions.

After modeling and simulation, the next task in the analysis phase is that of service decomposition. Service decomposition is covered in Chapter 3 and, at a high level, breaks the fundamental tasks and functions of the proposed system into services for implementation. This phase brings in the existing facility technology for the first time, as it includes the conceptual analysis of APIs that could be used for integration. The goal of this decomposition is not to have a service model complete with detailed interface definitions and wrapper designs, but rather to have a comprehensive list of services needed and an idea of the applications that might be used to implement these services. During this phase, the project team should be heavily focused on service reuse; an enterprise should leverage its existing SOA assets whenever possible. If this project is third or fourth in the SOA/BPM enterprise roadmap, then a good percentage of the services needed to accomplish the goals of the project will probably already exist in the facility.

Next comes the selection of the Key Performance Indicators (KPIs) that dictate project success. Even in scenarios where these KPIs will not be automatically measured by some business monitoring technology, it is still vital for the project team to identify and define them. KPIs tell a team when the system they have built is working properly, both from a technical and business standpoint. If the key performance goals of the system are not achieved, that means that either the system does not function correctly or the business requirements of the project do not match the business goals of the project. Defining KPIs fully at this stage of the project life cycle helps to avoid the latter situation, because the project team will be forced to determine how a given KPI is measured based on the performance of the system.

## FINDING THE RIGHT KPIs

A project team should attempt to define at least one KPI for each business goal of the project. For example, if one of the goals of the project is to reduce time to air by 10%, then time to air should be one of the KPIs defined at this stage. They are not always that straightforward; for example, if one business goal is to raise user satisfaction with the system, then some potential KPIs are used to accomplish specific tasks, number of process exceptions thrown, or number of trouble tickets opened.

After the identification of KPIs, the project team should also produce more traditional project documentation as well. A requirements document outlining the functional and non-functional requirements of the proposed system is always useful, SOA or no; a detailed project timeline and budget is a necessity simply to get the project off the ground.

To best serve the project team in the detailed design phase of the project, the requirements documentation produced in the analysis stage of an SOA/BPM project should feature a conceptual systems design that includes high-level middleware architecture, service interfaces, and business process definitions. This information helps to validate the service decomposition performed as part of analysis and the business models produced after elicitation. Apart from this, all of the traditional components of a project requirements document (scope, use cases, unit tests, etc.) can and should be included. This may seem like a lot of information for a project team to produce at the outset of a project, but since SOA is a top-loaded architecture, the more information the team has, the better.

The timeline and budget of the development parts of the project should be split by service and business process, if possible. SOA includes a wonderful functional boundary for project teams in the service horizon. If everyone agrees on the service interfaces after the design phase, services and processes can be delegated separately during the construction and integration phases. Project timelines oriented this way are also easier to produce, because a service (which represents a single unit of business functionality) has a defined scope and, often, a defined set of implementing technologies to limit individual project development stages.

Table 8-2 lists the deliverables of this stage of project development.

## 8.3.2 Detailed Design

A good project analysis leads to good project design. In fact, to a certain extent, the analysis phase of an SOA/BPM project covers many design needs. Business models that will eventually become executable process models are created during analysis, as are service interfaces that will (in Web service environments) eventually become WSDL documents to control message communication. The next phase of project development is really more of a design *completion* phase; that is, building on the initial design concepts created in analysis and bringing them to fruition. There are many aspects to this.

First of all, there is the physical detailed design to be considered. As much fun as it is to consider these service-oriented systems in the abstract (as much of the analysis phase is spent doing), for the project to be successful, these systems must be realized. Physical detailed design entails both platform selection (choosing the technology that the systems will be built on) and tool selection (choosing the technology that the project team will use to build the systems). In projects where the underlying applications that are providing the business functionality do not yet exist in the enterprise, these must be chosen as well. Although it is the first instinct of many project teams to pick a

**TABLE 8-2**

Deliverables from the Analysis Phase of the SOA/BPM Project Life Cycle

Analysis deliverables

Business Process Models

Business Process Simulations

Service Model

Key Performance Indicators

Functional/Non-Functional Requirements Document

Project Timeline/Plan

Project Budget

favorite SOA vendor or a favorite media application supplier, the number one influencer of technology selection must be the project analysis. A team should pick the best tools and technologies for the job, even if that means going with a vendor that is new or under-represented in the enterprise. Of course, the usual considerations of the stability of the vendor, availability of support, and other factors should also be considered at this stage.

The other aspects of detailed design focus instead on the software components to be developed or repurposed. One major part of this is the detailed designs of service implementations. In this phase of the project, project teams must take the high-level service interfaces and models developed during analysis and completely flesh them out. Service interfaces must be completely defined down to operations and business data, and the design of the service wrapper must be finalized. One decision that must be made by the project team at this stage is how to best implement various service wrappers. In some situations, a thin or pass-through wrapper design is best to capture the business logic of the underlying application; in other cases, a thick wrapper that implements as much functionality as it pulls from implementing systems is appropriate. More information about wrappers and wrapper design is found in Chapter 3.

Detailed design includes infrastructure-level architecture as well as design at the service level. The project team may opt to implement a simplistic middleware layer that only utilizes one or two message patterns and not many bells and whistles, or it may choose to go all out and throw lots of middleware components at the problem. Either way, this decision must be discussed and finalized during the detailed design phase. Middleware is an area where multiple SOA/BPM projects can all use the same components, so it is expected that after a few crucial initial projects, the enterprise can focus on reusing existing middleware rather than developing more middleware functionality. This does not remove the need for a middleware focus in detailed design. On the contrary, it heightens the importance of determining what components are necessary for a successful project, because the ability of existing components to fulfill these needs must be carefully considered.

A more business-focused aspect of middleware detailed design is the initial authoring of any and all business process used in the completed system. Business process writing — whether using BPMN, BPEL, or some other method — is an exacting science. Project teams will find it impossible to finalize processes at this stage of the game, because the non-functional aspects of services have not been worked out and there are no systems in place with which to test the written processes. However, a BPMN-level representation of all processes is suggested and entirely achievable during detailed design. These processes will assist with service and wrapper construction and give the project team an overall view of how the end product will work at a detailed level.

Table 8-3 lists the deliverables of this stage of project development.

## 8.3.3 Service and Wrapper Construction

Once the design of the solution is complete, it is time to start building some services! The service construction phase of the SOA/BPM project life cycle is the most interesting phase, especially because no other style of architecture requires such a phase. Certainly, there are parallels, especially to pure software development projects that will require the construction of software objects and classes, but building services is a unique task. In traditional or tightly coupled media engineering integration projects, the closest thing to service construction is the selection of product vendors (which, really, bears little resemblance). The goal of this phase of the project is to turn service designs and interfaces into working software components. This involves application integration and the SOA technologies discussed in Chapter 5.

The thing to remember about building SOA services is this: it is a software project! Wrapper building may not be as intensive as other

**TABLE 8-3**

Deliverables from the Detailed Design Phase of the SOA/BPM Project Life Cycle

Design deliverables
Tool and platform selection
Service implementation design
Wrapper design
Middleware architecture design
Business processes

software projects (unless the wrappers are especially involved), but they are custom software none the less. This means that all of the corollary stuff that helps out in software development will be useful here: code management, programming methodologies, etc. In media enterprises that have not done true software development in the past (and many have not), this may be a bit of a paradigm shift. However, the more the project team can learn about the best practices of software development, the better off they will be. While this is not a book on the best practices of software development, there are many such books out there. Any enterprise serious about SOA should begin to get a solid understanding of these best practices. Like it or not, the M&E industry is becoming more software-based, and while SOA is designed to shield the business user from much of that, this does not mean that the development team can ignore it.

One aspect of software development especially useful for service building is unit testing. In SOA, each individual service is independent from the next. This means that the testing of any one service is very straightforward, because it involves no other components of the architecture. Certainly, many services may use the interfaces of a single underlying application, but these services will be dependent upon that application only, not upon each other. So, as the project team completes services, they can immediately be tested regardless of the state of the other services in the system or the middleware layer. Even though there is a whole phase of the SOA/BPM project life cycle focused on testing, some amount of testing should be done throughout the cycle. Doing unit testing as services are developed is a great way to catch little problems that would otherwise trip up project teams in less obvious ways during integration.

## 8.3.4 Integration

The main goal of the integration phase is to tie the services developed in the previous phase to the middleware and process layers of the overall solution. For many first-time project teams, this is the most difficult phase of the project, because they either did not spend enough time in the analysis phase or did not produce the right information out of the analysis and design phases to integrate the overall system effectively and efficiently. In projects with complex middleware layer components, there may be some software development in this phase of the life cycle. However, in the majority of projects, the integration phase is spent installing middleware components and writing (if not done already) and testing business processes.

To tie process to service, the project team must take the process designs done in the detailed design phase and complete them. If they are using BPEL as an orchestration technology, this means identifying specific services (built in the previous phase) as business partners in individual business processes and calling their service interfaces in the process. All of the data transformation necessary must be developed and implemented in this phase as well, because information received from one service may need to be transformed in some way before it can be passed along to another service. In projects that are built on top of an existing SOA infrastructure, completing the business process and tying it to the implemented services is the primary responsibility of the integration phase. However, in projects building the first or second stages of a new SOA implementation, the completion of business processes is a secondary responsibility of this phase. The primary responsibility of integration in such projects is the construction of the middleware layer.

The project team should be building and installing the middleware layer in a test environment during this phase of the project, and they should be setting up the middleware layer in its final configuration before deploying any processes or services on it. In other words, if the underlying application servers are intended to be redundant or secured, this configuration should be done now to avoid surprises during deployment. Again, although the testing phase of the project is where the overall system is tested, smaller, unit tests should be done at all phases to ensure that design and development is proceeding correctly and that, when it comes time to test the integrated system, the problems encountered will be integration problems and not service development problems.

At the completion of the integration phase of the project, the project team should have a test system built and deployed with processes and services running on it. Also, in environments where this is possible, it is also advisable to implement the production middleware layer at this phase as well. Although no services or processes will be running on it yet, having the infrastructure in place will make deployment smoother.

## 8.3.5 Testing

Apart from initial analysis, the testing of the completed solution is the most important step in an SOA/BPM project. No one needs to tell media engineers that, of course, in production systems everything must be exhaustively tested. During integration, a test environment is created to facilitate this phase of the project life cycle and to smooth the deployment phase for all users of the system. Test environments are discussed further in Chapter 4. The project team should ensure that the test environment developed for the SOA system mirrors the production environment as closely as possible. The project team should then proceed to test as thoroughly as humanly possible in that environment.

In addition to repeating all of the standard unit tests for each component and process, the project testing phase should include systematic tests of the entire solution, as well as tests of all of the outlier conditions that come up during analysis. The project team should test for exception cases and not just the ones that are compensated for in the various business processes used. They should also test the exception cases that are truly exceptions to the business processes: losing components, time crunch, resource unavailability, etc. In addition, testing should include various unusual configurations that might be possible with the completed system. This includes, but is not limited to, oddly formatted service calls, process-intensive requests to the middleware layer, and unusual system uses that stress particular components. Finally, since one of the main benefits of SOA and BPM is system agility, the project team should test configurations that replace certain components with backups or reconfigured services and ensure that the system still responds as expected. After all, the biggest barrier to true agility in SOA is not a technology barrier, it is an interface design barrier. The project team should ensure that the services they designed are SOA agile.

## 8.3.6 Deployment

At the conclusion of testing, the system is finally ready for deployment. While the term "deployment" gives the impression of a single step or a moment in time, anyone who has deployed an integration project of any sort knows that this is not the case. A number of steps must be followed to successfully deploy a developed system. This is the stage of the SOA/BPM project life cycle where the rubber hits the road and the end users finally get a taste of the completed solution, so it is the job of the project team to ease those users into the solution. Changes must be announced and set up, and the team must be prepared for roll-back should something go wrong.

SOA projects in particular can be presented to the user incrementally on a service-by-service basis if necessary. In fact, one of the best practices of SOA deployment is to deploy services and processes in a backward compatible way to ensure the minimum amount of harsh adjustment for users. This means that new services and processes (such as the ones that are part of the project at hand) should be put into place alongside existing services and processes, even if some of the new components are simply updated versions of the current components. Initially, users should have the choice to revert back to the old workflow as they adjust to the new one.

For example, a project that introduces a new, streamlined ingest process to a facility along with new services that log incoming assets more effectively should be deployed in the following manner: the new logging services should be put into place alongside the existing ones, and the a process should be deployed for all new ingests (leaving the currently executing ones on the current process) that treats the two services equally and load balances. Then, once the department has adjusted to the change in a few weeks, the old service can be rolled out and the process altered to only refer to the new service. This is backward compatibility in SOA.

The timing of deployment is also crucial. In the above example, it is assumed that the facility will require a few weeks to adjust to the new services and processes. In more complex project deployments (that may have more than one phase), this could mean a few weeks in between each new batch of components. Deployment could take a couple of months if the facility is large enough and the changes are major. The project team is responsible for correctly timing process and service deployment to best help users train and adjust to the new systems. The team should take note: end users must be sold on any systemic change; they cannot be expected to follow along unless they see the benefit.

The expression "user adoption" is the business-friendly way of explaining this process of selling the user on the new system. Unless the users see the benefits of the solution, they will be wary of making any significant changes to their workflow. Therefore, a major part of project deployment must be dedicated to user adoption of the new solution. One of the ten commandments of workflow analysis (as presented in Chapter 6) is that all process participants should feel business value from the given process. This holds true for SOA/BPM solutions as a whole. Thankfully, if the project team followed the best practices of BPM during the analysis phase of the project life cycle, then they have captured processes in such a way as to ensure that every process participant feels both ownership of the process and value in the process. This simple idea can mean the success or failure of project deployment.

The only remaining task after the solution is in the enterprise is to effectively train the user. Training users on a new solution is the job of the project team, but it is a good idea for the high-level Service-Oriented Media Enterprise team to also be involved in this activity. The best way to train users for most SOA solutions is through overseen on-the-job use of the new system. The project team and SOA/BPM team should expect to spend a couple of weeks simply answering questions from end users about the new system until they feel comfortable enough to continue using it on their own. If the project team deploys the solution in a backward compatible way, then both the team and the end user have an easy way to revert back to older workflows during crunch time or if difficulty is experienced. Training is a facet of deployment that could even be shared among several concurrent projects being deployed — no sense in training the same user twice!

Because the project team has spent the last several weeks building and integrating the solution and is excited to see it in use, having a multi-week deployment phase may seem to some like an overly cautious move. However, a small amount of effort here can abate a large amount of effort soon after if the deployed solution does not work as planned.

Once the deployed system is in place and in operation, the project team has completed its required duties. The project cannot yet be considered a success, however, because the conditions for success (the KPIs) have not been met. At this point in the project life cycle, the Service-Oriented Media Enterprise team has one more responsibility.

## 8.3.7 Monitoring

The final piece of the SOA/BPM project life cycle is to monitor the deployed system. This is not a very active process, and can overlap with the beginning stages of other SOA/BPM projects, if desired. However, this is an important phase, because it is the phase that dictates project success and validates the overall enterprise SOA/BPM roadmap.

The central goal of this phase is for the SOA/BPM team to keep an eye on the project KPIs that were defined earlier in project analysis. These KPIs inform both the SOA/BPM team and the management of the enterprise whether or not the project was a success. For example, if the goal of the integration was to reduce production time of individual news stories by 20%, then that time should be a KPI and it should be monitored to ensure that it drops by at least 20% and stays there. In the initial weeks after project deployment there will no doubt be major fluctuation in KPI levels, so it is important for the SOA/BPM team to wait it out for a bit. Once the enterprise workflow stabilizes, KPIs will provide good information on the status of the new system.

In addition to the non-functional requirements defined by KPIs, the SOA/BPM team should also be looking to ensure the new solution meets its functional requirements (as outlined in the analysis phase). In other words: is the system doing what it is supposed to do? One good way to tell this is by monitoring exception cases. If the project team did a good job at both analysis and integration, than many exception cases will have been accounted for in process design. However, no team catches every single exception case (since there are so many of them, even in the simplest cases), so even air-tight architectures will have to deal with a few such cases after a couple of months into the process. The SOA/BPM team should be on the lookout for such situations, and make sure that the system reacts to them well and does not prevent the end users from doing their work.

All of this end-of-project analysis supports another goal of the Service-Oriented Media Enterprise team: continuous process improvement. By monitoring the deployed system, the team is finding new business requirements that the system does not address and discovering areas where additional efficiency might be inserted into the process. These issues can be addressed in later SOA/BPM projects and, as noticed, should be included in the enterprise roadmap. The team should be setting the stage for continuous process improvement by keeping an eye on all deployed SOA systems. If they do, then the SOA and BPM projects, as well as the SOA and BPM benefits, will come more quickly and easily.

## CASE STUDY

### The Service-Oriented Media Enterprise Project Life Cycle

A media archive facility wishes to use BPM and SOA to improve operations and to increase collaboration with other archives at studios and educational facilities. An SOA/BPM team was formed, and, after extensive elicitation and business planning, that team produced an enterprise roadmap outlining the facility's SOA/BPM strategy. Using SOA risk-benefit analysis as described in this chapter, the SOA/BPM team has decided that an optimal first project to tackle is the service-enablement of the facility's cataloging and creation of a new media browsing UI, giving a service-oriented view into media metadata in the enterprise (a combination of legacy and opportunistic integration). A separate project team is formed to address this solution, featuring both members of the SOA/BPM team, in-house integrators, and cataloging-specific managers.

1. **Analysis**
The project team took the initial business goals from the SOA/BPM team — speed up cataloging, reduce cataloging mistakes, and provide a browsing interface that is more user-friendly than existing functionality — and used these to further refine the project requirements. They met with catalogers and future end users of the browsing application to develop workflows and business models for browsing and cataloging media. They carried out simulations on different variations of the cataloging process to determine which was fastest. Using these models, the team identified four services: a media metadata access service, a new media entry service, a search service, and a cataloging service. KPIs were defined that determine throughput of individual catalogers, average number of media accesses per day, average time between initial media entry and cataloging, and time spent browsing media. The team captured all of this information in a requirements document, including estimated budget and timeline.

## 2. Detailed Design

The team took the models and requirements developed in the previous stage and used them to fully define the project. The four services identified were given exact operations and documented in WSDL format. Their implementation was considered and designed (including the selection of tools to implement the new functionality of the media browsing interface). In addition, a middleware architecture was selected and a rollout plan was developed and approved by the SOA/BPM team. Finally, the team took the business processes developed in the previous phase and made BPEL representations of them for orchestration in a process engine. This entire phase took two weeks of work by the team.

## 3. Service and Wrapper Construction

The team acquired all of the new components necessary for the solution and began construction of custom wrappers in a lab environment. Three of the four services — new media entry, metadata access, and cataloging — required implementation using existing cataloging tools, so copies of these tools were brought into the lab environment to be wrapped. The other service, media search, was to be built on top of a new Web management platform (a Web-based UI was decided upon for the new browsing interface). So this platform was brought in as well. Drop-down menus in the UI were used to reduce mistakes on the part of the cat-alogers. The team used traditional software project management techniques to develop and document the custom wrappers. This phase took six weeks to complete.

## 4. Integration

In this phase, the project team brought their selected middleware solution into the lab and configured it for the environment. The business processes developed during the detailed design phase were modified to work with the four recently built services, and these processes were deployed to the middleware. Some processes had to be slightly  redesigned based on details of the final services and configuration  quirks of the middleware components, so these changes were also made. This phase took the project team roughly two weeks to complete.

## 5. Testing

Once the lab environment is completely implemented, the team can begin to test the completed solution. Testing revealed unaccounted for exception cases in both the processes and the service interfaces, so these each had to be altered to address all possible scenarios. The testing plan which the project team developed also required significant documentation of the service interfaces and process components, so the team used the results of tests to produce manuals for system use. This phase took the team three weeks to complete because of the amount of changes necessary.

## 6. Deployment
For putting the solution into the enterprise, the team opted for a tiered deployment plan. Four catalogers would be instructed to use the new cataloging and new media entry services while the others remained on the existing infrastructure. In addition, all users were made aware of the new media browsing capabilities of the system, but no existing interfaces were removed, allowing any users to return to the way they were used to doing things. This setup was used for one week and monitored by the project team. After this time, four more catalogers were brought into the system and were monitored for an additional week. Finally, all catalogers were migrated to the new services and the various facility departments were instructed to use the new media browsing interface as a primary means of accessing media. The project team planned for the removal of the old cataloging clients in six weeks.

## 7. Monitoring
While the project team closed out various aspects of the project, the SOA/BPM team watched the KPIs made available to them and the facility managers through a Web-based dashboard. It was determined after three weeks of using the new system that there were significantly fewer cataloging mistakes made and that overall speed of the cataloging process was up. In addition, most end users liked the new browsing interface, but now wanted to be able to view media proxies while browsing. The SOA/BPM team took this feedback and refined the enterprise roadmap, adding proxy viewing to a later project.

## 8.4 CONCLUSION

The key lesson of this chapter is this: building the Service-Oriented Media Enterprise does not happen overnight. It takes education (a process that readers have already begun by getting through this book), persistence, and commitment. Going from a tightly coupled, point-to-point media infrastructure to one that is as agile, visible, and service-oriented as possible will likely take years. A team must be assembled, a roadmap developed, and a series of projects undertaken that embody the best practices of Business Process Management. It is not a path that a media enterprise takes on a whim. However, the road to SOA and BPM is very achievable, it is good for the enterprise, and, above all, it is increasingly necessary in an industry where competition is tough and technology moves fast.

Many integrators, even in the IT industry, are nervous about undertaking Service-Oriented Architecture. However, the tenets of SOA are more accessible and doable than it may seem at first glance. If this book is not enough to convince an integrator of this fact, then there are countless IT books on the subject that will do so. The Service-Oriented Media Enterprise is not just a pipe dream, it is an achievable goal for the M&E industry. Those media enterprises that are fearless in their pursuit of this goal will be the ones that succeed both in terms of SOA/BPM adoption and in terms of technological edge in the industry.

The central reason for this is that SOA and BPM are ultimately very good ideas. There is nothing truly groundbreaking in either philosophy, and because they are sets of best practices and not new technologies, there is no particular advancement here that cannot be found elsewhere. Certainly technologies such as Web services and business process orchestration represent new advancements in business functionality, and these were made in the name of SOA and BPM. At their heart, SOA and BPM are just good ideas, so they are healthy systems for a media enterprise to consider. The tenets contained in this book benefit the enterprise in fundamental ways. Any media enterprise that considers adoption of SOA and BPM is not abandoning their current workflows or methodologies, but streamlining and improving them. Because of this, all organizations should look into SOA and BPM simply to see if any of their best practices resonate.

Increasing expenses and shrinking revenues are also beginning to force media enterprises into looking for these kinds of solutions. The Service-Oriented Media Enterprise, therefore, is not simply a possibility, it is an increasing necessity. Facilities that jump on the idea now will not only have an edge on the competition as they are running to catch up later, but will also be embracing the future of the M&E industry in a proactive way. SOA and BPM are this future. This is happening now.

The importance of the Service-Oriented Media Enterprise is so immediate, in fact, that to a certain extent, this book is already out of date. More and more media enterprises are adopting SOA best practices, and, as they do so, they are able to move beyond the restrictions of legacy technology and begin to face new business challenges that no one could have predicted ten or even five years ago. Outside forces are allowing concepts like Web 2.0, media convergence, and federated, standards-based collaboration to worm their way into the M&E industry. Appendix F is dedicated to discussing some of these topics that will be important in the next phase of the media industry. The fact is, there is a vibrant and interesting conversation going on right now at the forefront of new media. Enterprises of all types and sizes should get to this forefront through the adoption of SOA and BPM best practices, and not only join in the conversation, but actually begin to lead it.

## WHAT TO TELL YOUR BOSS

- Building the Service-Oriented Media Enterprise is achievable, healthy, and increasingly necessary in a competitive industry landscape.
- The enterprise should form a specialized SOA/BPM team to create a roadmap and oversee project work.
- Media enterprises that wait to upgrade their infrastructures following the best practices of SOA and BPM will soon be rushing to catch up with more agile and productive companies.

# APPENDIX A: MEDIA-SPECIFIC SERVICE EXAMPLES

This book has focused on describing some of the core ideas and technologies behind Service-Oriented Architecture. However, often the best way to explain a concept is to give concrete examples. Thus, this appendix aims to provide some generic example services to demonstrate some core ideas about SOA. To those readers who are raring to build their own SOA infrastructures, the caveat is this: these examples are not intended to be complete pictures of everything these business services may need to do in an enterprise. The details of any service interface is specific to the business goals of the media enterprise implementing it.

The following services give a taste, but not the complete picture (which requires enterprise-specific details). Their interfaces are included; they meet the WS-I specification and are defined in WSDL 1.1 because this standard is generally compatible with most Web services development tools. There are also no additions to the interface such as WS-Policy. These are basic Web services definitions to give a simple idea of how services might look.

## A.1 TRANSCODING SERVICE

Transcoding could be considered the media industry's perfect service. It is easy to envision and often straightforward to implement because transcoding engines are fairly self-contained. Chapter 7 discusses the need to abstract transcoding out of the business domain through the use of a media layer, but until that time (or in media enterprises with business concerns in the transcoding space), it will be a business service.

A transcoding service is an excellent demonstration of the separation of interface and implementation in SOA. For though a transcoding engine may consider any work it does as a generic "job," different jobs may have different business meanings. In the service below, two types of jobs — transcoding an asset and moving an asset — are specifically called out in the service interface. Regardless of their implementation (which may be the same generic job underneath), they are separate business operations. A service wrapper may simply route both calls to the same API function with slightly different parameters, but this action is invisible to the service consumer.

In addition, the transcoding service described here is demonstrative of an asynchronous service without polling. In contrast to the edit service later in this appendix, this transcoding service expects that the service consumer implements a callback interface for completed jobs. The WS-Addressing standard is used to tell the service where to notify of job completion. If the consumer does not wish to implement the callback interface, it can poll the service for job completion instead using the status operations.

## A.1.1 Service Description

The transcoding service described here has only six operations:

**transcodeAsset** — Submit a media asset for transcoding by supplying the location of the asset and the details of the transcode to be carried out. It is an asynchronous operation that immediately returns a transcode job ID that can be used to reference the job in other operations. The asset, when complete, will be deposited in a destination location of the requester's specification.

**getTranscodeStatus** — Check on the status of any transcode job in progress. This operation will return one of five states: "not found," "job error," "canceled," "complete," or "in progress" (with the actual percentage completed returned as well). If job ID is for a move job, will return business fault.

**cancelTranscode** — Cancel any in progress or errored job in the transcoding queue.

**moveAsset** — Submit a media asset for movement from one location to another by supplying the source and destination locations. This is a simpler version of the transcodeAsset operation, in that it does not process the media asset in any way, only moves it. It is an asynchronous operation that immediately returns a move job ID that can be used to reference the job in other operations.

**getMoveStatus** — Check on the status of a move job in progress. Has the same states as getTranscodeStatus. If job ID is for a transcode job, will return business fault.

**cancelMove** — Cancel any in progress or errored job in the move queue.

In addition to these operations, the transcode service will make outgoing service calls for the completion of a job, if the service consumer provides the service with a callback location using the WS-Addressing standard. These callbacks provide the job ID completed back to the requester.

The transcoding service can be used in different ways depending on the status of the asset in question. A guideline to how a status query might return is shown in Fig. A-1. Without a media layer, this is the best way that a Web service can deal with media management.

## A.1.2 Service Interfaces

The transcoding service has two WSDL interfaces associated with it, one to describe the service itself, and one to describe the callback interface that it expects the service consumer to implement.

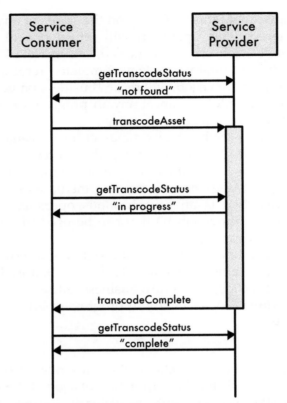

**FIGURE A-1**   This UML diagram demonstrates the possible responses from a getTranscodeStatus service call at different stages of a job. It also depicts the callback functionality of the transcoding service. The service is therefore not stateless, which is why the ideal SOA solution for transcoding involves a media layer.

## A.1.2.1  transcodingService.wsdl

```
<?xml version="1.0" encoding="UTF-8"?>
<wsdl:definitions name="transcodingService"
  targetNamespace="http://www.example.tv/transcodingService"
  xmlns:soapenc="http://schemas.xmlsoap.org/soap/encoding/"
  xmlns:soap="http://schemas.xmlsoap.org/wsdl/soap/"
  xmlns:tns="http://www.example.tv/transcodingService"
  xmlns:wsdl="http://schemas.xmlsoap.org/wsdl/"
  xmlns="http://schemas.xmlsoap.org/wsdl/"
  xmlns:xsd="http://www.w3.org/2001/XMLSchema">
```

```
<wsdl:types>
  <xsd:schema>

    <xsd:complexType name="transcodeDetailsObject">
      <xsd:sequence>
        <xsd:element minOccurs="0" name="fromCodec"
          type="xsd:string" />
        <xsd:element minOccurs="0" name="toCodec"
          type="xsd:string" />
        <xsd:element minOccurs="0" name="toResolution"
          type="xsd:string" />
        <xsd:element minOccurs="0" name="toWrapper"
          type="xsd:string" />
        <xsd:element minOccurs="0" name="toFPS"
          type="xsd:string" />
        <xsd:element minOccurs="0" name="watermark"
          type="xsd:string" />
      </xsd:sequence>
    </xsd:complexType>

    <xsd:complexType name="statusObject">
      <xsd:sequence>
        <xsd:element minOccurs="1" name="value">
          <xsd:simpleType>
            <xsd:restriction base="xsd:string">
              <xsd:enumeration value="not found" />
              <xsd:enumeration value="job error" />
              <xsd:enumeration value="cancelled" />
              <xsd:enumeration value="in progress" />
              <xsd:enumeration value="complete" />
            </xsd:restriction>
          </xsd:simpleType>
        </xsd:element>
        <xsd:element minOccurs="0" name="percentComplete"
          type="xsd:int" />
      </xsd:sequence>
    </xsd:complexType>

    <xsd:element name="transcodeAsset">
      <xsd:complexType>
        <xsd:sequence>
          <xsd:element name="assetTitle" nillable="true"
            type="xsd:string" />
```

```
        <xsd:element name="assetLocation"
          nillable="true" type="xsd:string" />
        <xsd:element name="assetDestination"
          nillable="true" type="xsd:string" />
        <xsd:element name="transcodeDetails"
          nillable="true" type="tns:transcodeDetailsObject" />
    </xsd:sequence>
  </xsd:complexType>
</xsd:element>

<xsd:element name="transcodeAssetResponse">
  <xsd:complexType>
    <xsd:sequence>
      <xsd:element name="jobID" nillable="true"
        type="xsd:int" />
    </xsd:sequence>
  </xsd:complexType>
</xsd:element>

<xsd:element name="getTranscodeStatus">
  <xsd:complexType>
    <xsd:sequence>
      <xsd:element name="jobID" nillable="true"
        type="xsd:int" />
    </xsd:sequence>
  </xsd:complexType>
</xsd:element>

<xsd:element name="getTranscodeStatusResponse">
  <xsd:complexType>
    <xsd:sequence>
      <xsd:element name="status" nillable="true"
        type="tns:statusObject" />
    </xsd:sequence>
  </xsd:complexType>
</xsd:element>

<xsd:element name="cancelTranscode">
  <xsd:complexType>
    <xsd:sequence>
      <xsd:element name="jobID" nillable="true"
        type="xsd:int" />
    </xsd:sequence>
```

```
          </xsd:complexType>
      </xsd:element>

      <xsd:element name="cancelTranscodeResponse">
        <xsd:complexType>
          <xsd:sequence>
            <xsd:element name="confirmation" nillable="true"
              type="xsd:boolean" />
          </xsd:sequence>
        </xsd:complexType>
      </xsd:element>

      <xsd:element name="moveAsset">
        <xsd:complexType>
          <xsd:sequence>
            <xsd:element name="assetTitle" nillable="true"
              type="xsd:string" />
            <xsd:element name="assetLocation"
              nillable="true" type="xsd:string" />
            <xsd:element name="assetDestination"
              nillable="true" type="xsd:string" />
          </xsd:sequence>
        </xsd:complexType>
      </xsd:element>

      <xsd:element name="moveAssetResponse">
        <xsd:complexType>
          <xsd:sequence>
            <xsd:element name="jobID" nillable="true"
              type="xsd:int" />
          </xsd:sequence>
        </xsd:complexType>
      </xsd:element>

      <xsd:element name="getMoveStatus">
        <xsd:complexType>
          <xsd:sequence>
            <xsd:element name="jobID" nillable="true"
              type="xsd:int" />
          </xsd:sequence>
        </xsd:complexType>
      </xsd:element>
```

```xml
    <xsd:element name="getMoveStatusResponse">
      <xsd:complexType>
        <xsd:sequence>
          <xsd:element name="status" nillable="true"
            type="tns:statusObject" />
        </xsd:sequence>
      </xsd:complexType>
    </xsd:element>

    <xsd:element name="cancelMove">
      <xsd:complexType>
        <xsd:sequence>
          <xsd:element name="jobID" nillable="true"
            type="xsd:int" />
        </xsd:sequence>
      </xsd:complexType>
    </xsd:element>

    <xsd:element name="cancelMoveResponse">
      <xsd:complexType>
        <xsd:sequence>
          <xsd:element name="confirmation" nillable="true"
            type="xsd:boolean" />
        </xsd:sequence>
      </xsd:complexType>
    </xsd:element>

    <xsd:element name="incorrectJobID">
      <xsd:complexType>
        <xsd:sequence>
          <xsd:element name="detail" type="xsd:string" />
        </xsd:sequence>
      </xsd:complexType>
    </xsd:element>

  </xsd:schema>
</wsdl:types>

<wsdl:message name="transcodeAssetRequestMsg">
  <wsdl:part element="tns:transcodeAsset"
    name="transcodeAssetParameters" />
</wsdl:message>
```

```
<wsdl:message name="transcodeAssetResponseMsg">
  <wsdl:part element="tns:transcodeAssetResponse"
    name="transcodeAssetResult" />
</wsdl:message>

<wsdl:message name="getTranscodeStatusRequestMsg">
  <wsdl:part element="tns:getTranscodeStatus"
    name="getTranscodeStatusParameters" />
</wsdl:message>

<wsdl:message name="getTranscodeStatusResponseMsg">
  <wsdl:part element="tns:getTranscodeStatusResponse"
    name="getTranscodeStatusResult" />
</wsdl:message>

<wsdl:message name="cancelTranscodeRequestMsg">
  <wsdl:part element="tns:cancelTranscode"
    name="cancelTranscodeParameters" />
</wsdl:message>

<wsdl:message name="cancelTranscodeResponseMsg">
  <wsdl:part element="tns:cancelTranscodeResponse"
    name="cancelTranscodeResult" />
</wsdl:message>

<wsdl:message name="moveAssetRequestMsg">
  <wsdl:part element="tns:moveAsset" name="moveAssetParameters" />
</wsdl:message>

<wsdl:message name="moveAssetResponseMsg">
  <wsdl:part element="tns:moveAssetResponse"
    name="moveAssetResult" />
</wsdl:message>

<wsdl:message name="getMoveStatusRequestMsg">
  <wsdl:part element="tns:getMoveStatus"
    name="getMoveStatusParameters" />
</wsdl:message>

<wsdl:message name="getMoveStatusResponseMsg">
  <wsdl:part element="tns:getMoveStatusResponse"
    name="getMoveStatusResult" />
</wsdl:message>
```

```
<wsdl:message name="cancelMoveRequestMsg">
  <wsdl:part element="tns:cancelMove" name="cancelMoveParameters" />
</wsdl:message>

<wsdl:message name="cancelMoveResponseMsg">
  <wsdl:part element="tns:cancelMoveResponse"
    name="cancelMoveResult" />
</wsdl:message>

<wsdl:message name="incorrectJobIDMsg">
  <wsdl:part element="tns:incorrectJobID" name="incorrectJobID" />
</wsdl:message>

<wsdl:portType name="transcodingService">

  <wsdl:operation name="transcodeAsset">
    <wsdl:input message="tns:transcodeAssetRequestMsg"
      name="transcodeAssetRequest" />
    <wsdl:output message="tns:transcodeAssetResponseMsg"
      name="transcodeAssetResponse" />
  </wsdl:operation>

  <wsdl:operation name="getTranscodeStatus">
    <wsdl:input message="tns:getTranscodeStatusRequestMsg"
      name="getTranscodeStatusRequest" />
    <wsdl:output message="tns:getTranscodeStatusResponseMsg"
      name="getTranscodeStatusResponse" />
    <wsdl:fault message="tns:incorrectJobIDMsg"
      name="incorrectJobID" />
  </wsdl:operation>

  <wsdl:operation name="cancelTranscode">
    <wsdl:input message="tns:cancelTranscodeRequestMsg"
      name="cancelTranscodeRequest" />
    <wsdl:output message="tns:cancelTranscodeResponseMsg"
      name="cancelTranscodeResponse" />
  </wsdl:operation>

  <wsdl:operation name="moveAsset">
    <wsdl:input message="tns:moveAssetRequestMsg"
      name="moveAssetRequest" />
    <wsdl:output message="tns:moveAssetResponseMsg"
```

```
        name="moveAssetResponse" />
  </wsdl:operation>

  <wsdl:operation name="getMoveStatus">
    <wsdl:input message="tns:getMoveStatusRequestMsg"
      name="getMoveStatusRequest" />
    <wsdl:output message="tns:getMoveStatusResponseMsg"
      name="getMoveStatusResponse" />
    <wsdl:fault message="tns:incorrectJobIDMsg"
      name="incorrectJobID" />
  </wsdl:operation>

  <wsdl:operation name="cancelMove">
    <wsdl:input message="tns:cancelMoveRequestMsg"
      name="cancelMoveRequest" />
    <wsdl:output message="tns:cancelMoveResponseMsg"
      name="cancelMoveResponse" />
  </wsdl:operation>

</wsdl:portType>

<wsdl:binding name="transcodingServiceBinding"
  type="tns:transcodingService">
  <soap:binding style="document"
    transport="http://schemas.xmlsoap.org/soap/http" />

  <wsdl:operation name="transcodeAsset">
    <soap:operation soapAction="" />
    <wsdl:input name="transcodeAssetRequest">
      <soap:body use="literal" />
    </wsdl:input>
    <wsdl:output name="transcodeAssetResponse">
      <soap:body use="literal" />
    </wsdl:output>
  </wsdl:operation>

  <wsdl:operation name="getTranscodeStatus">
    <soap:operation soapAction="" />
    <wsdl:input name="getTranscodeStatusRequest">
      <soap:body use="literal" />
    </wsdl:input>
    <wsdl:output name="getTranscodeStatusResponse">
      <soap:body use="literal" />
```

```
    </wsdl:output>
    <wsdl:fault name="incorrectJobID">
      <soap:fault name="incorrectJobID" use="literal" />
    </wsdl:fault>
</wsdl:operation>

<wsdl:operation name="cancelTranscode">
  <soap:operation soapAction="" />
  <wsdl:input name="cancelTranscodeRequest">
    <soap:body use="literal" />
  </wsdl:input>
  <wsdl:output name="cancelTranscodeResponse">
    <soap:body use="literal" />
  </wsdl:output>
</wsdl:operation>

<wsdl:operation name="moveAsset">
  <soap:operation soapAction="" />
  <wsdl:input name="moveAssetRequest">
    <soap:body use="literal" />
  </wsdl:input>
  <wsdl:output name="moveAssetResponse">
    <soap:body use="literal" />
  </wsdl:output>
</wsdl:operation>

<wsdl:operation name="getMoveStatus">
  <soap:operation soapAction="" />
  <wsdl:input name="getMoveStatusRequest">
    <soap:body use="literal" />
  </wsdl:input>
  <wsdl:output name="getMoveStatusResponse">
    <soap:body use="literal" />
  </wsdl:output>
  <wsdl:fault name="incorrectJobID">
    <soap:fault name="incorrectJobID" use="literal" />
  </wsdl:fault>
</wsdl:operation>

<wsdl:operation name="cancelMove">
  <soap:operation soapAction="" />
  <wsdl:input name="cancelMoveRequest">
    <soap:body use="literal" />
```

```
      </wsdl:input>
      <wsdl:output name="cancelMoveResponse">
        <soap:body use="literal" />
      </wsdl:output>
    </wsdl:operation>

  </wsdl:binding>

  <wsdl:service name="transcodingService">
    <wsdl:port name="transcodingServicePort"
      binding="tns:transcodingServiceBinding">
      <soap:address
        location="http://www.example.tv/transcodingService" />
    </wsdl:port>
  </wsdl:service>

</wsdl:definitions>
```

## A.1.2.2  transcodingServiceCallback.wsdl

```
<?xml version="1.0" encoding="UTF-8"?>
<wsdl:definitions name="transcodingServiceCallback"
  targetNamespace="http://www.example.tv/transcodingService"
  xmlns:soapenc="http://schemas.xmlsoap.org/soap/encoding/"
  xmlns:soap="http://schemas.xmlsoap.org/wsdl/soap/"
  xmlns:xsd="http://www.w3.org/2001/XMLSchema"
  xmlns:tns="http://www.example.tv/transcodingService"
  xmlns:wsdl="http://schemas.xmlsoap.org/wsdl/"
  xmlns="http://schemas.xmlsoap.org/wsdl/">

  <wsdl:types>
    <xsd:schema>

      <xsd:element name="transcodeComplete">
        <xsd:complexType>
          <xsd:sequence>
            <xsd:element name="jobID" nillable="true"
              type="xsd:int" />
            <xsd:element name="location" nillable="true"
              type="xsd:string" />
          </xsd:sequence>
```

```
            </xsd:complexType>
        </xsd:element>

        <xsd:element name="transcodeCompleteResponse">
            <xsd:complexType>
                <xsd:sequence>
                    <xsd:element name="confirmation" nillable="true"
                        type="xsd:boolean" />
                </xsd:sequence>
            </xsd:complexType>
        </xsd:element>

        <xsd:element name="moveComplete">
            <xsd:complexType>
                <xsd:sequence>
                    <xsd:element name="jobID" nillable="true"
                        type="xsd:int" />
                    <xsd:element name="location" nillable="true"
                        type="xsd:string" />
                </xsd:sequence>
            </xsd:complexType>
        </xsd:element>

        <xsd:element name="moveCompleteResponse">
            <xsd:complexType>
                <xsd:sequence>
                    <xsd:element name="confirmation" nillable="true"
                        type="xsd:boolean" />
                </xsd:sequence>
            </xsd:complexType>
        </xsd:element>

    </xsd:schema>
</wsdl:types>

<wsdl:message name="transcodeCompleteRequestMsg">
    <wsdl:part element="tns:transcodeComplete"
        name="transcodeCompleteParameters" />
</wsdl:message>

<wsdl:message name="transcodeCompleteResponseMsg">
    <wsdl:part element="tns:transcodeCompleteResponse"
        name="transcodeCompleteResult" />
</wsdl:message>
```

```
<wsdl:message name="moveCompleteRequestMsg">
  <wsdl:part element="tns:moveComplete"
    name="moveCompleteParameters" />
</wsdl:message>

<wsdl:message name="moveCompleteResponseMsg">
  <wsdl:part element="tns:moveCompleteResponse"
    name="moveCompleteResult" />
</wsdl:message>

<wsdl:portType name="transcodingServiceCallback">

  <wsdl:operation name="transcodeComplete">
    <wsdl:input message="tns:transcodeCompleteRequestMsg"
      name="transcodeCompleteRequest" />
    <wsdl:output message="tns:transcodeCompleteResponseMsg"
      name="transcodeCompleteResponse" />
  </wsdl:operation>

  <wsdl:operation name="moveComplete">
    <wsdl:input message="tns:moveCompleteRequestMsg"
      name="moveCompleteRequest" />
    <wsdl:output message="tns:moveCompleteResponseMsg"
      name="moveCompleteResponse" />
  </wsdl:operation>

</wsdl:portType>

<wsdl:binding name="transcodingServiceCallbackBinding"
  type="tns:transcodingServiceCallback">
  <soap:binding style="document"
    transport="http://schemas.xmlsoap.org/soap/http" />

  <wsdl:operation name="transcodeComplete">
    <soap:operation soapAction="" />
    <wsdl:input name="transcodeCompleteRequest">
      <soap:body use="literal" />
    </wsdl:input>
    <wsdl:output name="transcodeCompleteResponse">
      <soap:body use="literal" />
    </wsdl:output>
  </wsdl:operation>
```

```
   <wsdl:operation name="moveComplete">
     <soap:operation soapAction="" />
     <wsdl:input name="moveCompleteRequest">
       <soap:body use="literal" />
     </wsdl:input>
     <wsdl:output name="moveCompleteResponse">
       <soap:body use="literal" />
     </wsdl:output>
   </wsdl:operation>

 </wsdl:binding>

 <wsdl:service name="transcodingServiceCallback">
   <wsdl:port name="transcodingServiceCallbackPort"
     binding="tns:transcodingServiceCallbackBinding">
     <soap:address
       location="http://www.yourdomain.com/changedAtRuntime" />
   </wsdl:port>
 </wsdl:service>

</wsdl:definitions>
```

## A.2  ASSET MANAGEMENT SERVICE

An asset management service is one of the more difficult service interfaces to assess in all of media. This is because asset management means so many different things to so many people. The service presented in this section handles the repository and cataloging aspects of asset management, but there are surely many more functions that a media enterprise might envision an asset management service doing.

This service demonstrates the differences between services at the application idealization horizon and the system idealization horizon (both described in Chapter 3). The asset management service described here would be found at the application idealization horizon in most media enterprises. It deals in systemic issues such as asset records and metadata entries. Though these things have business value and therefore belong in a service interface, they are often lower level details than the business domain needs. A media enterprise would want to delete an asset, not an asset record. Therefore, readers can imagine a higher level asset management service that abstracts this and other asset management services away from the business process layer.

In addition, some operations in the asset management service (namely, requestAsset and archiveAsset) may even be implemented manually on the application side. This interface does not distinguish, and treats them as it does all of the other operations.

## A.2.1 Service Description

The asset management service exposes seven operations to access media.

**searchForAsset** — Searches through the media repository using either generic search terms or exact metadata fields. Consumers are able to request a specific number of asset records back from the service, which provides both specified metadata fields and asset UUIDs.

**requestAsset** — Submits a request for the transfer of a media asset to a particular location. Depending on the current format of the asset, this could either be a physical location or a location in a file system. This is an asynchronous operation, and so only returns a confirmation (or a business fault if the request cannot be completed as submitted). Managing the status of the submitted request is not within the realm of the asset management service.

**getAssetProxy** — Returns the URI location of an asset proxy if one exists for the given UUID. If one does not exist, returns a business fault.

**getAssetMetadata** — Provides the consumer with all metadata fields for a given media asset. The consumer must know the asset's UUID to request this operation.

**setAssetMetadata** — Sets specific metadata fields for a given media asset. The consumer must know the asset's UUID to request this information.

**createNewAssetRecord** — Creates a new record for a media asset within the asset management system. The consumer of this operation can provide a filename or a physical media identifier for the asset so that the asset management system can locate the asset. In the case of digital media assets, the asset management system will create a stored copy and, if appropriate, make a proxy file.

**deleteAssetRecord** — Deletes the record with the specified UUID from the asset management system. All full-res and proxy video (if-desired) is removed from the system.

**archiveAsset** — Requests that a given asset be moved off of online storage. Like requestAsset, this operation is asynchronous and simply returns a confirmation. In an ideal world, this would not need to be part of a business service, as it deals with implementation. However, because media storage is a major business concern still, this can be considered a useful business function.

## A.2.2 Service Interface: assetManagementService.wsdl

```
<?xml version="1.0" encoding="UTF-8"?>
<wsdl:definitions name="assetManagementService"
  targetNamespace="http://www.example.tv/assetManagementService"
  xmlns:soapenc="http://schemas.xmlsoap.org/soap/encoding/"
  xmlns:soap="http://schemas.xmlsoap.org/wsdl/soap/"
  xmlns:xsd="http://www.w3.org/2001/XMLSchema"
  xmlns:tns="http://www.example.tv/assetManagementService"
  xmlns:wsdl="http://schemas.xmlsoap.org/wsdl/"
  xmlns="http://schemas.xmlsoap.org/wsdl/">

  <wsdl:types>
    <xsd:schema>

      <xsd:complexType name="metadataObject">
        <xsd:sequence>
          <xsd:element minOccurs="0" name="field"
            type="xsd:string" />
          <xsd:element minOccurs="0" name="value"
            type="xsd:string" />
        </xsd:sequence>
      </xsd:complexType>

      <xsd:complexType name="metadataListObject">
        <xsd:sequence>
          <xsd:element minOccurs="0" name="metadata"
            type="tns:metadataObject" maxOccurs="unbounded" />
        </xsd:sequence>
      </xsd:complexType>
```

```xsd
<xsd:complexType name="resultObject">
  <xsd:sequence>
    <xsd:element minOccurs="0" name="uuid"
      type="xsd:string" />
    <xsd:element minOccurs="0" name="metadata"
      type="tns:metadataObject" maxOccurs="unbounded" />
  </xsd:sequence>
</xsd:complexType>


<xsd:complexType name="resultListObject">
  <xsd:sequence>
    <xsd:element minOccurs="0" name="result"
      type="tns:resultObject" maxOccurs="unbounded" />
  </xsd:sequence>
</xsd:complexType>


<xsd:complexType name="searchQueryObject">
  <xsd:sequence>
    <xsd:element minOccurs="0" name="genericSearch"
      type="xsd:string" />
    <xsd:element minOccurs="0" name="specificSearch"
      type="tns:metadataObject" maxOccurs="unbounded" />
  </xsd:sequence>
</xsd:complexType>


<xsd:element name="searchForAsset">
  <xsd:complexType>
    <xsd:sequence>
      <xsd:element name="search" nillable="true"
        type="tns:searchQueryObject" />
    </xsd:sequence>
  </xsd:complexType>
</xsd:element>


<xsd:element name="searchForAssetResponse">
  <xsd:complexType>
    <xsd:sequence>
      <xsd:element name="results" nillable="true"
        type="tns:resultListObject" />
    </xsd:sequence>
  </xsd:complexType>
</xsd:element>
```

```
<xsd:element name="requestAsset">
  <xsd:complexType>
    <xsd:sequence>
      <xsd:element name="uuid" nillable="true"
        type="xsd:string" />
      <xsd:element name="toLocation" nillable="true"
        type="xsd:string" />
    </xsd:sequence>
  </xsd:complexType>
</xsd:element>

<xsd:element name="requestAssetResponse">
  <xsd:complexType>
    <xsd:sequence>
      <xsd:element name="confirmation" nillable="true"
        type="xsd:boolean" />
    </xsd:sequence>
  </xsd:complexType>
</xsd:element>

<xsd:element name="getAssetProxy">
  <xsd:complexType>
    <xsd:sequence>
      <xsd:element name="uuid" nillable="true"
        type="xsd:string" />
    </xsd:sequence>
  </xsd:complexType>
</xsd:element>

<xsd:element name="getAssetProxyResponse">
  <xsd:complexType>
    <xsd:sequence>
      <xsd:element name="proxyLocation"
        nillable="true" type="xsd:string" />
    </xsd:sequence>
  </xsd:complexType>
</xsd:element>

<xsd:element name="getAssetMetadata">
  <xsd:complexType>
    <xsd:sequence>
      <xsd:element name="uuid" nillable="true"
        type="xsd:string" />
```

```
      </xsd:sequence>
    </xsd:complexType>
  </xsd:element>

  <xsd:element name="getAssetMetadataResponse">
    <xsd:complexType>
      <xsd:sequence>
        <xsd:element name="metadataList" nillable="true"
          type="tns:metadataListObject" />
      </xsd:sequence>
    </xsd:complexType>
  </xsd:element>

  <xsd:element name="setAssetMetadata">
    <xsd:complexType>
      <xsd:sequence>
        <xsd:element name="uuid" nillable="true"
          type="xsd:string" />
        <xsd:element name="metadataList" nillable="true"
          type="tns:metadataListObject" />
      </xsd:sequence>
    </xsd:complexType>
  </xsd:element>

  <xsd:element name="setAssetMetadataResponse">
    <xsd:complexType>
      <xsd:sequence>
        <xsd:element name="confirmation" nillable="true"
          type="xsd:boolean" />
      </xsd:sequence>
    </xsd:complexType>
  </xsd:element>

  <xsd:element name="createNewAssetRecord">
    <xsd:complexType>
      <xsd:sequence>
        <xsd:element name="assetLocation"
          nillable="true" type="xsd:string" />
        <xsd:element name="metadataList" nillable="true"
          type="tns:metadataListObject" />
      </xsd:sequence>
    </xsd:complexType>
  </xsd:element>
```

```xml
<xsd:element name="createNewAssetRecordResponse">
  <xsd:complexType>
    <xsd:sequence>
      <xsd:element name="uuid" nillable="true"
        type="xsd:string" />
    </xsd:sequence>
  </xsd:complexType>
</xsd:element>

<xsd:element name="deleteAssetRecord">
  <xsd:complexType>
    <xsd:sequence>
      <xsd:element name="uuid" nillable="true"
        type="xsd:string" />
    </xsd:sequence>
  </xsd:complexType>
</xsd:element>

<xsd:element name="deleteAssetRecordResponse">
  <xsd:complexType>
    <xsd:sequence>
      <xsd:element name="confirmation" nillable="true"
        type="xsd:boolean" />
    </xsd:sequence>
  </xsd:complexType>
</xsd:element>

<xsd:element name="archiveAsset">
  <xsd:complexType>
    <xsd:sequence>
      <xsd:element name="uuid" nillable="true"
        type="xsd:string" />
    </xsd:sequence>
  </xsd:complexType>
</xsd:element>

<xsd:element name="archiveAssetResponse">
  <xsd:complexType>
    <xsd:sequence>
      <xsd:element name="confirmation" nillable="true"
        type="xsd:boolean" />
    </xsd:sequence>
  </xsd:complexType>
</xsd:element>
```

```
    <xsd:element name="noProxyExists">
      <xsd:complexType>
        <xsd:sequence>
          <xsd:element name="detail" type="xsd:string" />
        </xsd:sequence>
      </xsd:complexType>
    </xsd:element>

    <xsd:element name="badLocation">
      <xsd:complexType>
        <xsd:sequence>
          <xsd:element name="detail" type="xsd:string" />
        </xsd:sequence>
      </xsd:complexType>
    </xsd:element>

    <xsd:element name="invalidSearchQuery">
      <xsd:complexType>
        <xsd:sequence>
          <xsd:element name="detail" type="xsd:string" />
        </xsd:sequence>
      </xsd:complexType>
    </xsd:element>

    <xsd:element name="invalidMetadataField">
      <xsd:complexType>
        <xsd:sequence>
          <xsd:element name="detail" type="xsd:string" />
        </xsd:sequence>
      </xsd:complexType>
    </xsd:element>

    <xsd:element name="incorrectUuid">
      <xsd:complexType>
        <xsd:sequence>
          <xsd:element name="detail" type="xsd:string" />
        </xsd:sequence>
      </xsd:complexType>
    </xsd:element>

  </xsd:schema>
</wsdl:types>
```

```
<wsdl:message name="searchForAssetRequestMsg">
  <wsdl:part element="tns:searchForAsset"
    name="searchForAssetParameters" />
</wsdl:message>

<wsdl:message name="searchForAssetResponseMsg">
  <wsdl:part element="tns:searchForAssetResponse"
    name="searchForAssetResult" />
</wsdl:message>

<wsdl:message name="requestAssetRequestMsg">
  <wsdl:part element="tns:requestAsset"
    name="requestAssetParameters" />
</wsdl:message>

<wsdl:message name="requestAssetResponseMsg">
  <wsdl:part element="tns:requestAssetResponse"
    name="requestAssetResult" />
</wsdl:message>

<wsdl:message name="getAssetProxyRequestMsg">
  <wsdl:part element="tns:getAssetProxy"
    name="getAssetProxyParameters" />
</wsdl:message>

<wsdl:message name="getAssetProxyResponseMsg">
  <wsdl:part element="tns:getAssetProxyResponse"
    name="getAssetProxyResult" />
</wsdl:message>

<wsdl:message name="getAssetMetadataRequestMsg">
  <wsdl:part element="tns:getAssetMetadata"
    name="getAssetMetadataParameters" />
</wsdl:message>

<wsdl:message name="getAssetMetadataResponseMsg">
  <wsdl:part element="tns:getAssetMetadataResponse"
    name="getAssetMetadataResult" />
</wsdl:message>

<wsdl:message name="setAssetMetadataRequestMsg">
  <wsdl:part element="tns:setAssetMetadata"
    name="setAssetMetadataParameters" />
</wsdl:message>
```

```
<wsdl:message name="setAssetMetadataResponseMsg">
  <wsdl:part element="tns:setAssetMetadataResponse"
    name="setAssetMetadataResult" />
</wsdl:message>

<wsdl:message name="createNewAssetRecordRequestMsg">
  <wsdl:part element="tns:createNewAssetRecord"
    name="createNewAssetRecordParameters" />
</wsdl:message>

<wsdl:message name="createNewAssetRecordResponseMsg">
  <wsdl:part element="tns:createNewAssetRecordResponse"
    name="createNewAssetRecordResult" />
</wsdl:message>

<wsdl:message name="deleteAssetRecordRequestMsg">
  <wsdl:part element="tns:deleteAssetRecord"
    name="deleteAssetRecordParameters" />
</wsdl:message>

<wsdl:message name="deleteAssetRecordResponseMsg">
  <wsdl:part element="tns:deleteAssetRecordResponse"
    name="deleteAssetRecordResult" />
</wsdl:message>

<wsdl:message name="archiveAssetRequestMsg">
  <wsdl:part element="tns:archiveAsset"
    name="archiveAssetParameters" />
</wsdl:message>

<wsdl:message name="archiveAssetResponseMsg">
  <wsdl:part element="tns:archiveAssetResponse"
    name="archiveAssetResult" />
</wsdl:message>

<wsdl:message name="badLocationMsg">
  <wsdl:part element="tns:badLocation" name="badLocation" />
</wsdl:message>

<wsdl:message name="noProxyExistsMsg">
  <wsdl:part element="tns:noProxyExists" name="noProxyExists" />
</wsdl:message>
```

```
<wsdl:message name="invalidSearchQueryMsg">
  <wsdl:part element="tns:invalidSearchQuery"
    name="invalidSearchQuery" />
</wsdl:message>

<wsdl:message name="invalidMetadataFieldMsg">
  <wsdl:part element="tns:invalidMetadataField"
    name="invalidMetadataField" />
</wsdl:message>

<wsdl:message name="incorrectUuidMsg">
  <wsdl:part element="tns:incorrectUuid" name="incorrectUuid" />
</wsdl:message>

<wsdl:portType name="assetManagementService">

  <wsdl:operation name="searchForAsset">
    <wsdl:input message="tns:searchForAssetRequestMsg"
      name="searchForAssetRequest" />
    <wsdl:output message="tns:searchForAssetResponseMsg"
      name="searchForAssetResponse" />
    <wsdl:fault message="tns:invalidSearchQueryMsg"
      name="invalidSearchQuery" />
  </wsdl:operation>

  <wsdl:operation name="requestAsset">
    <wsdl:input message="tns:requestAssetRequestMsg"
      name="requestAssetRequest" />
    <wsdl:output message="tns:requestAssetResponseMsg"
      name="requestAssetResponse" />
    <wsdl:fault message="tns:badLocationMsg" name="badLocation" />
    <wsdl:fault message="tns:incorrectUuidMsg"
      name="incorrectUuid" />
  </wsdl:operation>

  <wsdl:operation name="getAssetProxy">
    <wsdl:input message="tns:getAssetProxyRequestMsg"
      name="getAssetProxyRequest" />
    <wsdl:output message="tns:getAssetProxyResponseMsg"
      name="getAssetProxyResponse" />
    <wsdl:fault message="tns:incorrectUuidMsg"
      name="incorrectUuid" />
    <wsdl:fault message="tns:noProxyExistsMsg"
```

```
        name="noProxyExists" />
    </wsdl:operation>

    <wsdl:operation name="getAssetMetadata">
      <wsdl:input message="tns:getAssetMetadataRequestMsg"
        name="getAssetMetadataRequest" />
      <wsdl:output message="tns:getAssetMetadataResponseMsg"
        name="getAssetMetadataResponse" />
      <wsdl:fault message="tns:incorrectUuidMsg"
        name="incorrectUuid" />
    </wsdl:operation>

    <wsdl:operation name="setAssetMetadata">
      <wsdl:input message="tns:setAssetMetadataRequestMsg"
        name="setAssetMetadataRequest" />
      <wsdl:output message="tns:setAssetMetadataResponseMsg"
        name="setAssetMetadataResponse" />
      <wsdl:fault message="tns:incorrectUuidMsg"
        name="incorrectUuid" />
      <wsdl:fault message="tns:invalidMetadataFieldMsg"
        name="invalidMetadataField" />
    </wsdl:operation>

    <wsdl:operation name="createNewAssetRecord">
      <wsdl:input message="tns:createNewAssetRecordRequestMsg"
        name="createNewAssetRecordRequest" />
      <wsdl:output message="tns:createNewAssetRecordResponseMsg"
        name="createNewAssetRecordResponse" />
      <wsdl:fault message="tns:invalidMetadataFieldMsg"
        name="invalidMetadataField" />
    </wsdl:operation>

    <wsdl:operation name="deleteAssetRecord">
      <wsdl:input message="tns:deleteAssetRecordRequestMsg"
        name="deleteAssetRecordRequest" />
      <wsdl:output message="tns:deleteAssetRecordResponseMsg"
        name="deleteAssetRecordResponse" />
    </wsdl:operation>

    <wsdl:operation name="archiveAsset">
      <wsdl:input message="tns:archiveAssetRequestMsg"
        name="archiveAssetRequest" />
      <wsdl:output message="tns:archiveAssetResponseMsg"
        name="archiveAssetResponse" />
```

```
      <wsdl:fault message="tns:incorrectUuidMsg"
        name="incorrectUuid" />
    </wsdl:operation>

  </wsdl:portType>

  <wsdl:binding name="assetManagementServiceBinding"
    type="tns:assetManagementService">
    <soap:binding style="document"
      transport="http://schemas.xmlsoap.org/soap/http" />

    <wsdl:operation name="searchForAsset">
      <soap:operation soapAction="" />
      <wsdl:input name="searchForAssetRequest">
        <soap:body use="literal" />
      </wsdl:input>
      <wsdl:output name="searchForAssetResponse">
        <soap:body use="literal" />
      </wsdl:output>
      <wsdl:fault name="invalidSearchQuery">
        <soap:fault name="invalidSearchQuery" use="literal" />
      </wsdl:fault>
    </wsdl:operation>

    <wsdl:operation name="requestAsset">
      <soap:operation soapAction="" />
      <wsdl:input name="requestAssetRequest">
        <soap:body use="literal" />
      </wsdl:input>
      <wsdl:output name="requestAssetResponse">
        <soap:body use="literal" />
      </wsdl:output>
      <wsdl:fault name="badLocation">
        <soap:fault name="badLocation" use="literal" />
      </wsdl:fault>
      <wsdl:fault name="incorrectUuid">
        <soap:fault name="incorrectUuid" use="literal" />
      </wsdl:fault>
    </wsdl:operation>

    <wsdl:operation name="getAssetProxy">
      <soap:operation soapAction="" />
      <wsdl:input name="getAssetProxyRequest">
        <soap:body use="literal" />
```

```
      </wsdl:input>
      <wsdl:output name="getAssetProxyResponse">
        <soap:body use="literal" />
      </wsdl:output>
      <wsdl:fault name="noProxyExists">
        <soap:fault name="noProxyExists" use="literal" />
      </wsdl:fault>
      <wsdl:fault name="incorrectUuid">
        <soap:fault name="incorrectUuid" use="literal" />
      </wsdl:fault>
    </wsdl:operation>

    <wsdl:operation name="getAssetMetadata">
      <soap:operation soapAction="" />
      <wsdl:input name="getAssetMetadataRequest">
        <soap:body use="literal" />
      </wsdl:input>
      <wsdl:output name="getAssetMetadataResponse">
        <soap:body use="literal" />
      </wsdl:output>
      <wsdl:fault name="incorrectUuid">
        <soap:fault name="incorrectUuid" use="literal" />
      </wsdl:fault>
    </wsdl:operation>

    <wsdl:operation name="setAssetMetadata">
      <soap:operation soapAction="" />
      <wsdl:input name="setAssetMetadataRequest">
        <soap:body use="literal" />
      </wsdl:input>
      <wsdl:output name="setAssetMetadataResponse">
        <soap:body use="literal" />
      </wsdl:output>
      <wsdl:fault name="invalidMetadataField">
        <soap:fault name="invalidMetadataField" use="literal" />
      </wsdl:fault>
      <wsdl:fault name="incorrectUuid">
        <soap:fault name="incorrectUuid" use="literal" />
      </wsdl:fault>
    </wsdl:operation>

    <wsdl:operation name="createNewAssetRecord">
      <soap:operation soapAction="" />
      <wsdl:input name="createNewAssetRecordRequest">
```

```
          <soap:body use="literal" />
        </wsdl:input>
        <wsdl:output name="createNewAssetRecordResponse">
          <soap:body use="literal" />
        </wsdl:output>
        <wsdl:fault name="invalidMetadataField">
          <soap:fault name="invalidMetadataField" use="literal" />
        </wsdl:fault>
      </wsdl:operation>

      <wsdl:operation name="deleteAssetRecord">
        <soap:operation soapAction="" />
        <wsdl:input name="deleteAssetRecordRequest">
          <soap:body use="literal" />
        </wsdl:input>
        <wsdl:output name="deleteAssetRecordResponse">
          <soap:body use="literal" />
        </wsdl:output>
      </wsdl:operation>

      <wsdl:operation name="archiveAsset">
        <soap:operation soapAction="" />
        <wsdl:input name="archiveAssetRequest">
          <soap:body use="literal" />
        </wsdl:input>
        <wsdl:output name="archiveAssetResponse">
          <soap:body use="literal" />
        </wsdl:output>
        <wsdl:fault name="incorrectUuid">
          <soap:fault name="incorrectUuid" use="literal" />
        </wsdl:fault>
      </wsdl:operation>

  </wsdl:binding>

  <wsdl:service name="assetManagementService">
    <wsdl:port name="assetManagementServicePort"
      binding="tns:assetManagementServiceBinding">
      <soap:address
        location="http://www.example.tv/assetManagementService" />
    </wsdl:port>
  </wsdl:service>

</wsdl:definitions>
```

# A.3  EDITING SERVICE

An editing service presents a different challenge to a media SOA integrator. This is because, more often than not, a human is at the core of such a service. There are very few programmatic editing systems in widespread use in the industry (at least, for now), and so the standard editing workflow involves task lists, manual processing, and editor instructions. The editing service, therefore, is a good example of how a media enterprise might wrap a human to be another service attached to the middleware layer.

The service interface described below could be the interface for a single editing workstation and a single editor, or it could be for a larger number of editing workstations, with load balancing or another scheduling mechanism attached (such as sorting each individual editor's jobs to specific edit bays). The rest of the infrastructure need not concern itself with the details of implementation because they do not affect functionality to the enterprise; this is just an editing service.

Unlike the transcoding service described above, an editing job must be polled for status; there is no callback interface that the service supports. A service consumer should treat a job asynchronously, calling the getEditStatus operation periodically if a completed editing job is required to continue the process. Unfortunately, this type of architecture is more common in services, especially Web services, today. BPEL integrators can expect to get familiar with polling for status.

## A.3.1  Service Description

This editing service exposes six operations to affect editor workflow:

**pushToEdit** — Supplies an editor with a new editing job. The instructions and data attached to this initial request can be incomplete; the updateEditJob operation can be called to provide additional detail. In an enterprise that implements this service using a portal with a task list, this would cause a new item to appear on the editor's task list. If no editor is specifically requested, the service will assign one automatically. This operation returns an editing job ID to be used to reference this particular editing job in the future.

**updateEditJob** — Provides additional detail for a particular job. All of the same data fields are available for this operation as for pushToEdit. The clip bin list and editorial instructions given in this service call will be appended to the lists supplied in the initial push and in previous updates. Singleton fields — the requested editor and title — will be updated to reflect the values supplied in the latest service call.

**getEditStatus** — Returns the status of a particular editing job. The return value can take five states: "not found," "not started," "complete," "canceled," "ready for review," and "in progress" (with the actual percentage complete returned as well). Note that the granularity of the "in progress" percentage is not specified, so that a simple editing solution can have just a few levels (perhaps allowing the editor to manually specify the percentage completed), while a much more complex editing implementation can use automatic metrics to determine this number (such as comparing the current length of the timeline to the requested Total Run Time or TRT).

**cancelEditJob** — Cancels a given job, which updates its status and (presumably, although since implementation is independent from interface there is no guarantee) stops the editor from working on the particular job.

**escalateJob** — Raises the priority of a particular editing job. Again, since interface is independent from implementation, this could have any number of meanings. Should the editing service actually utilize the priorities associated with jobs to ensure faster completion or have them rise to the top of the editor's task list, this operation will change the processing of the specified editing job. In editing services that do not have this functionality, this operation should either be not present or do nothing. This difference should be called out in policy documentation (either WS-Policy or otherwise) and potentially used alongside business rules when routing calls to various editing services.

**getCurrentProxy** — Provides the service consumer with the location of a proxy asset of the current editing job, should one exist. This operation allows the editing job to go through several approval cycles through this service interface. Fig. A-2 describes a possible process using only the editing service to go through an entire edit workflow.

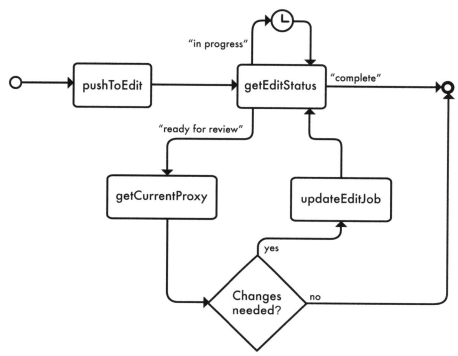

**FIGURE A-2**  This BPMN process shows a possible use case of the editing service to assign, review, and approve an edit. The service consumer in all cases is the producer reviewing the edit, and the service provider is the editor or edit system itself.

## A.3.2  Service Interface: editingService.wsdl

```xml
<?xml version="1.0" encoding="UTF-8"?>
<wsdl:definitions name="editingService"
  targetNamespace="http://www.example.tv/editingService"
  xmlns:soapenc="http://schemas.xmlsoap.org/soap/encoding/"
  xmlns:soap="http://schemas.xmlsoap.org/wsdl/soap/"
  xmlns:tns="http://www.example.tv/editingService"
  xmlns:wsdl="http://schemas.xmlsoap.org/wsdl/"
  xmlns="http://schemas.xmlsoap.org/wsdl/"
  xmlns:xsd="http://www.w3.org/2001/XMLSchema">

  <wsdl:types>
    <xsd:schema>
```

```
<xsd:complexType name="statusObject">
  <xsd:sequence>
    <xsd:element minOccurs="1" name="value">
      <xsd:simpleType>
        <xsd:restriction base="xsd:string">
          <xsd:enumeration value="not found" />
          <xsd:enumeration value="not started" />
          <xsd:enumeration value="in progress" />
          <xsd:enumeration
            value="ready for review" />
          <xsd:enumeration value="cancelled" />
          <xsd:enumeration value="complete" />
        </xsd:restriction>
      </xsd:simpleType>
    </xsd:element>
    <xsd:element minOccurs="0" name="percentComplete"
      type="xsd:int" />
  </xsd:sequence>
</xsd:complexType>

<xsd:complexType name="clipBinAssetObject">
  <xsd:sequence>
    <xsd:element minOccurs="1" name="clipTitle"
      type="xsd:string" />
    <xsd:element minOccurs="0" name="clipLocation"
      type="xsd:string" />
  </xsd:sequence>
</xsd:complexType>

<xsd:complexType name="clipBinAssetListObject">
  <xsd:sequence>
    <xsd:element minOccurs="0" name="clipBinAsset"
      type="tns:clipBinAssetObject" maxOccurs="unbounded" />
  </xsd:sequence>
</xsd:complexType>

<xsd:element name="pushToEdit">
  <xsd:complexType>
    <xsd:sequence>
      <xsd:element name="jobTitle" nillable="true"
        type="xsd:string" />
      <xsd:element name="editorRequested"
        nillable="true" type="xsd:string" />
      <xsd:element name="editorialInstructions"
```

```
                    nillable="true" type="xsd:string" />
           <xsd:element name="clipBinAssets"
                    nillable="true" type="tns:clipBinAssetListObject" />
        </xsd:sequence>
      </xsd:complexType>
    </xsd:element>

    <xsd:element name="pushToEditResponse">
      <xsd:complexType>
        <xsd:sequence>
          <xsd:element name="jobID" nillable="true"
                    type="xsd:int" />
        </xsd:sequence>
      </xsd:complexType>
    </xsd:element>

    <xsd:element name="updateEditJob">
      <xsd:complexType>
        <xsd:sequence>
          <xsd:element name="jobID" nillable="true"
                    type="xsd:int" />
          <xsd:element name="jobTitle" nillable="true"
                    type="xsd:string" />
          <xsd:element name="editorRequested"
                    nillable="true" type="xsd:string" />
          <xsd:element name="editorialInstructions"
                    nillable="true" type="xsd:string" />
          <xsd:element name="clipBinAssets"
                    nillable="true" type="tns:clipBinAssetListObject" />
        </xsd:sequence>
      </xsd:complexType>
    </xsd:element>

    <xsd:element name="updateEditJobResponse">
      <xsd:complexType>
        <xsd:sequence>
          <xsd:element name="confirmation" nillable="true"
                    type="xsd:boolean" />
        </xsd:sequence>
      </xsd:complexType>
    </xsd:element>

    <xsd:element name="getEditStatus">
      <xsd:complexType>
```

```xml
      <xsd:sequence>
        <xsd:element name="jobID" nillable="true"
          type="xsd:int" />
      </xsd:sequence>
    </xsd:complexType>
</xsd:element>

<xsd:element name="getEditStatusResponse">
  <xsd:complexType>
    <xsd:sequence>
      <xsd:element name="status" nillable="true"
        type="tns:statusObject" />
    </xsd:sequence>
  </xsd:complexType>
</xsd:element>

<xsd:element name="cancelEditJob">
  <xsd:complexType>
    <xsd:sequence>
      <xsd:element name="jobID" nillable="true"
        type="xsd:int" />
    </xsd:sequence>
  </xsd:complexType>
</xsd:element>

<xsd:element name="cancelEditJobResponse">
  <xsd:complexType>
    <xsd:sequence>
      <xsd:element name="confirmation" nillable="true"
        type="xsd:boolean" />
    </xsd:sequence>
  </xsd:complexType>
</xsd:element>

<xsd:element name="escalateJob">
  <xsd:complexType>
    <xsd:sequence>
      <xsd:element name="jobID" nillable="true"
        type="xsd:int" />
    </xsd:sequence>
  </xsd:complexType>
</xsd:element>
```

```xml
<xsd:element name="escalateJobResponse">
  <xsd:complexType>
    <xsd:sequence>
      <xsd:element name="newPriority" nillable="true"
        type="xsd:int" />
    </xsd:sequence>
  </xsd:complexType>
</xsd:element>

<xsd:element name="getCurrentProxy">
  <xsd:complexType>
    <xsd:sequence>
      <xsd:element name="jobID" nillable="true"
        type="xsd:int" />
    </xsd:sequence>
  </xsd:complexType>
</xsd:element>

<xsd:element name="getCurrentProxyResponse">
  <xsd:complexType>
    <xsd:sequence>
      <xsd:element name="proxyLocation"
        nillable="true" type="xsd:string" />
    </xsd:sequence>
  </xsd:complexType>
</xsd:element>

<xsd:element name="unknownEditor">
  <xsd:complexType>
    <xsd:sequence>
      <xsd:element name="detail" type="xsd:string" />
    </xsd:sequence>
  </xsd:complexType>
</xsd:element>

<xsd:element name="incorrectJobID">
  <xsd:complexType>
    <xsd:sequence>
      <xsd:element name="detail" type="xsd:string" />
    </xsd:sequence>
  </xsd:complexType>
</xsd:element>
```

```
      <xsd:element name="noProxyExists">
        <xsd:complexType>
          <xsd:sequence>
            <xsd:element name="detail" type="xsd:string" />
          </xsd:sequence>
        </xsd:complexType>
      </xsd:element>

    </xsd:schema>
  </wsdl:types>

  <wsdl:message name="pushToEditRequestMsg">
    <wsdl:part element="tns:pushToEdit" name="pushToEditParameters" />
  </wsdl:message>

  <wsdl:message name="pushToEditResponseMsg">
    <wsdl:part element="tns:pushToEditResponse"
      name="pushToEditResult" />
  </wsdl:message>

  <wsdl:message name="updateEditJobRequestMsg">
    <wsdl:part element="tns:updateEditJob"
      name="updateEditJobParameters" />
  </wsdl:message>

  <wsdl:message name="updateEditJobResponseMsg">
    <wsdl:part element="tns:updateEditJobResponse"
      name="updateEditJobResult" />
  </wsdl:message>

  <wsdl:message name="getEditStatusRequestMsg">
    <wsdl:part element="tns:getEditStatus"
      name="getEditStatusParameters" />
  </wsdl:message>

  <wsdl:message name="getEditStatusResponseMsg">
    <wsdl:part element="tns:getEditStatusResponse"
      name="getEditStatusResult" />
  </wsdl:message>

  <wsdl:message name="cancelEditJobRequestMsg">
    <wsdl:part element="tns:cancelEditJob"
      name="cancelEditJobParameters" />
  </wsdl:message>
```

```
<wsdl:message name="cancelEditJobResponseMsg">
  <wsdl:part element="tns:cancelEditJobResponse"
    name="cancelEditJobResult" />
</wsdl:message>

<wsdl:message name="escalateJobRequestMsg">
  <wsdl:part element="tns:escalateJob"
    name="escalateJobParameters" />
</wsdl:message>

<wsdl:message name="escalateJobResponseMsg">
  <wsdl:part element="tns:escalateJobResponse"
    name="escalateJobResult" />
</wsdl:message>

<wsdl:message name="getCurrentProxyRequestMsg">
  <wsdl:part element="tns:getCurrentProxy"
    name="getCurrentProxyParameters" />
</wsdl:message>

<wsdl:message name="getCurrentProxyResponseMsg">
  <wsdl:part element="tns:getCurrentProxyResponse"
    name="getCurrentProxyResult" />
</wsdl:message>

<wsdl:message name="unknownEditorMsg">
  <wsdl:part element="tns:unknownEditor" name="unknownEditor" />
</wsdl:message>

<wsdl:message name="incorrectJobIDMsg">
  <wsdl:part element="tns:incorrectJobID" name="incorrectJobID" />
</wsdl:message>

<wsdl:message name="noProxyExistsMsg">
  <wsdl:part element="tns:noProxyExists" name="noProxyExists" />
</wsdl:message>

<wsdl:portType name="editingService">

  <wsdl:operation name="pushToEdit">
    <wsdl:input message="tns:pushToEditRequestMsg"
      name="pushToEditRequest" />
```

```
    <wsdl:output message="tns:pushToEditResponseMsg"
      name="pushToEditResponse" />
    <wsdl:fault message="tns:unknownEditorMsg"
      name="unknownEditor" />
</wsdl:operation>

<wsdl:operation name="updateEditJob">
    <wsdl:input message="tns:updateEditJobRequestMsg"
      name="updateEditJobRequest" />>
    <wsdl:output message="tns:updateEditJobResponseMsg"
      name="updateEditJobResponse" />
    <wsdl:fault message="tns:incorrectJobIDMsg"
      name="incorrectJobID" />
    <wsdl:fault message="tns:unknownEditorMsg"
      name="unknownEditor" />
</wsdl:operation>

<wsdl:operation name="getEditStatus">
    <wsdl:input message="tns:getEditStatusRequestMsg"
      name="getEditStatusRequest" />
    <wsdl:output message="tns:getEditStatusResponseMsg"
      name="getEditStatusResponse" />
</wsdl:operation>

<wsdl:operation name="cancelEditJob">
    <wsdl:input message="tns:cancelEditJobRequestMsg"
      name="cancelEditJobRequest" />
    <wsdl:output message="tns:cancelEditJobResponseMsg"
      name="cancelEditJobResponse" />
</wsdl:operation>

<wsdl:operation name="escalateJob">
    <wsdl:input message="tns:escalateJobRequestMsg"
      name="escalateJobRequest" />
    <wsdl:output message="tns:escalateJobResponseMsg"
      name="escalateJobResponse" />
    <wsdl:fault message="tns:incorrectJobIDMsg"
      name="incorrectJobID" />
</wsdl:operation>

<wsdl:operation name="getCurrentProxy">
    <wsdl:input message="tns:getCurrentProxyRequestMsg"
      name="getCurrentProxyRequest" />
```

```
      <wsdl:output message="tns:getCurrentProxyResponseMsg"
        name="getCurrentProxyResponse" />
      <wsdl:fault message="tns:incorrectJobIDMsg"
        name="incorrectJobID" />
      <wsdl:fault message="tns:noProxyExistsMsg"
        name="noProxyExists" />
    </wsdl:operation>

</wsdl:portType>

<wsdl:binding name="editingServiceBinding"
  type="tns:editingService">
  <soap:binding style="document"
    transport="http://schemas.xmlsoap.org/soap/http" />

  <wsdl:operation name="pushToEdit">
    <soap:operation soapAction="" />
    <wsdl:input name="pushToEditRequest">
      <soap:body use="literal" />
    </wsdl:input>
    <wsdl:output name="pushToEditResponse">
      <soap:body use="literal" />
    </wsdl:output>
    <wsdl:fault name="unknownEditor">
      <soap:fault name="unknownEditor" use="literal" />
    </wsdl:fault>
  </wsdl:operation>

  <wsdl:operation name="updateEditJob">
    <soap:operation soapAction="" />
    <wsdl:input name="updateEditJobRequest">
      <soap:body use="literal" />
    </wsdl:input>
    <wsdl:output name="updateEditJobResponse">
      <soap:body use="literal" />
    </wsdl:output>
    <wsdl:fault name="unknownEditor">
      <soap:fault name="unknownEditor" use="literal" />
    </wsdl:fault>
    <wsdl:fault name="incorrectJobID">
      <soap:fault name="incorrectJobID" use="literal" />
    </wsdl:fault>
  </wsdl:operation>
```

```
<wsdl:operation name="getEditStatus">
  <soap:operation soapAction="" />
  <wsdl:input name="getEditStatusRequest">
    <soap:body use="literal" />
  </wsdl:input>
  <wsdl:output name="getEditStatusResponse">
    <soap:body use="literal" />
  </wsdl:output>
</wsdl:operation>

<wsdl:operation name="cancelEditJob">
  <soap:operation soapAction="" />
  <wsdl:input name="cancelEditJobRequest">
    <soap:body use="literal" />
  </wsdl:input>
  <wsdl:output name="cancelEditJobResponse">
    <soap:body use="literal" />
  </wsdl:output>
</wsdl:operation>

<wsdl:operation name="escalateJob">
  <soap:operation soapAction="" />
  <wsdl:input name="escalateJobRequest">
    <soap:body use="literal" />
  </wsdl:input>
  <wsdl:output name="escalateJobResponse">
    <soap:body use="literal" />
  </wsdl:output>
  <wsdl:fault name="incorrectJobID">
    <soap:fault name="incorrectJobID" use="literal" />
  </wsdl:fault>
</wsdl:operation>

<wsdl:operation name="getCurrentProxy">
  <soap:operation soapAction="" />
  <wsdl:input name="getCurrentProxyRequest">
    <soap:body use="literal" />
  </wsdl:input>
  <wsdl:output name="getCurrentProxyResponse">
    <soap:body use="literal" />
  </wsdl:output>
  <wsdl:fault name="noProxyExists">
    <soap:fault name="noProxyExists" use="literal" />
```

```
      </wsdl:fault>
      <wsdl:fault name="incorrectJobID">
        <soap:fault name="incorrectJobID" use="literal" />
      </wsdl:fault>
    </wsdl:operation>

  </wsdl:binding>

  <wsdl:service name="editingService">
    <wsdl:port name="editingServicePort"
      binding="tns:editingServiceBinding">
      <soap:address
        location="http://www.example.tv/editingService" />
    </wsdl:port>
  </wsdl:service>
</wsdl:definitions>
```

## A.4  INGEST SERVICE

This ingest service is the type that might be exposed by a single ingest server connected to one or many VTRs, or it might be exposed by an entire ingest department. It exposes many of the same operations that are similar to those exposed by other services discussed above: moving assets and setting metadata. However, these operations, though they look familiar, have different business meaning for an ingest service than they would for a transcoding or asset management service. For example, entering or extracting asset metadata in an ingest service may refer to the metadata included in the wrapper of the digital asset in question, whereas in an asset management service, this will no doubt refer to the metadata stored in the asset management system. Business context is important in service definition, which is why service providers should include policies, descriptions, and semantics whenever possible to avoid confusion. If a media integrator only gets service descriptions like the WSDLs below, he or she could have a hard time determining the purpose of the service in question.

This ingest service also shows the challenges of doing out-of-band media transfer. To move assets in or out of local ingest storage, a supported transfer mechanism must be specified. One ingest service may only support FTP, while others may support a handful of technologies. Specifying these restrictions is the theoretical job of a UDDI registry or other such information repository. Out-of-band media transfer is also where a media layer becomes incredibly useful by handling the details of the transaction.

Also, like the transcoding service specified above, this ingest service provides a callback mechanism for those consumers that wish to take advantage of it. Unlike the transcoding service, the ingest service requires the consumer to implement the callback interface, because it does not provide any status-checking operations for synchronous feedback. Between this service, the transcoding service, and the editing service, the entire gamut of asynchronous messaging has been discussed. An orchestration engine can often hide the details of this type of asynchronous messaging (so that, for example, the business user never has to deal with a job ID), and SOA integrators should look for opportunities to shield this from the rest of the enterprise. One of the faults of the current incarnation of Web services, unfortunately, is its inability to handle this type of asynchronous messaging gracefully.

## A.4.1  Service Description

The ingest service exposes seven operations to the rest of the enterprise.

**ingestAsset** — Schedules a physical media asset for ingest through the use of a unique identifier. This ingest is given a deadline/priority and is treated asynchronously by the service. The asset, once ingested, exists as a digital media file in the local ingest storage, where it can be moved out through other service calls or accessed out-of-band by other services. The filename of the asset, once ingested, is used as a unique job identifier, although the requested filename cannot always be the actual filename due to potential naming conflicts.

**cancelIngest** — Uses a filename to cancel a specific ingest request. If the ingest has not yet occurred, it will be removed from the schedule. If it has already occurred, the operation will return a false confirmation.

**moveAssetIn** — Moves a digital media asset into local ingest storage from an external location. The method of out-of-band transfer must be specified. This operation would be used to bring in external media assets if the local ingest storage was used like a holding pen for incoming digital assets (both tapes and files). It is managed asynchronously, with a job ID.

**moveAssetOut** — Moves a digital media asset out of local ingest storage to another location, such as an asset management or transcoding watch folder. The method of out-of-band transfer must be specified by the consumer.

**cancelMove** — Cancels a pending on in-process move request (either in or out). If the move has already occurred, this operation returns a false confirmation.

**extractMetadata** — Returns the metadata stored in the wrapper of a given digital media asset (in local storage), using the asset filename as a unique identifier. This operation could be used in tandem with the moveAssetOut operation to register an incoming file with an asset management system and move it into long-term storage. Since the ingest service does not advertise its own metadata storage, it is expected that the metadata returned by this operation is only that which can be stored in the media wrapper.

**enterMetadata** — Stores the provided metadata in the wrapper of the specified digital media asset in local storage. This operation can be used in tandem with moveAssetOut if the asset had been given a placeholder in an asset management system that was populated with metadata prior to the video asset itself arriving. Since it is expected that the metadata is stored directly in the media wrapper, any fields provided that cannot be stored in the wrapper will result in a business fault by this operation.

## A.4.2 Service Interfaces

In addition to its regular operations, the ingest service expects its consumer to implement interfaces for a moveComplete and ingestComplete operation. Should the consumer not implement these interfaces and use WS-Addressing to provide their location to the service, that consumer will receive no feedback when their move or ingest requests are completed.

### A.4.2.1  ingestService.wsdl

```
<?xml version="1.0" encoding="UTF-8"?>
<wsdl:definitions name="ingestService"
  targetNamespace="http://www.example.tv/ingestService"
  xmlns:soapenc="http://schemas.xmlsoap.org/soap/encoding/"
  xmlns:soap="http://schemas.xmlsoap.org/wsdl/soap/"
  xmlns:tns="http://www.example.tv/ingestService"
  xmlns:wsdl="http://schemas.xmlsoap.org/wsdl/"
  xmlns="http://schemas.xmlsoap.org/wsdl/"
  xmlns:xsd="http://www.w3.org/2001/XMLSchema">

  <wsdl:types>
    <xsd:schema>

      <xsd:complexType name="metadataObject">
        <xsd:sequence>
          <xsd:element minOccurs="0" name="field"
            type="xsd:string" />
          <xsd:element minOccurs="0" name="value"
            type="xsd:string" />
        </xsd:sequence>
      </xsd:complexType>

      <xsd:complexType name="metadataListObject">
        <xsd:sequence>
          <xsd:element minOccurs="0" name="metadata"
            type="tns:metadataObject" maxOccurs="unbounded" />
        </xsd:sequence>
      </xsd:complexType>

      <xsd:element name="ingestAsset">
        <xsd:complexType>
          <xsd:sequence>
            <xsd:element name="physicalMediaID"
              nillable="true" type="xsd:string" />
            <xsd:element name="physicalMediaLocation"
              nillable="true" type="xsd:string" />
            <xsd:element name="deadline" nillable="true"
              type="xsd:date" />
            <xsd:element name="requestedFilename"
              nillable="true" type="xsd:string" />
          </xsd:sequence>
```

```
        </xsd:complexType>
    </xsd:element>

    <xsd:element name="ingestAssetResponse">
      <xsd:complexType>
        <xsd:sequence>
          <xsd:element name="filename" nillable="true"
            type="xsd:string" />
        </xsd:sequence>
      </xsd:complexType>
    </xsd:element>

    <xsd:element name="cancelIngest">
      <xsd:complexType>
        <xsd:sequence>
          <xsd:element name="filename" nillable="true"
            type="xsd:string" />
        </xsd:sequence>
      </xsd:complexType>
    </xsd:element>

    <xsd:element name="cancelIngestResponse">
      <xsd:complexType>
        <xsd:sequence>
          <xsd:element name="confirmation" nillable="true"
            type="xsd:boolean" />
        </xsd:sequence>
      </xsd:complexType>
    </xsd:element>

    <xsd:element name="moveAssetIn">
      <xsd:complexType>
        <xsd:sequence>
          <xsd:element name="externalLocation"
            nillable="true" type="xsd:string" />
          <xsd:element name="internalFilename"
            nillable="true" type="xsd:string" />
          <xsd:element name="transferMethod"
            nillable="true" type="xsd:string" />
        </xsd:sequence>
      </xsd:complexType>
    </xsd:element>
```

```
<xsd:element name="moveAssetInResponse">
  <xsd:complexType>
    <xsd:sequence>
      <xsd:element name="filename" nillable="true"
        type="xsd:string" />
      <xsd:element name="jobID" nillable="true"
        type="xsd:int" />
    </xsd:sequence>
  </xsd:complexType>
</xsd:element>

<xsd:element name="moveAssetOut">
  <xsd:complexType>
    <xsd:sequence>
      <xsd:element name="externalLocation"
        nillable="true" type="xsd:string" />
      <xsd:element name="internalFilename"
        nillable="true" type="xsd:string" />
      <xsd:element name="transferMethod"
        nillable="true" type="xsd:string" />
    </xsd:sequence>
  </xsd:complexType>
</xsd:element>

<xsd:element name="moveAssetOutResponse">
  <xsd:complexType>
    <xsd:sequence>
      <xsd:element name="jobID" nillable="true"
        type="xsd:int" />
    </xsd:sequence>
  </xsd:complexType>
</xsd:element>

<xsd:element name="cancelMove">
  <xsd:complexType>
    <xsd:sequence>
      <xsd:element name="jobID" nillable="true"
        type="xsd:int" />
    </xsd:sequence>
  </xsd:complexType>
</xsd:element>

<xsd:element name="cancelMoveResponse">
  <xsd:complexType>
```

```xml
    <xsd:sequence>
      <xsd:element name="confirmation" nillable="true"
        type="xsd:boolean" />
    </xsd:sequence>
  </xsd:complexType>
</xsd:element>

<xsd:element name="extractMetadata">
  <xsd:complexType>
    <xsd:sequence>
      <xsd:element name="filename" nillable="true"
        type="xsd:string" />
    </xsd:sequence>
  </xsd:complexType>
</xsd:element>

<xsd:element name="extractMetadataResponse">
  <xsd:complexType>
    <xsd:sequence>
      <xsd:element name="metadataList" nillable="true"
        type="tns:metadataListObject" />
    </xsd:sequence>
  </xsd:complexType>
</xsd:element>

<xsd:element name="enterMetadata">
  <xsd:complexType>
    <xsd:sequence>
      <xsd:element name="filename" nillable="true"
        type="xsd:string" />
      <xsd:element name="metadataList" nillable="true"
        type="tns:metadataListObject" />
    </xsd:sequence>
  </xsd:complexType>
</xsd:element>

<xsd:element name="enterMetadataResponse">
  <xsd:complexType>
    <xsd:sequence>
      <xsd:element name="confirmation" nillable="true"
        type="xsd:boolean" />
    </xsd:sequence>
  </xsd:complexType>
</xsd:element>
```

```
<xsd:element name="inappropriateDeadline">
  <xsd:complexType>
    <xsd:sequence>
      <xsd:element name="detail" type="xsd:string" />
    </xsd:sequence>
  </xsd:complexType>
</xsd:element>

<xsd:element name="unknownLocation">
  <xsd:complexType>
    <xsd:sequence>
      <xsd:element name="detail" type="xsd:string" />
    </xsd:sequence>
  </xsd:complexType>
</xsd:element>

<xsd:element name="unknownID">
  <xsd:complexType>
    <xsd:sequence>
      <xsd:element name="detail" type="xsd:string" />
    </xsd:sequence>
  </xsd:complexType>
</xsd:element>

<xsd:element name="cannotAccessLocation">
  <xsd:complexType>
    <xsd:sequence>
      <xsd:element name="detail" type="xsd:string" />
    </xsd:sequence>
  </xsd:complexType>
</xsd:element>

<xsd:element name="transferMethodNotSupported">
  <xsd:complexType>
    <xsd:sequence>
      <xsd:element name="detail" type="xsd:string" />
    </xsd:sequence>
  </xsd:complexType>
</xsd:element>

<xsd:element name="filenameNotFound">
  <xsd:complexType>>
    <xsd:sequence>
```

```
            <xsd:element name="detail" type="xsd:string" />
          </xsd:sequence>
        </xsd:complexType>
      </xsd:element>

      <xsd:element name="inappropriateMetadata">
        <xsd:complexType>
          <xsd:sequence>
            <xsd:element name="detail" type="xsd:string" />
          </xsd:sequence>
        </xsd:complexType>
      </xsd:element>

    </xsd:schema>
  </wsdl:types>

  <wsdl:message name="ingestAssetRequestMsg">
    <wsdl:part element="tns:ingestAsset"
      name="ingestAssetParameters" />
  </wsdl:message>

  <wsdl:message name="ingestAssetResponseMsg">
    <wsdl:part element="tns:ingestAssetResponse"
      name="ingestAssetResult" />
  </wsdl:message>

  <wsdl:message name="cancelIngestRequestMsg">
    <wsdl:part element="tns:cancelIngest"
      name="cancelIngestParameters" />
  </wsdl:message>

  <wsdl:message name="cancelIngestResponseMsg">
    <wsdl:part element="tns:cancelIngestResponse"
      name="cancelIngestResult" />
  </wsdl:message>

  <wsdl:message name="moveAssetInRequestMsg">
    <wsdl:part element="tns:moveAssetIn"
      name="moveAssetInParameters" />
  </wsdl:message>

  <wsdl:message name="moveAssetInResponseMsg">
    <wsdl:part element="tns:moveAssetInResponse"
```

```
      name="moveAssetInResult" />
</wsdl:message>

<wsdl:message name="moveAssetOutRequestMsg">
  <wsdl:part element="tns:moveAssetOut"
    name="moveAssetOutParameters" />
</wsdl:message>

<wsdl:message name="moveAssetOutResponseMsg">
  <wsdl:part element="tns:moveAssetOutResponse"
    name="moveAssetOutResult"/>
</wsdl:message>

<wsdl:message name="cancelMoveRequestMsg">
  <wsdl:part element="tns:cancelMove" name="cancelMoveParameters" />
</wsdl:message>

<wsdl:message name="cancelMoveResponseMsg">
  <wsdl:part element="tns:cancelMoveResponse"
    name="cancelMoveResult" />
</wsdl:message>

<wsdl:message name="extractMetadataRequestMsg">
  <wsdl:part element="tns:extractMetadata"
    name="extractMetadataParameters" />
</wsdl:message>

<wsdl:message name="extractMetadataResponseMsg">
  <wsdl:part element="tns:extractMetadataResponse"
    name="extractMetadataResult" />
</wsdl:message>

<wsdl:message name="enterMetadataRequestMsg">
  <wsdl:part element="tns:enterMetadata"
    name="enterMetadataParameters" />
</wsdl:message>

<wsdl:message name="enterMetadataResponseMsg">
  <wsdl:part element="tns:enterMetadataResponse"
    name="enterMetadataResult" />
</wsdl:message>
```

```
<wsdl:message name="inappropriateDeadlineMsg">
  <wsdl:part element="tns:inappropriateDeadline"
    name="inappropriateDeadline" />
</wsdl:message>

<wsdl:message name="unknownLocationMsg">
  <wsdl:part element="tns:unknownLocation" name="unknownLocation" />
</wsdl:message>

<wsdl:message name="unknownIDMsg">
  <wsdl:part element="tns:unknownID" name="unknownID" />
</wsdl:message>

<wsdl:message name="cannotAccessLocationMsg">
  <wsdl:part element="tns:cannotAccessLocation"
    name="cannotAccessLocation" />
</wsdl:message>

<wsdl:message name="transferMethodNotSupportedMsg">
  <wsdl:part element="tns:transferMethodNotSupported"
    name="transferMethodNotSupported" />
</wsdl:message>

<wsdl:message name="filenameNotFoundMsg">
  <wsdl:part element="tns:filenameNotFound"
    name="filenameNotFound" />
</wsdl:message>

<wsdl:message name="inappropriateMetadataMsg">
  <wsdl:part element="tns:inappropriateMetadata"
    name="inappropriateMetadata" />
</wsdl:message>

<wsdl:portType name="ingestService">

  <wsdl:operation name="ingestAsset">
    <wsdl:input message="tns:ingestAssetRequestMsg"
      name="ingestAssetRequest" />
    <wsdl:output message="tns:ingestAssetResponseMsg"
      name="ingestAssetResponse" />
    <wsdl:fault message="tns:inappropriateDeadlineMsg"
      name="inappropriateDeadline" />
    <wsdl:fault message="tns:unknownLocationMsg"
      name="unknownLocation" />
```

```
      <wsdl:fault message="tns:unknownIDMsg" name="unknownID" />
</wsdl:operation>

<wsdl:operation name="cancelIngest">
  <wsdl:input message="tns:cancelIngestRequestMsg"
    name="cancelIngestRequest" />
  <wsdl:output message="tns:cancelIngestResponseMsg"
    name="cancelIngestResponse" />
</wsdl:operation>

<wsdl:operation name="moveAssetIn">
  <wsdl:input message="tns:moveAssetInRequestMsg"
    name="moveAssetInRequest" />
  <wsdl:output message="tns:moveAssetInResponseMsg"
    name="moveAssetInResponse" />
  <wsdl:fault message="tns:cannotAccessLocationMsg"
    name="cannotAccessLocation" />
  <wsdl:fault message="tns:transferMethodNotSupportedMsg"
    name="transferMethodNotSupported" />
</wsdl:operation>

<wsdl:operation name="moveAssetOut">
  <wsdl:input message="tns:moveAssetOutRequestMsg"
    name="moveAssetOutRequest" />
  <wsdl:output message="tns:moveAssetOutResponseMsg"
    name="moveAssetOutResponse" />
  <wsdl:fault message="tns:cannotAccessLocationMsg"
    name="cannotAccessLocation" />
  <wsdl:fault message="tns:transferMethodNotSupportedMsg"
    name="transferMethodNotSupported" />
  <wsdl:fault message="tns:filenameNotFoundMsg"
    name="filenameNotFound" />
</wsdl:operation>

<wsdl:operation name="cancelMove">
  <wsdl:input message="tns:cancelMoveRequestMsg"
    name="cancelMoveRequest" />
  <wsdl:output message="tns:cancelMoveResponseMsg"
    name="cancelMoveResponse" />
</wsdl:operation>

<wsdl:operation name="extractMetadata">
  <wsdl:input message="tns:extractMetadataRequestMsg"
```

```
            name="extractMetadataRequest" />
      <wsdl:output message="tns:extractMetadataResponseMsg"
        name="extractMetadataResponse" />
      <wsdl:fault message="tns:filenameNotFoundMsg"
        name="filenameNotFound" />
    </wsdl:operation>

    <wsdl:operation name="enterMetadata">
      <wsdl:input message="tns:enterMetadataRequestMsg"
        name="enterMetadataRequest" />
      <wsdl:output message="tns:enterMetadataResponseMsg"
        name="enterMetadataResponse" />
      <wsdl:fault message="tns:filenameNotFoundMsg"
        name="filenameNotFound" />
      <wsdl:fault message="tns:inappropriateMetadataMsg"
        name="inappropriateMetadata" />
    </wsdl:operation>

  </wsdl:portType>

  <wsdl:binding name="ingestServiceBinding"
    type="tns:ingestService">
    <soap:binding style="document"
      transport="http://schemas.xmlsoap.org/soap/http" />

    <wsdl:operation name="ingestAsset">
      <soap:operation soapAction="" />
      <wsdl:input name="ingestAssetRequest">
        <soap:body use="literal" />
      </wsdl:input>
      <wsdl:output name="ingestAssetResponse">
        <soap:body use="literal" />
      </wsdl:output>
      <wsdl:fault name="unknownLocation">
        <soap:fault name="unknownLocation" use="literal" />
      </wsdl:fault>
      <wsdl:fault name="unknownID">
        <soap:fault name="unknownID" use="literal" />
      </wsdl:fault>
      <wsdl:fault name="inappropriateDeadline">
        <soap:fault name="inappropriateDeadline" use="literal" />
      </wsdl:fault>
    </wsdl:operation>
```

```
<wsdl:operation name="cancelIngest">
  <soap:operation soapAction="" />
  <wsdl:input name="cancelIngestRequest">
    <soap:body use="literal" />
  </wsdl:input>
  <wsdl:output name="cancelIngestResponse">
    <soap:body use="literal" />
  </wsdl:output>
</wsdl:operation>

<wsdl:operation name="moveAssetIn">
  <soap:operation soapAction="" />
  <wsdl:input name="moveAssetInRequest">
    <soap:body use="literal" />
  </wsdl:input>
  <wsdl:output name="moveAssetInResponse">
    <soap:body use="literal" />
  </wsdl:output>
  <wsdl:fault name="cannotAccessLocation">
    <soap:fault name="cannotAccessLocation" use="literal" />
  </wsdl:fault>
  <wsdl:fault name="transferMethodNotSupported">
    <soap:fault name="transferMethodNotSupported"
      use="literal" />
  </wsdl:fault>
</wsdl:operation>

<wsdl:operation name="moveAssetOut">
  <soap:operation soapAction="" />
  <wsdl:input name="moveAssetOutRequest">
    <soap:body use="literal" />
  </wsdl:input>
  <wsdl:output name="moveAssetOutResponse">
    <soap:body use="literal" />
  </wsdl:output>
  <wsdl:fault name="cannotAccessLocation">
    <soap:fault name="cannotAccessLocation" use="literal" />
  </wsdl:fault>
  <wsdl:fault name="filenameNotFound">
    <soap:fault name="filenameNotFound" use="literal" />
  </wsdl:fault>
  <wsdl:fault name="transferMethodNotSupported">
    <soap:fault name="transferMethodNotSupported"
```

```
            use="literal" />
      </wsdl:fault>
   </wsdl:operation>

   <wsdl:operation name="cancelMove">
     <soap:operation soapAction="" />
     <wsdl:input name="cancelMoveRequest">
       <soap:body use="literal" />
     </wsdl:input>
     <wsdl:output name="cancelMoveResponse">
       <soap:body use="literal" />
     </wsdl:output>
   </wsdl:operation>

   <wsdl:operation name="extractMetadata">
     <soap:operation soapAction="" />
     <wsdl:input name="extractMetadataRequest">
       <soap:body use="literal" />
     </wsdl:input>
     <wsdl:output name="extractMetadataResponse">
       <soap:body use="literal" />
     </wsdl:output>
     <wsdl:fault name="filenameNotFound">
       <soap:fault name="filenameNotFound" use="literal" />
     </wsdl:fault>
   </wsdl:operation>

   <wsdl:operation name="enterMetadata">
     <soap:operation soapAction="" />
     <wsdl:input name="enterMetadataRequest">
       <soap:body use="literal" />
     </wsdl:input>
     <wsdl:output name="enterMetadataResponse">
       <soap:body use="literal" />
     </wsdl:output>
     <wsdl:fault name="filenameNotFound">
       <soap:fault name="filenameNotFound" use="literal" />
     </wsdl:fault>
     <wsdl:fault name="inappropriateMetadata">
       <soap:fault name="inappropriateMetadata" use="literal" />
     </wsdl:fault>
   </wsdl:operation>

</wsdl:binding>
```

```
    <wsdl:service name="ingestService">
      <wsdl:port name="ingestServicePort"
        binding="tns:ingestServiceBinding">
        <soap:address
          location="http://www.example.tv/ingestService" />
      </wsdl:port>
    </wsdl:service>

  </wsdl:definitions>
```

## A.4.2.2 ingestServiceCallback.wsdl

```
<?xml version="1.0" encoding="UTF-8"?>
<wsdl:definitions name="ingestServiceCallback"
  targetNamespace="http://www.example.tv/ingestService"
  xmlns:tns="http://www.example.tv/ingestService"
  xmlns="http://schemas.xmlsoap.org/wsdl/"
  xmlns:wsdl="http://schemas.xmlsoap.org/wsdl/"
  xmlns:soap="http://schemas.xmlsoap.org/wsdl/soap/"
  xmlns:soapenc="http://schemas.xmlsoap.org/soap/encoding/"
  xmlns:xsd="http://www.w3.org/2001/XMLSchema">

  <wsdl:types>
    <xsd:schema>

      <xsd:element name="ingestComplete">
        <xsd:complexType>
          <xsd:sequence>
            <xsd:element name="filename" nillable="true"
              type="xsd:string" />
          </xsd:sequence>
        </xsd:complexType>
      </xsd:element>

      <xsd:element name="ingestCompleteResponse">
        <xsd:complexType>
          <xsd:sequence>
            <xsd:element name="confirmation" nillable="true"
              type="xsd:boolean" />
          </xsd:sequence>
        </xsd:complexType>
      </xsd:element>
```

```
    <xsd:element name="moveComplete">
      <xsd:complexType>
        <xsd:sequence>
          <xsd:element name="jobID" nillable="true"
            type="xsd:int" />
        </xsd:sequence>
      </xsd:complexType>
    </xsd:element>

    <xsd:element name="moveCompleteResponse">
      <xsd:complexType>
        <xsd:sequence>
          <xsd:element name="confirmation" nillable="true"
            type="xsd:boolean" />
        </xsd:sequence>
      </xsd:complexType>
    </xsd:element>

  </xsd:schema>
</wsdl:types>

<wsdl:message name="ingestCompleteRequestMsg">
  <wsdl:part element="tns:ingestComplete"
    name="ingestCompleteParameters" />
</wsdl:message>

<wsdl:message name="ingestCompleteResponseMsg">
  <wsdl:part element="tns:ingestCompleteResponse"
    name="ingestCompleteResult" />
</wsdl:message>

<wsdl:message name="moveCompleteRequestMsg">
  <wsdl:part element="tns:moveComplete"
    name="moveCompleteParameters" />
</wsdl:message>

<wsdl:message name="moveCompleteResponseMsg">
  <wsdl:part element="tns:moveCompleteResponse"
    name="moveCompleteResult" />
</wsdl:message>

<wsdl:portType name="ingestServiceCallback">
```

```
    <wsdl:operation name="ingestComplete">
      <wsdl:input message="tns:ingestCompleteRequestMsg"
        name="ingestCompleteRequest" />
      <wsdl:output message="tns:ingestCompleteResponseMsg"
        name="ingestCompleteResponse" />
    </wsdl:operation>

    <wsdl:operation name="moveComplete">
      <wsdl:input message="tns:moveCompleteRequestMsg"
        name="moveCompleteRequest" />
      <wsdl:output message="tns:moveCompleteResponseMsg"
        name="moveCompleteResponse" />
    </wsdl:operation>

</wsdl:portType>

<wsdl:binding name="ingestServiceCallbackBinding"
  type="tns:ingestServiceCallback">
  <soap:binding style="document"
    transport="http://schemas.xmlsoap.org/soap/http" />

    <wsdl:operation name="ingestComplete">
      <soap:operation soapAction="" />
      <wsdl:input name="ingestCompleteRequest">
        <soap:body use="literal" />
      </wsdl:input>
      <wsdl:output name="ingestCompleteResponse">
        <soap:body use="literal" />
      </wsdl:output>
    </wsdl:operation>

    <wsdl:operation name="moveComplete">
      <soap:operation soapAction="" />
      <wsdl:input name="moveCompleteRequest">
        <soap:body use="literal" />
      </wsdl:input>
      <wsdl:output name="moveCompleteResponse">
        <soap:body use="literal" />
      </wsdl:output>
    </wsdl:operation>

</wsdl:binding>
```

```
<wsdl:service name="ingestServiceCallback">
  <wsdl:port name="ingestServiceCallbackPort"
    binding="tns:ingestServiceCallbackBinding">
    <soap:address
      location="http://www.yourdomain.com/changedAtRuntime" />
  </wsdl:port>
</wsdl:service>

</wsdl:definitions>
```

# APPENDIX B: FOR MORE INFORMATION

As discussed in the introduction, the audience of this book is intended to be both IT engineers who are engaging in SOA and BPM initiatives in media enterprises as well as media engineers who are engaged in the same pursuits.

Either side of the house can drive projects in an enterprise and in many cases they can be the same organization. This appendix is intended to provide a source of references and other materials that can be of value.

The first section lists information that an IT engineer may find useful to become current on some of the basics of the media space. The second section lists some additional sources of information that can be valuable for media engineers hoping to gain greater insight on the subjects discussed in this book. Both types of engineers can certainly find information of value in the other section as well.

Of course, this is not comprehensive, but should represent a good start for anyone wanting to explore more.

## B.1  FOR THE IT-ORIENTED ENGINEER

The Media and Entertainment (M&E) vertical is clearly not the easiest vertical for an IT person to get their arms around. There is quite a bit of information that is truly special to the industry. It is important, however, to understand at least the basics of both the business and the technology to be successful at making changes in the media areas of an organization.

## B.1.1  Web Sites

**Site:** www.smpte.org
**Description:** SMPTE is the leading technical society for the motion imaging industry. This site can provide information about SMPTE events, membership, and standards. At www.smpte.org/about/industry_links/ a great number of links to related industry Web sites can be found.

**Site:** www.amwa.tv
**Description:** The Advanced Media Workflow Association (AMWA) is the only M&E industry group tackling SOA and BPM topics. Their Web site has information about AMWA events and membership. The Media Services Architecture Group (MSAG) specifically addresses SOA within AMWA.

**Site:** www.nab.org
**Description:** The National Association of Broadcasters (NAB) is an organization involved in a number of important activities associated with broadcasting. Perhaps the most important to someone new to the industry is a trade show held in April. This is the largest trade show for professional media in the world. Information on this show and other interesting information can be found on their Web site.

**Site:** www.ibc.org
**Description:** IBC is an organization that runs the second largest professional media conference in the world every September in Amsterdam. Their Web site provides information on upcoming conferences as well as free, downloadable audio of past conferences.

**Site:** www.broadcastengineering.com
**Description:** *Broadcast Engineering* is a major industry publication and Web site in the media space. The Web site contains a wealth of valuable information such as news articles, press releases, webinars, blogs, whitepapers, and a newsletter. They also offer online training.

**Site:** www.tvtechnology.com
**Description:** TV Technology is another major provider of media news coverage. In addition to excellent news coverage and columns, the site features webinars, newsletters, and other features.

**Site:** www.digitalcontentproducer.com
**Description:** This site is another major provider of media news coverage, and it is more likely to have information about technologies that affect film studios and other media industries. There are podcasts, blogs, newsletters, and more.

**Site:** www.variety.com
**Description:** This is an online newspaper that covers the business of film and television. The site features daily news articles, video clips, blogs, reviews, and more.

**Site:** www.broadcastingcable.com
**Description:** This is an online newspaper that covers the business of television. The site caries extensive coverage of ratings and other business stories. It also features video, newsletters, blogs, and polls.

**Site:** www.tvbeurope.com
**Description:** This is an online magazine that covers broadcasting from a European perspective. It features news articles, white papers, press releases, and more.

**Site:** www.bbctraining.com
**Description:** This site offers extensive training resources from the British Broadcasting Corporation (BBC). They cover nearly all aspects of television. It also offers a number of free online training courses.

## B.1.2 Books

**Title:** *Video Systems in an IT Environment*
**Author:** Al Kovalick
**Publisher:** Focal Press
**Description:** This book is an excellent description of how audio/video systems and IT technology are working together. Topics include networking for video, storage, SOA, and a review of A/V basics.

**Title:** *How Video Works, Second Edition*
**Author:** Marcus Weise
**Publisher:** Focal Press
**Description:** This book covers the basics of video technology. Topics include MPEG, video recording, transmission, and playback.

**Title:** *Television Production Handbook*
**Author:** Herbert Zettl
**Publisher:** Wadsworth Publishing
**Description:** This is a comprehensive textbook on television production and technology that covers all aspects from pre- to post-production. Topics include production techniques, digital technology, television basic, and HDTV.

**Title:** *Video Editing: A Post-Production Primer*
**Author:** Steven E. Browne
**Publisher:** Focal Press
**Description:** This book focuses on the tools and techniques used in video editing. Topics include editing techniques, non-linear editing, DTV formats, and procedures to make the editing process easier.

**Title:** *Television Technology Demystified: A Non-Technical Guide*
**Author:** Aleksandar Louis Todorovic
**Publisher:** Focal Press
**Description:** This book presents the basics of television technology in an easy-to-digest way. Topics include interlace scanning, digital compression, technical quality evaluation, and human visual characteristics.

**Title:** *Film Technology in Post-Production, Second Edition*
**Author:** Dominic Case
**Publisher:** Focal Press
**Description:** This book focuses on film-related technology and while it mainly covers post-production, many of the same technological issues are relevant in film production. Topics include film stocks, film processing, film printing, and telecines.

**Title:** *Digital Cinema, The Revolution in Cinematography, Post-Production, and Distribution*
**Author:** Brian McKernan
**Publisher:** McGraw-Hill/TAB Electronics
**Description:** This book is a comprehensive guide to all aspects of digital cinema. Topics include digital compression, digital intermediates, audio, and the business of digital cinema.

**Title:** *The Filmmaker's Handbook: A Comprehensive Guide for the Digital Age*
**Authors:** Steven Ascher/Edward Pincus
**Publisher:** Plume

**Description:** This is a general film and television production textbook that is used in a number of film schools. Topics include techniques for making a number of different types of films, video formats, non-linear video editing, and lighting.

**Title:** *Tech Terms, Third Edition: What Every Telecommunications and Digital Media Professional Should Know*
**Author:** Jeff Rutenbeck
**Publisher:** Focal Press
**Description:** Essentially the most comprehensive glossary/dictionary of technical terms in media and telecommunications. Contains more than 1000 words.

## B.2 FOR THE MEDIA ENGINEER

Any engineer who has been in this business for some time now clearly understands the degree to which IT technologies are becoming more and more a part of daily life. Becoming knowledgeable on a variety of technical subjects in IT is important. The information sources that follow are not only valuable for more information on the subjects covered in this book, but also for other IT topics as well.

### B.2.1 Web Sites

**Site:** www.omg.org
**Description:** The Object Management Group (OMG) is an industry consortium that develops integration standards for a wide range of technologies and industries. Their site features information on specifications and standards as well as webinars and podcasts.

**Site:** www.oasis-open.org
**Description:** OASIS (Organization for the Advancement of Structured Information Standards) is a body that develops numerous standards in Web services. Their Web site features news on OASIS activities and technical information on standards.

**Site:** www.w3.org
**Description:** The World Wide Web Consortium (W3C) develops diverse standards for the Web. Their Web site features news about the activities of the W3C as well as technical reports.

**Site:** www.w3schools.com
**Description:** This Web site contains free online training on diverse and important Web technologies, including Web services.

**Site:** www.infoworld.com
**Description:** Infoworld is an online newspaper featuring news reports about technologies from the IT industry. Their Web site features blogs, columns, podcasts, video, newsletters, white papers, and strategy guides. There is much information on a great number of IT topics to be found here.

**Site:** www.xml.com
**Description:** Run by the O'Reilly publishing company, this site offers a number of resources for XML development, including Web services development. Of particular interest are the XML technology tutorials describing various standards such as XSLT, XQuery, and XML Schema and webservices.xml.com, a subsection of the site devoted to Web services technology.

**Site:** www.osoa.org
**Description:** A fascinating project led by a consortium of IT industry leaders, the Open SOA Collaboration aims to produce a set of completely language-neutral SOA programming standards. This is the group that is, at the time of this writing, pioneering the SCA and SDO standards in the IT industry.

## B.2.2 Books

**Title:** *Service-Oriented Architecture*
**Authors:** Eric A. Marks/Michael Bell
**Publisher:** Wiley
**Description:** This book provides an overview of the subject of SOA. Topics covered in the book include services, business modeling, governance, and ROI.

**Title:** *Service-Oriented Architecture (SOA): Concepts, Technology, and Design*
**Author:** Thomas Erl
**Publisher:** Prentice Hall

**Description:** This book is really a tutorial on building a system with SOA end to end. Topics include service-oriented analysis, service-oriented design, Web services, and business modeling.

**Title:** *Service-Oriented Enterprises*
**Author:** Setrag Khoshafian
**Publisher:** Auerbach
**Description:** This book is a comprehensive resource of tools, techniques, and technologies that make up a service-oriented enterprise. Topics include standards, portal integration, service management, and business rules.

**Title:** *Enterprise Service Bus*
**Author:** David Chappell
**Publisher:** O'Reilly Media, Inc.
**Description:** This book covers SOA by the man who coined the term ESB. Topics include Web service specifications, event-driven SOA, message-oriented middleware, and business drivers from several verticals (not M&E).

**Title:** *Web Services Platform Architecture: SOAP, WSDL, WS-Policy, WS-Addressing, WS-BPEL, WS-Reliable Messaging, and More*
**Authors:** Sanjiva Weerawarana/Francisco Curbera/Frank Leymann/ Tony Storey/Donald F. Ferguson
**Publisher:** Prentice Hall
**Description:** This is a comprehensive book covering significant details of Web services and related technologies. Topics include service-orientation, WSDL, UDDI, and BPEL.

**Title:** *Applied Cryptography: Protocols, Algorithms, and Source Code in C*
**Author:** Bruce Schneier
**Publisher:** Wiley
**Description:** This is often considered to be the ultimate primer book on building secure enterprise infrastructures. It covers a number of cryptographic techniques, including the Data Encryption standard and the RSA Public Key Infrastructure (PKI).

**Title:** *Networking Explained*
**Authors:** Michael Gallo/William M. Hancock
**Publisher:** Digital Press

**Description:** This book gives the reader an overview of computer networking techniques and technologies. It covers a number of networking standards, up to the latest developments in the area.

**Title:** *Business Process Management: The Third Wave*
**Authors:** Howard Smith/Peter Fingar
**Publisher:** Meghan Kiffar Press
**Description:** This book documents the so-called "third wave" of BPM, which is a shift toward agile, process-managed enterprises. It presents the ideas behind BPM in an engaging way that embodies the importance of moving toward a process-centric way of doing business.

# APPENDIX C: SECURITY AND RELIABILITY

One of the most common complaints (or, rather, observations) that media engineers make about the enterprise IT systems marketed in the Media & Entertainment (M&E) industry is their relative unreliability. However, IT professionals may sometimes underestimate the importance of security and reliability in media systems (mostly due to inexperience in the field). This is a mistake on both sides because, while it is true that reliability and security are very important facets of all media systems, the enterprise software described in this book and many of the IT systems panned by media engineers are capable of high levels of both reliability and security.

First of all, the enterprise systems described in this book are not like those e-mail servers at the office that are down for chunks of time. While they are built on top of the same hardware as those IT servers, SOA systems can be made extremely reliable with a little bit of effort. It is often the software pieces themselves that provide this reliability, not the hardware. Much of it comes from the middleware layer — specifically the application server component of that middleware layer. It ultimately comes down to a question of intent. Because a corporation can abide with a ten-minute loss in e-mail or HR system availability, there is less pressure to make these systems high-reliability. When the servers in question are involved with the air chain, the situation is very different.

In addition, SOA systems are not like the desktop computer at home that might get a virus from time to time. Again, the reason for this is mostly intent; with a little bit of effort, enterprise systems, even those that require Internet connectivity, can be secured. The first step for an integrator is to reduce the chance of a security hole. Systems should only be networked to the extent that is required, and, if it is possible to completely isolate integrated systems away from the greater enterprise network or the Internet, these systems should be isolated. Many business requirements necessitate Internet connectivity, however, and in these situations the servers should only open those ports necessary for integration.

The ultimate lesson with enterprise SOA system security and reliability is to not treat these systems like personal computers or low-reliability corporate systems. These systems must be high-availability and secure, and the appropriate steps to ensure this must be taken.

This is not a concept entirely unique to the M&E industry, either. Many computer systems running the very same application servers and enterprise software stacks discussed in this book are used in critical situations. For example, transactions at nearly every major bank run on these types of systems as do other, more life-critical applications (space travel, medical, military, etc.). The importance of media availability, while prudent for the success of the media enterprise, pales in comparison to the importance of these activities. If they can do it, then media can as well.

## C.1  RELIABILITY

Ensuring maximum SOA system reliability means building a reliable platform at every level, starting with the hardware level. The tactics used to ensure hardware reliability in a computer-based enterprise infrastructure should be very familiar to media engineers of all types, for they are really the same tactics used in media systems. Redundant power supplies, mirrored hard disks, and backup servers are all good ways to increase the reliability of the hardware layer. The goal here is to have no single point of failure in the system (as shown in Fig. C-1) — a concept well-understood in media.

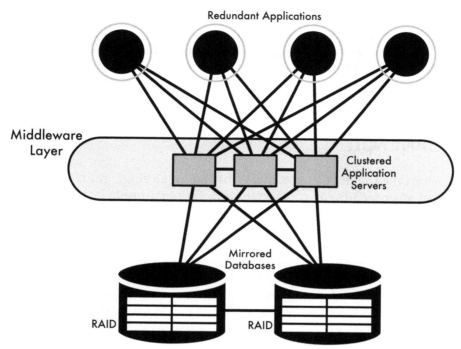

**FIGURE C-1**   An architecture with no single point of failure ensures that any one hardware failure can be endured with no downtime. Components (such as RAID hard drives) that may fail often or need long periods of time to recover should have even greater hardware redundancy.

The software application layer, too, should be fully reliable in a high-availability media system; with a little work, they can be. The number one tool in the integrator's toolbox to ensure software reliability is server clustering, which makes multiple redundant hardware platforms appear as a unified platform from the point of view of the enterprise software. Other, higher level load balancing techniques can be used to reduce the amount of stress on any one system as well by distributing messages to multiple endpoints. To this end, having redundant services in a Service-Oriented Architecture (and configuring a messaging model or ESB that supports load balancing across these services) is also a very good idea.

Application server clustering ensures that no downtime is experienced by system users in the case of a failure of a cluster node. All messages are immediately rerouted to the nodes still online (so users may see some level of performance hit if the clustered server was also load balancing a large amount of traffic). Once the failed server comes back online, its peer servers initiate a cluster recovery process, which makes it operational again. Different application servers will feature clustering in different ways, but due to its importance in enterprise software, all major app server vendors support it in some way.

## IMPORTANT NOTE

A pervasive belief with SOA systems is that having a single middleware layer means that an enterprise also has a single point of failure in its infrastructure. This is not the case. A middleware layer is a logical construct, not a physical one. It is composed of many software pieces, and these can be logically and geographically separated to ensure safety. In addition, these pieces can often be clustered or replicated. Application servers are a fine example of a single logical layer that has many physical components. Most process orchestration engines on the market have clustering capabilities equal to those of app servers, so building a redundant, secure middleware layer is easier than many people think.

In SOA, the messaging/middleware layer itself is the best place to put components that ensure reliability. This is because all communication between services is sent through this layer. Communication patterns can be established that assist with the overall reliability of the infrastructure. In fact, Web service standards exist to achieve these goals. The most popular of these is known as WS-ReliableMessaging.

WS-ReliableMessaging (and its precursor, WS-Reliability) is a standard that hopes to impose a reliability layer on top of normal Web service communication. The idea works much like TCP communication: a "reliable messaging source" delivers messages from an application to a destination, and can impose its own logic on how the message is transmitted and confirmed. A reliable messaging source as outlined in WS-ReliableMessaging can provide any of four guarantees to the application/service taking advantage of its functionality:

- Deliver every message to the destination at least once. Guarantee delivery and allow for multiple deliveries.

- Deliver every message to the destination no more than once. Do not guarantee delivery, but do guarantee that the destination will not receive multiple copies.
- Deliver every message to the destination exactly once.
- Deliver every message to the destination in the order they were provided.

These are the sorts of guarantees that are necessary to have a robust, reliable messaging infrastructure. A truly reliable software stack is very achievable, but requires a commitment to high-availability at every level of abstraction. This includes hardware, middleware, and software.

## C.2  SECURITY

Security is also gaining in importance in the M&E industry, and is rightfully a major concern. In an SOA, there are essentially two types of security that can be implemented SOA-wide: agent-based security and message-based security. A good security model will include elements of both. However, the most important aspect of a security model is that it meets the needs of the enterprise implementing it. If the enterprise is only shipping media files from point to point inside a closed network, then encrypting these files is not as important as ensuring that they cannot leave the facility. However, if the enterprise workflow entails sending files across the Internet to remote sites, then encryption suddenly becomes a major concern. Integrators should closely examine their situation before making decisions regarding security technologies, especially in an SOA.

### C.2.1  Agent-Based Security

Agent-based security in an SOA is essentially security at the endpoint. This may mean requiring a username token with every message received at a given service, or it may mean only accepting messages from particular sources. It is essentially keeping track of the various participants in the SOA, and doing this correctly will no doubt require some sort of identity management infrastructure.

## IDENTITY MANAGEMENT

The computerized management of user and system identity dates back to the development of the X.500 directory service standards. These defined how a computer system might query a directory for identity data and how it might transfer that data from one place to another (the certificate standard, X.509, is still in widespread use today). This paved the way for the enterprise directory server (popular examples include Microsoft ActiveDirectory, Novell eDirectory, and IBM Tivoli Directory Server), which has since become an IT staple.

The modern view of identity management is a robust and agile framework for provisioning new users, systems, and external domains, and transferring that identity or the trust conferred through that identity across enterprise networks. Much focus has been placed on identity federation (the subject of Appendix E) and on providing single sign-on and role-based content to users across multiple systems.

Some form of identity management is necessary to ensure user-level security in a media enterprise, because this infrastructure will inform the systems of who it is using them. In order to effectively shield content from particular users, an enterprise needs a way to identify what users are out there. An enterprise should determine its identity management scheme early on in the integration process so that directory servers and identity provisioning technology can be put in place to serve as a platform for the applications and services to come.

Regardless of the type of identity management employed in the infrastructure (whether it be a well-founded standard or simply a master list of authorized users mirrored to every server), the primary security responsibility for an enterprise integrator is then ensuring that every participant in the workflow uses this infrastructure. The best way to ensure proper SOA security is to be vigilant about its enforcement. If security policies are constantly circumvented in favor of getting the job done quickly or easily, then that means that (1) the security methods are not transparent enough and are interfering with user experience and (2) the enterprise is not actually secure. Agent-based security is essentially keeping tabs on the components in a system; this should be a facet of every enterprise system, regardless of the actual security requirements.

## WHAT NOT TO DO: ADMINISTRATOR LOGINS

Do not leave all workstations logged on as "administrator" all the time. This is sadly common practice in many media enterprises. While this may be the easiest way to avoid any pesky permissions or forgotten password issues, it opens up a fundamental security hole in the enterprise infrastructure. The best idea is to implement an identity management scheme that uniquely identifies all system users and provides them with the permissions necessary to do their work (and an agile process with which to change these permissions, known as "provisioning" users).

### C.2.2 Message-Based Security

The other major type of security model used in SOA is message-based security. Message-based security entails encrypting or otherwise securing the messages that pass between services. Some technology to achieve this (such as XML encryption and signature) is covered in Chapter 5, Web Services. In addition, the most well-accepted technique for achieving message-based security in a Web services based SOA is to use a standard known as WS-Security.

WS-Security goes hand-in-hand with SOAP technology to secure messages and endpoints. It provides end-to-end security, which means that a message is secured even if it has to go through a number of layer 7 routing steps in between its source and destination. While lower level security protocols such as SSH or HTTPS can be used to secure a Web service message on one hop of its journey, an end-to-end solution such as WS-Security is required to ensure that a message's security is not compromised at any point in its path.

WS-Security forms the basis of a number of other WS-* standards, such as WS-SecureConversation, WS-Federation, and WS-Trust. It is also heavily intertwined with the WS-I's development of a Basic Security Profile, which was released in early 2007 and complements its existing Basic Profile.

## C.3  CONCLUSION

The ultimate lesson to media engineers giving themselves migraines over security and reliability concerns in enterprise software is this: relax, M&E is not the only industry with these concerns, and they are certainly not the only industry to ever solve these problems. What M&E is in the running for is perhaps being the last industry to adopt these technologies in a widespread way, which gives it the benefit of having well-established methods from which to choose. With a little bit of effort, software-based media systems can be just as secure and reliable as their hardware-based counterparts. The only real reason for poor reliability and security in a media enterprise is poor planning and execution.

# APPENDIX D: INFORMATION FOR VENDORS

The majority of this book is catered to the in-house integrator that faces the challenging task of designing and implementing a new enterprise architecture. While this is an important audience to address, there are others who can learn from the Service-Oriented Media Enterprise: the vendors. The default position of SOA is to assume an application that does not meet the business requirements directly and flexibly must be wrapped to exist in a middleware environment. This does not have to be the case, as many media vendors have shown through their service-oriented approach and exposure of Web service interfaces for use in enterprise integration. In fact, the SOA-aware vendor is the best friend an enterprise integrator has, and more media system providers should be looking for ways to service-orient their products. This will be an important challenge in the future, and, like enterprise adoption of SOA and BPM, vendors that meet this challenge head-on will be much better off than their competitors.

## D.1 THE COMMODITIZATION CONCERN

SOA (and BPM) are focused on reuse and business agility. In the ideal SOA architecture, an enterprise should be able to replace one application with another that meets the same business need (even if it is structured or presented differently) without the end user noticing a thing. This may appear to be unwelcome news for any software vendor, because it raises the concern of commoditization. Suddenly, vendors can no longer leverage their application suites as a whole or their laundry list of other products with which they work out of the box. Instead, the decision for the media enterprise comes down to two things: cost and functionality.

At least, in an ideal world, that is how it would be. But for the most part, this concern is unfounded. First of all, it is not as easy as picking just the right functionality because available interfaces are still important. Vendors that make wrapper design easy for popular SOA technologies such as Web services will go far in their customers' eyes as they will reduce the total cost of integration. No one wants to pull directly from database tables to achieve integration if they do not have to. Second of all, even if product selection came down to pure functionality, there is less overlap here than most people think. Individual products tend to offer specific (and useful) functionality that other in-class vendors do not have. These "bonus features" can often be the deciding factor for a customer.

It is also critical to recognize that key deciding factors for the purchase of technology such as support and service do not change in the service-oriented model. Even as functionality may be componentized to smaller bites, there is still a need to receive support regarding the integration or operation of these services. It has been seen in the IT space that a growing differentiating factor is the types and levels of support offered by a vendor.

So, to a certain extent, vendors should not worry about SOA commoditizing their specialty product into just an "edit service" or "media management service." However, there is some amount of business that vendors will have to fight harder for with service-enabled customers. One good thing about SOA (from the media enterprise point of view) is that it does not lock an architecture into any silo, including vendor silos. An SOA-based architecture allows an integrator to choose a different provider if desired for each individual service, and vendors that have certain weaker products "along for the ride" with their stronger product offerings will find sales of these products dropping. This is what many vendors fear when they hear about SOA — a fear that is not completely without basis. On the other hand, by removing the need to produce these "side" products, which had been

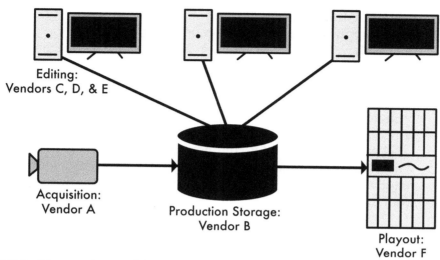

Editing:
Vendors C, D, & E

Acquisition:
Vendor A

Production Storage:
Vendor B

Playout:
Vendor F

**FIGURE D-1**   The near future of the Media & Entertainment industry is one where media enterprises will pick an architecture that suits their functionality and expect vendors to interoperate within the scope of that architecture.

needed in the past to maintain sales of the core technologies of a vendor, it is now possible to focus valuable R&D resources completely on those areas where the vendor is strongest. No longer does a vendor need to be all things to all people!

So, is there a commoditization concern with SOA? Yes and no. If it were not SOA, though, it would be a different enterprise architecture that presented this concern. The truth of the matter is, as software-based media systems become more prevalent in the industry, media enterprises are going to demand more in terms of interoperability and product modularity. This shift to a service-based orientation, therefore, is inevitable. Other industries have experienced the same issues, and vendors in these industries have risen to the challenge. Look, for example, at the enterprise platform vendors such as IBM, BEA, and Oracle, who have standards-based products that compete with and interoperate with each other. This is the future landscape of the M&E industry as well, shown in Fig. D-1.

## D.2  SERVICE-ENABLING PRODUCTS

Chapter 3 of this book discusses the best ways to wrap applications and present service interfaces to the middleware layer. The lesson for vendors to learn is that there are basically two ways in which to service-enable applications from the vendor perspective: the right way and the quick way. Service-orientation is not created by a technology, it is created through good design decisions and product architecture. If a media vendor makes the decision to service-orient its product (and all media vendors should!), then it should devote an appropriate amount of time and effort to this initiative. Unlike specific media enterprises, which need to wrap applications to expose only those services used, vendors need to consider common use cases for their product when wrapping. This is a significantly greater task, and will probably require some degree of re-envisioning of the product architecture from the ground up.

Service-orienting a product requires this level of effort because it reconsiders how different product components communicate with each other. Instead of just having modules with tightly coupled interfaces to one another, a service-oriented media application has independent services with published interfaces. The right way to service-orient a product is to open up each of these services to the customer. That's right: if a vendor determines that its best-selling application is actually five separate business services interacting with one another, it should continue to sell those services as a package, but allow customers to replace one of the services with a different service that presents the same interface.

So, if a major asset management vendor re-architects its product to present five business services instead, what does it ship to the customer? The service-oriented method is to implement these services in an independent way — ship five separate application installations to the customer with a configuration utility to set them up to interact with one another. Interface-level documentation is appropriate (if Web services is the communication standard among the services, then WSDLs are a must), along with some idea of what these services represent and how they interact with one another. Basically, the vendor wants to provide the customer enough information to replace one of the vendor's services with another. This is a new and counterintuitive way of thinking about product packaging and interaction, but, if done correctly, the flexibility this approach grants product customers will increase the popularity and sales of the product.

## EXAMPLE DOCUMENTATION

A vendor that follows the SOA model for service orientation and exposure will put a great deal of integration responsibility in the hands of the customer. A vendor's service-oriented product might feature a user guide with the following table of contents:

I. Product Overview
   A. Installation
   B. Service Configuration

II. The User Interfaces
   A. Views Offered and Their Functionality
   B. Running the Application

III. The Service Interfaces
   A. Services Offered and Their Functionality
   B. Connecting to the Service Interfaces
   C. Service Policies
   D. Service QoS and Guarantees

IV. Appendix A: WSDL Files

V. Appendix B: Example Integration Scenarios

It may be difficult for media vendors to get started down this road. Assuming that the design team has buy-in to evaluate service orientation (not necessarily a safe assumption, but one that can increasingly be made as SOA becomes pervasive in M&E), the first step is to look at the system-level functionalities that the product provides. These will become a list of operations that product services will expose. Splitting into services then becomes a formality based on the resources needed for each use case. Perhaps there is a database that exposes data access functionality that becomes a service. Vendors should shoot for application-level services. Media applications should not feign to know the specific business requirements of the facility in which they are installed, but present their base functionality in such a way that it can be orchestrated to meet many business requirements.

## D.3  THE FUTURE SOA VENDOR LANDSCAPE

SOA provides a fairly clear view of where the media industry will be in the next five years, and the steps that need to be taken for it to get there. For example, there is a strong need for enhanced communication standards in M&E. Efforts like the SMPTE BXF standard for automation and traffic systems help pave the way for a world where common media operations are formalized, and the data needed to carry out these operations are well understood. The more such standards exist, the greater opportunity there is for vendors to provide a solution that will more closely meet a customer's needs, because it will "snap in" to a media architecture using standards-based interfaces.

There are not many such standards out there; however, this should not deter media vendors from beginning the work of service exposure and defining their own published standards for common operations. At the same time as standards-based service definition is getting more and more important in the industry, the specifics of *how* those standards look is getting less and less important. Technologies such as XML transformation and Enterprise Service Buses are enabling media enterprises to translate any one interface into another with minimal effort. This means that it is easy to "bootstrap" these standards, and work initial efforts into a later standards-based architecture. Starting this work now will serve to increase the success of standards efforts and support the move to SOA as a whole.

How does this affect the media vendor landscape? Well, one common feature of many enterprise media products that goes away in the SOA future is the long list of supported product integrations. Everyone knows this list: it is the one often ill-documented that reassures customers that the product works with 50-odd other products (one of which the customer surely has!) in some way or another. This goes away because, in a service-oriented landscape, every product is interoperable with every other product! The only restriction is what makes sense from a business point of view — maybe a playout system cannot work too closely with an HR system simply because there is no logical way for them to interact beyond the validity of users on the system. However, technology is ideally no longer the restriction for system integration.

This integration now falls squarely into the hands of the customer as well. The massive service organizations attached to many media vendor companies are no longer required on every single install. Because everything is standards-based, product integration could just as easily be done in-house or by an independent third party as it could by the vendor itself. This allows vendors the opportunity to streamline their organizations, and evaluate the need for the bulky service arms that have grown organically out of interoperability issues. On the other hand, it can also allow vendors the opportunity to expand those service arms and begin to tackle the transformation from application-level to business-level services for customers as well.

Support models change too in this new landscape. Since the integration, even among multiple services provided by the same vendor, is possibly handled independently from the service implementation, there is no longer any ownership by the vendor over this connection. A number of support models spin off from this paradigm. There are now three support "boundaries" in the media application space (as shown in Fig. D-2) and the opportunity by vendors to offer all three to their customers. Currently, vendors that provide their product in a box and walk away provide the lowest level of support: to the application API. Those vendors that make the effort to service-enable their products and to support these wrappers through standards updates and integration by their customers offer application-level service support. Finally, by offering integration services between their products and other services, vendors have the opportunity to offer business-level service support.

## D.4  THE INEVITABILITY OF SOA

Media vendors are understandably cautious about the whole concept of SOA. For vendors that were making a living out of providing little business functionality and a lot of tightly coupled integration functionality or vendors that were making a living out of being especially difficult to integrate with, SOA threatens commoditization. For vendors that make a solid product providing specific business value to the customer, SOA signals an opportunity to re-envision this product along the lines of the functionality it offers and the support the vendor can provide to the media enterprise.

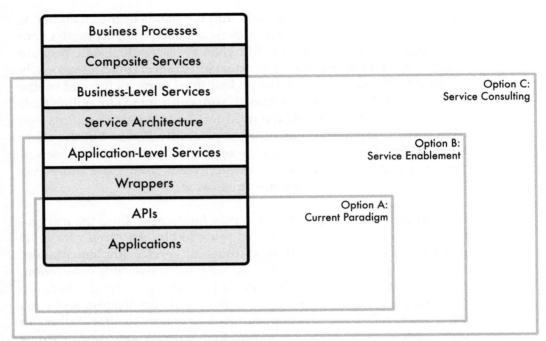

**FIGURE D-2**  This figure presents the three SOA support models for applications. Vendors have the opportunity to stop at the API level (installing the product as is), to support the application-level services (service-orienting the products and supporting this wrapper), or to provide integration support all the way up to the business service level (providing custom integration services between their services and other application-level services).

The elephant in the room of this discussion is the inevitability of SOA. Adoption by other industries signals a change in M&E, and media enterprises are beginning to take notice. Vendors that refuse to adopt this new architectural mode will find their customer base slowly shifting over to those vendors that provide easy integration with their middleware layers. The truth of the matter is that SOA is more than just a good idea, it is the future of the M&E industry and one that every vendor will need to embrace.

# APPENDIX E: FEDERATION

One topic that comes up often in a discussion of enterprise architectures in general is that of federation. Federation is a software concept where many components interact without the direction of a central authority. These components might be individual software systems, or they might be entire facilities. Federated communication may arise in any number of situations in the M&E industry, but is perhaps most often encountered when multiple facilities or media enterprises need to collaborate in a software-assisted way.

Experienced media professionals may balk at the idea that programmatic collaboration between entities like this even occurs at all. It is certainly not the norm in the industry. While collaboration between different business entities is a major part of Media & Entertainment (studios outsourcing to post houses, television networks renting production trucks, the prevalence of freelancing, etc.), this collaboration often occurs in the traditional way, with paper contracts and the media going back and forth. However, with the advent of SOA and BPM technology, federation has the opportunity to re-envision this collaboration.

There are many reasons why an increase in federated collaboration is a benefit to a media enterprise (and to the industry as a whole). For one, maintaining a software-led relationship between two media entities helps to ensure an efficient collaboration, because negotiations can occur more programmatically, instead of through the time-consuming process of passing paper back and forth. Secondly, establishing systematic connections between facilities forces formalization over their interaction, which can help to better define the scope and quality of work.

Media enterprises should consider this model in appropriate situations, even situations within the enterprise! While the concept of federation is heard most often in the IT world in relation to the idea of propagating user identity across domains (a problem hopefully solved within most enterprises through the use of unified directory servers), it can be extended to other data such as schedules, status, or asset metadata. These concepts can have use even among business units or departments.

## FEDERATED ASSET MANAGEMENT

Asset management serves as an excellent example of how a federated media system might function. In infrastructures where there are multiple asset management systems, but no single authoritative asset manager, keeping track of the assets available can be a challenge. Each asset management system might use a separate identifier to describe the same asset, and there might be metadata for that asset in one system that does not exist in any other system. In addition, there is no guarantee that an asset that is in one system will be in any other system. How could a media enterprise develop a search that stretches across all of these systems? How do these systems interact?

One common way to deal with this architecture is to impose a new, authoritative system that catalogues the assets from all other systems. This might be the easiest way to brute-force a solution, but it is not always possible. What if, for example, the various systems were located in different organizations around the world, and some of these organizations were wary about giving up their entire records to an authoritative party?

Instead, the asset management systems could be put into a federated relationship with one another, which means that each individual system would have the capacity to search its records and the records of other, federated systems as authorized. This would be enabled through shared technology or trust relationships among systems. Whether these assets are video files, books, or anything else, federation is a good way to share data among domains. Such an architecture can be seen right now in libraries worldwide, in hospitals (with patient data), and in airline partnerships such as the Star Alliance.

Federation is no cakewalk. Security is the number one issue in an architectural scenario with no central authority. How does one domain in a federation (whether it is a business unit, facility, or entire enterprise) verify the claims of another domain without a master list or governing body? How can two domains establish a trust relationship so that they may collaborate? To put it in media-specific terms, if a major studio is sending material out to a little post house, how does it know that the post house is legitimate, and how does it know that its media will be secure both in transmission and while in the purview of the post house? These are not easy questions, and they represent the forefront of IT security thought.

SOA technologies are assisting in this discussion. Web services standards such as WS-Trust and WS-Federation are hoping to address the security and logistical issues with federated collaboration. In addition, SOA as an architectural construct eases the transition to a federated environment by formalizing enterprise interfaces. If an external domain is going to take advantage of functionality within a given enterprise, they will need to establish a contract that dictates the boundaries of what they can and cannot do. They will also need to establish policies that will provide the service requestor with some guarantee of service quality. These requirements sound exactly like the use cases of Web services standards such as WSDL and WS-Policy. SOA technologies such as these are a natural fit for the needs of federation.

## FEDERATED IDENTITY

Federation today is heavily focused on the propagation of user identity from one domain to another. A user in one domain might have the rights to access data in another domain, but since that other domain has no knowledge of the user, how is this proven? Many methods of achieving trust and authentication across domains have been put forth, notably by the Liberty Alliance (http://www.projectliberty.org) in 2001 and more recently by the Higgins project (http://www.eclipse.org/higgins). The way many of these architectures work is to have each domain offer an identity provider through which other domains can authenticate external users. Standards such as SAML, OpenID, and Shibboleth can be used to express this identity and this identity provider in a widely understood way so that many domains can authenticate against each other.

The Web services world also has its own standard in this space: WS-Federation. WS-Federation dictates the use of security tokens, using WS-Security, WS-Trust, and SOAP to pass identity back and forth. In a Web services based SOA, federated communication can be enabled through the use of this standard.

## E.1 FEDERATION MODELS AND ARCHITECTURES

There are many established models to enable federation in enterprise IT architectures. This section will briefly discuss some of relevance to the M&E industry. The M&E industry has differing requirements to the average federated enterprise for one reason: the need to transport large media files from domain to domain. While most other federated entities need only worry about security and message passing, media domains (it is expected) will also have media transfer requirements. Since federated domains can be continents apart from each other, in different administrative domains, and forming and dissolving in an ad-hoc fashion, it is expected that these transfers will take long periods of time and occur over a switched network.

Required for this type of federation is some way to initiate and monitor these transfers. One such model would have a third party of equal standing to each individual media domain that had a trust relationship with every domain. This central entity, shown in Fig. E-1, would not have any administrative control over the various media domains other than the ability to broker transactions among them. It would serve

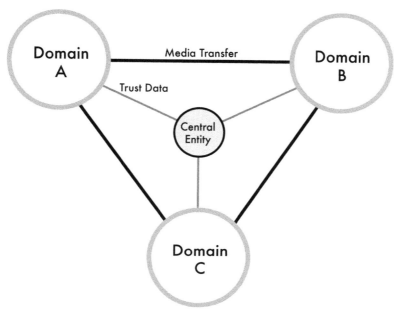

**FIGURE E-1**    A central entity could broker federated communication among media domains.

much the same purpose that the service registry does in the Web services roles discussed in Chapter 5. No media transfers need to specifically move through the central entity, it would just need to broker and manage most federated communication. In a media landscape, with studios, smaller production entities, distributors, and individuals all exchanging media assets, this role would ideally be played by an independent entity that could be equally trusted by all domains.

One benefit of such a model is that it reduces the amount of work needed by any one domain to participate in federated collaboration. In today's world, where media enterprises need to collaborate to quickly turn around product, this type of a model would allow for a much lower buy-in, thus increasing total participation. There is of course the concern that no such useful central entity could be established without the participation of many domains, thus creating a bit of a chicken-and-egg problem for bootstrapping such an architecture. However, should the need for federated collaboration be great enough (as it surely will be), a trusted central entity provides a good solution to the problem of monitoring and brokering media transformation.

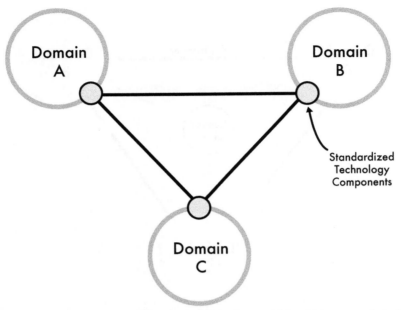

**FIGURE E-2** A federated communication technology that resides within every domain would allow for more effective business integration among federated partners.

Another model for federation that may be achievable in a heterogeneous landscape is to unify all domains on a single technology instead of on a single administrative entity. Media enterprises could install a "federation-in-a-box," which sits within the enterprise infrastructure and handles all federated communication with other, similar devices in other domains. This type of architecture, shown in Fig. E-2, is nothing new; media vendors have had file-sharing servers with similar functionality for quite some time. However, a federation technology would not only have to broker file transfers, but also serve as a registry for secured communication with other domains. In a SOA, it would act as a service gateway to federated services exposed by external entities. All service messages to business partners would be funneled through this gateway.

With such an architecture, the challenges are mostly technical. A single vendor or coalition of vendors would be able to provide the technology for the box in every domain, but to be a successful model, the communication among domains must be standardized. The actual medium could leverage existing standards such as Web services (for communication) and FTP or MDP (for media transfer), but the operations and the data that a domain shares must also be standardized. Otherwise, no domain will know how to talk to any other domain, even though they have the means.

## E.2 CONCLUSION

For multiple enterprise entities to work together, they must either all report to a single authority that can impose communication (the null federation case), all agree to contribute to the same third-party organization (the central entity architecture), or all agree upon the same technology and interface standard (the box in every domain architecture). The increasing business demands of the M&E industry dictate that more collaboration is required among media enterprises to keep production costs low. The industry will need to increase its support of operational federation to facilitate this need. SOA helps to facilitate this federation. As the spread of SOA and BPM across the industry is inevitable, it may also be the right time to begin to move toward this federated ideal.

# APPENDIX F: THE FUTURE

Service-Oriented Architecture (SOA) and Business Process Management (BPM) are very contemporary concepts in the computer industry. In the Media & Entertainment (M&E) industry, they are cutting-edge. Still, with the pace of technology increasing rapidly, it will not be long until they are widely adopted across the industry and considered an integral part of product and system design. With that said, the question arises: What are the other characteristics of this service-oriented world? What are the integration and technology challenges of the ideal SOA environment? What are the business concerns of a media enterprise that has a comprehensive BPM policy in place to formalize and streamline workflow? What are, in other words, the challenges of the industry in five years?

Well, no one is truly able to answer that question with any degree of certainty (especially with the quick pace of change), but there are a number of theories, technologies, and models that are just appearing on the edges of the collective consciousness, and are moving toward the center. This appendix simply documents some of these newer or lesser known software ideas that have not yet become mainstream. It is, essentially, a collection of cool-sounding futuristic stuff.

## F.1 NEW SOA/BPM CONCEPTS

There is a surprising amount of agreement in the IT industry about the direction in which enterprise architectures will go in the next several years. SOA has been communally hailed as a great idea (although some feel that it is currently too large-scale and enterprise-focused), but everyone is looking to the Web for the next big idea in software architecture. This is reflected in the SOA world through the growing prevalence of Representational State Transfer (REST) as both a technology and as a competing architecture. REST is Web-focused in its concepts, as it uses the existing HTTP architecture to call operations without bulkier SOAP communication on top. This type of infrastructure is leaner and can be easily parsed by low-impact Web technologies such as PHP, ASP, or servlets without needing bulky Java or C# applications backing them up.

What is discussed here is a lightweight version of SOA that is well suited for Web-based applications. Gartner has coined the term "Web-Oriented Architecture" to describe this area of focus and, though it does not advocate any new technologies (with the exception of REST), it is indicative of the direction in which the IT industry is turning — low impact, Web-based apps. They see the enterprise of the future hosting everything on remote Web servers. Web technology (such as portals, AJAX, and social networking) is getting to the point that it is replacing professional technology (mainframes, siloed applications, etc.) in the enterprise. So the professional IT world is facing a glut of traditionally consumer-side technology taking over. This should sound familiar to anyone in the media industry (which, incidentally, should be looking out for a new generation of Web-based media apps — including editing — in the next few years as well).

The biggest buzzword migrating from the consumer level to the enterprise level is Web 2.0. Web 2.0, the name given to the movement toward collaboration- and networking-focused services and technologies, stands for more end-user interaction, more feedback mechanisms, and more Web-based utilities. To give a media example, an asset management system built under the precepts of Web 2.0 would not organize any of its video assets at the outset (with the exception of automatically generated metadata), but let users determine optimal organization schemes themselves through ranking, linking, and inserting metadata. Web 2.0 applications are all over the Internet, with social networking sites booming and content filtering sites such as Digg (http://www.digg.com) allowing end users to drive the news headlines. For these Web sites, Web 2.0 means less focus on controlling content and letting the mob take over (although this means increased publicity for pictures of kittens over actual news items). In the media enterprise, it means increased collaboration and content sharing, less tightly scripted metadata schemas, and important content floating to the top. It will be interesting to watch where the value of "editorial" lands in the coming years.

Web 2.0 and SOA collide in the world of Web application hybrids that are known as "mash-ups." Mash-ups are user-defined applications that combine the functionality of multiple applications, exposed as services. These hybrids are essentially composite services — they take basic business functionality from Web 2.0 software enterprises such as Google and Flickr and orchestrate them together to create new functionality. Enterprises are beginning to take this model to the corporate world in combination with an enterprise SOA, which allows one business group to orchestrate the functionality of other business groups together to create new functionality. This is relevant to the M&E world as well. Providing programmatic hooks into business functionality at an enterprise level is a good way to encourage resource reuse and innovation. For example, should an asset management system at a cable news network expose semantic metadata about production media and a production or master control department expose detailed rundown information on the assets aired, then a sales department could write a mash-up that lists topics for each hour of broadcast and cater their ad sales to this list to make them even more relevant. They would be able to do this on their own, without the involvement of an enterprise integration department or team.

In addition to an increasing Web- and collaboration-focus, SOA and BPM have also become a little more people-focused. An architecture such as SOA, which was founded on the principle of abstracting technology to the business functionality that it provides, should have no problem envisioning a world where human participants in processes and systems are equally abstracted to business functionality. Indeed, it does not; however, the technology to enable this abstraction has still been running to catch up. The recent SOA/BPM standard BPEL4People (an extension of BPEL to account for human workflows, escalation of ownership, etc.) is an excellent example of the type of advancement that is necessary for human integration to become seamless in enterprise architecture. There is a WS-* specification to correspond with this human workflow as well: WS-HumanTask, which suggests some ways in which humans might be exposed as services. In the next few years, enterprise integrators will see more such technology-independent human interfaces into system architecture being developed.

## WS-HUMANTASK

If SOA and BPM are increasing their support of human-based workflow, what exactly does a Web-services-based interface look like to a human participant? The WS-HumanTask specification has some suggestions on that front. It defines sets of interactions between humans, calling out the groups of people involved and how best to reach them. A WS-HumanTask document might look as follows:

```
<htd:humanInteractions>
   <htd:logicalPeopleGroups>
      <htd:logicalPeopleGroup name="producers" reference="prod">
         <htd:parameter name="" type="" />
      </htd:logicalPeopleGroup>
   </htd:logicalPeopleGroups>
   <htd:tasks>
      <htd:task name="schedule production">
         <htd:peopleAssignments>...</htd:peopleAssignments>
         <htd:deadlines>...</htd:deadlines>
      </htd:task>
   </htd:tasks>
   <htd:notifications>
      <htd:notification name="overdue schedule">
         <htd:priority>...</htd:priority>
      </htd:notification>
   </htd:notifications>
</htd:humanInteractions>
```

## F.2 THE DECREASING IMPORTANCE OF STANDARDS

Another macro-trend in the IT industry that is just about to hit (and will slowly, but surely, seep over to the media industry as well) is the simultaneous proliferation and decreasing necessity of standard data representation. This may be odd for an industry that has recently completed building the immense MXF standard to hear, but this trend is occurring more in data/IT standards than in media standards.

Media standards such as MXF are just as vital as they have ever been. However, with the architectural construct of data transformation becoming a part of every enterprise architecture, it becomes less and less important what format control data, business data, and metadata take as they move throughout an enterprise, as long as they are formalized in some easily understood way. Standardization becomes less of a concern once an integrator can easily transform any data representation to any other.

What does then become a concern is parsing through the many standards that will exist in a single facility. This is where the burgeoning realm of semantics comes into play.

Semantic standards and technologies attempt to capture the true, human-understandable *meaning* behind all of those countless metadata standards and models. Semantics would capture that "number of frames," "duration," and "total runtime" are all representing the same kinds of information about an asset. They are necessary for transforming one metadata or messaging schema to another, although they do not necessarily have to be formalized to do that. Even so, there is a large area of study around formalizing these semantics to make such transformations easier. A semantic SOA would take advantage of such standards to communicate interface information in a dynamic way to allow for automatic discovery and binding to services.

There are two standards by the W3C in this area already that show great promise in enabling the so-called "Semantic Web": the resource description framework (RDF) and the Web ontology language (OWL). RDF is a language that allows for the definition of ideas using subject-predicate-object relationships. A media library might define the predicate "uses material from," and then be able to make computer parsable statements such as "Asset A184739 uses material from asset A018456." Then, a rights management system could automatically identify any of the inherited rights from any given asset. This is the type of infrastructure that RDF aims to support.

OWL extends RDF to provide a library of defined classes and relationships. This gives catalogers a base language from which to start building semantic relationships among data. Together, RDF and OWL can represent fairly in-depth meaning relationships between resources, whether those resources are users, applications, Web pages, media assets, or simply ideas. They are the base of a much larger menagerie of semantic standards, such as simple protocol and RDF query language (SPARQL) for searching based on semantic data and gleaning resource descriptions from dialects of languages (GRDDL) for transforming one data standard to another using semantic relationships.

GRDDL is becoming the basis of a larger movement to facilitate enhanced representation of enterprise assets. For example, a grassroots movement called Microformats (http://microformats.org) has sprung up to define a whole series of XML schemas for various types of data (locations, calendars, resumes, lists, etc.), which are lower impact than more formalized data schemas. GRDDL can be used to programmatically transform assets in any XML-based, proprietary language to one of these Microformats or to any other standard, thus allowing enterprises to begin cataloging assets in any way that they want, knowing that they have the means to transform that catalog to another semantic format in the future.

The Semantic Web is a powerful idea that is taking the IT industry by storm. The M&E industry, since it already deals so heavily in the creative expression of data and meaning, should take note and find ways to leverage the semantic technologies currently out there to develop enhanced library and asset management systems.

## F.3  THE BLACK HOLE OF SOFTWARE

This book is almost entirely about the trends and technologies in the IT industry (such as SOA and BPM), and how they affect the development of the media industry in the near future. However, there is a trend in the media industry today that has never occurred in the IT industry due to the fact that IT has basically been all about software since its inception. That trend is the collapsing of media hardware chains into software.

Since the beginning of the modern media industry, engineers and other media professionals have needed separate, specialized equipment for production that was custom-built, expensive, and not that useful for anything other than its specific purpose. The technology of film- and tape-based production has given way to the video servers and non-linear editing systems of file-based production, but the same fact remains: production technology is custom-purpose and dedicated.

This fact is changing. As the software-based systems that this book evangelizes become more prevalent in the M&E industry, they will be replacing, in many cases, dedicated hardware-based systems. The reason that many media engineers are wary about SOA in the first place is because this industry is in the early stages of production-chain equipment becoming software-based. Never before could computers guarantee the type of real-time, high-quality throughput that is necessary in a broadcast chain. Never before could software encode and decode media fast enough to have it happen live. Never before could consumer applications handle the types of professional functionality that media enterprises require. But this is all happening now.

One excellent example of the collapse of the media hardware infrastructure into software is an automation product by Omnibus called iTX. iTX is a software-based automation and playout system for television broadcasters. It is the component in a media enterprise that handles the real-time, can't-drop-a-frame feed out to the consumer, and it is running on commodity, IT hardware (even handling multiple separate channels!). The product provides a cheaper and easier alternative to the bulky, hardware-based playout systems of the past. iTX was arguably the first of its kind, and there are already several others that are similar out there. In truth, all aspects of the media hardware chain are collapsing. Soon a media enterprise will literally be able to run an entire channel in a single box.

Ironically, it is this very convergence that will be the ultimate downfall of SOA in the M&E industry. Yes, the end of SOA is discussed in book extolling the virtues of a Service-Oriented Architecture. At some point, building a media facility will mean downloading an installation file onto a PC workstation and running it. Convergence kills SOA. Thankfully for SOA advocates, however, that point is still far off. For the near, foreseeable future, the industry will still have heterogeneous environments and require standards-based communication among disparate systems; SOA will be a very necessary thing.

So here is a plan for the industry: move toward open standards and interoperable, heterogeneous environments. Move toward software-based media chains and continue moving toward file-based production. Reduce production costs wherever possible and do not be afraid of commoditization. The future of the M&E industry is a bright one, and these enterprise technologies will be the ones that help get us there!

# GLOSSARY

**Accidental Architecture** — Describes those integrated systems that have organically grown to respond to a series of business needs without regards to an overall architectural model or pattern. In many cases, an enterprise will intend to use a specific integration architectural model, but time or monetary constraints will force an accidental architecture.

**Adapter** — In SOA, an adapter is a component that translates from one middleware standard to another. Software that turns SOAP messages into SQL calls for access to a database would be one such example. The term adapter may also denote the wrapper around the service.

**API (Application Programming Interface)** — APIs are the (often) proprietary methods through which an application can be programmatically accessed. Vendors will provide APIs to enterprises looking to integrate with their application. In SOA, APIs are the components that wrappers use to expose service operations.

**Application Server** — The fundamental component of a modern middleware layer. It provides communication, enterprise reliability, and scalability to middleware. The two major application server technologies are .NET and Java EE.

**Asynchronous** — An asynchronous message pattern is one by which messages are sent out by a consumer without expecting an immediate reply from a provider. This is used in the fire-and-forget style of service call.

**BPEL (Business Process Execution Language)** — The most widely accepted XML-based process representation language. It can be used to represent business processes for execution within an orchestration engine. BPEL includes the tasks in a process, the data that moves between tasks, and the services that are called to implement these tasks.

**BPMN (Business Process Modeling Notation)** — A graphical business process representation that can be used to communicate process detail in a standardized way. Process development or orchestration software may use BPMN to represent their processes. The XPDL standard can be used to transform BPMN to a machine-readable format.

**Business Activity Monitoring (BAM)** — Used in architectures such as SOA that use BPM to represent business-level data in the systems infrastructure. BAM technology aggregates business data such as process metrics and KPIs and presents this data to authorized users.

**Business Agility** — The ability to change business processes without changing the technology that implements those processes. This quality is important for an enterprise that wants to respond quickly to business changes.

**Business Process** — A cross-functional, formalized method of representing work done in an enterprise. Business processes might use programmatic representations such as BPEL or BPMN to orchestrate activity within a middleware layer. They serve as the basis of Business Process Management (BPM).

**Business Process Management (BPM)** — A business process-oriented methodology for understanding and organizing work within an enterprise. It is focused on process agility and business visibility. See Chapter 6 for more information.

**Business Rules** — Business rules are transactional, business-level logic components that exist within the middleware layer of an SOA. Business rules can be used to allow a business rules engine or other such middleware technology to make business-level message processing decisions automatically and therefore speed up programmatic communication within an enterprise.

**Business Service** — A transactional component within an architecture that provides business value to the enterprise. It has an interface that is independent from its underlying implementation. Services are the basis of a Service-Oriented Architecture (SOA). See Chapter 3 for more information.

**Business Silo** — Many enterprises arrange their technology and processes in vertical business silos. Silos are systems that, while they may operate very well internally, do not have the capability to effectively communicate with external systems. Silos are often described as "vertical" because they each have all layers required for operation, which means they have little dependence on external entities.

**C#** ("cee sharp") — A programming language developed by Microsoft to facilitate enterprise programming on their .NET platform. It is equivalent in functionality to Java, and both have ample enterprise resources to support middleware components.

**COM (Component Object Model)** — An SOA precursor developed by Microsoft. It introduced the concept of an Interface Description Language (IDL), which became the precursor for the modern WSDL.

**CORBA (Common Object Request Broker Architecture)** — An open, standardized architecture from the 1990s that took the best practices of COM and DCOM and made them generally available to many platforms. Like COM/DCOM, it allowed for software components with independent interface and implementation. It is a precursor to SOA.

**CRUD (Create, Read, Update, Delete)** — CRUD functionality is the basic functionality that a programmatic interface can have over a data object. Users of this interface are able to create new instances of that object, read instances, update instances, or delete them. In a Service-Oriented Architecture, business objects may expose services that have CRUD functionality.

**Dashboard** — A business monitoring user interface that presents disparate business data to the user in a unified way. They are useful in presenting information from many systems in one place. Many dashboard solutions will feature graphical lights, gauges, and graphs.

**Data Aggregation** — The architectural concept of collecting all business data in an integrated system in a single place so that it can be viewed and analyzed by software or humans. Software architectures that support data aggregation are easily monitored and can provide important feedback to users about the health of the overall system.

**Data Transformation** — A requisite task of an SOA middleware layer wherein data (for example, in XML format) is moved from one standard or published representation to another. Data transformation is necessary when multiple services in an SOA require the same business data, but in a different representational format.

**DCOM (Distributed Component Object Model)** — DCOM is the successor to the COM architecture and a precursor to SOA. It was ultimately more popular than COM and also became a basis for .NET and the NT operating system.

**Decomposition** — The logical act of turning a system or group of systems into a business service or group of business services (the physical act of doing this is called "wrapping"). To expose an application as a service, an enterprise must determine the level of business abstraction that is appropriate. It must also determine how the service will be represented in the overreaching SOA. These are both aspects of decomposition. See Chapter 3 for further information.

**Encapsulation**—Services are encapsulated because they have their implementations hidden behind an interface. Encapsulation is "black boxing" a software component so that the user does not have visibility into its infrastructure. This is a crucial part of SOA.

**Encryption**—The alteration of data so that it cannot be compromised by outside parties, but still read by all of its intended recipients using a key to de-encrypt the data. It is a necessary part of any security architecture. Most SOA technologies, such as Web services, have methods for encrypting important data.

**Enterprise Application Integration (EAI)**—A movement within the IT industry popular prior to SOA. EAI is based on the precepts of maximizing the functionality of systems through integration, but not necessarily doing so in a distributed, loosely coupled way. Theoretically, SOA is a type of EAI, although the term is commonly associated with tightly coupled (albeit heavily integrated) infrastructures.

**Enterprise Java Beans (EJBs)**—The fundamental programming component of enterprise Java. They utilize the resources of a Java EE application server to be reliable, responsive, and scalable. There has been a recent trend in the IT industry to move away from the bulkier EJB model to a more lightweight, Web-based model of Java programming, and an SOA can be built using either one.

**Enterprise Service Bus (ESB)**—This began as a buzzword used by middleware vendors to describe the SOA-relevant capabilities of their middleware platforms. It has since become a catch-all term to refer to a set of middleware components that provide necessary functionality to Service-Oriented Architectures.

**Extensibility**—A quality of XML by which message parts that are not understood by recipients are ignored. This way, providers are able to add to their schemas without affecting consumers of that data, allowing for seamless transition to newer versions.

**Federation**—A software architecture in which many components interact without the assistance of a governing entity. This has applicability in the business world as well, when multiple enterprises need to work together in a decentralized way. See Appendix E for more information.

**Governance**—In the context of SOA it refers to the management of services, including their versions, structure, policies, and reuse. It is oversight of the entire architecture, and it is a necessary component of an enterprise SOA plan, otherwise what starts as an SOA may end as a tightly coupled, point-to-point architecture that happens to use SOA technology.

**IDE (Integrated Development Environment)** — A software tool used by developers and integrators alike to speed development of software components. As software integration gets more complex (with XML messaging and middleware involved), IDEs are increasingly necessary for a successful project.

**Identity Management** — An important aspect of enterprise security policy, deals with the authorization, authentication, and auditing of system users. Identity management technology facilitates the provisioning and sharing of user accounts, and the management of such things as passwords and system rights.

**IDL (Interface Description Language)** — A COM and DCOM standard that allowed developers to write an interface to a component that was independent from its implementation. This model served as the basis for a wrapper in SOA. IDL itself was the precursor to the WSDL standard.

**Java** — A programming language originally developed by Sun but then made open so that others could contribute to its libraries. It has become the basis of modern, Web-enabled enterprise programming (although .NET and its C# have been catching up) and forms the basis of many SOA tools and components.

**Java Community Process (JCP)** — The primary way in which the open source community contributes to the development of the Java language. Participants create JSRs covering various Java functional enhancements, and many of these become widespread through use and adoption. The process has produced a number of useful technologies for enterprise software.

**Java EE/J2EE (Enterprise Java)** — The EE in Java EE is an acronym for "enterprise edition." This term is used to describe the Java runtime and libraries that, together, make up a Java application server. The application server is the basis of middleware, and the Java standard for an app server is the one most widely available by vendors. Many enterprise software components (and, therefore, many SOA components) are based on Java EE.

**JSR (Java Specification Request)** — JSRs are the standards and libraries that are submitted as part of the Java Community Process (JCP) that offer extensions to the Java language to cover new functionality. They are numbered for identification purposes. For example, JSR 224 is the Java API for XML Web services.

**Key Performance Indicator (KPI)** — A metric that measures the business performance of a system or facility. A KPI is normally constructed from business data aggregated across many systems and addresses a specific business need. KPIs determine whether or not a system or architecture is successful.

**Layer of Abstraction** — SOA, as an enterprise architecture, introduces layers of abstraction into the infrastructure. A layer of abstraction is a level at which all infrastructure components more detailed are encapsulated and hidden from the integrator. These layers are crucial in enterprise integration, because they allow the integrator to focus on business need instead of technical detail.

**Loose Coupling** — An infrastructure in which components are independent from one another, and the "ripple effect" of changes to architecture is minimized. A loosely coupled system allows for easy replacement or upgrading of components, giving the implementing facility more agility.

**Mash-Up** — Web-based applications that leverage (through service calls) the functionality of two or more underlying business applications, commonly associated with Web 2.0 technology. These can be used to produce hybrid functionality without a lot of original programming.

**Message-Oriented Middleware (MOM)** — The term used to describe enterprise middleware that is focused on the delivery and routing of messages. It predates the usage of "Enterprise Service Bus," which is a MOM optimized for SOA. MOMs often implement a number of different messaging models.

**Message Queue (MQ)** — A messaging model wherein messages will queue up in the middleware layer until they can be delivered. This model provides reliability, because the queue guarantees that a message will be delivered and not dropped due to excessive traffic, although delays may be inevitable.

**Middleware Layer** — A middleware layer is an important component to SOA (and, indeed, to most enterprise architectures). It is a collection of components that provide a communication infrastructure to enterprise software. Services or other components attaching to the middleware layer can take advantage of the functionality or benefits that it provides. See Chapter 4 for additional information.

**.NET** ("dot net") — Microsoft's proprietary version of the application server. It was developed in the late 1990s and has since become a very popular way to program enterprise applications. .NET provides all of the benefits of application servers, including reliability, scalability, and a messaging infrastructure.

**OASIS (Organization for the Advancement of Structured Information Standards)** — A standards body that advanced the use of SGML in the IT industry and today supports a number of Web-based information technologies, including UDDI and BPEL.

**Object-Oriented Programming (OOP)** — A software concept by which data components can be organized into objects. It has been extremely influential in the IT space, spawning countless programming languages, and is considered to be an ancestor to SOA.

**OMG (Object Management Group)** — An IT-industry consortium that is responsible for many of the SOA standards. They developed both the CORBA standard and the UML standard. Currently they are focused on industry-specific business modeling.

**Orchestration**—The act of automating the execution of a business process. Orchestration engines can be put into SOA middleware layers so that communication from service to service can follow the enterprise's specified process without needing to wait for human interaction. Process orchestration is an important trend in BPM.

**OWL (Web Ontology Language)**—A new specification which expands upon the RDF specification and provides a number of ways to associate semantics with data models. It is an important part of Web 2.0, in addition to being potentially useful to service designers.

**Portal**—An enterprise component that is useful for organizing data from multiple sources in a single user interface. Portals use portlets as fundamental presentation components. Many SOA implementations will use portal technology to present dashboards, task lists, administrative interfaces, and other views to users.

**Publish/Subscribe (pub/sub)**—A messaging model where service providers will specify channels to which consumers can subscribe. Messages are then published to the middleware and delivered to all interested consumers.

**RDF (Resource Description Framework)**—A standard that allows for the definition of semantics for a given data schema. This allows enterprise integrators to understand the intention of particular interfaces and facilitates data transformation. It is a major Web 2.0 technology as well.

**REST (Representational State Transfer)**—Considered both an implementing technology of, and a competitor to, SOA. It uses simple HTTP technology to communicate with resources occupying specific URIs. It competes with SOA because it advocates a resource-oriented infrastructure as opposed to a service-oriented one.

**RPC (Remote Procedure Call)**—The RPC method of calling Web services is much more similar to a programming-language specific model. It specifies methods and the parameters necessary to invoke those methods. It is not part of the WS-I specification, and so many do not consider the RPC architecture to be SOA-compliant.

**Schema**—In XML it is the definition of the data model used in the document. In Web services, the WSDL file will contain or refer to an XML schema to define the makeup of service messages.

**Semantics**—Literally refers to the meanings behind terms. In software integration, the semantics is used to describe the intent behind a particular messaging schema. Standards such as RDF and OWL have been developed to translate from one semantic representation to another.

**Service Consumer**—The service consumer in Web services interaction is the entity that requests an operation from a service provider. It is the client in the Web services transaction.

**Service Gateway**—A component in an SOA that exposes a subset of functionality of one SOA for the benefit of other, external consumers. Gateways are important to enable federation and interaction with outside parties. They may also be necessary as a protective measure if the security model changes from one domain to the next.

**Service-Oriented Architecture (SOA)**—An architecture of independent, wrapped services communicating via published interfaces over a common middleware layer. See Chapter 3 for more information.

**Service Provider**—The entity in Web services interaction that presents an interface and allows consumers to call its operations. The service provider is also commonly referred to as simply the service.

**Service Registry**—An SOA component that catalogs service locations and interfaces so that consumers interested in using a service can find one. It is distinguished from a service repository because a repository holds service interfaces and contracts while a registry simply refers to them. UDDI is the Web services standard for the registry.

**SGML (Standard Generalized Markup Language)**—The precursor to HTML and XML alike. It was an early technology to use readable "tags" to mark data.

**SOAP**—An XML standard and the most popular transport protocol for Web services. It defines a message that is split into an envelope with instructional metadata and a body that contains the business data. SOAP also supports a number of security and addressing methodologies popular in the Web services world. See Chapter 5 for additional information.

**Swimlane**—An organizational construct in a BPM business process (defined in BPMN) that is used to group tasks by role, service, or domain. Using swimlanes as part of an enterprise process definition effort can increase the quality of elicitation.

**Synchronous**—A synchronous message pattern is one in which an immediate response is expected. Clients implementing this type of messaging will often wait for a response before proceeding. The faster a provider can return a message to the consumer, the better.

**Technical Agility** — The ability to make changes to underlying enterprise technology without affecting the manner in which this technology is used by the enterprise. It is an important quality for enterprises looking to react to business changes.

**Tight Coupling** — Tight coupling (as opposed to loose coupling) describes an enterprise infrastructure that is heavily integrated and heavily dependent on the structure and location of its various components. A tightly coupled architecture is not easy to change or expand, and is difficult to manage.

**tModel** — (short for "technical model") A UDDI construct that is used to group individual services by interface, policy, or any other arbitrary business data. tModels are especially useful for searching a registry or supporting runtime discovery of services.

**UDDI (Universal Description, Discovery, and Integration)** — Web services technology used to implement a service registry. While it has not been widely accepted or used within the IT industry, a good replacement technology has yet to be developed. See Chapter 5 for more information.

**UML (Unified Modeling Language)** — A set of specifications developed by the OMG to represent software concepts visually in a unified way. It is useful for enterprise integration in general, and is used throughout this book.

**W3C (the World Wide Web Consortium)** — The standards body behind some of the most influential IT standards of the last 20 years. They continue to remain relevant and have helped the SOA effort along considerably. For example, they developed the WSDL standard used with Web services.

**Web 2.0** — The name given to the latest movement in the IT industry toward Web-based, community-driven technology. This movement is relevant to SOA (and leverages many SOA standards and technologies), and also relevant to the media industry in the near future.

**Web Services** — An XML-based technology for communicating between loosely coupled systems. It is optimized for transactional, document-style messaging and uses the WSDL standard to represent service interfaces. See Chapter 5 for more information.

**Wrapper** — A software component that "surrounds" an application and exposes that application's functionality as a service interface. Wrappers are important components of an SOA, and are necessary when dealing with legacy applications.

**WS-*** ("w-s-star") — A set of specifications that are important extensions to Web services technology addressing such needs as security, reliability, addressing, and semantics.

**WS-Addressing**—One of the WS-* standards that allows service consumers and providers to include specific address and routing information in the header of the SOAP message sent out. This information can be used by an ESB or by service gateways to process messages.

**WSDL (Web Service Description Language)**—The XML-based technology used to represent interfaces for Web services business services. WSDL documents describe the data and operations necessary for a service consumer to interact with a business service provider.

**WS-Federation**—One of the WS-* standards, and it facilitates federated communication among service domains. Its main purpose is with propagating identity across these domains, so that federated collaboration using Web services can be secured.

**WS-I**—The Web Services Interoperability group is a coalition dedicated to improving the use of Web services. They most notably published a specification which advocated a particular use of Web service technology to guarantee interoperability.

**WS-Policy**—One of the WS-* standards used to specify additional interface details in a WSDL document. Service providers that want to inform consumers of usage restrictions or non-functional requirements can use this method to do so.

**WS-ReliableMessaging**—A WS-* standard that allows consumers and providers to guarantee message delivery in particular ways. When used in combination with a reliable middleware layer, this standard can enforce reliable delivery of business data.

**WSRP (Web Services for Remote Portlets)**—This specification (outlined in JSR 168) facilitates the interoperability of Web service-based business services and portal platforms. Using WSRP, an integrator could easily create portlets that serve as interfaces to Web services.

**WS-Security**—A WS-* standard that is used in conjunction with XML encryption and signature to secure SOAP messages traveling between Web services. It is increasingly used as part of an SOA-wide security policy.

**XForms**—An XML standard used to represent form-based data. It is useful for standardized data entry or the representation of structured data objects in a form to be presented to a user.

**XLink**—Used to link and correlate various XML documents together. It is one of the many XML standards that allow XML to be as widespread and useful in enterprise integration as it is today.

**XML (Extensible Markup Language)** — A language used to represent structured data in an extensible, formalized, and human-readable way. It is the basis of practically every Web-based enterprise technology of the last ten years, including Web services. See Chapter 5 for additional information.

**XPath** — One of the XML standards that facilitates XML's interoperability with so many enterprise technologies. It provides a simple way to identify individual elements within an XML document, allowing applications to drill down to exactly the data they need.

**XPDL (XML Process Description Language)** — A new language that allows for the XML representation of BPMN business processes, which facilitates the transfer of these processes between development tools and organizations. Without XPDL, there would be no non-graphical (and therefore computer-readable) way of representing BPMN.

**XSLT (Extensible Stylesheet Language Transformations)** — Allows integrators to define data transformation schemes for XML documents. Running an XML document through an XSLT processor converts it to a different XML schema. This is especially useful for the data transformation components that are often found in middleware layers.

# INDEX

For Product Safety Concerns and Information please contact our EU
representative  GPSR@taylorandfrancis.com
Taylor & Francis Verlag GmbH, Kaufingerstraße 24, 80331 München, Germany